Interdisciplinarity

The idea that research should become more interdisciplinary has become commonplace. According to influential commentators, the unprecedented complexity of problems such as climate change or the social implications of biomedicine demand interdisciplinary efforts integrating both the social and natural sciences. In this context, the question of whether a given knowledge practice is too disciplinary, or interdisciplinary, or not disciplinary enough has become an issue for governments, research policymakers and funding agencies. Interdisciplinarity, in short, has emerged as a key political preoccupation; yet the term tends to obscure as much as illuminate the diverse practices gathered under its rubric.

This volume offers a new approach to theorising interdisciplinarity, showing how the boundaries between the social and natural sciences are being reconfigured. It examines the current preoccupation with interdisciplinarity, notably the ascendance of a particular discourse in which it is associated with a transformation in the relations between science, technology and society. Contributors address attempts to promote collaboration between, on the one hand, the natural sciences and engineering and, on the other, the social sciences, arts and humanities. From ethnography in the IT industry to science and technology studies, environmental science to medical humanities, cybernetics to art-science, the collection interrogates how interdisciplinarity has come to be seen as a solution not only to enhancing relations between science and society, but the pursuit of accountability and the need to foster innovation.

Interdisciplinarity is essential reading for scholars, students and policymakers across the social sciences, arts and humanities, including anthropology, geography, sociology, science and technology studies and cultural studies, as well as all those engaged in interdisciplinary research. It will have particular relevance for those concerned with the knowledge economy, science policy, environmental politics, applied anthropology, ELSI research, medical humanities and art-science.

Andrew Barry is Professor of Political Geography at the University of Oxford.

Georgina Born is Professor of Music and Anthropology at the University of Oxford.

Culture, Economy and the Social

A new series from CRESC – the ESRC Centre for Research on Socio-cultural Change

Editors

The *Culture, Economy and the Social* series is committed to innovative contemporary, comparative and historical work on the relations between social, cultural and economic change. It publishes empirically based research that is theoretically informed, that critically examines the ways in which social, cultural and economic change is framed and made visible, and that is attentive to perspectives that tend to be ignored or sidelined by grand theorising or epochal accounts of social change. The series addresses the diverse manifestations of contemporary capitalism, and considers the various ways in which the 'social', 'cultural' and 'economic' are apprehended as tangible sites of value and practice. It is explicitly comparative, publishing books that work across disciplinary perspectives, cross-culturally, or across different historical periods.

The series is actively engaged in the analysis of the different theoretical traditions that have contributed to the development of the 'cultural turn' with a view to clarifying where these approaches converge and where they diverge on a particular issue. It is equally concerned to explore the new critical agendas emerging from current critiques of the cultural turn: those associated with the descriptive turn for example. Our commitment to interdisciplinarity thus aims at enriching theoretical and methodological discussion, building awareness of the common ground that has emerged in the past decade, and thinking through what is at stake in those approaches that resist integration to a common analytical model.

Series titles include:

The Media and Social Theory (2008)
Edited by David Hesmondhalgh and Jason Toynbee

Culture, Class, Distinction (2009)
Tony Bennett, Mike Savage, Elizabeth Bortolaia Silva, Alan Warde,
Modesto Gayo-Cal and David Wright

Material Powers (2010)
Edited by Tony Bennett and Patrick Joyce

The Social after Gabriel Tarde: Debates and Assessments (2010)
Edited by Matei Candea

Cultural Analysis and Bourdieu's Legacy (2010)
Edited by Elizabeth Silva and Alan Ward

Milk, Modernity and the Making of the Human (2010)
Richie Nimmo

Creative Labour: Media Work in Three Cultural Industries (2010)
Edited by David Hesmondhalgh and Sarah Baker

Migrating Music (2011)
Edited by Jason Toynbee and Byron Dueck

Sport and the Transformation of Modern Europe: States,
Media and Markets 1950–2010 (2011)
Edited by Alan Tomlinson, Christopher Young and Richard Holt

Inventive Methods: The Happening of the Social (2012)
Edited by Celia Lury and Nina Wakeford

Understanding Sport: A Socio-Cultural Analysis (2012)
By John Horne, Alan Tomlinson, Garry Whannel and Kath Woodward

Shanghai Expo: An International Forum on the Future of Cities (2012)
Edited by Tim Winter

Diasporas and Diplomacy: Cosmopolitan Contact Zones at the BBC World Service (1932–2012)
Edited by Marie Gillespie and Alban Webb

Making Culture, Changing Society
Tony Bennett

Interdisciplinarity: Reconfigurations of the Social and Natural Sciences (2013)
Edited by Andrew Barry and Georgina Born

Rio de Janeiro: Urban Life through the Eyes of the City (forthcoming)
Beatriz Jaguaribe

Devising Consumption: Cultural Economies of Insurance, Credit and Spending (forthcoming)
Liz Mcfall

Unbecoming Things: Mutable Objects and the Politics of Waste (forthcoming)
By Nicky Gregson and Mike Crang

E·S·R·C
ECONOMIC
& SOCIAL
RESEARCH
COUNCIL

Centre for Research on
Socio-Cultural Change

Interdisciplinarity
Reconfigurations of the social and natural sciences

Edited by Andrew Barry and Georgina Born

Routledge
Taylor & Francis Group

LONDON AND NEW YORK

First published 2013
by Routledge
2 Park Square, Milton Park, Abingdon, Oxfordshire OX14 4RN

Simultaneously published in the USA and Canada
by Routledge
711 Third Avenue, New York, NY 10017

First issued in paperback 2014

Routledge is an imprint of the Taylor & Francis Group, an informa business

British Library Cataloguing in Publication Data
A catalogue record for this book is available from the British Library

Library of Congress Cataloging in Publication Data
  Interdisciplinarity : reconfigurations of the social and natural sciences/
  edited by Andrew Barry and Georgina Born.
      p. cm. — (Culture, economy and the social)
  Includes bibliographical references and index.
  1. Interdisciplinary approach to knowledge. 2. Research. I. Barry,
  Andrew, 1960- II. Born, Georgina.
  BD255.I566 2013
  001—dc23
                                                    2012037097

ISBN 978-0-415-57892-9 (hbk)

ISBN 978-1-138-84334-9 (pbk)

ISBN 978-0-203-58427-9 (ebk)

Typeset in Times New Roman
by Keystroke, Station Road, Codsall, Wolverhampton

For Helga Nowotny and Marilyn Strathern
and in memory of Beatriz da Costa (1974–2012)

Contents

Notes on Contributors   xi
Acknowledgements   xv

1   **Interdisciplinarity: Reconfigurations of the
    social and natural sciences**   1
    ANDREW BARRY AND GEORGINA BORN

2   **How Disciplines Look**   57
    SIMON SCHAFFER

3   **Inter that Discipline!**   82
    THOMAS OSBORNE

4   **Fields and Fallows: A political history of STS**   99
    SHEILA JASANOFF

5   **Unexpected Consequences and an Unanticipated Outcome**   119
    MARILYN STRATHERN AND ELENA KHLINOVSKAYA ROCKHILL

6   **Consuming Anthropology**   141
    LUCY SUCHMAN

7   **Where Natural and Social Science Meet? Reflections on an
    experiment in geographical practice**   161
    SARAH J. WHATMORE

8   **Multiple Environments: Accountability, integration and ontology**   178
    GISA WESZKALNYS AND ANDREW BARRY

9   **Ontology and Antidisciplinarity**   209
    ANDREW PICKERING

10   Logics of Interdisciplinarity: The case of medical humanities   226
MONICA GRECO

11   Art-Science: From public understanding to public experiment   247
GEORGINA BORN AND ANDREW BARRY

Index   273

Notes on Contributors

Andrew Barry is Professor of Political Geography at the University of Oxford. He is the author of *Political Machines: Governing a Technological Society* (2001), co-editor of *Foucault and Political Reason* (ed. with T. Osborne and N. Rose, 1996), and *The Technological Economy* (ed. with D. Slater, 2005). He collaborated with Lucy Kimbell in the design of an interactive installation, 'Pindices', first exhibited at the 'Making Things Public' exhibition at ZKM in 2005. His research focuses primarily on the relations between science, technology and politics including, most recently, the politics of energy.

Georgina Born is Professor of Music and Anthropology at the University of Oxford. She researches cultural production – including music, television, new media art and art-science – often in institutional form. Her books include *Rationalizing Culture: IRCAM, Boulez and the Institutionalization of the Musical Avant-Garde* (1995), *Uncertain Vision: Birt, Dyke and the Reinvention of the BBC* (2005) and *Music, Sound and Space: Transformations of Public and Private Experience* (ed., 2013). She currently directs the research programme 'Music, Digitisation, Mediation: Towards Interdisciplinary Music Studies', funded by the European Research Council.

Monica Greco is Senior Lecturer in the Department of Sociology at Goldsmiths College, University of London. She is the author of *Illness as a Work of Thought* (1998) and of articles on different aspects of medical rationality, vitalism and health promotional discourse. She has a long-standing interest in internalist critiques of medical dualism/biomedical reductionism and their ethico-political implications. Her current research interests focus on the sociology of medically unexplained symptoms and on medical humanities.

Sheila Jasanoff is Pforzheimer Professor of Science and Technology Studies at the Harvard Kennedy School. She is the author or editor of a dozen books including *The Fifth Branch* (1994), *Science at the Bar* (1997) and *Designs on Nature* (2005). Her work explores the role of science and technology in law, politics and policy, with particular attention to the nature of public reason. She was founding chair of the STS Department at Cornell University and has held a number of distinguished visiting appointments in the US, Europe and Japan.

Thomas Osborne is Professor of Social and Cultural Theory and Head of the School of Sociology, Politics and International Studies in the Faculty of Social Science and Law at the University of Bristol. He is the author of *Aspects of Enlightenment: Social Theory and the Ethics of Truth* (1998), *The Structure of Modern Cultural Theory* (2008) and co-editor of *Foucault and Political Reason* (ed. with A. Barry and N. Rose, 1996). His research has been particularly concerned with the history of social thought and with the analysis of literature, ethics and aesthetics.

Andrew Pickering is Professor of Sociology and Philosophy at the University of Exeter. He is the author of *Constructing Quarks: A Sociological History of Particle Physics* (1984), *The Mangle of Practice: Time, Agency and Science* (1995) and, most recently, *The Cybernetic Brain: Sketches of Another Future* (2010), and the editor of *Science as Practice and Culture* (1992) and (with Keith Guzik) *The Mangle in Practice: Science, Society and Becoming* (2008). His current research grows out of his work on cybernetics and looks at non-standard approaches to art, agency and the environment.

Elena Khlinovskaya Rockhill is a social anthropologist with an area interest in Russia and particularly the Russian Far North. She has research interests in the anthropology of the state, childhood, parenting, relatedness and kinship. She was a Research Associate in the Department of Social Anthropology, University of Cambridge on the ESRC project, 'Interdisciplinarity and Society: A Critical Comparative Study' (2004–2006), and is currently an Associate of the Scott Polar Research Institute, University of Cambridge.

Simon Schaffer is Professor of History of Science at the University of Cambridge. He has co-edited studies of innovation and inquiry in early modern Europe and of the role of go-betweens in global knowledge networks in the age of revolutions. He is a principal investigator for an AHRC project on science, empire and innovation in the Georgian world. His chapter in this book has been awarded the Ivan Slade prize of the British Society for the History of Science.

Marilyn Strathern, DBE, Emeritus Professor of Social Anthropology, University of Cambridge, has recently been made Life President of the (UK and Commonwealth) Association of Social Anthropologists. Her interests have long been divided between Melanesian and British ethnography. Projects over the last twenty years are reflected in publications on reproductive technologies, and intellectual and cultural property rights, while 'critique of good practice' has been the umbrella under which she has written about audit, accountability and interdisciplinarity. Some of these themes are brought together in her book *Kinship, Law and the Unexpected* (2005).

Lucy Suchman is Professor of Anthropology of Science and Technology in the Department of Sociology at Lancaster University and Co-Director of Lancaster's Centre for Science Studies. Before taking up her present post she spent twenty years as a researcher at Xerox's Palo Alto Research Center. In 2010 she received the ACM Special Interest Group in Computer–Human Interaction Lifetime Research Award. Her writings include *Human–Machine Reconfigurations* (2007).

Gisa Weszkalnys is Lecturer in Anthropology at the London School of Economics. Among her previous positions she was a Research Associate on the ESRC project, 'Interdisciplinarity and Society: A Critical Comparative Study' (2004– 2006). In addition to interdisciplinarity, her research has addressed urban planning, natural resource extraction, and the ways that expert knowledge articulates with and shapes the contexts of its application. She is the author of *Berlin, Alexanderplatz: Transforming Place in a Unified Germany* (2010). Her current work focuses on the temporality and materiality of oil exploitation, specifically in West Africa.

Sarah Whatmore is Professor of Environment and Public Policy at the University of Oxford. Her research addresses the interface between cultural geography, political theory and science and technology studies. She is the author of *Hybrid Geographies* (2002) and the editor (with Bruce Braun) of *Political Matter: Technoscience, Democracy and Public Life* (2010) and of *Using Social Theory: Thinking Through Research* (2003). Following recent research on environmental knowledge controversies and the science and politics of flood risk (knowledge-controversies.ouce.ox.ac.uk), she is working on a book for Minnesota University Press on *Remaking Environmental Expertise.*

Acknowledgements

The preparation of this book, and the research on which it is based, have left us with a number of debts. Our thanks are due first to our contributors, who endured with good humour lengthy delays in the production of the book. We hope they find the results worth waiting for. We thank also those who participated in the conference held at St Catherine's College, Oxford that led to the book, including Don Brenneis, Diana Liverman, Nigel Thrift and Brian Wynne. For their generous feedback and suggestions on the introduction, as well as their contributions to our broader arguments, we thank Gail Davies, Paul Dourish, Monica Greco, Mike Hulme, Sheila Jasanoff, Lucy Kimbell, Antoinette Lafarge, Patrice Maniglier, Bill Maurer, Susan Owens and Simon Penny.

The research informing the introduction (Chapter 1), as well as Chapters 5, 8 and 11, was funded by the Economic and Social Research Council under the Science in Society Programme: our overarching project was titled 'Interdisciplinarity and Society: A Critical Comparative Study' (RES-151-25-0042-A, 2004-2006). Our warm thanks are due to the colleagues with whom we worked on this research: Marilyn Strathern, who conceived of the initiative with Andrew Barry, whose work on interdisciplinarity has been an inspiration, and who made numerous illuminating interventions, as well as Elena Khlinovskaya Rockhill and Gisa Weszkalnys, both of whom undertook demanding fieldwork with energy and contributed insightfully to the resulting analyses. We remember with pleasure how stimulating and enjoyable were the conversations between the team. Since we ourselves worked primarily in a team of three (Barry, Born and Weszkalnys), Gisa's contributions to our work were particularly significant and we are immensely grateful for her vital input into the research and thinking reported here.

Our final debt is to those individuals and institutions who allowed us to carry out ethnographic fieldwork on them and in dialogue with them. Without the cooperation, reciprocal enthusiasm and openness of our ethnographic subjects, fieldwork just can't take place. As Marilyn Strathern has memorably written of the prospective, emergent nature of ethnography, 'rather than devising research protocols that will purify the data in advance of analysis, the anthropologist embarks on a participatory exercise which yields material for which analytical protocols are often devised after the fact'. In an era characterised by attempts to rationalise and instrumentalise the fragile and hopeful mutuality, the dialogical pact, at the heart of fieldwork, we remain enormously grateful to those interlocutors who enabled us – without guarantees – to participate in their lives and work.

Chapter 1 is a substantially rewritten and extended version of A. Barry, G. Born, and G. Weszkalnys (2008), 'Logics of Interdisciplinarity', *Economy and Society*, 37 (1): 20–49. Chapter 11 is a significantly revised and extended version of G. Born and A. Barry (2010), 'Art-Science: From Public Understanding to Public Experiment', *Journal of Cultural Economy*, 3 (1): 103–20. We are grateful to Taylor and Francis for permission to republish these articles.

This book is dedicated to two colleagues whose astonishing imaginations and powerful work have inspired us throughout its production.

It is, however, with enormous sadness that, in the very last stages of editing the book, we note the untimely death of an outstanding young artist, Beatriz da Costa, whose work has been inspirational for our research on art-science. The book is also, therefore, dedicated to her memory.

1   Interdisciplinarity

Reconfigurations of the social and natural sciences

Andrew Barry and Georgina Born

The idea of discipline opens up a nexus of meaning. Disciplines discipline disciples.[1] A commitment to a discipline is a way of ensuring that certain disciplinary methods and concepts are used rigorously and that undisciplined and undisciplinary objects, methods and concepts are ruled out. By contrast, ideas of interdisciplinarity imply a variety of boundary transgressions, in which the disciplinary and disciplining rules, trainings and subjectivities given by existing knowledge corpuses are put aside.

In this introduction we interrogate the current preoccupation with interdisciplinarity and transdisciplinarity, in particular the ascendance in recent years of a particular discourse on interdisciplinarity where it is associated with a more generalised transformation in the relations between science, technology and society. We are therefore less concerned with interdisciplinarity in general than with the contemporary formation of interdisciplinarity: how it has come to be seen as a solution to a series of current problems, in particular the relations between science and society, the development of accountability, and the need to foster innovation in the knowledge economy. The present situation, we will suggest, can be understood as a problematisation:[2] the question of whether a given knowledge practice is too disciplinary, or interdisciplinary, or not disciplinary enough has become an issue and an object of enquiry for governments, funding agencies and researchers.

An influential manifestation of this problematisation was the publication by Helga Nowotny, Peter Scott and Michael Gibbons of *Re-Thinking Science: Knowledge and the Public in an Age of Uncertainty* in 2001. The book took as its focus the evolving institutionalisation of knowledge in the guise of science and research policy, research funding and evaluation, and the nature of the university. Nowotny and her collaborators suggested that the concern with interdisciplinarity is part of a shift from what they call Mode-1 science to Mode-2 knowledge production (Gibbons et al 1994, Nowotny et al 2001, Nowotny 2003a, Strathern 2004b). The latter was said to include: (1) the growth of transdisciplinary research which, unlike interdisciplinary research, is not derived from pre-existing disciplines; (2) the development of novel forms of quality control which undermine disciplinary forms of evaluation; (3) the displacement of a 'culture of autonomy of science' by a 'culture of accountability'; (4) the growing importance of the 'context of application' as a site for research; and (5) a growing diversity of sites at which knowledge is produced. In a subsequent online forum on interdisciplinarity Nowotny reiterated these views:

> We introduced the idea of Mode-2 in order to bring in a new way of thinking about science, which is often described in strictly disciplinary terms. [. . .] We identified some attributes of the new mode of knowledge production, which we think are empirically evident, and argued that, all together, they are integral or coherent enough to constitute something of a new form of production of knowledge.
>
> (Nowotny 2003b: 48–9)[3]

Other commentators broadly concur with this account, and we return later to consider the significance of the distinction between transdisciplinarity and interdisciplinarity. Leading figures in the Interdisciplinary Studies Project at Harvard University, for example, note that there is a 're-emerging awareness of interdisciplinarity as a pervasive form of knowledge production' (Mansilla and Gardner 2003: 160), while a major report on 'facilitating interdisciplinary research' sponsored by the US National Academies[4] claims that

> as a mode of discovery and education, [interdisciplinary research] has delivered much already and promises more – sustainable environment, healthier and more prosperous lives, new discoveries and technologies to inspire young minds, and deeper understanding of our place in space and time.
>
> (National Academy of Sciences 2004: 1)

This collection therefore responds to the emergence and prominence of the contemporary discourse on interdisciplinarity. It has its origins in a research programme, 'Interdisciplinarity and Society: A Critical Comparative Study', which, given the considerable claims, took its initial impetus from the paucity of empirical studies of how interdisciplinarity unfolds in practice. The programme encompassed ethnographic studies of interdisciplinary fields that cut across the boundaries between the natural sciences and engineering, on the one hand, and the social sciences, humanities and arts, on the other. It is these kinds of interdisciplinary research that are understood to have the greatest significance in the transition to a new mode of knowledge production, auguring closer relations between science and society (Strathern 2004a).

The programme had two main empirical components. First, studies undertaken by Andrew Barry, Georgina Born and Gisa Weszkalnys of three salient and contrasting interdisciplinary fields identified by an Internet-based mapping survey: environmental and climate change research (Weszkalnys and Barry, this volume); ethnography in the IT industry (this introduction);[5] and art-science (Born and Barry 2010, Born and Barry, this volume). We carried out ten case studies of interdisciplinary institutions and initiatives and the practices they supported, in different national settings, across the three fields[6] – institutions chosen because they were understood to be influential in or symptomatic of the respective fields (Born 2010a: 19–20).[7]

The second component was an ethnographic study carried out by Elena Khlinovskaya Rockhill in dialogue with Marilyn Strathern of an institution, the Cambridge Genetics Knowledge Park, created to implement an experiment in collaboration between the biosciences and studies of the ethical, legal and social implications of research (or ELSI) (Strathern 2004c, 2006, 2011, Khlinovskaya Rockhill 2007, Strathern and Khlinovskaya Rockhill, this volume).

A conference held at the completion of the programme brought together colleagues working on adjacent research questions, and led to initial publications by the editors of this volume (Barry, Born and Weszkalnys 2008, Born and Barry 2010).[8] After the conference we invited a number of participants, as well as scholars who responded to our initial publications, to contribute to this collection. The book thus emerges from iterative dialogues between a loose 'community of critics' (Strathern 2006) concerned in distinctive ways with the problematisation of the disciplines. At the heart of our concerns is the question of the articulation between contemporary programmatic statements and practices of interdisciplinarity and the reconfiguration of the relations between the social and natural sciences.

Two inflections of the discourse on interdisciplinarity are particularly apparent. The first portrays interdisciplinarity as offering new techniques for accountability, or even as itself an index of knowledge practices that are accountable to society (Strathern 2004b, Doubleday 2007). The second lays emphasis on the capacity of interdisciplinarity to assist in forging closer relations between scientific research and the requirements of the economy through fostering innovation (Mirowski and Mirjam Sent 2002). In contrast, disciplinarity tends to be associated with a defence of academic autonomy. Assertions of a link between interdisciplinarity and accountable science responsive to user needs can be found in the US Gulbenkian Commission's report on the restructuring of the social sciences (Wallerstein 1996), and the 2000 report of the German Science Council (Wissenschaftsrat 2000). In the UK, an influential paper by HM Treasury argued that interdisciplinarity should lie at the heart of the government's research strategy: 'In order to maintain the UK's world-class university system, the [g]overnment is keen to ensure that excellent research of all types is rewarded, including user-focused and interdisciplinary research' (HM Treasury 2006). For the British Treasury, by releasing research from the restrictions of disciplinary boundaries (Weingart and Stehr 2000: 270), interdisciplinarity enables research to be more readily connected to the needs of industrial users and market demands (Nowotny 2005).

In interrogating the contemporary preoccupation with interdisciplinarity, it is important to avoid two temptations. The first temptation is to imagine that interdisciplinarity is historically novel – that in the past knowledge production has primarily taken place within autonomous and unified disciplines, and that it no longer does so (*Social Epistemology* 1995, Galison and Stump 1996, Weingart and Stehr 2000, Schaffer, this volume). Without doubt, knowledge production has always occurred in a variety of institutional sites and geographically dispersed assemblages, not only in the scientific laboratory or the apparently enclosed space of the humanist's study (Livingstone 2003, Osborne 2004). Moreover, the evolution of disciplines has often occurred in the form of what would now be identified as interdisciplinary phases. Even an apparently 'pure' discipline such as astronomy has been transformed historically through the development of practices and methods that might now be considered interdisciplinary (Schaffer 1996, 2007). In other cases, what were once interdisciplines may themselves become progressively established as distinct disciplines (Fuller 2002, Jasanoff, this volume). If the appearance of what is now called interdisciplinarity is a historical constant, then, what is novel is the contemporary sense that greater interdisciplinarity is a necessary response to intensifying demands that research should become more integrated than before with society and the economy.[9] Interdisciplinarity has come to be at once a governmental demand, a reflexive orientation within the academy and an object of knowledge.[10]

Second, and relatedly, there is a temptation to read the contemporary concern with interdisciplinarity too politically in the conventional sense of the term: to view it entirely as an emanation from current governmental preoccupations with accountability, the knowledge economy or innovation, or as driven by commercial imperatives. Here, in other words, the temptation is to unify interdisciplinarity excessively. Others have rightly pointed to the force of these dynamics, as noted above (e.g. Mirowski and Mirjam Sent 2002, Nowotny 2005). Yet it is critical to recognise that these developments coexist with, and may reinforce the importance of, a series of other dynamics. One of the arguments that we will propose is that the current burgeoning of varieties of interdisciplinarity has not led straight-forwardly to a reduction in the autonomy of research. As we shall argue, interdisciplinarity is equally associated with the development of fields, initiatives and sites in which new types of autonomy are created and defended against a reduction of research to the imperatives of accountability or innovation. Interdisciplinarity is certainly a key term in present efforts to transform the relations between research, economy and society, and the promotion of interdisciplinarity has come to be central to the government of research (cf. Power 1996, Barry 2001). Yet despite this, we want to suggest that interdisciplinarity may on occasion generate knowledge practices and forms, and may have effects, that cannot be understood merely as instrumental or as a response to broader political demands, social or economic transformations. In short, autonomy can be associated as much with interdisciplinary as with disciplinary research.

In light of these temptations, the starting point of our research programme was a dissatisfaction with the teleological account of interdisciplinarity in much of the literature. Certainly, the notion that we are witnessing a progressive decline in the significance of disciplines as institutions of knowledge production has been highly influential. Indeed, during our research we found that the narrative of 'Mode-2' was not only echoed in assessments of research policy and practice (e.g. Century 1999, Becker 2003), but that it had become performative: folded into the research institutions and practices that we were studying, and even offered by some interviewees as a kind of 'local' framework of understanding (Weszkalnys and Barry, this volume). Rather than accept this framing, we strove to get a sense of the multiplicity of interdisciplinary forms and their diverse histories, to interrogate the unity of interdisciplinarity – fostered through a series of apparently interrelated or mimetic initiatives, analyses and claims[11] – but also to grasp its heterogeneity, evident not only in the proliferation of a variety of interdisciplinary fields, institutions, practices and experiments, but also in the specificity of their trajectories (Weszkalnys and Barry, this volume, Pickering, this volume, Greco, this volume, Born and Barry, this volume).

Following Foucault's injunction, we do not take interdisciplinarity or transdisciplinarity to be a sign of 'culture in its totality' or an indicator of a generalised transformation in science and society, but a particular configuration of programmatic statements, interventions and practices (Foucault 1972: 159). Nor do we imagine that this configuration emanates from a specific source or series of authors (ibid.: 205), or that it could be analysed simply as a discourse of science policy that bears little relation to the conduct of research. Given this approach to the analysis of interdisciplinarity, we confronted a series of problems: how can we give any coherence to interdisciplinarity if it takes such specific forms, and what other unities might be revealed that are not immediately apparent? If the claim that there is a discontinuity in the mode of production of knowledge has been influential, what other 'differences, relations, gaps, shifts, independences, autonomies' might be occluded by such a claim (ibid.: 191)? Is it possible to map some of the diverse ways in which interdisciplinarity is invoked, promoted and contested, and the extent to which analyses of interdisciplinarity have been performative (cf. MacKenzie et al 2007)? How might one understand interdisciplinarity less as a unity and more as a field of differences, a multiplicity?

Critics have rightly argued that dominant accounts of interdisciplinarity have often understood its value in largely instrumental terms, terms that may inhibit rather than foster novelty. In these circumstances, rather than interdisciplinarity, what may be required is a certain degree of antidisciplinarity (Pickering 1995a)[12] or indiscipline (Rancière 2006, cf. Althusser 1990, Guattari 1992). At the same time, others maintain that it is the disciplines that continue to sustain intellectual change through their capacity both to foster productive forms of internal disagreement and dissent (Strathern 2006) and to generate new ways of interrogating an exteriority (Osborne, this volume). We do not disagree with these arguments. Our pronounced scepticism about the value of interdisciplinarity 'in general' is matched only by incredulity towards any claim for the infallible intellectual and creative vitality of the established disciplines. Nonetheless, in what follows we argue that interdisciplinary research has the potential to be inventive. By this we mean two things.

First, the notion of invention points to the openness of the contemporary historical situation. An invention can be understood as the introduction of a form of novelty within a specific domain, one that cannot be explained away as the consequence of pre-existing factors or forces, and that serves to protend or open up the space of future possibilities (Barry 2001, 2005, Born 2005b, 2010b, Connolly 2011). As we shall suggest, while the call for greater interdisciplinarity today is often understood in terms of the needs of society or stakeholders or the demands of the economy, interdisciplinary research can lead to forms of novelty that cannot be assumed to follow from governmental demands nor from any given historical tendency. Novelty, of course, can also be anti-inventive in so far as it closes down rather than opens up the space of possibilities. Indeed we have argued elsewhere that it is possible to identify 'defensive innovation' when anti-invention, or the creation of stasis and avoidance of significant change, becomes a deliberate or indirect aim of cultural, artistic, technological, industrial or political strategy (Born 1995: 325–7, Barry 2001: 212).

Our second argument is that in order for inventiveness not only to open up possibilities but to bring about an event, it is necessary for it to be recognised and taken up by others (Feltham and Clemens 2003: 27, Stengers 1997, Tarde 2001). Invention should not be understood as a moment in time, but as a process. But while the anticipation or protention of the future by those engaged in invention may lead to the recognition, reception and development of this inventiveness by others, this is not inevitable; invention is a fragile and contested quality and some inventive practices fail to be recognised (Born 2005b: 20–4). In referring to the question of invention, then, we highlight a critical issue in relation to the chapters that follow. Rather than describe the formation of a new mode of production of knowledge, our interest is in heightening awareness of what is potentially inventive, or anti-inventive, in the emergence of interdisciplinarity in particular eras and fields.

The chapters in this volume do not provide a unified account of interdisciplinarity, nor do their authors necessarily agree with the analyses advanced in this introduction. However, despite the differences between them, all of the authors gathered together in this collection insist on the need to attend to the specificity and the history of the disciplines and interdisciplines that they interrogate, rather than assume that there has been a generalised movement from a disciplinary to an interdisciplinary or transdisciplinary mode of knowledge production. The volume develops a sustained portrait of interdisciplinarity as a problematisation, but one that must be traced through a series of strikingly distinctive vectors across an array of practices, institutions and events – vectors that are local and specific to the fields at issue. In this way the volume issues a profound challenge to earlier accounts of interdisciplinarity and propels research in new directions.

In the remainder of this introduction we probe the limits of the existing literature on interdisciplinarity with reference both to our own research and that of our contributors. In the next section we address the status of disciplinarity, multidisciplinarity, interdisciplinarity and transdisciplinarity. In the second section we examine the different types of interrelations between disciplines that are embodied in interdisciplinary assemblages. We question the idea that interdisciplinary research should be understood simply in terms of the synthesis between two or more disciplines and distinguish between three modes of interdisciplinarity. In the third section we describe and interrogate three different logics that are manifest in contemporary interdisciplinarity, drawing a distinction between what we term the logics of accountability, innovation and ontology. An overview of each of the chapters follows, and in this and the concluding part of the introduction we bring out some core themes running through the analyses presented in them, including the nature of the ecologies that support or inhibit interdisciplinarity, the importance of pedagogy and of the formation of interdisciplinary subjects, how certain interdisciplinary assemblages can be associated with the logic of ontology and thus with the generation of novel objects, subjects and relations of research, and the enduring challenges posed by the evaluation of interdisciplinary work.

Disciplinarity – Interdisciplinarity – Transdisciplinarity

Much of the heat generated by debates about interdisciplinarity stems from the existence of polarised judgements about the creative or repressive status of disciplinary knowledge. On one side are those for whom disciplines are generative and enabling, the repositories of a responsible kind of epistemological reflexivity. Marilyn Strathern gives voice to such a perspective when she writes that 'the value of a discipline is precisely in its ability to account for its conditions of existence and thus . . . how it arrives at its knowledge practices' (2004a: 5). On the other side are those who see disciplines as 'inherently conventional', 'artificial "holding patterns" of inquiry' sustained by historical casts of mind 'that cannot imagine alternatives to the current [disciplinary] regime'. In this view the significance of interdisciplinary research lies in the contrast with what are taken to be the more restrictive structures of disciplinary knowledge. Only interdisciplinarity holds out the promise of 'sustained epistemic change' (Fuller 2003: 125, 128; 1993).

In thinking about the relations between disciplinarity and interdisciplinarity, however, it would be a mistake to contrast the homogeneity and closure of disciplines with the heterogeneity and openness of interdisciplinarity. On the one hand, interdisciplinary research can involve closure, limiting as well as transforming the possibilities for new forms, methods and sites of research (Weingart and Stehr 2000). On the other hand, disciplines themselves are often remarkably heterogeneous or even internally divided (Bensaude-Vincent and Stengers 1996, Galison 1996a, 1996b, Clifford 2005). Consider, for example, the differences between theoretical and experimental high-energy physics (Knorr-Cetina 1999), between computational and laboratory medicinal chemistry (Barry 2005), or between neoclassical, Keynesian and Marxian economics (Amariglio et al 1993). Even more radical internal differences exist between social and biological anthropology (Ingold 2001, Segal and Yanagisako 2005, Eriksen 2007, Harkin 2010) and between the sub-disciplines of geography (Harrison et al 2004, Castree 2005, Bracken and Oughton 2009). Indeed, disciplines are routinely characterised by internal differences; the existence of a discipline does not always imply that there is acceptance of an agreed set of problems, objects, practices, theories or methods, nor even a shared language or common institutional forms. Yet this heterogeneity is not necessarily a source of instability. In Peter Galison's words, 'the disunified, heterogeneous assemblage of the subcultures of science is precisely what structures its strength and coherence' (Galison 1996a: 13).

Disciplines exhibit clear inertial tendencies, and differences within them may exist over long periods of time.[13] They may develop ways of translating across or negotiating not only internal boundaries, but the boundaries between the diverse social worlds involved in any scientific work (Star and Griesemer 1989); or chronic internal intellectual divisions may persist unaddressed through pragmatic working arrangements, and may even be collectively denied. Disciplines should not therefore be regarded as homogeneous, but as multiplicities or heterogeneous unities marked by differences that are themselves enacted in numerous ways (cf. Laclau and Mouffe 1985: 96). The existence of disciplines tends to revolve around a historically evolving and heterogeneous nexus of problems, methods, canonical texts, theories and institutions that it is thought to be worth both contesting and defending. The boundaries of disciplines and the forms in which they should exist, then, are in question and in play. Disciplinary boundaries are neither entirely fixed nor fluid; rather, they are relational and in formation.[14] These dynamics are captured by Stefan Collini in a powerful metaphor when discussing the emergence of cultural studies from its disciplinary progenitors: 'Cultural studies is part of the noise made by the great academic ice-floes of Literature, Sociology and Anthropology . . . , as their mass shifts and breaks apart' (Collini 1994: 3).

Further conceptual ground-clearing is necessary in the face of efforts to define three types of cross-disciplinary practice: interdisciplinarity, multidisciplinarity and transdisciplinarity. Commonly, a distinction is made between multidisciplinarity, in which several disciplines cooperate but continue to work with standard disciplinary framings, and interdisciplinarity, in which there is an attempt to integrate or synthesise perspectives from several disciplines.[15] The case for multidisciplinarity is made by Ian Hacking when he argues for 'collaborating disciplines that do not need to be . . . "interdisciplinary"' and that presume a strong disciplinary base in the study of complex objects (Hacking 2004: 197).

Less clear distinctions are made between interdisciplinarity and transdisciplinarity, and in practice their meanings are often conflated;[16] perhaps the clearest is the assumption that the latter term bears stronger and more radical implications. Yet the terms are also rooted in particular national and transnational traditions. In the Anglo-American academy, the concept of interdisciplinarity has been dominant and has been widely adopted by researchers and funding organisations alike. In this context, interdisciplinarity is often closely linked not only to notions of accountability and innovation, but also to ideas of problem solving; indeed, the demands of problem solving are taken to provide 'axiomatic evidence of the need for multiple perspectives and collaborative work' (Strathern 2004c: 80, 2011).

The idea of transdisciplinarity, in contrast, has wider currency in the French and German speaking worlds. It is said to have been coined at an OECD meeting in Nice in 1970 and was articulated in a subsequent volume, *Interdisciplinarity: Problems of Teaching and Research in Universities* (1972), edited by the Belgian philosopher Leo Apostel and others. Apostel himself developed a radical proposal that the 'socialist manager of a non-bureaucratic society constantly breaking up monopolies' should 'rotate' persons between production and research, in this way attempting 'to realise a strongly interdisciplinary science' (Apostel 1972: 145).

In the same volume, the idea of transdisciplinarity was explicitly linked to the putatively transdisciplinary status of structuralism and systems theory, as well as to what was imagined to be the transdisciplinary practice of 'mathematic' (sic).

The term transdisciplinarity itself was introduced by three authors. The systems theorist Erich Jantsch articulated it as a yet-to-be-realised ideal associated with his vision of a cybernetic university (Jantsch 1972). André Lichnerowicz, a professor of mathematics at the Collège de France, proposed that transdisciplinarity should be based on the kinds of structuralist analyses already established in mathematics, which, he argued, were also developing in the human sciences, indicating that the social sciences were beginning to realise 'the way in which science is built up' (Lichnerowicz 1972: 125). The developmental psychologist Jean Piaget, for his part, looked forward to the emergence of a type of transdisciplinarity that would allow specialised research projects to be 'placed within a total system without any firm boundaries between disciplines' (Piaget 1972: 138).[17] As an alternative to the formalism of the continental thinkers, the historian Asa Briggs, the only British contributor to the volume, outlined the liberal curriculum of the recently founded University of Sussex (Briggs and Michaud 1972), which drew some inspiration from the innovative model of education that had already long been offered to Oxford undergraduates in Greats and Philosophy, Politics and Economics. Indeed, according to another Sussex academic, the University's institutionalised interdisciplinarity had the merit of adapting 'the tutorial system, as developed in Oxford and Cambridge, to the conditions of the modern university' (Corbett 1964: 27).

It is therefore in the French and German speaking worlds that the idea of transdisciplinarity has been most prevalent in recent decades (e.g. Morin 1997, Nowotny 2003a, Hirsch Hadorn et al 2008, Osborne 2011). In comparison with interdisciplinarity, transdisciplinarity is taken to involve a transgression against or transcendence of disciplinary norms; in some influential writings, as we have seen, it is linked to wider directions in twentieth-century thought including structuralism, systems theory and quantum mechanics (Nicolescu 2008, Schmidt 2010). Against this background, Nowotny et al's bold thesis linking transdisciplinarity to Mode-2 knowledge production went further than earlier formulations by endowing the concept with greater sociological and historical significance than hitherto. In their summarising words, '[i]ts reflexivity, eclecticism and contextualization mean that Mode-2 knowledge is inherently transgressive. . . . [It] transcends disciplinary boundaries. It reaches beyond interdisciplinarity to transdisciplinarity' (Nowotny et al 2001: 89). Following Nowotny et al, recent discussions of transdisciplinarity have tended to place less emphasis on the importance of systemic theories, stressing instead the need to reduce the distance between specialised and lay knowledge in problem solving (Lawrence and Després 2004: 398–400, Klein 2004). Whatever the strengths of the concept of transdisciplinarity, in view of the continuing disputes both over its provenance and over its kinship with or difference from interdisciplinarity, in this introduction we attempt neither to define nor to arbitrate between the two terms. Instead, we take 'interdisciplinarity' to be a generic expression, while recognising that interdisciplinarity and transdisciplinarity are indigenous concepts with variable significance in particular circumstances.

Yet despite the varied meanings attributed to them, many accounts of interdisciplinarity and transdisciplinarity are united by the conviction that they proffer a privileged means for the solution of complex 'real-world problems' (Krohn 2010: 31–2) that are taken as given (Klein 2004: 523, Klein 2010: 26, National Academy of Sciences 2004, Baerwald 2010: 495). Rather than taking this conviction as self-evident, it is productive to distinguish between two ways of conceptualising problems (Maniglier 2012). One is to view problems negatively, as obstacles that need to be overcome or as issues that need to be managed or that require a solution. This is the customary stance adopted by many writers on interdisciplinarity. Against this, we want to pose a positive conception of problems, one that directs us to the way that the problematisation of certain situations may demand and generate novel responses (Foucault 1994: 118, Maniglier 1997, 2012, Laurent 2011, Barry 2012).[18] As we shall see, one of the issues raised in contemporary debates is whether the promotion of interdisciplinarity is better understood as a response to given problems or as a means of generating questions around which new forms of thought and experimental practice can coalesce.

Modes of Interdisciplinarity

It should be obvious that interdisciplinarity should not be thought of as a historical given, but as mobilising in any instance an array of programmatic statements, policy interventions, institutional forms, theoretical statements, instruments, materials and research practices – interdisciplinary assemblages that have acquired a remarkable and growing salience. Such assemblages enact a variety of interrelations between disciplines. Yet for all this apparent diversity, we propose in this section that it is possible to identify three modes of interdisciplinarity, by which we mean three ideal-typical arrangements of the interrelations between disciplines.

In broad terms, recent policy interventions and theoretical literatures on interdisciplinarity have tended to assume an integrative or synthesis model of interdisciplinarity, in which a given interdisciplinary practice proceeds through the integration of two or more 'antecedent disciplines' in relatively symmetrical form (Tait and Lyall 2001, Mansilla and Gardner 2003: 162–3, Ramadier 2004, Mansilla 2006a). A prominent study of interdisciplinarity articulates this position clearly:

> Our goal was to understand qualities of expert interdisciplinary work in order to inform educational practice that fosters interdisciplinary understanding. In this study we defined 'interdisciplinary work' as work that integrates knowledge and modes of thinking from two or more disciplines. Such work embraces the goal of advancing understanding (e.g. explain phenomena, craft solutions, raise new questions) in ways that would have not been possible through single disciplinary means.
>
> (Mansilla and Gardner 2003: 160)[19]

This model, and the view that interdisciplinary research should lead to the integration of different disciplinary approaches, has been performative. In climate change research, for example, there is a widespread view that social scientists should provide an account of social factors ('society', 'the economy') that impact on climate change, and that in turn are impacted by climate change (Jasanoff and Wynne 1998: 3). In principle, it is thought that natural scientific and social scientific accounts of impacts should be integrated into a more general model of climate change. The creation of mathematical models provides one set of ways in which such a synthesis or integration can be achieved. Yet it is also notable that far from leading to the formation of novel heterogeneous fields, the development of increasingly 'universal' models can lead to new forms of closure effected through synthesis (Bowker 1993).

In our view, however, interdisciplinary practice should not necessarily be understood additively as the sum of two or more 'disciplinary' components or as achieved through a synthesis of different disciplinary approaches, whether through a process of integration or negotiation (Petts et al 2008). If we take the *integrative-synthesis* mode as a first type, we want to propose two additional ideal-typical modes of interdisciplinary practice, both of which figure prominently in our research and which may coexist in some fields. In the second, *subordination-service* mode, interdisciplinarity takes a form in which one or more disciplines occupy a subordinate or service role in relation to other component disciplines. This points to the hierarchical division of labour that characterises many forms of interdisciplinarity (and that may indeed be the nature of the articulation in putatively 'integrative' interdisciplinarity). In this mode the service discipline(s) are typically conceived as making up for, or filling in for, an absence or lack in the other, (master) discipline(s). In some cases the social sciences are understood precisely in such terms. They appear to make it possible for the natural sciences and engineering to engage with 'social factors' that had hitherto been excluded from analysis or consideration (Marcus 2002). Social scientists are expected to 'adopt the "correct" natural science definition of an environmental problem "and devise relevant solution strategies"' (Leroy 1995, quoted in Owens 2000: 1143, n. 3); or they may be called upon to assess and help to correct a lack of public understanding of science (Irwin and Wynne 1996).

In a nuanced analysis of his role as a social scientist working in an interdisciplinary nanotechnology research centre, Robert Doubleday suggests that in these circumstances '"social science" runs the risk of taking on the role of protecting an inner experimental core from wider complexities of the public meanings of nanotechnology research' (Doubleday 2007: 173). In effect, the social scientist can come to represent 'society' in the laboratory, leaving the conduct of natural scientific research both largely unaffected by the presence of the social scientist and remote from any wider social engagement. While in the field of art-science, particularly in the UK, funding has often been predicated on the notion that the arts are expected to provide a service to science, rendering it more popular or accessible to the lay public, or enhancing and publicising aesthetic aspects of scientific materials or imagery that might not otherwise be appreciated or known.

Ironically, our research suggests that in the microsocial space of interdisciplinary practice the hierarchy entailed in the subordination-service mode can be inverted. In art-science, for example, scientists sometimes adopt a service role for their artist collaborators, providing resources and equipment that are used to further a project conceived largely in artistic terms (cf. Born 1995).

In the third, *agonistic-antagonistic* mode, in contrast, interdisciplinarity takes the form neither of a synthesis nor of a disciplinary division of labour; rather, it is driven by an agonistic or antagonistic relation to existing or prior forms of disciplinary knowledge and practice. Here, interdisciplinarity springs from a self-conscious dialogue with, criticism of or opposition to the limits of established disciplines, or the status of academic research or instrumental knowledge production in general. This does not mean that what is produced can be reduced to these antagonisms, nor that it is necessarily 'oppositional' or 'critical'. By pointing to the *agonistic-antagonistic* mode we highlight how this kind of interdisciplinarity commonly stems from a commitment or desire to contest or transcend the given epistemological and/or ontological assumptions of specific historical disciplines, a move that makes the new interdiscipline irreducible to its 'antecedent disciplines'.[20] This indicates in turn how such a move can only be grasped diachronically by tracing a genealogy of the relevant field, one that is attentive to the particular problematisation entailed, which may generate interdisciplinarity. We might note, for example, how certain advocates of ethnography in the IT industry, faced with the instrumental expectations of the corporation, challenge the view that ethnography should have any direct utility for engineers or designers. Indeed, as we will argue, some industry ethnographers seek explicitly to constitute ethnography as a field that may, to a greater or lesser extent, be antagonistic both to existing sociological approaches to the study of technology[21] and to narrowly scientific and technical understandings of the properties and uses of technical objects and devices (Suchman 2007 [1987], Suchman this volume, Dourish 2001).

An intriguing aspect of our research was ethnographic engagement with informants who themselves had cogent analyses of interdisciplinary practice.[22] One such account was articulated by a key art-science figure: Simon Penny, an artist-engineer and the founding director of the Arts, Computation and Engineering Masters program at the University of California at Irvine (n. 6). Simon distinguished between three kinds of interdisciplinary practice corresponding broadly to our three modes. The first is akin to the integrative-synthesis mode; for Simon it is the least interesting form and one that tends to be officially licenced since it is the least troubling. This is when 'interdisciplinarity [occurs] between separate disciplines which at root have exactly the same commitments; so, for instance, to establish an interdisciplinary project between electrical engineering and material science doesn't really challenge the basic assumptions of the practitioners. The commitments to the nature of knowledge are much the same'.

His second form, corresponding to our subordination-service mode, is when 'practitioners who are firmly rooted in one discipline, and have a strong internal sense of [its] authority – who feel that they hold the master discourse, as it were – go on looting expeditions to grab some subject matter or [methodology] from some outlying discipline and drag it back to mine or exploit or reprocess it'. Simon contrasted these types with a third form, analogous to our agonistic-antagonistic mode, on which he founded the ACE program. This is when,

> coming in as an outsider to a discipline, with a different set of values, the fundamental assumptions by which that discipline is structured are revealed – assumptions that remain largely invisible to insiders. . . . This kind of interdisciplinarity can be fruitful . . . in enabling a context for the mutual critique of the fundamental assumptions of the different disciplines, and indeed of how the disciplines are in fact identified as disciplines. . . . [At stake is a readiness] to accept that one's commitments in one's own discipline may be revealed to be faulty or unreliable.

Simon continued by drawing out the personal implications: 'I'm in an odd position professionally in having been hired half in the Electrical Engineering Department and half in the Studio Art Department. I don't really identify with the practices of either, and nor do they recognise me as one of them'.[23] In Simon's eyes, the ACE program's commitment to an agonistic-antagonistic interdisciplinarity was a test bed for a pedagogy that cut against the grain of the disciplinary values and procedures of the university. The ACE program returns as a focus of Chapter 11.

We have suggested that interdisciplinarity enacts an array of interrelations between disciplines, with distinctive effects – a diversity that the discourse of Mode-2, with its focus on an epochal shift in the forms of knowledge production, tends to overlook. If the integrative-synthesis mode can augur epistemic transformations, and if the service-subordination mode, with its disciplinary division of labour, is unlikely to afford even this, then what is striking about the agonistic-antagonistic mode is that it can be associated with more radical shifts in knowledge practices, shifts that may be epistemic and/or ontological. Indeed in what follows, with reference to the interdisciplinary fields that we studied and certain chapters in this volume, we propose that a privileged relation can be discerned between the agonistic-antagonistic mode and what we will call the logic of ontology. To demonstrate this it is necessary to employ the framework outlined earlier and specifically to do two things: first, through an account of the genealogies of each field, to indicate how the agonistic-antagonistic mode can only be understood diachronically in terms of a dynamic imperative to supersede prior epistemological and/or ontological commitments; and second, to convey how this dynamic cannot be grasped by attributing a spurious unity. Instead, each interdisciplinary field must be analysed as precisely in formation and 'in play' – as a multiplicity.

Logics of Interdisciplinarity

If the identification of modes of interdisciplinarity highlights the diverse ways in which the interrelations between disciplines can be configured, it tells us little about why interdisciplinarity is thought to be necessary, nor about the transformations in research practice that it aims to bring about. In what follows we address these issues by pointing to three distinctive logics guiding the present burgeoning of interdisciplinarity. We call these the logics of accountability, of innovation and of ontology. In distinguishing between them, we wish to make three initial points. First, we do not imply that the list is exhaustive. It might well be possible to multiply the number of logics governing the development of interdisciplinarity and to make further differentiations within them. Nor do we imply that interdisciplinary research has always been guided by them. Rather, we point to the three logics in order to emphasise the particular nature of the rationales and techniques governing the contemporary development of interdisciplinarity which, as mentioned, are sometimes elided in earlier discussions. We want to retain here a sense of the multiplicity of logics, but also to make visible differences that matter for our analysis.

Secondly, when writing of logics, we do not think of them merely as states of mind or ideas. What we have called the logic of accountability has been fostered and developed through an array of technologies and devices that take specific material and immaterial forms – including voluntary agreements, websites, legislation, public inquiries, public consultations and voting procedures (Barry 2002, 2006, Latour and Weibel 2005). We therefore understand the logic of accountability through its relation to a range of practices and technologies of government oriented towards the conduct of research. Similarly, the logic of innovation depends on the activity of researchers, designers, engineers, marketers, accountants, economists and journalists in their practical engagement with a series of material and informational objects. Through this activity, certain investments in new practices and technologies become possible, desirable and visible (Power 1996, Callon et al 2007). The logics that we discern, then, are imagined, empractised and worlded: they come to exist in material, informational and social forms, and they may have inventive and anti-inventive consequences (Barry 2007).

Thirdly, the logics of interdisciplinarity that we describe here can be interdependent; they may also be confused. It is notable, for instance, that concepts of 'users', 'user needs' and 'user engagement' have migrated and may now be taken to index not only accountability to publics but the involvement of stakeholders or a responsiveness to consumers or to industry. Our aim in identifying the three logics, then, is to indicate how they are imbricated in the interdisciplinary fields that we studied. If accountability and innovation are often linked to the contemporary discourse on interdisciplinarity, in what follows our primary focus is their heterogeneous practico-material and discursive expression in these fields, and how they can be entangled with a logic of ontology.

According to a number of authors and policy initiatives, interdisciplinary research can be governed by a logic of accountability (Nowotny et al 2001, Strathern 2004b). In this view, as already noted, interdisciplinarity is understood to foster a culture of accountability, breaking down the barriers between science and society and leading to greater interaction, for instance, between scientists and various publics. In Nowotny's terms, 'science can no longer assume that support for its activities are self-evident. . . . The culture of autonomy of science has shifted to a culture of accountability which can take many different forms' (Nowotny 2003a: 211–12). In our research this logic appeared in several guises. It could be a matter of defending or legitimising the sciences by providing them with a protective layer of social scientific expertise or public 'engagement' – in this way deflecting potentially more disruptive criticisms, or meeting legislative requirements or guidelines for public consultation.[24] In some cases, as we have seen, it appeared as though the minimal performance of interdisciplinarity through the employment of social scientists in a natural scientific laboratory could be taken as an indicator of accountability (Doubleday 2007). An analogous situation pertained in the British art-science field, which emerged in the 1990s in response to a series of funding schemes including the Wellcome Trust's Sciart programme and Arts Council England/Arts and Humanities Research Board's Art-Science Fellowships.[25] Prominent in the rationale for such funding was the 'public understanding of science' paradigm: that art can be used to popularise or communicate science and its social, cultural and ethical dimensions, whether through aesthetic elaboration or by rendering scientific discovery exciting or palatable by expressive means. Here, artists' collaboration with scientists was expected to effect a wider social engagement, on occasion providing an aesthetic legitimation (Born and Barry, this volume).

But it would be wrong to contend that the social sciences or arts invariably function as instruments of legitimation, defending against the possibility of public criticism or enabling legislative guidelines to be met. There is evidence that critical social movements, in alliance with social scientists, can play an active role in directing or conducting scientific research (Irwin 1995, Epstein 1996, Rabeharisoa and Callon 1999, Callon et al 2001). Moreover, social scientists have developed potentially inventive ways of engaging publics in scientific debate through practices such as deliberative mapping and participatory integrated assessment (Davies 2006, Weszkalnys and Barry, this volume). These interventions can be justified both on the basis that they encourage publics and governments to 'buy into' the results of the research, and on the grounds that they can make scientific institutions more responsive to the demands and concerns of non-scientists.

In our study of environmental research, the German Öko-Institut can be seen as representing a radical vision of 'accountability' through its inversion of the standard hierarchy of relations between the natural sciences and social sciences or political activism. When it was founded in 1977, the Öko-Institut was understood by environmental activists and civic action groups in south-western Germany to be serving their movements through the production of scientific research – what they termed a counter-science (*Gegen-Wissenschaft*) – that would endow their protests with strong foundations. We see a similar inversion in some areas of art-science. On the one hand, the idea of public understanding of science represents the hierarchical arrangement in which art serves to render science communicable, comprehensible or non-alienating. On the other hand, in an alternative lineage of art-science, such instrumental orientations are resisted: instead, the field is contaminated by a series of troubling genealogies, notably certain conceptual art and art and technology movements, which animate practices and events that are incommensurable with disciplinary art or science. In this way art-science is caught up in a nexus of imperatives stemming from conceptual art's refusal of notions of autonomous art and its foregrounding of art's social embeddedness, including public art as social research, art that probes mediation and publicity, and art that engages with the politics of science and technology (Osborne 2002, Corris 2004, 2005, Buchmann 2006, Da Costa and Philip 2008). A multiplicity of accountabilities are therefore manifest in interdisciplinary assemblages, from legitimation and regulation to critical and radically militant forms.

Yet while accountability has been central to a variety of initiatives involving social scientists and artists in the environmental, techno- and biosciences, this is not the exclusive logic governing such interdisciplinary engagements. Arguments for the involvement of social scientists, and sometimes artists, in natural science and engineering research have been guided also by a logic of innovation. In our research the logic of innovation was most pronounced in the growth of ethnographic research in the IT industry, where ethnography has been widely promoted as a solution to the problem of connecting businesses to the unarticulated desires of their customers – desires that are not sufficiently identified or evoked by more conventional methods of market research and that, it is believed, can drive innovation (Thrift 2006, Barry and Thrift 2007). We might say that ethnography in the IT industry offers a set of techniques through which businesses are expected to be able to transform their knowledge of and engagement with those micro-spaces of social life, replete with social and cultural difference, to which they previously did not have access (Thrift 2005, 2006: 283).[26] To this end, ethnographers in industry may collaborate closely with designers and engineers in small teams, forging relations with different communities of practice within the firm (Amin and Cohendet 2004). They may attempt to fine-tune the design of products by offering analyses of how they are likely to be of value to users. The interdisciplinary teams may also develop prototypes, as this ethnographer describes:

> Some people did actually do designs, prototypes, that ended up being transferred into the product divisions – but that's very hard to do. We tried to do it with the end-user programming stuff. We had a prototype that my group worked on, and we thought it was good, but we couldn't convince the product divisions that they wanted to put their money into it. The idea with research groups is that you find a bunch of smart people, and maybe 10 to 15 per cent of the designs they come up with are going to end up in the product divisions – and that's true at any company.[27]

Ethnography can therefore have implications that depart from any immediate utility for the corporation, providing, for example, portraits of diverse contexts of consumption that feed into thinking about long-term strategies such as openings in and demands from emerging markets (Thrift 2005). Moreover, in directing corporations to consider the ways and contexts in which technology is used, ethnography can be employed to challenge narrowly technology-driven investment strategies (Miller and O'Leary 2007). According to a leading IT corporate innovation strategist,

> Success exists at the intersection . . . of three domains [user value, business value, technology] and reaching the center is inherently a mixed-discipline process. It requires that the technologist or engineer be able to constructively interact with these other, non-technical disciplines [ethnography and market analysis]. That typically requires having a good understanding of why other domains matter, what vocabulary they use, and how their work relates to the engineer's work.
>
> (D'Hooge 2005: 4)

In an era in which businesses have increasingly mediated relations with their customers, there is an escalating demand for ethnography to proffer what may appear to be direct and naturalistic connections to those intimate and exotic spaces, relations, practices, bodies and affects that are perceived to be missing or to have been lost – or at least to stage that connection, or provide a proxy for it (Suchman 2012, this volume). In this way, by elucidating the 'real value' of technological products for users, ethnography is expected to access some of those 'external excesses' that are vital to capitalism and the condition of its success (Mitchell 2002: 303).

Likewise, the problem-focused orientation of interdisciplinary environmental and energy research can also entail the logic of innovation. For example, social scientists may be drawn into dialogue with natural scientists and engineers involved in the development of increasingly efficient, affordable and environmentally sustainable technologies such as renewables, carbon capture and storage, and smart grids.[28] This orientation towards innovation may, of necessity, engender a pragmatic approach to the challenge of fostering interdisciplinary research. As an interdisciplinary team manager put it: 'I don't think we sat down and worked out a model of interdisciplinarity. We learned as we went along, and consequently, if you talk to people in different parts of the team, they have different experiences of how interdisciplinarity has evolved'.[29] At the same time, the logic of innovation is likely to be entangled with the logic of accountability in so far as research funding bodies are now convinced that if new energy and environmental technologies are to be successfully introduced, they need to be acceptable to interested publics.

Ontologies and Entanglement

The examples of interdisciplinary environmental research and ethnography in the IT industry might appear to support the contention that interdisciplinarity arises primarily in response to wider social and economic demands. But what is striking across a range of interdisciplinary fields today is how they are understood to be governed not only by a logic of accountability or of innovation, but by what we are identifying as an ontological logic.[30] As we emphasised earlier, we should not understand this logic simply as a set of ideas about what the world is, but rather as encompassing a diverse range of rationales, techniques, practices and interventions. It is manifest in an array of efforts to transform the practice of research and training, inside and outside the academy, leading to the generation of novel problems, objects and relations of research, as well as interdisciplinary subjectivities (Greco this volume, Born and Barry this volume). The logic of ontology, as we have insisted, is neither an historical constant nor universal; it exists in relation to other logics, and it responds to and may be elicited by material circumstances and historical currents.

In the chapters that follow we discern various manifestations of the logic of ontology. Crucially, in each case what is at stake are interdisciplinary practices whose orientation to the world cannot be grasped merely in the terms of epistemology, as though they were separate from the world with which they engage. The limits of epistemology as a way of understanding scientific practices has been central to recent developments in the history and sociology of science. A number of writers including Lorraine Daston, Bruno Latour and Annemarie Mol have advanced the proposition that scientific research does not simply represent its objects, but has the effect of generating new entities or enhancing and adding to the properties of existing ones (Latour 1999: 124). Scientific research practices therefore enter into the world, enacting it in multiple forms (Barry 2005). For Mol, this observation leads to the possibility of what she terms an 'ontological politics' such that the question of which entities are brought into being and what relation they have to one another should be recognised as a political matter (Mol 2002). For Daston, rejecting the sterile dichotomy between realism and constructionism, historians must attend to

> how a heretofore unknown, ignored, or dispersed set of phenomena is transformed into a scientific object that can be observed and manipulated, that is capable of theoretical ramifications and empirical surprises, and that coheres, at least for a time, as an ontological entity.
>
> (Daston 2000: 5)

In tracing the historicity of scientific objects, she advocates an 'applied metaphysics' (ibid.: 3), one that revives 'ontology for historians', thereby enabling them to avoid 'slipping back into' the familiar tropes of neo-Kantian epistemology (ibid.: 14). This is a project, Daston says, that stands orthogonally to the realism–constructionism debates, while being attentive to the ways in which scientific research can make entities 'grow more richly real as they become entangled in webs of cultural significance, material practices, and theoretical derivations' (Daston 2000: 13). Latour, for his part, criticises those philosophies of science that draw a radical distinction between epistemology and ontology, contending that it is necessary to chart how in the course of scientific practice (for example, Pasteur's experimentation with lactic acid fermentation) the entities involved (both Pasteur and the ferment) '*mutually exchange and enhance their properties*' (Latour 1999: 124, emphasis in original). Thus, 'an experiment is an event' in which all the elements are partially transformed (ibid.: 126). Rather than maintain, with the philosophers of science, that 'we should never confuse epistemological questions (what our representation of the world is) and ontological questions (what the world is really like)', Latour avers that 'confusing those two supposedly separate domains is precisely what scientists spend much of their time doing' (ibid.: 93).

Andrew Pickering (this volume) comes at these issues from another direction, drawing attention to what he calls nonmodern ontologies. His example is cybernetics and its ramifying influence from the mid-twentieth century. If the Cartesian modern sciences – physics preeminent among them – 'presume a knowable world, of identifiable entities in specifiable interaction with one another', the nonmodern sciences, Pickering suggests, envisage a world replete with non-dualist couplings of the human and nonhuman, one 'that is ultimately not fully knowable – a world of endless unpredictable emergence and becoming' (ibid.: 209). In this sense his perspective converges with that espoused by neo-vitalist social theory (Fraser et al 2006, Connolly 2011). As Pickering makes clear, nonmodern ontologies are not merely ideas or conceptions of the world driven by an antagonistic relation to the ontology of the moderns. Rather, nonmodern ontologies have been worked through and demonstrated in a series of practical devices and experimental and control techniques in an expansive array of fields.

We find these perspectives compelling. But in proposing the existence of the logic of ontology, our arguments are both more specific and more historically situated than those advanced by these writers. In this book we are concerned not with the practice of modern science in general, but with the recent burgeoning of interdisciplinarity. We wish therefore to differentiate between general arguments for an applied metaphysics or for the existence of nonmodern ontologies and the idea of a logic of ontology manifest in contemporary forms of interdisciplinarity which necessitates that we attend – through the genealogy of particular interdisciplinary practices and fields – to its path-dependency and historicity and to the distinctive style in which it is empractised.

Four propositions follow. The first is that the logic of ontology can be discerned in the way that certain forms of interdisciplinarity take as a focus of concern how knowledge practices intervene in the world, bringing the subjects and objects of research into a relational existence. Second, and relatedly, the logic of ontology is manifest in those interdisciplinary practices that are oriented towards the generation of hybrid or relational objects that cannot be broken down into distinct natural, technical and social components. Conversely, it may be that it is the hybridity or relationality of the problem that resists the efforts of disciplinary practitioners to distil them into distinct natural and social fractions; and it is this resistance that may engender interdisciplinary practices that reconfigure or cut across the borders between the natural and social sciences (Latour 1993).

A third proposition is that the logic of ontology is evident when interdisciplinary practices arise in response to, or encounter, the problem of what the philosopher A. N. Whitehead called the 'bifurcation of nature'. In this way Whitehead pointed to a division between two aspects of nature: namely, the 'nature which is the cause of awareness' and 'the nature apprehended in awareness' (Whitehead 1920: 31) or, in Michael Halewood's exegesis, the 'ostensibly unbridgeable gap between reality as conceived by science and reality as experienced by humans' (Halewood 2011: 8). Once again, our observation here about the logic of ontology is historically specific. It is that we can speak about the logic of ontology to the extent that interdisciplinary practices today address, or are forced to address, the bifurcation of nature. Responses to this challenge can take many forms, such as a recognition of the importance of attending to the aesthetic, affective or social qualities of events as well as their physical or biological dynamics. It is striking in this regard that Whitehead perceived a connection between the philosophical problem of the bifurcation of nature and the organisation of university education into distinct departments or faculties (Whitehead 1926).

A fourth proposition regarding the logic of ontology, which integrates the three previous points, concerns the social arrangements mobilised by distinctive forms of interdisciplinarity. The involvement in scientific research of non-experts, citizens or lay publics, as others have noted, can generate both different objects and different ways of proposing problems (Callon et al 2001, Stengers 2005). In this book we build on this insight by drawing a contrast between practices of 'public understanding' that are intended to interpellate an absent but preformed public, a public that is assumed to exist, which tends to be associated with a logic of accountability, and the potential for participatory practices such as those invoked by ideas of 'public engagement' or user involvement, which can be associated both with accountability and with a logic of ontology (Weszkalnys and Barry, this volume, Born and Barry, this volume). As the chapters by Lucy Suchman and Sarah Whatmore (this volume) suggest, such participatory methods may engender novel arrangements and can lead to inventive effects; they should not be understood simply as a means of fostering accountability. Rather, the alternative modes of knowledge and experience characteristic of lay publics and non-experts are likely to enlarge and enrich what must be taken into account. And if it is accepted that the affective and aesthetic dimensions of experience enter as much as physical or biological processes into the constitution of the world, then not only the knowledge of non-experts and lay participants but the contributions to world-making of these dimensions of experience should also be recognised.

Ethnography in the IT industry and the logic of ontology

To discern how the logic of ontology is imbricated in any interdisciplinary field, as we have said, requires a genealogical grasp of its path dependence, and this is so even in apparently applied fields of research. Consider ethnography in the IT industry: a field that might seem most closely oriented to the logic of innovation and the commercial imperatives of the firm. Ethnography in the IT industry has a long history with multiple genealogies. It developed, in particular, from ethnomethodological studies of work (Suchman 2007 [1987], Bowker et al 1997), as well as sociological and phenomenological critiques of artificial intelligence. It drew additional inspiration from the Scandinavian Participatory Design movement (Schuler and Namioka 1993). In human–computer interaction (HCI) research in the IT industry and academia, efforts to bring ethnomethodological and other ethnographic approaches together with design led, in the mid-1980s, to the emergence of the interdisciplinary field of computer-supported cooperative work (CSCW). Within the broader space of HCI, ethnography appeared to offer 'a means by which the complexity of real-world settings could be apprehended, and a toolkit of techniques for studying technology "in the wild"' (Dourish 2006: 2). More recently, some ethnographers in the IT industry have drawn extensively on academic research in cultural anthropology (e.g. Clifford and Marcus 1986) and the sociology and anthropology of technology (e.g. Silverstone and Hirsch 1994, Miller and Slater 2000), while others have been influenced by interaction design (e.g. Gaver, Dunne and Pacenti 1999). The success and visibility of ethnography in the IT industry has caused the techniques to be imitated across new domains, notably in market research and other industries including banking, media and pharmaceuticals (Born 2005a, ch. 7, Barry 2005).[31]

The result of these complex genealogies is a heterogeneous field dispersed across a range of commercial and academic sites, one that is in formation and the boundaries of which are animated by continuing controversies and differences. These vibrant controversies reveal the extent to which ethnography in the IT industry manifests the agonistic-antagonistic mode of interdisciplinarity. The most prominent area of controversy centres on the imbrication of the logic of ontology and that of innovation. It has two modalities. First, there is a spectrum of positions on the question of the relation between ethnography and design (Salvador, Bell and Anderson 1999). For some, ethnography in the IT industry should be thoroughly integrated into a practice of user-centred design; for others, the theoretical claims of ethnography should be clearly distinguished from any particular design implications (Dourish 2006). Second, there is an ongoing debate amongst ethnographers in the IT industry, involving multiple perspectives, over the relative merits of different theoretical and methodological accounts of the social, including those derived from the traditions of ethnomethodology, science and technology studies, and social and cultural anthropology, and how they can be articulated with industry and HCI research. A core current concerns the evolving relations between ethnography as it is practised in industry, including ethnomethodology and conversation analysis, and 'anthropological ethnography'. According to one informant, for example, tensions exist between 'old-fashioned, . . . broad-based' ethnography – by implication holistic, exhaustive and sustained – and what he portrayed as the more attenuated focus of the ethnomethodologists, whose research time frames are much shorter and where analysis may dwell exclusively on transcripts or on twenty minutes of video.[32] Yet other actors point to a distinction between those who defend the integrity of ethnography as an established historical body of anthropological theory and methodology and those who claim that ethnography in industry has itself evolved and diffused in recent years to become a pluralistic field – a set of techniques that have been utilised in and refined by different traditions and settings, and that are now quite distinct from ethnography as it is practised academically (Randall et al 2005):[33]

> My argument is that ethnography in different practices [such as CSCW] has built up caucuses and reasoning, and that the reason you do [academic] anthropology at Cambridge is to learn what it is that prior anthropologists have argued about, but also to learn the analytic sensibility. . . . But likewise, . . . ethnography in CSCW is different from what it was twenty years ago. I mean, ethnography in CSCW: there's no reason why you should turn to [academic] anthropology; you should just turn to the caucus of stuff that's there.[34]

Within ethnography in industry there are therefore quite conscious, and contested, attempts to distinguish the affordance of interdisciplinary research from demands for better design or new products or organisational forms. Collectively, this question of establishing a distance between the field and demand, or not, has been staged since 2005 in the organisation of the annual EPIC conference (n. 26), a forum where the emerging field performs its reflexive professionalisation and where these and other controversies are agonistically aired. In individual research groups, meanwhile, the performance of distance from the immediate demands of the IT corporation for improved product or process takes diverse forms. It can involve orienting research towards the production of academic journal articles and conference papers rather than industrial prototypes or designs; it can take the form of a critique of the politics of industrial ethnographic practice (Anderson and Nafus 2006); it can entail the development of designs that are not intended to be the basis for products; and it can take the form of research with no discernible relation to consumer demand or design: 'Our role is not to design a new and better application for X or a new and better gadget'.[35]

There is much to be said about why some ethnographers distance their work from expectations that it should impact on design. It may be difficult for them to demonstrate any direct impact, and even when their work does have implications for design it may be problematic to discuss these in public because of commercial confidentiality. At the same time, ethnographers are more likely to achieve such distance in those corporations able to pursue a long-term research strategy, as well as those that collaborate with universities or fund university-linked research outfits. In this situation the corporation gains by having researchers that act as a porous interface with their academic counterparts, picking up currents across the Chinese walls (Amin and Cohendet 2004). Moreover, the corporation accrues legitimacy by supporting and being seen to support an interstitial zone of hybrid research, demonstrating its commitment to the generation of research with no immediate economic utility:

> The primary reason I was attracted to the Lab was this open policy of collaboration not just with [corporate] researchers but outside individuals – we are encouraged to bridge those kinds of connections. . . . It's obvious that

there are lots of other people and other disciplines that have looked at this phenomenon [interactions between social life and technology]. They should be part of the dialogue. The main thing is the open policy: it's a great model. I wanted to be able to share things. In the same way this is a very academic-feeling environment, being close to academia.[36]

It would be a mistake to reduce these demonstrations of autonomy from the logic of innovation merely to legitimation or public relations, even if they may sometimes be seen as such by corporate managers (cf. Latour and Weibel 2002). On the one hand, they demonstrate the possible contribution of ethnography in the IT industry to debates that are not oriented towards industrial applications or innovation. Indeed, some industry researchers argue that the corporate context makes it possible to carry out inventive types of ethnography that it would be difficult or impossible to undertake in academia, including sustained and intensive collaborations with designers and computer scientists (Cefkin 2009). On the other hand, they express a sense that the justification of the role of ethnographer is in large part ontological: that s/he must effect an ontological transformation. The rationale for carrying out ethnography, then, is not just that it may impact on design, but that it has the potential to transform the technological object from being merely an object or product into something which, depending on the approach, is locally situated, socially contextualised, encultured or emotionally attached (e.g. Suchman 2007 [1987], Bowker et al 1997, Nardi and O'Day 1999, Dourish 2001, Suchman et al 2002, Harper 2003, Nafus and Anderson 2009, Dourish and Bell 2011). In this respect ethnography in the IT industry draws on and, through collaboration with designers and computer scientists, contributes to much longer traditions of philosophical and social enquiry concerning the nature of technology. Of course, the ontological contribution of the ethnographer may nonetheless have implications for design, or contribute to increasingly sophisticated market research.

In an irony that is not lost on the actors, the ontological chemistry of corporate ethnography is crystallised in a highly developed rhetoric of naturalism (Anderson and Nafus 2006). We can distinguish at least five techniques by which the ethnographer is able to achieve this chemistry in practice:

- Through *metonymy*: the ethnographer reports on social reality indexically through the use of audio-visual recordings, photographs and ethnographic vignettes – bringing back to the corporation a small part of the real (Salvador, Bell and Anderson 1999, Anderson and Nafus 2006);
- Through *contagion*: the ethnographer as 'I-witness' (Geertz 1988), in direct contact with the real, gives personal testimony and acts as a proxy for social reality – standing in for society in design meetings and conversations with engineers and management;
- Through *transportation*: the ethnographer acts as a guide who takes the executive, engineer or designer physically outside the corporation/the US for a direct experience of the real (D'Hooge 2005: 7);

- Through *collaboration*: the ethnographer engages in an interdisciplinary practice of user-centred design, transforming socio-technical reality through processes of collaboration; and
- Through *scientific observation*: the ethnographer acts as an observer, whose descriptions and findings may or may not have subsequent implications for design (Dourish 2001, 2006).

In these and other ways, ethnography can be employed in efforts to catalyse a transformation of the ontological imagination of the firm towards a conception of the industrial object as a socio-cultural-technical assemblage (Bell, Brooke and Churchill 2003, Dourish 2006, Thrift 2006: 288, Dourish and Bell 2011). The problem faced by corporate ethnographers in seeking to effect such transformations at the level of corporate strategy and imagination is at base, then, a rhetorical one. The challenge may not be how to provide a detailed and nuanced description of the way that IT mediates the routines of an Indian middle-class home, an American public library or a Russian street, but how to demonstrate the ontological truth that technical objects have to be understood as situated in particular microsocial, encultured and affective assemblages (Deleuze 1988). Corporate ethnography may be marked by an emphasis on rhetoric and display, but, as Barbara Cassin argues, rhetoric can be necessary for truth to survive in harsh conditions (Cassin 2005).

Interdisciplinary environmental research and the logic of ontology

The logic of ontology is at work in a different guise in the field of environmental and climate change research. As we have noted, interdisciplinary environmental research institutions tend to have a problem-solving orientation, and their development has largely been guided by a logic of accountability: because environmental problems are multidimensional they demand interdisciplinary approaches, and because they are objects of government and of immense public political concern, they raise issues of accountability.

Yet, along with accountability and problem solving, it is possible to discern several new arguments and techniques emerging both in environmental and climate change research and in related fields, including environmental geography. A particularly influential set of arguments was associated with the emergence of the field of climate science in the 1970s. As Paul Edwards argues, climatologists in the 1960s represented climate change primarily using long-term statistical databases. However, by the late 1970s computer-based models had become dominant. Since then, in the context of the developing interdisciplines of climate science and earth systems science, the global environment has come to be understood and modelled as a set of systems of varying scales, levels of resolution and complexity (Edwards 2001: 32–3). Within this framework, the contribution of the social sciences was expected to be the provision of one element of an integrated analysis of the global environment. At the same time, the global environment has increasingly been addressed not just as a system or set of systems, but as an object of global government:[37] '[earth systems analysis] is a diagnostic instrument, generating evidence necessary for treatment. This means that we are ultimately confronted with a control problem, a geo-cybernetic task' (Schellnhuber 1999: 20).

More recently, however, a different set of rationales and techniques have emerged in interdisciplinary environmental research influenced by a range of intellectual traditions including political ecology, science and technology studies, social anthropology and cultural geography. Although these arguments have a long history, they did not become visible in environmental research until the late 1990s (Liverman 1999). There are three strands to these arguments, which are sometimes elided. The first proposes that established understandings of natural science models of the environment have failed to address the ways in which such models are shaped by political assumptions and cultural values: 'it is not that the scientific models and ensuing knowledge are empty of culture and politics, but that they are impregnated with them without even recognising it, let alone the implications' (Shackley and Wynne 1985: 124, Hulme 2009). At the same time, in this view, the uncertainties of scientific knowledge claims, including climate change models, are seldom acknowledged in public debate (Jasanoff and Wynne 1998).

The second strand originated in an awareness of the limitations of scientific expertise as well as recognition of the importance of local and indigenous knowledge with respect to the environment. In this view, lay and non-expert accounts of environmental problems should not be understood merely as perceptions, but recognised as an expression of a kind of 'citizen science' (Irwin 1995, Wynne 1996, Callon et al 2001, Berkhout et al 2005: 12, Leach et al 2005). Both environmental science and policy are understood in this perspective to be immanently cultural and political. Indeed, Brian Wynne contends that non-experts can contribute knowledge and expertise concerning the local, social and historical nature of environmental issues that scientific experts do not possess (Wynne 1996). In this view, while devices such as public consultations and public inquiries may often be anti-inventive, legitimising the authority of established sources of scientific expertise, other techniques for engaging non-experts in environmental debate and research practice can be more generative (Callon et al 2001, Stirling 2005, Turnpenny et al 2005, Davies 2006, Whatmore 2009, this volume). Such inventive modes of inter- and extra-disciplinary practice involving non-experts are frequently justified in terms of their contribution to greater accountability. At the same time, however, both experts and non-experts must perform the difficult task of demonstrating the autonomy of these new interdisciplinary practices from a logic of accountability. That is to say, the involvement of non-experts in research and public debate may have critical implications for policy and practice precisely in so far as it cannot be dismissed either as an expression of a predetermined politics or as a response to the need for accountability.

Together, these two strands of rationales and techniques suggest that closer attention should be paid to the politics of research and the manner in which non-experts participate in the production of environmental knowledge and in the dynamics of environmental knowledge controversies. In this respect they resonate with Nowotny et al's (2001) general claims about the erosion of boundaries between experts and non-experts, as well as the need for scientific knowledge claims to stand up to scrutiny in the public arena. However, together these arguments point to a third, more encompassing ontological orientation evident in recent environmental research according to which the environment can no longer be cognised as presenting a given set of problems that demand to be acted upon or solved. In this account, environmental research does not confront an external nature or a given set of problems, but itself contributes to the problematisation of the environment (Castree 2005, Anderson and Braun 2008). Nor can publics and stakeholders be understood as distinct from the existence of environmental problems which they define and to which they respond (Latour 1999, Liverman 1999, Callon et al 2001, Jasanoff 2004). Instead, the practice of environmental research is understood as animated by and as entering into the ongoing formation and re-formation both of environmental problems and of their publics. Conversely, environmental problems may engender interdisciplinary research practices not because the environment is a complex system containing a number of distinct social and natural subsystems, nor because of demands for greater public accountability, but because the hybridity of environmental problems resists purification into distinct natural and social elements (Latour 2004, Whatmore 1999). These encompassing ontological and political arguments have been articulated primarily by researchers in science and technology studies, social anthropology and geography (Hinchliffe 2007, Braun and Whatmore 2010). Their implications for the practice and politics of interdisciplinary environmental research, as well as for policy and politics, remain contested and in process (Whatmore, this volume, Weszkalnys and Barry, this volume).

Overall, the practice of interdisciplinary environmental research appears more fragmented as a field than ethnography in the IT industry. Where ethnography provides a core method around which ontological issues arise, and which, however interpreted, serves to give some sense of unity to the interdiscipline, there is no such core method in interdisciplinary environmental research. Instead, there are a multitude of different ways of researching the environment associated with different social scientific approaches and techniques, including computer modelling, systems analysis, scenario analysis, focus groups, interactive assessment, competency groups and ethnography (Whatmore, this volume, Weszkalnys and Barry, this volume). In these circumstances, interdisciplinary environmental research institutions are often marked by divisions not only between the natural and social sciences, but between alternative interdisciplinary perspectives associated with the different environmental social sciences and their particular articulation of the logic of ontology.

Art-science and the logic of ontology

Of our three interdisciplinary fields, perhaps the clearest manifestation of the logic of ontology occurs in the burgeoning field of art-science: an exemplary instance of interdisciplinary endeavour across the 'two cultures' (Snow 1959). Art-science is a field recognised by practitioners, funders and arts institutions alike. It emerged in its current guise in the mid-1990s, but its identity continues to evolve through its close association with an array of other practices – including installation and robotic art, bio art and wet art – that occupy the borderlands between the arts, sciences and technologies (Wilson 2002, Popper 2007, da Costa and Philip 2008, Reichle 2009). We might consider art-science, then, as an emergent interdiscipline.[38] At its core lie retentions of long-standing currents dating from the mid-twentieth century that problematise the ontological grounds of what art is or can be, causing this to be cast into doubt and to be radically transformed. Such ontological transformations can be grasped by tracing its plural genealogies, in particular through diachronic analysis of the unfurling in recent decades of an evolving set of concerns with the interconnections and mediations between both art and technology and art and the social. Although the perspective varies according to individual and institutional commitment and location, the genealogy of art-science encompasses the mutual entanglement of at least three currents, notably (post-)conceptual art, movements articulating art and technology, and practices in which art engages with the bio, computational and information sciences.

Conceptual art, which originated in the post-Second World War period in a wave of heterogeneous rejections of formalist modernisms, generated a series of directions that remain influential across a range of contemporary art practices, including art-science. Its basic premise is a commitment to an entirely distinctive ontology of art, indeed to pluralising art's ontologies (Newman 2002, Doherty 2004, Skrebowski 2009, Born and Barry, this volume). This premise is evident both in art-science practices that have taken materials and media as the locus of experimentation, and in those practices that have been oriented more towards social and political experiment (Buchmann 2006). In the politicised lineages of art-science, both science and technology studies and critical and feminist theories may be brought into the mix in an attempt to build a systematic critical reflexivity into the new practices. Art-science engages science, then, in plural ways: in terms of mining the conceptual and material armouries of the sciences, in terms of convergent interests in experimentation and innovation, and in the guise of animating critiques of science. Together, the genealogies of art-science etch out a decidedly artistic space, but one that intersects with technological and scientific experimentation and controversy, such that art is retooled – as one practitioner put it – as a kind of 'interdisciplinary production'.

Prominent in Britain, as mentioned earlier, are currents linking art-science to accountability. Whether in the Wellcome Trust's 'public understanding of science' funding paradigm or its 'public engagement' successor, art-science 'has been sold around a very pragmatic and instrumentalist notion' of reaching new audiences for science (see Born and Barry, this volume).[39] Despite efforts to combat this limiting image, there is a perception that this instrumental conception, along with the limited collaborations allowed by project-based funding for art-science, make for conditions that prey on artists' precarious financial standing and can result in poor work.[40] This points to a key line of dissent within the field, in which the output from such project-based funding schemes – where collaboration between artist and scientist is often short-lived and the division of labour remains intact; that is, where art-science labours in a subordination-service mode under the logic of accountability – is commonly characterised as 'decorative', 'celebratory' or superficial. In contrast, originality and invention in art-science are invariably associated by those in the field with practices in which the engagement or confrontation between art and science is deeper and sustained, and in which artists are able – or are trained – to make full and knowledgeable use of the 'special facilities of the scientific lab', engineering workshop or computer workstation.[41]

While art-science has often been justified as contributing to the public understanding of science, the field has also been prominently associated with the logic of innovation. This is exemplified by an influential report, commissioned by the Rockefeller Foundation, which emphasises the 'studio-lab' as a site of experimental activity in which artistic practices can 'co-evolve' with new technologies and new media, engendering creative applications (Century 1999, cf. Born 1995). Here the studio-lab is portrayed as a key site for fostering innovation, while science is seen as proffering new subject matters, concepts, imagery, technologies and materials that elicit artistic experimentation.

More generally, artists' engagements with scientific and technological research are taken by commentators to offer a range of potential stimuli or aids to innovation. Collaborative projects between artists and scientists may provoke and enrich scientific research, triggering unforeseen directions; they may assemble an unconventional mix of disciplinary skills and talents; the artist can offer the content required for the testing of new technological tools; artists' responses to new research, concepts or materials can allow scientists to observe human responses and behaviour; artists may act as particularly acute or creative 'lead users', generating further research or development; or the artistic exhibition of research outcomes may act as a test bed for their launch in the real world (cf. Naimark 2003). In Britain an Art and Science Research Fellowship programme initiated in 2003 by Arts Council England and the AHRB was founded on the conviction that art-science could embody the entanglement of the logics of innovation and ontology. The scheme responded explicitly to calls from government bodies such as the 2001 Council on Science and Technology for the arts and humanities to contribute to the knowledge economy (Ferran 2006: 443). Yet at the same time, collaborations between artists and scientists funded by the programme were expected to be guided by an ontological logic in which the collaborative endeavour was envisaged both as methodology and as the 'work': 'we consider our overall objective as a new kind of social "material", aiming to create new cultures of technological collaboration and artistic production' (Blackwell and Biggs 2006: 471).

In our institutional case studies these inventive modalities of art-science, combining the logics of ontology and innovation, were particularly apparent in the US and Australia. In these settings, university-based salaried artists were able to achieve intensive collaborations with scientist colleagues through prolonged encounters with or immersion in scientific environments, thereby incorporating scientific problematics into their work to occasionally extraordinary synergistic effect (Born and Barry, this volume). Such conditions provided the basis for transcending the disciplinary division of labour, sometimes through a commitment to the cultivation of 'interdisciplinarity in one person'. It was this approach that motivated the pedagogy of the Arts, Computation and Engineering (ACE) Masters program at UC Irvine described in Chapter 11. Transcending mere 'decorative' art-science, the ACE program was engaged in subjectifying a new generation of art-science practitioners with the resources to imagine and navigate new ontologies in the fertile borderlands between artistic, technological and scientific practice.

The Chapters

The following chapters offer contrasting challenges to dominant understandings of interdisciplinarity. Simon Schaffer's starting point is the recognition that the discourse of interdisciplinarity 'evidently, if oddly, takes as accurate history the stories disciplines have told about themselves'. To question these stories, Schaffer probes the period of the late eighteenth through the mid-nineteenth century, a period that was 'key for disciplinary society' and for the constitution of disciplines as well as the labile relations between them. His aim is to undermine the functionalist view 'that the order of disciplines is simply the expression of a utilitarian division of intellectual labour set up in the early nineteenth century . . . [a functionalism resting] on a kind of forgetting of discipline's indisciplined history'. In place of such a view, Schaffer offers a genealogy of discipline that traces its connection back through the work of Jeremy Bentham to the practice of colonial education. Bentham's *Chrestomathia* educational project fuelled a metropolitan experiment in schooling involving 'up-to-date principles of utility, accountancy, economy, the division of labour, surveillance and a monitorial system'.

But Schaffer's primary focus is the 'Madras System', an exemplary institution of pedagogic discipline developed by the Scottish natural philosophy lecturer Andrew Bell in the 1790s, which greatly influenced Bentham. Schaffer shows how Bell's project had hybrid origins, drawing extensively on the disciplined pedagogic practices of Tamil culture. Only later would this pedagogic technology be brought to the imperial metropolis. Tracing the complex and recursive circuits of mimesis in this history, Schaffer highlights, not without irony, how Bell's

> system of training had originally been adopted and adapted from Halle pietism and Tamil pedagogy. It was turned into a form of economic and scientific discipline for 'half-caste' Indo-European trainees destined for service in the East India Company's administration and surveys. Later, within the imperial metropolis, utilitarian and romantic writers then saw in this system powerful tools for securing social discipline, moral order and scientific advance.

Eventually, 'British administrators and historians saw such disciplinary systems as the necessary means by which what they saw as Indian culture could at last be redirected and modernised'. If Bentham has been taken by readers of Foucault as one of discipline's most ardent proponents, then the origins of discipline are to be found in the Indian subcontinent as much as in Britain or France. Schaffer directs our attention to the 'genealogy of global networks and their entanglements throughout the histories of disciplinary formation', as well as the close interrelations between the history of the disciplines and the history of colonialism and its aftermath. At the same time he issues a timely reminder, before we make too many assumptions about interdisciplinarity today, that it would be wise to interrogate the stereotypes of disciplinary history, homogeneity and hegemony that are shared by the proponents of disciplines and their interdisciplinary and transdisciplinary critics alike.

In the following chapter, Thomas Osborne offers a lively rejoinder to the present enthusiasm for interdisciplinarity, probing the nature of disciplinarity particularly in the social sciences with a focus on sociology, economics and social anthropology. His argument begins with the observation that the natural sciences continue today to have 'more circumscribed epistemological profiles' than the social sciences and humanities. Taking off from this 'backward brand of C. P. Snowism', he takes issue with ideas of disciplinary insulation or indeed any notion 'that disciplines are implicitly akin to monads'. Rather, 'all disciplines are hybrid'; indeed 'there is a basic transparency or porosity to disciplines, and some more so than others'. The social sciences, he suggests, are especially porous and even promiscuous in their aptitude for certain kinds of mobility across, and cross-fertilisation with, other areas of inquiry; but this is a mark precisely of their disciplinarity, not of interdisciplinarity.

Osborne's key concern is to identify the distinctive styles of mobility exhibited by the social sciences – to excavate the ways in which, as part of their normal operation, these disciplines produce relations of exteriority. In this sense he adds to the project of this book by pointing to what might be called characteristic modes not of interdisciplinary but of (inter-)disciplinary practice, along with their epistemological entailments. Osborne dwells on three such modes: parasitism, which he identifies primarily with anthropology; trespassing (and its big brother, imperialism), which he associates with economics; and poaching, which he links to postmodern social theory and sees as the product of 'disciplinary deficit'.

Anthropology, for instance, exemplifies a creative parasitism (in a descriptive rather than pejorative sense): ethnographers go into the field these days to study scientific laboratories, businesses or indeed interdisciplinary research projects, aiming to develop an intimate knowledge of the domain being studied, to be 'absorbed' into it whilst 'leaving their own disciplinary core intact'; and an analogous parasitism, Osborne points out, occurs in some branches of the philosophy of science. In comparison, the trespassing that characterises the work of economists, according to Osborne, involves the imposition of their 'own view of the terrain on another disciplinary area', thereby 'bringing the other discipline into [their] own'. Indeed rational choice theory is what eventuates, he argues, 'when utilitarian economics trespasses on domains other than economics in the social sciences'. This can be a reductive exercise, but such 'reductiveness can be part of the creativity and usefulness of the endeavour itself'. For Osborne, 'interdisciplinarity is not the opposite of disciplinarity', nor does it pose a threat to those disciplines that have a strong identity (such as, quite differently, anthropology and economics). But it may pose a threat to certain disciplines (his example is sociology) that are weakly formed or lack a clear sense of their distinctive disciplinarity.

While Osborne considers how established disciplines are, in different ways, immanently (inter-)disciplinary, Sheila Jasanoff gives an account of the emergence out of a ferment of interdisciplinary activity of what she regards as a new discipline, Science and Technology Studies (STS) – a process in which she played an influential part. Her chapter therefore initiates a series of reflexive contributions to the volume. Although Jasanoff recognises that there are external pressures for greater interdisciplinarity, she makes a strong case for the importance of bottom-up initiatives from scholars who, 'possibly at the margins of their own disciplinary enclaves, start asking questions that demand new modes of inquiry'. Her account of the gradual disciplining of STS revolves around three phases in the history of the field. The first centres on the so-called 'science wars' that erupted in the US in the 1990s following publication both of Paul Goss and Norman Levitt's broadside against the academic left, *Higher Superstition*, and of the physicist Alan Sokal's hoax contribution to the journal *Social Text*. Crucially, she argues, the science wars undermined the commitment of STS scholars to the principle of symmetry, according to which true and false claims to scientific knowledge should be analysed in identical terms.

If the science wars tell us about the potential for antagonistic relations between STS and the natural sciences, Jasanoff's second phase centres on the continuing existence of unresolved and agonistic relations between STS and its cognate fields, including history, sociology and philosophy. Here her analysis dwells on differences between the contents of two major collections that aspired to be definitive of STS: the 1995 *Handbook of Science and Technology Studies* (of which she was an editor) and the 1999 *Science Studies Reader*. Jasanoff notes that while the latter presented the field as a combination of contributions from distinct disciplines, the editors of the *Handbook* sought to map the contours of an emerging disciplinary form. In an evocative metaphor, Jasanoff argues that the formation of STS should be likened to the charting of the high seas, rather than the construction of a highway between clearly defined fields. But her contribution also foregrounds another theme of this volume, evident in the chapters by Schaffer, Greco, and Born and Barry: the critical importance of pedagogy in the formation of interdisciplines and disciplines, embodied in the development of teaching programs and departments and, for STS, the publication of handbooks. In the course of what Jasanoff suggests is a third phase, STS has become an established discipline marked by increasing engagement with politics and policy. In tracing these three phases in the history of STS, Jasanoff suggests that the formation of any discipline is likely to be marked by disagreement over whether it should coalesce as a distinct discipline or remain an interdiscipline. Importantly, her analysis points to the politics of the relations between disciplines as their proponents struggle for authority, institutional standing, resources and intra- and extra-academic influence.

The chapter by Marilyn Strathern and Elena Khlinovskaya Rockhill introduces a group of contributions that respond, in various ways and to different degrees, to the framework set out in this introduction. It focuses on a particular institution, the Cambridge Genetics Knowledge Park (CGKP), on which they carried out research in the mid 2000s.[42] The approach taken by Strathern and Khlinovskaya Rockhill is ethnographic and methodologically internalist. Their study opens an important seam of analysis running through this collection, uncovering how the intellectual, social, institutional and economic conditions within which interdisciplinarity is cultivated make a difference. Specifically, their analysis shows that even if funding is provided and research policies are conducive, if interdisciplinarity is implanted within unresponsive or hostile organisational surroundings, it will fail to thrive.

In terms of the expression and imbrication of the logics of accountability and ontology, the CGKP provides a striking contrast to our studies of interdisciplinary environmental and art-science research; indeed, it presents a negative case. The CGKP was an institution that laid claim to its interdisciplinarity as an index of its accountability to society. Yet the institution was so purely driven by the logic of accountability that there was in practice no commitment to what else interdisciplinarity might deliver in epistemological or ontological terms. Thus, despite the CGKP's avowed and explicit remit to consider the ethical, legal and social implications of scientific studies of genetics for public health and policy, at the heart of their account is an analysis of the marginalisation within the CGKP of 'research' in general and of the social scientific research represented by ELSI in particular. There was therefore little support for interdisciplinary collaboration, nor any attempt to reconfigure the relations between the social sciences and natural sciences. The marginalisation of social science in this context was evidence of what the authors term a 'ricochet effect', occurring in several directions. One manifestation of this effect was difficulty in evaluating the CGKP: the problem of demonstrating the value of social research internally was both mirrored and amplified externally in the difficulty the CGKP had in demonstrating its value to those bodies required to assess its performance. Another manifestation was that the internal marginalisation of ELSI within the institution was magnified in the intensified marginalisation of the most 'social' of ELSI's component disciplines: sociology.

While the CGKP appears to exemplify the subordination-service mode, in that social research was required to take a service role with respect to its dominant orientation towards public health genetics, Strathern and Khlinovskaya Rockhill insist on the need to retain an interest in its singularity. Indeed, they report an unexpected finding: 'for all its protested aversion to research, there were many features of [the CGKP management's] open-horizons ideology and equal aversion to the micro-management of performance indicators that brought it closer to a research ethos than its directorate would have admitted'.

Lucy Suchman's chapter traces reflexively, in part through her own experience and pioneering work at the Xerox Corporation's Palo Alto Research Center (PARC), how anthropology and its method of ethnography entered the world of the IT corporation and became part of the means of constituting markets. Overall, her argument is that in recent decades, through such interdisciplinary engagements, anthropology has itself become an 'object of consumption within the worlds of commercial research and development', playing its part in the promotion of the 'cultural turn' in the global economy, and assisting in the era of lifestyle marketing and branding in 'the expansion and deeper penetration of cultures of capitalism'. Interrogating the media's 'discovery' of and fascination with corporate ethnography from the early 1990s, Suchman finds in it an echo of Strathern and Khlinovskaya Rockhill's fractal-like 'ricochet effect': an ironic juxtaposition in which the ethnographer as investigator of those exotic others sought by the global corporation when expanding into new markets is mirrored by the anthropologist as herself an exotic other within the corridors of the corporate workplace.

But lest we collapse this history into teleology, Suchman is at pains to show how, in the early period of the 1980s to mid 1990s, ethnography in industry as it was being invented at PARC was able to incubate – in part through connections to the Department of Anthropology at the University of California at Berkeley – a space for 'critical anthropology'. Indeed, her account of the period suggests that the logic of innovation and the logic of ontology were entwined at PARC. On the one hand PARC's ethnographers, through collaborative experiments with computer scientists and co-workers from other disciplines, engaged in the development of prototype commercial information systems. On the other hand, influenced by the Scandinavian participatory design movement and its advocacy of workplace democracy, PARC's ethnographers and their collaborators cultivated an 'agonistic interdisciplinarity'. Through the example of a participatory project in the mid-1990s with the California Department of Transportation, she shows how such projects were crafted by the actors to pursue the design-oriented and commercial requirements of the corporation while also engaging in dialogical and material exchange practices that, in the terms of Michel Callon (1998), 'overflowed' any market rationale. By reframing technologies as socio-material practices and enriching the corporate engagement with the social embeddedness of information systems, they opened up 'margins of manoeuvre . . . that exceeded the conventional market frame'; although in doing so, she admits, it was often necessary to make implicit the political values that underlay 'superior design outcomes'. This was a phase of possibility, as Suchman makes clear, that was eventually eclipsed by more purely commercial imperatives. The story of ethnography at PARC is therefore one in which such practices were at times afforded and at other times foreclosed by changing institutional conditions as they refracted in turn the evolving political economy.

Geography, as an interdisciplinary discipline, is apparently well-placed to respond to the escalating research initiatives demanding interdisciplinarity. In her chapter, Sarah Whatmore documents her experience as a geographer of another set of institutional conditions: a call for proposals from the UK Research

Council-funded Rural Environment and Land Use (RELU) research programme in 2004, 'the first and largest programme in the UK to make collaboration between natural and social scientists a precondition of project funding'. As she explains, the call posed applicants the challenge of giving as much attention 'to promoting novel cross-disciplinary couplings' and 'involving stakeholders in all stages' as to 'further refinement of established interdisciplinary methods and techniques'. In their response to the call, Whatmore and her colleagues sought to develop a novel interdisciplinary approach to the problem of flood risk, one that involved not just physical and human geographers but also 'competency groups': an experimental practice trialled by the project that brought local people with direct experience of flooding into the research collective. In this way her contribution pursues another theme of this volume, evident also in Suchman's chapter: the place of participatory practices and, in particular, the involvement not only of lay or non-expert knowledges but of lay participants' practical and experiential competencies in experimental forms of interdisciplinarity.

Whatmore poses the terms of the situation starkly through a dualism in which the normative interdisciplinarity envisaged by the RELU programme, where 'research is positively allied to governmental and business agendas . . . in the name of environmental "problem-solving"', was reshaped in their successful application into an alternative, 'inventive interdisciplinarity [premised on] a practised attentiveness to the ontological demands of the complex artefacts and processes assembled in/as "environmental problems"'. Where the first Interdisciplinarity entails 'an *a priori* separation of "human society" from "the environment"', she contends, 'the second insists on "the ontological impossibility of sustaining the binary conception – human and environment"'. Here she takes as a compass Jane Bennett's argument that 'humans are always in composition with nonhumanity, never outside a sticky web of connections or an ecology' (2004: 365). In this light, a core aim of Whatmore's project is to reframe the research agenda so as to 'direct attention to the techno-scientific practices of environmental "problem-solving" as ecologically constitutive themselves and, hence, as matters of crucial analytical (and political) concern'. Indeed, counterposing the two interdisciplinarities, Whatmore argues, exemplifies the 'perpetual interaction' evoked by Deleuze and Guattari between 'royal' (machinic) and 'minor' (or nomadic) science. Interweaving the logics both of ontology and of accountability, the task of Whatmore's flood-risk project was not to address already defined problems, nor to engage in critique, but to generate positive problems through an intervention that responded to the need to invent novel practices and engagements. Her contention is that 'the ontological logic of our experiment in geography's interdisciplinary inventiveness allies research with the potential for knowledge controversies to act as democratic force-fields'.

Where Whatmore's project formed one element of a much larger research programme that was explicitly interdisciplinary, Gisa Weszkalnys and Andrew Barry report the findings of a comparative study of three major interdisciplinary research institutions, all three of which were concerned, in Whatmore's terms, with 'environmental problem solving'. They are the German Öko-Institut, the

Tyndall Centre for Climate Change Research in the UK, and the Earth Institute located at Columbia University in New York.

The chapter develops two general arguments, while stressing the need to attend to the particular genealogies and institutional trajectories of the three institutions. The first argument focuses on the specificity of the relations between the development of these institutions, each of which brings together researchers in the natural sciences and social sciences, and the logic of accountability. The authors link the emergence of the Öko-Institut in the 1970s both to Nowotny's notion of transdisciplinarity and to the practice of what was called counter-science (*Gegen-Wissenschaft*), an idea encapsulated in Ulrich Beck's contention that radical environmental politics is not possible without 'the aid of the entire arsenal of scientific measurement, experimental and argumentative instruments' (Beck 1992: 162–3). The formation of the Tyndall Centre drew on a longer British history of interdisciplinary research in the new universities founded in the 1960s, but it also reflected a growing stress in the UK in the 1990s and 2000s on the importance of involving users and stakeholders in environmental research. The interdisciplinarity of the Earth Institute, in contrast, developed as a response to the complexity of the global policy problems that its researchers were expected to address. Reflecting on the researchers' experience of the continuing importance of disciplinary forms of peer review at the Earth Institute and the Tyndall Centre, Weszkalnys and Barry point to the contingency of the relation between interdisciplinary research and 'society' that is associated with the logic of accountability.

The authors' second argument focuses on the centrality of the common trope of 'integration' in interdisciplinary environmental research. 'Integration', they argue, should not be understood as an end result, but as a set of practices that take multiple and often agonistic forms; what is called 'integration' in this field, then, may or may not correspond to what we have termed the integrative-synthesis mode of interdisciplinarity. For many researchers, the challenges posed by integration are oriented towards the solution of problems and are primarily organisational and methodological. However, Weszkalnys and Barry contend that there are incipient signs of the logic of ontology in 'integrated' environmental research. This is evident, for example, in the ways that stakeholders have been brought into the research process through the development of such methods as interactive assessment and scenario analysis, suggesting that 'environmental research has come explicitly to interrogate its own entanglement in the world that it analyses'. The authors conclude by observing that, despite the growing attention paid to the bifurcation of nature and notably to the importance of affective and aesthetic experience in geographical research on the environment, a concern with the realm of experience still appears to be marginal to the work of environmental research institutions.

In the next chapter, Andrew Pickering offers a quite different exploration of the 'ontological thread' spun by this introduction, following it through a series of fields that he identifies as antidisciplines and that he associates with varieties of 'ontological nonmodernity'. Examples include alchemy, *naturphilosophie*, those fields grouped under the heading of 'complexity', and certain interpretations of quantum mechanics. For Pickering, such 'nonmodern sciences' evidence 'not so much [a] combination of distinct disciplines, but . . . the eruption of a relatively unified approach to the world across the disciplinary map'. The focus of Pickering's paper is a particular and exemplary antidiscipline: cybernetics. As he shows, the emergence of cybernetics was bound up with the development of models, machines and assemblages, notably the homeostat, which figured as the centrepiece of Ross Ashby's *Design for a Brain* (1952). In Ashby's account, the cybernetic brain was performative and adaptive, not representational; it should be regarded, Pickering argues, not only as a contribution to brain science but to ontology. In turn, the implications of multi-homeostat assemblages could not be confined to brain science but rapidly radiated out to infect a multiplicity of fields, among them philosophy, aeronautics, engineering, robotics, psychiatry, management and biological computing. In the work of Stafford Beer, cybernetic ambitions spanned interactions with pond ecosystems – where 'the idea was that nature is already full of adaptive systems which one could seek to entrain in human projects' – to the application of Beer's Viable System Model to the entire Chilean economy under Allende's socialist regime in the 1970s. For Pickering, such antidisciplinarity was not built on antipathy to specific disciplines or to disciplinarity per se; rather, it was an effect of the 'working out of a nonmodern ontological stance', one that fuelled the 'transformative displacement' of the disciplines it encountered.

Pickering nonetheless acknowledges an antagonistic moment in cybernetics, arguing that if the modern sciences 'lend themselves readily to projects of domination', then 'cybernetics . . . problematised this stance'. Such a problematisation is signalled by the prefix 'anti' commonly attached to cybernetic forays into other fields, for example in the anti-psychiatry movement that coalesced around Gregory Bateson's critique of the social relations of psychiatry and Ronald Laing's experiments in non-hierarchical therapeutic communities. In sociological and institutional terms, Pickering's cybernetics appears to be the opposite of Jasanoff's STS: if the burgeoning discipline of STS is bedding down in the heartlands of the academy, Pickering shows that cybernetics has always been antithetical to institution-building and PhD programmes, flourishing at the margins of academia where disciplinary policing is at its weakest. Cyberneticists, Pickering notes, came together 'almost orthogonally to their modern counterparts'. If cybernetics is one incarnation of a logic of ontology, it should not be understood, according to Pickering, as an interdiscipline at all.

Many accounts of interdisciplinarity focus on the conduct of research, or on relations between research and the arena of its application. Rather than take these as her starting point, Monica Greco places at the centre of her analysis of the interdisciplinary field of medical humanities its gathering around a 'sense of a "mission" whose practical expression is primarily pedagogical'. Her contribution foregrounds a theme of this book pursued also in the chapter that follows. It is the role of pedagogical initiatives in catalysing and consolidating interdisciplinarity through the formation of interdisciplinary subjects. In part, Greco's interest is in charting how this novel 'pedagogical agenda . . . aims to be effective at a capillary level'. But in addition, in a particularly acute exploration of how the logic of ontology 'blurs into' the logic of accountability, her critical insight is that an ontological logic 'is apparent in the pedagogical intention that lies at the core of medical humanities. Contrary to the expectation that an ontological commitment should refer to the nature of the medical *object* – leaving the subject of knowledge un-problematised – this logic is addressed in the first instance to fostering processes of "aesthetic and ethical self-forming"'. The intention is to produce medical 'doctors as different kinds of *subjects* . . . reflexive practitioners educated in the dangers of "misplaced concreteness" . . . and in the creative use of their imagination'. Certainly, the field realises the long-standing contention that medicine must include 'an irreducible element of "art"'. Yet at the same time, by highlighting the 'multiple dimensions of subjectivity in medicine' as well as the 'uncertainty and indeterminacy of clinical situations', medical humanities also shows its commitment to a different understanding of the object of medical knowledge.

Overall, Greco suggests, medical humanities arose from a problematisation of the assumption that the mechanistic and reductive 'scientific approach currently employed in the context of medicine is adequate to its purpose'. In developing her case, Greco's chapter exemplifies the method of genealogy advocated in this introduction as a means of charting the moments and types of critique, difference or détournement, as well as the continuities, that signal an agonistic-antagonistic interdisciplinarity, which can in turn be associated – as it is in this case – with a logic of ontology. She traces through the appearance in recent decades of new programmes and institutions as well as changes to key journals the emergence of medical humanities from its several progenitors, notably the opening up of medical ethics and bioethics beyond traditional moral philosophy to such techniques as narrative ethics. Greco stresses both the heterogeneity of the emergent interdiscipline and its problem of individuation, of becoming more than just '"parasitic" upon medical education'. Arguing against those who are sceptical about the significance of medical humanities, she insists that such a view 'overlooks how [the field's] pedagogical intention not only does point to an ontological commitment, but also transforms how we might understand and what we might expect as the expression of such a commitment'. In this way she offers a compelling portrait of how medical humanities enacts a logic of ontology, while criticising the 'anti-political' (Barry 2001) effects of reducing the field merely to accountability or public relations.

While Greco touches on the importance of the arts in medical pedagogy, in the final chapter Born and Barry examine another interdisciplinary borderland between the arts and humanities, on the one hand, and the natural sciences, on the other: the emergent field of art-science. Their account draws on ethnographic research on practitioners and initiatives in the US, UK and Australia, including an experimental pedagogical program. Two themes run through the chapter. Of all the chapters in the volume it develops at greatest length, in a way comparable to Greco's, an account of the logic of ontology as it can be manifest in art-science and its interdisciplinary pedagogy, and as it is entangled with the logics of innovation and accountability. The second theme concerns the distinctive public-making propensities of interdisciplinarity, highlighting through the example of art-science alternative ways in which publics may be assembled. At the outset of the chapter Born and Barry draw out the heterogeneity of art-science through its multiple genealogies and their mutual interference. In particular, the authors trace two broad genealogies subtending the field: one stemming from the growing concern in the scientific community from the mid-1980s with the 'public understanding of science', the other from the diverse movements spawned from the late 1960s by conceptual art. If the former trajectory led by the 1990s to a spate of art-science funding programmes in which art was enrolled to enhance the public communication of science, the latter disturbed such 'aestheticising' rationales by mobilising an alternative history, one that problematised art's entanglement with science and technology.

At the heart of the chapter is an ethnographic analysis of one contemporary manifestation of the latter trajectory: the Arts, Computation and Engineering (ACE) Masters program at UC Irvine. ACE was devoted to cultivating interdisciplinary subjects through a training that encompassed not only aspects of the arts, computation and engineering, but their articulation with a range of critical theories. The program foresaw a generation possessed of a growing intimacy with these disciplines, equipped to develop rich 'interlanguages' (Galison 1997) between them, and endowed with a reflexive sense of the epistemological and ontological implications of this project: subjects empowered to negotiate a transition to a novel, potentially inventive ontological space. Through the case of an art-science work, PigeonBlog, by the ACE faculty member Beatriz da Costa, the third part of the chapter expounds the concept of a public experiment. Drawing on Barbara Cassin's distinction between two rhetorical forms, Born and Barry point to the difference between an interdisciplinary practice of public understanding and one of public experiment, as exemplified by PigeonBlog. 'Public experiments', they argue, 'do not so much present existing scientific knowledge to the public, as forge relations between new knowledge, things, locations and persons that did not exist before – in this way producing truth, public and their relation at the same time'. In an epilogue, the authors anatomise the difficulties of legitimising as interdisciplinary an entity as ACE. They chart forces leading to the recent closure of the ACE program, notably the 'ricochet effect' embodied in contradictory values and structural processes bearing both on the program and on its individual faculty that caused chronic problems of evaluation. Despite favourable institutional conditions signalled by a university-wide commitment to interdisciplinarity that enabled the experimental ACE program briefly to flourish, within a few years – in this increasingly neoliberal public university – those conditions were eclipsed.

Conclusions

The case of art-science encapsulates four key themes running through this collection. The first centres on the relation between interdisciplinarity and the generation of novel objects and practices that are irreducible to their antecedent conditions and disciplinary progenitors. Andrew Pickering's account of the wild antidiscipline of cybernetics, which has drawn inspiration throughout its history from the creation of experimental models; Lucy Suchman's depiction of the potentially inventive collaborative and participatory practices of ethnography in the IT industry; Sarah Whatmore's analysis of the vital potential of competency groups; and Monica Greco's excavation of the subtle and evolving ontological project of medical humanities: all draw attention to the inventiveness of specific forms of interdisciplinarity and their relation to the logic of ontology. In all of these cases, moreover, interdisciplinary practices address the problem of how to reconfigure the relations between the natural and social sciences, albeit in distinctive ways.

A second theme of the book concerns the variant, often unstable and sometimes surprising ecologies within which interdisciplinarity is cultivated. The chapters show how the historical and institutional conditions within which interdisciplinary initiatives are implanted make a difference. They indicate, as we have remarked, how such initiatives can fail to take root or grow even when research policies and funding are supportive, while also suggesting that initiatives that emerge from the 'bottom up' or that are fomented in the academic margins may be especially fertile, resilient and long lasting – perhaps fuelled by counter-hegemonic energies.

A third, related theme arising from the chapters concerns the chronic difficulty posed by the evaluation of interdisciplinarity. This problem lies at the heart of Strathern and Khlinovskaya Rockhill's analysis of the marginalisation of 'social' research at the Cambridge Genetics Knowledge Park; it is recapitulated in Weszkalnys and Barry's account of interdisciplinary environmental research, and in Born and Barry's depiction of experimental art-science in the ACE program. In each of these instances interdisciplinarity has a fragile existence due in part to tensions stemming from the submission of interdisciplinary practices to disciplinary evaluation. If interdisciplinarity is sustained, it is often only in very particular and temporary ecological niches, niches that may dissolve under various pressures – of legitimation, or of perceived lack of economic or cultural value or policy relevance.

A fourth seam running through the collection is the critical importance of pedagogy, highlighted in the chapters by Schaffer, Greco, and Born and Barry. Auspicious interdisciplinarity, as we have seen, is associated not only with the constitution of new objects, but with the cultivation of interdisciplinary subjectivities and skills – sometimes as its primary orientation.

At the start of this introduction we contrasted our approach with the analysis of the transition to Mode-2 knowledge production developed by Nowotny et al (2001). Nowotny and her collaborators emphasise the correlations between changes in knowledge production, on the one hand, and broader societal changes on the other. But if the approach advocated in this book differs from the externalist account of scientific change offered by Nowotny et al, it differs also from the internalism propounded by other influential writers. Exemplary in this regard is Andrew Abbott's *Chaos of Disciplines* (2001) which, with reference to the social sciences, portrays interdisciplinarity as a recurrent feature of an essentially disciplinary academic system that is subject to cycles of disciplinary division and subdivision, producing a fractal effect. Abbott dwells in particular on the mutating relations between history and sociology and the reasons why, over a period of time, they have never led to a synthesis of the two disciplines (Abbott 2001: 119). His analysis of interactions between history and sociology is not intended to provide a general model of interdisciplinarity. For he goes on to argue that 'interdisciplinarism' in the social sciences has largely been driven by the appearance of problems that 'have their own life cycle' (ibid.: 134); and it is the proliferation of such problems that, in his view, generates short-lived interdisciplinary fragments. In these circumstances, he argues, two obstacles prevent what might be called the chaotic proliferation of such interdisciplinary fragments. One is the enduring structure of the academic labour market and the resilient departmental organisation of undergraduate programs in the United States. The other obstacle is that 'a university organized around problems of investigation would be hopelessly balkanized', and therefore unmanageable (ibid.: 135). Moreover, in contrast to interdisciplines, he contends, disciplines have the virtue that they generate 'problem-portable knowledge' (ibid.). Thus, according to Abbott, 'a long historical process has given rise to a more or less steady, institutionalised social structure in American academia: a structure of flexibly stable disciplines, surrounded by a perpetual hazy buzz of interdisciplinarity' (ibid.: 136).

In many ways Abbott's account of interdisciplinarity is a mirror image of that given in *Re-Thinking Science*. Where Nowotny et al. (2001) understand the growth of transdisciplinary research as bound up with wider social and economic changes, Abbott views the disciplinarity–interdisciplinarity couplet as a perennial product of the internal organisation of the American university system. Nowotny et al's sense of the systemic relations between changes in society, economy and politics and transitions in the mode of production of knowledge is in marked contrast to Abbott's preoccupation with the internal structure and reward system of the American disciplines;[43] just as, in an irony that would not be lost on Abbott, Nowotny et al's emphasis on discontinuity in the history of the institutions of knowledge production contrasts strikingly with Abbott's stress on cyclical continuity.

In pointing to the existence in the present conjuncture of three modes and three logics of interdisciplinarity, the framework outlined in this introduction and embodied in a number of the chapters in this collection departs from the models espoused both by Abbott and by Nowotny et al. On the one hand, this framework does not ignore the need to take account of dynamics internal to the emergence of specific interdisciplinary fields, by tracing their field-specific (and sometimes multiple) genealogies, the irreducible departures and novel directions augured by the agonistic-antagonistic mode of interdisciplinarity, and the problematisation that often marks particular interdisciplinary turns. At the same time, the contributions to this book indicate the manner in which interdisciplinarity has emerged in varied institutional and political conditions, some of which differ considerably from the singular ecology of the American university system. On the other hand, rather than trace the co-evolution of two entities, science and society, by drawing attention to the logics of accountability, innovation and ontology the framework developed here highlights three prevalent and unlike, if entangled, ways in which the 'social' is mediated by practices of interdisciplinarity. A number of chapters also detail the complex nexus of circumstances bearing on the growth and demise of heterogeneous interdisciplinary assemblages.

In this way the framework advanced in this volume also offers a different account of the temporalities of interdisciplinarity than that provided both by Abbott, with his portrayal of a dominant disciplinarity that cyclically begets but then reincorporates its interdisciplinary splinters, and by Nowotny et al (2001), with their periodisation in which Mode-2 knowledge and society have progressively superseded their Mode-1 counterparts. The chapters in this book offer cogent analyses of more diverse temporal processes, encompassing various speeds, gradients and curves of the waxing and waning of interdisciplinary institutions and initiatives in particular conditions (Barry 2010, Born 2010b). Remarkable in this regard are three examples of what appeared at the outset in each case to be sustainable interdisciplinary programmes with extraordinary promise – the early period of ethnographic research at Xerox PARC, art-science in the ACE program at UC Irvine, and the ELSI unit in the Cambridge Genetics Knowledge Park – of which, arguably, the first two were wound up after a short period despite having 'delivered' considerable successes in their own terms, while the third was effectively stillborn. However, equally strikingly, the collection includes important examples of new interdisciplines (and possibly disciplines) that, *contra* Abbott, have gathered pace cumulatively over long periods of time and show no immediate signs of dissolution. Particularly salient in this regard is the establishment of both science and technology studies and medical humanities as recognised interdisciplinary academic fields with their own teaching programmes, journals and conferences, as well as the proliferation of the various interdisciplines that compose environmental research, and the enduring inter-/anti-disciplinarity and extra-academic history of cybernetics.

In this introduction, while recognising the importance of their intervention, we have questioned some of the claims made by Nowotny et al (2001) concerning the emergence of Mode-2 knowledge production. But we are more sceptical about Abbott's general suggestion that the history of interdisciplinarity is a continuous one, and that it can be understood largely as problem-driven. Both accounts – as this collection makes plain – make it difficult to recognise the diversity of the recent animated engagements with interdisciplinarity and transdisciplinarity on the part of funding organisations, research and teaching programmes, scientific labs and artists' workshops, research collaborations and individual practitioners alike. Moreover, instead of assuming that there is an underlying similarity between the strategies and interests guiding different forms of interdisciplinarity, the chapters in this book attest to the heterogeneity that characterises both disciplines and interdisciplines and the necessity of probing the genealogies of particular interdisciplinary problematics. Our typology of modes and logics of interdisciplinarity is intended neither to be exhaustive, nor fine-grained, nor ahistorical; rather, it is intended to provide the basis for illuminating the singularity and the particular historicity of the emergence of distinct interdisciplinary formations.

At the heart of this collection is a topic that does not figure at all in Abbott's analysis. This is the question of the reconfiguration of the relations between the natural sciences, the social sciences, and the arts and humanities. Abbott's contention is that 'sociology provides within a single disciplinary compass examples of many of the processes I am discussing at the level of social science in general' (ibid.: 3). He is therefore quite unconcerned with those disciplines and interdisciplines – some with long histories, others burgeoning particularly strongly in recent decades – that traverse the boundaries between the social and natural sciences. Geography and anthropology provide instructive examples, for both disciplines were formed around the idea that it was necessary in principle, and possible in practice, to establish fields that brought together the sciences of the natural and the material, on the one hand, and the social and the cultural, on the other. Despite their multiplicity and their persistent lack of 'integration', the continuing existence of these interdisciplinary disciplines is a reminder that a concern with the interaction between the social and natural sciences, although it has taken varied forms, is far from new (Livingstone 1992, Ingold 2001, Castree 2005, Segal and Yanagisako 2005). A key interest of the topic of interdisciplinarity is therefore that it directs us to consider the diverse ways in which the reconfiguration of the relations between the social and natural sciences is today being posed anew, whether this is manifest in the emergence and evolution of science and technology studies, ELSI research, ethnography in the IT industry, environmental research, medical humanities, art-science, or in the latest flowering of the recurrent interest in materiality and experimentation across geography, anthropology and sociology (Fraser 2002, Latour and Weibel 2005, Henare et al 2006, Küchler 2008, Bennett and Joyce 2010, Braun and Whatmore 2010, Hicks and Beaudry 2010, Thrift 2011, Harvey et al 2012). While research policymakers tend to emphasise the link between interdisciplinarity and innovation or accountability, a significant proportion of these interdisciplinary developments, as we have insisted, are oriented as much towards variants of the logic of ontology.

Finally, we want to raise the prospect of a re-evaluation of interdisciplinarity. It should be plain that we are emphatically not enthusiasts for interdisciplinarity per se; nor do we mean to suggest that there is a necessary or privileged affinity between interdisciplinary research and invention. As we have indicated, any analysis of the inventiveness of interdisciplinarity must attend to the path-dependence of specific interdisciplines, their genealogies and multiplicity, and in this light the extent to which any particular interdisciplinary practice can be judged inventive (Barry and Born 2007, Born 2010b: 242–6). At the same time, it may be tempting to posit a straightforward equation between the disruption of disciplinary boundaries and the erosion of autonomy. The links made between interdisciplinarity and the logics of accountability and innovation certainly encourage that belief. In these circumstances it is perhaps not surprising that, in reaction against the drive in science and research policy to expand interdisciplinarity, some scholars and authorities seek to defend disciplinary purity as a way of protecting a threatened academic autonomy. But, as we stated at the outset, disciplines are not infallibly autonomous or inventive: they have unproductive phases and may exhibit inertial and anti-inventive dynamics. In this introduction we refer to autonomy not in order to criticise this ideal, but to point to the existence of forms of *inter*disciplinary autonomy and rigorous interdisciplinarity that can lead to the production of new objects, subjects and relations of knowledge, practices that are irreducible both to previous disciplinary formations and to accountability and innovation.

Notes

1 *Discipline*: 'a system of rules governing conduct' and 'a field of study'; 'to train . . . by instruction and exercise, *esp.* in obedience and self-control' and 'to punish or penalize . . . for the sake of discipline'; *disciple*: 'a pupil or follower', *New Penguin English Dictionary* (2000). We are indebted to Simon Schaffer for drawing to our attention the aggregate of meaning around 'discipline' (Schaffer 2007). On Foucault's theoretical contributions to the historiography of the 'disciplines', by favourable contrast with the historical sociology of the professions, see Goldstein (1984).
2 For Foucault, 'Problematisation doesn't mean the representation of a pre-existent object, nor the creation through discourse of an object that doesn't exist. It's the set of discursive or nondiscursive practices that makes something enter into the play of the true and false, and constitutes it as an object for thought (whether under the form of moral reflection, scientific knowledge, political analysis, etc.)' (Foucault 2001: 1489; see also Rabinow 2005: 43). In order for this to occur, something 'must have happened to introduce uncertainty, a loss of familiarity; that loss, that uncertainty is the result of difficulties in our previous way of understanding' (Foucault 1994: 598).
3 The website to which Nowotny was contributing, 'Interdisciplines' (www. interdisciplines.org), was sponsored by the CNRS in 2003 and devoted to the reflexive discussion and enhancement of interdisciplinary exchange and research.
4 National Academy of Science, National Academy of Engineering and the Institute of Medicine.
5 While our empirical study focused on ethnographic research in the IT industry, later in this introduction we refer to 'ethnography in industry'. As we note, ethnographic approaches that first developed in the IT industry are now increasingly used across a wide range of industrial sectors.
6 The ten case studies were: (1) environmental and climate change research: the Tyndall Centre, University of East Anglia; the Earth Institute, Columbia University; the Öko-Institut, Darmstadt and Freiburg; (2) ethnography in the IT industry: three major IT corporations; the Institute for Software Research at the University of California at Irvine; and (3) art-science: the Arts, Computation and Engineering (ACE) Masters program, University of California, Irvine, and Digital Arts Research network (DARnet) of the University of California; the SymbioticA lab, University of Western Australia; and project-based funding programmes supported by the Wellcome Trust and Arts Council England.
7 In the project we did not analyse the growth of interdisciplinary and transdisciplinary research outside corporate and university research institutions in other potentially inventive locations such as think-tanks (Osborne 2004), business schools (Thrift 2005), firms more generally (Amin and Cohendet 2004), or consultancies and NGOs (Barry 2004).
8 This introduction is a revised and extended version of Barry et al (2008).
9 The historical particularity of these proposals is apparent through comparison with the importance of interdisciplinary research in the development of military science and

technology in the 1940s and 1950s (Pickering 1995b). There is, of course, nothing new in the idea that scientific research should be directed towards social and economic goals.

10 There are an escalating number of studies of contemporary interdisciplinarity, among them a burgeoning reflexive and empirical literature in geography and the environmental sciences, as well as surveys of the literature and handbooks on interdisciplinary research. Recent examples include: Tait and Lyall (2001); Bruce et al (2004); Rhoten (2004); Mansilla (2006a, 2006b); Strathern (2005); Tompkins (2005); Buller (2009); Baerwald (2010); Donovan et al (2010); Friman (2010); Frodeman et al (2010); Huutoniemi et al (2010); Lyall et al (2011).

11 On the importance of imitation in social and political change see Tarde (2001); Barry and Thrift (2007); Born (2010b).

12 Pickering (1995a) coined the term 'antidiscipline' when anatomising the 'border wars' within science studies between philosophy, history and sociology of science, divisions that fostered what he saw as an unsatisfactory 'eclectic multidisciplinarity' that left the traditional division of intellectual labour intact. Instead, at this time, Pickering advocated what he called the 'antidisciplinary synthesis' proffered by cultural studies of science.

13 Turner (2000), however, points to the role in the bureaucratisation of modern knowledge of 'the relatively short history of disciplinarity, the historical uniqueness [and conservative effects] of the vast expansion of university education over the last fifty years', arguing that these conditions – regarded by Gibbons et al (1994) as 'normal' or Mode-1 – are in fact 'entirely anomalous' (ibid.: 61–2).

14 For an overview of research on the contribution of material and symbolic boundaries in the formation of scientific disciplines and social knowledges, see Lamont and Molnar (2002: 177–81).

15 See, *inter alia*, Petts et al (2008); Lawrence and Després (2004: 400); Huutoniemi et al (2010); and the discussion on www.interdisciplines.org.

16 Petts et al make the helpful observation that the various definitions point to a spectrum: 'at its weakest, interdisciplinarity constitutes barely more than cooperation, while at its strongest, it lays the foundation for a more transformative recasting of disciplines' (2008: 8).

17 The original author of the term transdiciplinarity still appears to be disputed. In recent texts, Basarab Nicolescu, a theoretical physicist employed by the CNRS and founder of the International Center for Transdisciplinary Research and Studies, claims that the French-speaking Jean Piaget first proposed the term (Nicolescu 2008: 2); while according to the German sociologist of science Peter Weingart, the Austrian Erich Jantsch 'first coined the term, which was taken up two decades later by Gibbons et al' (Weingart 2010: 12).

18 The notion of problematisation, introduced by Foucault (Note 2), implies a positive conception of problems. In this collection, we understand the relevance of problematisation in the analysis of interdisciplinarity to have two aspects. On the one hand, the proliferation of different forms and practices of interdisciplinarity is bound up with the problematisation of the conduct of research, as we have already observed. On the other hand, interdisciplinary research in specific fields may both respond to and lead to the generation of new problems.

19 A similar idea is suggested by the US National Academy of Sciences: 'Interdisciplinary research (IDR) is a mode of research by teams or individuals that integrates information, data, techniques, tools, perspectives, concepts, and/or theories from two or more disciplines or bodies of specialised knowledge to advance fundamental understanding or to solve problems whose solutions are beyond the scope of a single discipline or field of research practice' (Committee on Facilitating Interdisicplinary Research 2004: 26).

20 It is notable, and lends general support to our argument here, that Nowotny et al (2001: 259) write of the 'antagonistic' epistemological relation between what they call

'socially robust' Mode-2 knowledge, involving a 'variety of knowledge traditions', and the universalistic claims of Western science. However we augment their observation by advocating the irreductive analysis of specific genealogies of antagonism, as defined here, that fuel interdisciplinarity.

21 See, for example, Randall et al's observation about the distance between Computer Supported Collaborative Work (CSCW), a form of what we have termed ethnography in the IT industry, and existing social science disciplines: 'Whether our view is right or wrong, it seems to us that an answer to CSCW's current dilemmas might be produced by considering the distinction between disciplinary assumptions about *method*, substantive disciplinary *concerns*, and disciplinary *sensibilities*. More particularly, we contend that to undertake ethnographic fieldwork for the home or for public spaces (and in other new or in some ways perplexing domains) and attending to the potentialities of new technologies requires a particular open-mindedness about method, a thoughtful selection of concerns, and an artful refinement of disciplinary, particularly design-oriented sensibilities. These cannot be taken lock, stock and barrel from other disciplines' (Randall et al 2005: 88, emphasis in original). See also Harper (2003: 6).

22 Holmes and Marcus (2005) coin the term 'para-ethnography' for this situation, arguing that it entails a particular kind of ethnographic collaboration where the researcher takes locally produced discourses and critiques to advance scholarly debate. Expert inform-ants become not only research partners, but 'epistemic partners'. For a discussion, see Born (2011).

23 Interview with Simon Penny, UCI, 2006.

24 For example, the Åarhus convention on 'Access to Information, Public-Participation in Decision-Making and Access to Justice in Environmental Matters' (UNECE 1998).

25 On the Wellcome Trust's Sciart initiatives, and detailing some of the projects funded, see Arends and Thackara (2003). On the ACE/AHRB Fellowship programme see Ferran (2006), together with other papers collected together in the special issue on art-science of the journal *Leonardo* (2006, volume 39, number 5).

26 The published work of industry ethnographers and our participation in the 2006 Ethnographic Praxis in Industry Conference (EPIC) throw up many examples of the evocation of such spaces. They include: the emotional life of the American middle-class home, notions of community on a Brazilian beach, the ways in which PCs are sited and used in Indian bedrooms or Chinese villages (D'Hooge 2005), the use of mobile phones on London buses, the social organisation of space in American public libraries, the mundane use of paper in offices (Sellen and Harper 2002), or how patients actually take medicine in South African townships (Jones 2006).

27 Interview, 2006.

28 See, for example, the work of the UK research council programmes 'Living with Environmental Change' (www.lwec.org.uk/) and 'Energy Research' (www.rcuk.ac.uk/research/xrcprograms/energy/) (accessed May 2012).

29 Interview, 2006.

30 In accord with our approach, Lawrence and Després mention 'ontological frameworks that do not embrace the complexity of the natural and human-made environment' in 'traditional scientific research' as a key obstacle to innovative approaches to the environment that might be redressed by transdisciplinarity (2004: 398).

31 For a reflexive overview of the emergent field of interdisciplinary corporate ethnography, see Cefkin (2009).

32 Interview, 2006.

33 '[W]e contend that to undertake ethnographic fieldwork for the home or for public spaces . . . and attending to the potentialities of new technologies requires a particular open-mindedness about method, a thoughtful selection of concerns, and an artful refinement of disciplinary, particularly design-oriented sensibilities' (Randall et al 2005: 88).

34 Interview, 2006.
35 Interview, 2006.
36 Interview, 2006.
37 See Jasanoff and Wynne (1998), Demeritt (2001) and Miller (2004) on the co-construction of the global environment as an object of both knowledge and government. On the lack of relation between climate change science and policy during the 1950s and the 1960s, see Hart and Victor (1993).
38 It is in the UK that 'science-art' appeared in the period of our fieldwork to have its most stable identity, called into being by the burgeoning of dedicated funding programmes from the mid-1990s which, because they were based on a project-based commissioning model, also rendered the field quite fragmentary and discontinuous.
39 Interview with a British art-science administrator, 2005.
40 The problem is sometimes also linked to perceived restrictions on artistic activities: the Wellcome Trust, for example, claimed that its science-art schemes tolerate projects that question the norms and power structures of science; but in interview it was conceded that it is difficult for the Trust to fund projects that are highly critical of science.
41 Interview, 2006.
42 The CGKP was one of several Genetics Knowledge Parks co-funded from 2002 on by the British Department of Health and Department of Trade and Industry.
43 His approach has some similarities to Bourdieu's analysis of the scientific field (1975), although Abbott chooses not to refer to Bourdieu's work, nor to that of other sociologists of science.

References

Abbott, A. (2001) *Chaos of Disciplines*, Chicago, IL: Chicago University Press.
Althusser, L. (1990) 'Philosophy and the Spontaneous Philosophy of the Scientists (1967)' in *Philosophy and the Spontaneous Philosophy of the Scientists and Other Essays* (pp. 69–165), London: Verso.
Amariglio, J., Resnick, S. and Wolff, R. D. (1993) 'Division and Difference in the "Discipline" of Economics', in E. Messer-Davidow, D. Shumway and D. Sylvan (eds.) *Knowledges: Historical and Critical Studies in Disciplinarity* (pp. 150–84), Charlottesville and London: University of Virginia Press.
Amin, A. and Cohendet, P. (2004) *Architectures of Knowledge: Firms, Capabilities and Communities*, Oxford: Oxford University Press.
Anderson, K. and Braun, B. (eds.) (2008) *Environment*, Aldershot: Ashgate.
Anderson, K. and Nafus, D. (2006) 'The Real Problem: Rhetorics of Knowing in Corporate Ethnographic Research', EPIC 2006 conference proceedings, American Anthropological Association.
Apostel, L. (1972) 'Conceptual Tools for Interdisciplinarity: An Operational Approach', in L. Apostel et al. (eds.) *Interdisciplinarity: Problems of Teaching and Research in Universities*, (pp. 141–84) Paris: Organisation for Economic Cooperation and Development.
Apostel, L., Berger, G., Briggs, A. and Michaud, G. (eds.) (1972) *Interdisciplinarity: Problems of Teaching and Research in Universities*, Paris: Organisation for Economic Cooperation and Development.
Arends, B. and Thackara, D. (eds.) (2003) *Experiment: Conversations in Art and Science*, London: Wellcome Trust.
Baerwald, T. (2010) 'Prospects for Geography as an Interdisciplinary Discipline', *Annals of the Association of American Geographers,* 100 (3): 493–501.
Barry, A. (2001) *Political Machines: Governing a Technological Society*, London: Athlone.
— (2002) 'The Anti-Political Economy', *Economy and Society*, 31 (2): 268–84.

— (2004) 'Ethical Capitalism', in W. Larner and W. Walters (eds.) *Global Governmentality* (pp. 195–221), London: Routledge.

— (2005) 'Pharmaceutical Matters: The Invention of Informed Materials', *Theory, Culture and Society*, 22: 51–69.

— (2006) 'Technological Zones', *European Journal of Social Theory*, 9: 239–53.

— (2007) 'Political Invention', in K. Asdal, B. Brenna and I. Moser (eds.) *Technoscience: The Politics of Interventions* (pp. 287–308), Oslo: Unipub.

— (2010) 'Tarde's Method: Between Statistics and Experimentation', in M. Candea (ed.) *The Social After Tarde: Debates and Assessments* (pp. 177–90), London: Routledge.

— (2012) 'Political Situations: Knowledge Controversies in Transnational Governance', *Critical Policy Studies*, 6 (3): 324–36.

Barry, A. and Born, G. (2007) 'Interdisciplinary Research and Evaluation', unpublished manuscript. Prepared for the Economic and Social Research Council, 5 pp.

Barry, A. Born, G. and Weszkalnys, G. (2008) 'Logics of Interdisciplinarity', *Economy and Society*, 37 (1): 20–49.

Barry, A. and Thrift, N. (2007) 'Gabriel Tarde: Imitation, Invention and Economy', *Economy and Society*, 36 (4): 509–25.

Beck, U. (1992) *The Risk Society: Towards a New Modernity*, London: Sage.

Becker, E. (2003) 'Soziale Ökologie: Konturen und Konzepte einer neuen Wissenschaft', in G. Matschonat and A. Gerber (eds.) *Wissenschaftstheoretische Perspektiven Für Die Umweltwissenschaften* (pp. 165– 195), Wikersheim: Margratf Publishers.

Bell, G., Brooke, T. Churchill, E. and Panlos, E. (2003) 'Intimate (Ubiquitous) Computing', Proc UbiComp workshop, www.citeseerx.ist.psu.edu (accessed September 2012).

Bennett, J. (2004) 'The Force of Things: Steps to an Ecology of Matter', *Political Theory*, 32 (3): 347–72.

Bennett, T. and Joyce, P. (2010) *Material Powers: Cultural Studies, History and the Material Turn*, London: Routledge.

Bensaude-Vincent, B. and Stengers, I. (1996) *The History of Chemistry*, Cambridge, MA: Harvard University Press.

Berkhout, F., Leach, M. and Scoones, I. (eds.) (2005) *Negotiating Environmental Change: New Perspectives from Social Science*, Cheltenham: Edward Elgar.

Blackwell, A. and Biggs, S. (2006) 'Making Material Culture', *Leonardo*, 39 (5): 471–3.

Boltanski, L. and Thévenot, L. (2006) *On Justification: Economies of Worth*, Princeton, NJ: Princeton University Press.

Born, G. (1995) *Rationalizing Culture: IRCAM, Boulez, and the Institutionalization of the Musical Avant-Garde*, Berkeley: University of California Press.

— (2005a) *Uncertain Vision: Birt, Dyke and the Reinvention of the BBC*, London: Vintage.

— (2005b) 'On Musical Mediation: Ontology, Technology and Creativity', *Twentieth Century Music*, 2 (1): 7–36.

— (2010a) 'The Social and the Aesthetic: For a Post-Bourdieuian Theory of Cultural Production', *Cultural Sociology*, 4 (2): 1–38.

— (2010b) 'On Tardean Relations: Temporality and Ethnography', in Candea, M. (ed.) *The Social After Gabriel Tarde: Debates and Assessments* (pp. 232–49), London: Routledge.

— (2011) 'Complexity as Method? Experimenting with Ethnographic Agonism in Research on Digital Musics', paper presented to the American Anthropological Association conference, Montreal, November.

Born, G. and Barry, A. (2010) 'Art-science: From Public Understanding to Public Experiment', *Journal of Cultural Economy*, 3 (1): 107–23.

Born, G. and Weszkalnys, G. (2007) 'Irreducible Heterogeneities and Interdisciplines In-formation, or the Possibility of Art-Science', paper presented to the colloquium, *Interdisciplinarity and Society*, St Catherine's College, Oxford, February 2007.

Bourdieu, P. (1975) 'The Specificity of the Scientific Field and the Social Conditions of the Progress of Reason', *Social Science Information*, 14 (6): 19–47.

Bowker, G. (1993) 'How to be Universal: Some Cybernetic Strategies, 1943–70', *Social Studies of Science*, 23: 107–27.

Bowker, G., Star, S. L., Turner, W. and Gasser, L. (eds.) (1997) *Social Science, Technical Systems and Cooperative Work*, Mawah, NJ: Lawrence Erlbaum.

Bracken, L. and Oughton, E. (2009) 'Interdisciplinarity Within and Beyond Geography: Introduction to Special Section', *Area*, 41 (4): 371–4.

Braun, B. and Whatmore, S. (eds.) (2010) *Political Matter: Technoscience, Democracy, and Public Life*, Minneapolis: Minnesota University Press.

Briggs, A. and Michaud, G. (1972) 'Problems and Solutions', in L. Apostel et al (eds.) *Interdisciplinarity: Problems of Teaching and Research in Universities* (pp. 185–280), Paris: Organisation for Economic Cooperation and Development.

Bruce, A., Lyall, C., Tait, J. and Williams, R. (2004) 'Interdisciplinary Integration in Europe: The Case of the Fifth Framework Program', *Futures*, 36 (4): 457–70.

Buchmann, S. (2006) 'From Systems-oriented Art to Biopolitical Art Practice', in M-A. Francis, J. Walsh, L. Sykes and M. Vishmidt (eds.) *Media Mutandis: Surveying Art, Technologies and Politics*, London: NODE.

Buller, H. (2009) 'The Lively Process of Interdisciplinarity', *Area*, 41 (4): 395–403.

Callon, M. (ed.) (1998) *The Laws of the Market*, Oxford: Basil Blackwell.

Callon, M., Lascoumes, P. and Barthe, Y. (2001) *Agir Dans un Monde Incertain: Essai Sur La Democratie Technique*, Paris: Seuil.

Callon, M., Millo, Y. and Muniesa, F. (eds.) (2007) *Market Devices*, Oxford: Basil Blackwell.

Cassin, B. (2005) 'Managing Evidence' in B. Latour and P. Weibel (eds.) *Making Things Public: Atmospheres of Democracy* (pp. 858–64), Cambridge, MA: MIT Press.

Castree, N. (2005) *Nature*, London: Routledge.

Cefkin, M. (ed.) (2009) *Ethnography and the Corporate Encounter: Reflections on Research In and Of Corporations*, New York and Oxford: Berghahn.

Century, M. (1999) *Pathways to Innovation in Digital Culture*, Report for the Rockefeller Foundation, www.nextcentury.ca/PI/PImain.html (accessed September 2012).

Clifford, J. (2005) 'Rearticulating Anthropology', in D. Segal and S. Yanagisako (eds.) *Unwrapping the Sacred Bundle: Reflections on the Disciplining of Anthropology* (pp. 24–48), Durham, NC: Duke University Press.

Clifford, J. and Marcus, G. (eds.) (1986) *Writing Culture: The Poetics and Politics of Ethnography*, Berkeley: University of California Press.

Collini, S. (1994) 'Escape from DWEMsville', *Times Literary Supplement*, 27 May.

Committee on Facilitating Interdisciplinary Research (National Academy of Sciences, National Academy of Engineering, Institute of Medicine) (2004) *Facilitating Interdisciplinary Research*, Washington, DC: National Academies Press.

Connolly, W. (2011) *A World of Becoming*, Durham, NC: Duke University Press.

Corbett, J. P. (1964) 'Opening the Mind' in D. Daiches (ed.) *The Idea of a New University: An Experiment in Sussex* (pp. 22–39), London: Andre Deutsch.

Corris, M. (2004) *Conceptual Art: Theory, Myth and Practice*, Cambridge: Cambridge University Press.

— (2005) 'Recoding of Information: Knowledge and Technology', paper presented to the *Open Systems: Rethinking Art c. 1970* conference, Tate Modern, September. www.publication.nodel.org/Recoding-of-Information (accessed February 2007).

Council of Science and Technology (2001) *Imagination and Understanding: A Report on the Arts and Humanities in Relation to Science and Technology* www.bis.gov.uk/assets/bispartners/cst/docs/files/whats-new/01-1051-imagination-understanding.pdf

da Costa, B. and Philip, K. (eds.) (2008) *Tactical Biopolitics: Art, Activism, and Technoscience*, Cambridge, MA and London: MIT Press.

Daston, L. (2000) 'The Coming into Being of Scientific Objects', in L. Daston (ed.) *Biographies of Scientific Objects* (pp. 1–14), Chicago, IL: Chicago University Press.

Davies, G. (2006) 'Mapping Deliberation: Calculation, Articulation and Intervention in the Politics of Organ Transplantation', *Economy and Society*, 35 (2): 232–58.

Deleuze, G. (1988) *Foucault*, London: Athlone.

Demeritt, D. (2001) 'The Construction of Global Warming and the Politics of Science', *Annals of the Association of American Geographers*, 91 (2): 307–37.

D'Hooge, H. (2005) 'User-Centred Research Fuels Technology Innovation at Intel', *Technology Intel Magazine*, April www.intel.com/technology/magazine/research/user-centered-innovation-0405.pdf, (accessed June 2006).

Doherty, C. (2004) *Contemporary Art: From Studio to Situation*, London: Black Dog.

Donovan, A., Ward, N. and Bradley, S. (2010) 'Mess Among Disciplines: Interdisciplinarity in Environmental Research', *Environment and Planning A*, 42 (7): 1521–36.

Doubleday, R. (2007) 'Organizing Accountability: Co-Production of Technoscientific and Social Worlds in a Nanoscience Laboratory', *Area*, 39 (2): 166–75.

Dourish, P. (2001) *Where the Action Is: Foundations of Embodied Interaction*, Cambridge, MA: MIT Press.

— (2006) 'Implications for Design', *CHI*, Montréal, 22–27 April 2006, www.dl.acm.org/citation.cfm?id=1124855, (accessed November 2012).

Dourish, P. and Bell, G. (2011) *Divining a Digital Future: Mess and Mythology in Ubiquitous Computing*, Cambridge, MA: MIT Press.

Edgerton, D. (2006) *Warfare State: Britain, 1920–1970*, Cambridge: Cambridge University Press.

Edwards, P. (2001) 'Representing the Global Atmosphere: Computer Models, Data, and Knowledge about Climate Change', in C. Miller and P. Edwards (eds.) *Changing the Atmosphere: Expert Knowledge and Environmental Governance* (pp. 31–66), Cambridge, MA: MIT Press.

Epstein, S. (1996) *Impure Science: AIDS, Activism, and the Politics of Knowledge*, Berkeley: University of California Press.

Eriksen, T. (2007) 'Tunnel Visions', *Social Anthropology*, 15 (2): 237–43.

Feltham, O. and Clemens, J. (2003) 'Introduction' to A. Badiou, *Infinite Thought* (pp. 1–38), London: Continuum.

Ferran, B. (2006) 'Creating a Program of Support for Art and Science Collaborations', *Leonardo*, 30 (5): 442–6.

Foucault, M. (1972) *The Archaeology of Knowledge*, London: Tavistock.

— (1994) 'Polemics, Politics, and Problematizations', in *Ethics: The Essential Works, Volume 1* (pp. 111–20), London: Penguin.

— (2001) 'Le Souci de la Vérité', in *Dits et Écrits II, 1976–1988* (pp. 1487–97), Paris: Gallimard.

Fraser, M. (2002) 'What is the Matter of Feminist Criticism?', *Economy and Society*, 31 (4): 606–25.

Fraser, M., Kember, S. and Lury, C. (eds.) (2006) *Inventive Life: Approaches to the New Vitalism*, London: Sage.

Friman, M. (2010) 'Understanding Boundary Work through Discourse Theory: Inter/disciplines and Interdisciplinarity', *Science Studies*, 23 (2): 5–19.

Frodeman, R., Klein, J. T. and Mitcham, C. (eds.) (2010) *The Oxford Handbook of Interdisicplinarity*, Oxford: Oxford University Press.

Fuller, S. (1993) *Philosophy, Rhetoric, and the End of Knowledge*, Madison: University of Wisconsin Press.

— (2002) *Social Epistemology*, Bloomington: Indiana University Press.

— (2003) 'Interdisciplinarity: The Loss of the Heroic Vision in the Marketplace of Ideas', www.interdisciplines.org/medias/confs/archives/archive_3.pdf (accessed September 2012), pp. 125–130.

Galison, P. (1996a) 'Introduction: The Context of Disunity' in P. Galison and D. Stump (eds.), pp. 1–36.

— (1996b) 'Context and Constraints' in J. Buchwald (ed.) *Scientific Practice*, pp. 13–41 Chicago, IL: Chicago University Press.

— (1997) *Image and Logic: A Material Culture of Microphysics*, Chicago, IL: University of Chicago Press.

Galison, P. and Stump, D. (eds.) (1996) *The Disunity of Science: Boundaries, Contexts, and Power*, Stanford, CA: Stanford University Press.

Gaver, W., Dunne, A. and Pacenti, E. (1999) 'Cultural Probes', *Interactions*, vi (1): 21–9.

Geertz, C. (1988) 'I-Witnessing: Malinowski's Children', in *Works and Lives: The Anthropologist as Author*, (pp. 73–101) Cambridge: Polity.

Gibbons, M., Limoges, C., Nowotny, M., Schwartzman, S., Scott, P. and Trow, M. (1994) *The New Production of Knowledge*: *The Dynamics of Science and Research in Contemporary Societies*, London: Sage.

Goldstein, J. (1984) 'Foucault Among the Sociologists: The "Disciplines" and the History of the Professions', *History and Theory*, 23 (2): 170–92.

Guattari, F. (1992) 'Félix Guattari et l'Art Contemporain', Interview with Olivier Zahm, *Chimères*, www.revue-chimeres.fr/drupal_chimeres/files/23chi04.pdf (accessed May 2012).

Hacking, I. (2004) 'The Complacent Disciplinarian', www.interdisciplines.org//medias/confs/archives/archive_3.pdf (accessed September 2012), pp. 194–97.

Halewood, M. (2011) *A. N. Whitehead and Social Theory: Tracing a Culture of Thought*, London: Anthem.

Harkin, M. (2010) 'Uncommon Ground: Holism and the Future of Anthropology', *Reviews in Anthropology*, 39 (1): 25–45.

Harper, R. (2003) *Inside the Smart Home*, London: Springer.

Harrison, S. et al (2004) 'Thinking Across the Divide: Perspectives on the Conservations Between Physical and Human Geography', *Area* 36: 435–42.

Hart, D. and Victor, D. (1993) 'Scientific Elites and the Making of US Policy for Climate Change Research 1957–74', *Social Studies of Science*, 23: 643–80.

Harvey, P., Casella, E., Evans, G., Knox, H., MacLean, C., Silva, E., Thoburn, N. and Woodward, K. (2013) *Objects and Materials: A Routledge Companion*, London: Routledge.

Henare, A., Holbraad, M. and Wastell, S. (2006) *Thinking Through Things: Theorising Artefacts Ethnographically*, London: Routledge.

Hicks, D. and Beaudry, M. (eds.) (2010) *The Oxford Handbook of Material Culture* Studies, Oxford: Oxford University Press.

HM Treasury (2006) *Science and Innovation Investment Framework 2004–2014: Next Steps*, London: HMSO, www.bis.gov.uk/files/file29096.pdf, (accessed November 2012).

Hinchliffe, S. (2007) *Geographies of Nature: Societies, Environments, Ecologies*, London: Sage.

Hirsch Hadorn, G., Hoffmann-Riem, H., Biber-Klemm, S., Grossenbacher-Mansuy, W., Joye, D., Pohl, C., Wiesmann, U. and Zemp, E. (eds.) (2008) *Handbook of Transdisciplinary Research*, Heidelberg: Springer.

Holmes, D. and Marcus, G. (2005) 'Cultures of Expertise and the Management of Globalization: Toward the Re-Functioning of Ethnography', in A. Ong and S. Collier (eds.) *Global Assemblages: Technology, Politics, and Ethics as Anthropological Problems* (pp. 235–52), Malden, MA: Blackwell.

Hulme, M. and Turnpenny, J. (2004) 'Understanding and Managing Climate Change: The UK Experience', *The Geographical Journal*, 170: 105–15.

Hulme, M. (2009) *Why We Disagree About Climate Change*, Cambridge: Cambridge University Press.

Huutoniemi, K., Klein, J. T., Bruun, H. and Hukkinen, J. (2010) 'Analyzing Interdisciplinarity: Typology and Indicators', *Research Policy*, 39 (1): 79–88.

Ingold, T. (2001) 'From Complementarity to Obviation: On Dissolving the Boundaries between Social and Biological Anthropology, Archaeology and Psychology', in S. Oyama, P. Griffiths and R. Gray (eds.) *Cycles of Contingency: Developmental Systems and Evolution* (pp. 255–79), Cambridge, MA: MIT Press.

Irwin, A. (1995) *Citizen Science*, London: Routledge.

Irwin, A. and Wynne, B. (eds.) (1996) *Misunderstanding Science*, Cambridge: Cambridge University Press.

Jantsch, E. (1972) 'Towards Interdisciplinarity and Transdisciplinarity in Education and Innovation', in L. Apostel, G. Berger, A. Briggs and G. Michaud (eds.) *Interdisciplinarity: Problems of Teaching and Research in Universities* (pp. 97–121), Paris: OECD.

Jasanoff, S. (ed.) (2004) *States of Knowledge: The Co-Production of Science and Social Order*, New York: Routledge.

Jasanoff, S. and Wynne, B. (1998) 'Science and Decisionmaking' in S. Rayner and E. Malone (eds.), *Human Choice and Climate Change v.1–4* (pp. 1–87), Columbus, OH: Batelle Press.

Jones, S. (2006) 'From Ancestors to Herbs: Innovation According to the "Protestant Re-Formation" of African Medicine', *Ethnographic Praxis in Industry Conference* (EPIC), pp. 177–97.

Khlinovskaya Rockhill, E. (2007) 'On Interdisciplinarity and Models of Knowledge Production', *Social Analysis*, 51 (3): 121–47.

Klein, J. T. (2004) 'Prospects for Transdisciplinarity', *Futures*, 36: 515–26.

— (2010) 'A Taxonomy of Interdisciplinarity', in R. Frodeman et al (eds.) *The Oxford Handbook of Interdisciplinarity*, (pp. 15–30), Oxford: Oxford University Press.

Knorr-Cetina, K. (1999) *Epistemic Cultures: How the Sciences Make Knowledge*, Cambridge, MA: Harvard University Press.

Krohn, W. (2010) 'Interdisciplinary Cases and Disciplinary Knowledge', in R. Frodeman et al (eds.) *The Oxford Handbook of Interdisciplinarity* (pp. 31–9), Oxford: Oxford University Press.

Küchler, S. (2008) 'Technological Materiality: Beyond the Dualist Paradigm', *Theory, Culture and Society*, 25 (1): 101–20.

Laclau, E. and Mouffe, C. (1985) *Hegemony and Socialist Strategy*, London: Verso.

Lamont, M. and Molnar, V. (2002) 'The Study of Boundaries in the Social Sciences', *Annual Review of Sociology*, 28: 167–95.

Lash, S., Swersznski, B. and Wynne, B. (eds.) (1996) *Risk, Environment and Modernity: Towards a New Ecology*, London: Sage.

Latour, B. (1993) *We Have Never Been Modern*, Hemel Hempstead: Harvester Wheatsheaf.

—— (1999) *Pandora's Hope: Essays on the Reality of Science Studies*, Cambridge, MA: Harvard University Press.

—— (2004) *The Politics of Nature*, Cambridge, MA: Harvard University Press.

Latour, B. and Weibel, P. (eds.) (2002) *Iconoclash: Beyond the Image Wars in Science, Religion, and Art*, Cambridge, MA: MIT Press.

—— (2005) *Making Things Public: Atmospheres of Democracy*, Cambridge, MA: MIT Press.

Laurent, B. (2011) *Democracy on Trial: Assembling Nanotechnology and its Problems*, Doctorat ParisTech, l'École Nationale Supérieure des Mines de Paris.

Lawrence, R. and Després, C. (2004) 'Introduction: Futures of Transdisciplinarity', *Futures*, 36 (4): 397–406.

Leach, M., Scoones, I. and Wynne, B. (eds.) (2005) *Science and Citizens: Globalisation and the Challenge of Engagement*, London: Zed Books.

Leroy, P. (1995) 'Environmental Science as a Vocation', inaugural lecture at the University of Nijmegen, 9 June.

Lichnerowicz, A. (1972) 'Mathematic and Transdisciplinarity', in. Apostel et al. (eds.) Interdisciplinarity: Problems of Teaching and Research in Universities, (pp. 121–7) Paris: Organisation for Economic Cooperation and Development.

Liverman, D. (1999) 'Geography and the Global Environment', *Annals of the Association of American Geographers*, 89 (1): 107–20.

Livingstone, D. (1992) *The Geographical Tradition*, Oxford: Basil Blackwell.

—— (2003) *Putting Science in its Place*, Chicago, IL: Chicago University Press.

Lyall, C., Bruce, A., Tait, J. and Meagher, L. (2011) *Interdisciplinary Research Journeys: Practical Strategies for Capturing Creativity*, London: Bloomsbury Academic.

MacKenzie, D., Muniesa, F. and Siu, L. (eds.) (2007) *Do Economists Make Markets?: On the Performativity of Economics*, Princeton, NJ: Princeton University Press.

Maniglier, P. (1997) *De la Position des Problèmes*, Diplôme d'Etudes Avancées, Université Paris X Nanterre/École Normale Supérieure.

—— (2012) 'Problem-Sharing: The Role of Problems in Transdisciplinarity from the Standpoint of the French Epistemological Tradition', paper presented at the workshop on *Transdisciplinarity and the Humanities*, Kingston University, January.

Mansilla, V. B. (2006a) 'Symptoms of Quality: Assessing Expert Interdisciplinary Work at the Frontier – an Empirical Exploration', *Research Evaluation*, 15 (1): 17–29.

—— (2006b) 'Interdisciplinary Work at the Frontier: An Empirical Examination of Expert Interdisciplinary Epistemologies', *Issues in Integrative Studies*, 24: 1–31.

Mansilla, V. B. and Gardner, H. (2003) 'Assessing Interdisciplinary Work at the Frontier: An Empirical Exploration of "Symptoms of Quality"', www.interdisciplines.org/medias/confs/archives/archive_ (accessed September 2012), pp. 160–66.

Marcus, G. (2002) 'Intimate Strangers: The Dynamics of (Non) Relationship between the Natural and Human Sciences in the Contemporary U.S. University', *Anthropological Quarterly*, 75 (3): 519–26.

Miller, C. (2004) 'Climate Change and the Making of a Global Political Order', in S. Jasanoff (ed.), *States of Knowledge: The Co-production of Science and Social Order*, (pp. 46–66), New York: Routledge.

Miller, D. and Slater, D. (2000) *The Internet: An Ethnographic Approach*, Oxford: Berg.

Miller, P. and O'Leary, T. (2007) 'Mediating Instruments and Making Markets: Capital Budgeting, Science and the Economy', *Accounting, Organizations and Society*, 32: 701–34.

Mirowski, P. and Mirjam Sent, E. (eds.) (2002) *Science Bought and Sold: Essays in the Economics of Science*, Chicago, IL: Chicago University Press.

Mitchell, T. (2002) *Rule of Experts: Egypt, Techno-Politics, Modernity*, Berkeley: University of California Press.

Mol, A. (2002) *The Body Multiple: Ontology in Medical Practice*, Durham, NC: Duke University Press.

Morin, E. (1997) 'Réforme de pensée, transdisciplinarité, réforme de l'Université', Communication au Congrès International, *Quelle Université Pour Demain? Vers Une Évolution Transdisciplinaire De l'Université*, Locarno, Switzerland, 30 April–2 May 1997. basarab.nicolescu.perso.sfr.fr/ciret/bulletin/b12/b12c1.htm (Accessed May 2012).

Nafus, D. and Anderson, K. (2009) 'Writing on Walls: The Materiality of Social Memory in Corporate Research', in K. Cefkin (ed.) *Ethnography and the Corporate Encounter: Reflections on Research In and Of Corporations* (pp. 137–57) New York and Oxford: Berghahn.

Naimark, M. (2003) 'Truth, Beauty, Freedom, and Money: Technology-Based Art and the Dynamics of Sustainability', a report for *Leonardo* journal, www.artslab.net, (accessed November 2012).

Nardi, B. and O'Day, V. (1999) *Information Ecologies*, Cambridge, MA and London: MIT Press.

National Academy of Sciences (2004) *Facilitating Interdisciplinary Research*, Washington, DC: National Academies Press.

Newman, M. (2002) 'Conceptual Art from the 1960s to the 1990s: An Unfinished Project?', in P. Osborne (ed.) *Conceptual Art*, London: Phaidon.

Nicolescu, B. (2008) 'In Vitro and In Vivo Knowledge – Methodology of Transdisciplinarity' in B. Nicolescu (ed.) *Transdisciplinarity: Theory and Practice*, (pp. 1–21) Cresskill, NJ: Hampton Press.

Nowotny, H. (2003a) 'Science in Search of its Audience', *Nova Acta Leopoldina*, NF, 87, 325: 211–15.

— (2003b) 'The Potential of Transdisciplinarity', www.interdisciplines.org/medias/confs/archives/archive_3.pdf (accessed September 2012), pp. 48–53.

— (2005) 'The Changing Nature of Public Science' in H. Nowotny, D. Pestre, B. Schmidt-Assmann, H. Schulze-Fielitz and H.-H. Trute (eds.) *The Public Nature of Science Under Assault: Politics, Markets, Science and the Law*, (pp. 1–28) Berlin: Springer.

Nowotny, H., Scott, P. and Gibbons, M. (2001) *Re-Thinking Science: Knowledge and the Public in an Age of Uncertainty,* Cambridge: Polity.

Osborne, P. (2002) *Conceptual Art*, London: Phaidon.

— (2011) 'From Structure to Rhizome: Transdisciplinarity in French Thought (1)', *Radical Philosophy*, 165: 15–16.

Osborne, T. (2004) 'On Mediators: Intellectuals and the Ideas Trade in the Knowledge Society', *Economy and Society*, 33 (4): 430–47.

Owens, S. (2000) '"Engaging the Public": Information and Deliberation in Environmental Policy', *Environment and Planning A*, 32: 1141–8.

Petts, J., Owens, S. and Bulkeley, H. (2008) 'Crossing Boundaries: Interdisciplinarity in the Context of Urban Environments', *Geoforum*, 39 (2): 593–601.

Piaget, J. (1972) 'The Epistemology of Interdisciplinary Relationships', in L. Apostel et al (eds.) *Interdisciplinarity: Problems of Teaching and Research in Universities* (pp. 127–39), Paris: OECD.

Pickering, A. (1995a) *The Mangle of Practice: Time, Agency and Science*, Chicago, IL: University of Chicago Press.

— (1995b) 'Cyborg History and the World War II Regime', *Perspectives on Science*, 3 (1): 1–48.

Popper, F. (2007) *From Technological to Virtual Art*, Cambridge, MA: MIT Press.

Power, M. (ed.) (1996) *Accounting and Science: Natural Inquiry and Commercial Reason*, Cambridge: Cambridge University Press.

Rabeharisoa, V. and Callon, M. (1999) *Le Pouvoir des Malades*, Paris: Les Presses de l'École des Mines.

Rabinow, P. (2005) 'Midst Anthropology's Problems', in A. Ong and S. Collier (eds.) *Global Assemblages: Technology, Politics, and Ethics as Anthropological Problems* (pp. 40–53), Oxford: Blackwell.

Ramadier, T. (2004) 'Transdisciplinarity and its Challenges: The Case of Urban Studies', *Futures*, 36 (4): 423–40.

Rancière, J. (2006) 'Thinking Between Disciplines: An Aesthetics of Knowledge', *Parrhesia*, 1: 1–12.

Randall, D., Harper, R. and Rouncefield, M. (2005) 'Fieldwork, Ethnography and Design: A Perspective from CSCW', in K. Anderson and T. Lovejoy (eds.) *EPIC 2005: Ethnographic Praxis in Industry Conference*, pp. 88–99, Redmond: WA, Seattle, American Anthropological Association, Arlington, VA.

Rayner, S. and Malone, E. (eds.) (1998) *Human Choice and Climate Change v.1–4*, Columbus, OH: Batelle Press.

Reichle, I. (2009) *Art in the Age of Technoscience: Genetic Engineering, Robotics, and Artificial Life in Contemporary Art*, Vienna: Springer.

Rhoten, D. (2004) 'Interdisciplinary Research: Trend or Transition', *Items and Issues*, 5: 6–12.

Salvador, T., Bell, G. and Anderson, K. (1999) 'Design Ethnography', *Design Management Journal*, 10 (4): 35–41.

Schaffer, S. (1996) 'Where Experiments End: Tabletop Trials in Victorian Astronomy', in J. Buchwald (ed.) *Scientific Practice* (pp. 257–99), Chicago, IL: Chicago University Press.

— (2007) 'On Disciplines and Interdisciplines', paper presented to the colloquium on *Interdisciplinarity and Society*, St Catherine's College, Oxford, February 2007.

Schellnhuber, H. J. (1999) '"Earth System" Analysis and the Second Copernican Revolution', *Nature* supplement, 402 (2 December): 19–23.

Schmidt, J. (2010) 'Prospects for a Philosophy of Interdisciplinarity', in R. Frodeman et al (eds.) *The Oxford Handbook of Interdisciplinarity*, Oxford: Oxford University Press.

Schuler, D. and Namioka, A. (eds.) (1993) *Particpatory Design: Principles and Practices*, Hillsdale, NJ: Lawrence Erlbaum

Segal, D. and Yanagisako, S. (eds.) (2005) *Unwrapping the Sacred Bundle: Reflections on the Disciplining of Anthropology*, Durham, NC: Duke University Press.

Sellen, A. and Harper, R. (2003) *The Myth of the Paperless Office*, Cambridge, MA: MIT Press.

Shackley, S. and Wynne, B. (1985) 'Integrating Knowledges for Climate Change: Pyramids, Nets and Uncertainties', *Global Environmental Change*, 5 (2): 113–26.

Silverstone, R. and Hirsch, E. (eds.) (1994) *Consuming Technologies*, London: Routledge.

Skrebowski, L. (2009) *Systems, Contexts, Relations: An Alternative Genealogy of Conceptual Art*, PhD thesis, Centre for Research in Modern European Philosophy/ History of Art and Design, Middlesex University (September).

Snow, C. P. (1959) *The Two Cultures*, Cambridge: Cambridge University Press.

Social Epistemology (1995) 'Special Issue on Boundary Rhetorics and the Work of Interdisciplinarity', *Social Epistemology*, 19 (2).

Star, S. L. and Griesemer, J. (1989) 'Institutional Ecology, "Translations" and Boundary Objects: Amateurs and Professionals in Berkeley's Museum of Vertebrate Zoology, 1901–39', *Social Studies of Science*, 19 (3): 387–420.

Stengers, I. (1997) *Power and Invention: Situating Science*, Minneapolis: Minnesota University Press.

— (2005) 'The Cosmopolitical Proposal', in B. Latour and P. Weibel (eds.), *Making Things Public: Atmosphere of Democracy* (pp. 994–1003), Cambridge, MA: MIT Press.

Stirling, A. (2005) 'Opening Up or Closing Down?: Analysis, Participation and Power in the Social Appraisal of Technology', in M. Leach, I. Scoones and I. Wynne (eds.) *Science and Citizens: Globalisation and the Challenge of Engagement* (pp. 218–31), London: Zed Books.

Strathern, M. (2004a) 'In Crisis Mode: A Comment on Interculturality', in M. Strathern, *Commons and Borderlands: Working Papers on Interdisciplinarity, Accountability and the Flow of Knowledge* (pp. 1–14), Wantage: Sean Kingston.

— (2004b) 'Accountability Across Disciplines', in M. Strathern, *Commons and Borderlands: Working Papers on Interdisciplinarity, Accountability and the Flow of Knowledge* (pp. 68–86), Wantage: Sean Kingston.

— (2004c) 'Social Property: An Interdisciplinary Experiment', *PoLAR (Political and Legal Anthropology Review)*, 27: 33–50.

— (2005) 'Experiments in Interdisciplinarity', *Social Anthropology*, 13 (1): 75–90.

— (2006) 'A Community of Critics? Thoughts on New Knowledge', *Journal of the Royal Anthropological Institute*, 12 (1): 191–209.

— (2011) 'An Experiment in Interdisciplinarity: Proposals and Promises', in C. Camic, N. Gross and M. Lamont (eds.) *Social Knowledge in the Making* (pp. 257–84), Chicago, IL: Chicago University Press.

Suchman, L. (2007 [1987]) *Human-Machine Reconfigurations: Plans and Situated Actions*, expanded edition, New York: Cambridge University Press.

— (2000) 'Anthropology as Brand: Reflections on Corporate Ethnography', www.lancs.ac.uk/fss/sociology/papers/suchman-anthropology-as-brand.pdf

Suchman, L., Blomberg, J. and Trigg, R. (2002) 'Working Artefacts: Ethnomethods of the Prototype', *British Journal of Sociology*, 53 (2): 163–79.

Tait, J. and Lyall, C. (2001) *Investigation into ESRC Funded Interdisciplinary Research*, www.supra.ed.ac.uk/Publications/ESRC_report_Interdisiplinary_research.pdf (accessed September 2012).

Tarde, G. (2001) *Les Lois de L'Imitation*, Paris: Les Empêcheurs de Penser en Rond.

Thompson, M. and Rayner, S. (1998) 'Risk and Governance Part I: The Discourse of Climate Change', *Government and Opposition*, 33: 139–66.

Thompson, M., Rayner, S. and Ney, S. (1998) 'Risk and Governance Part II: Policy in a Complex and Plurally Perceived World', *Government and Opposition*, 33: 330–54.

Thrift, N. (2005) *Knowing Capitalism*, London: Sage.

— (2006) 'Re-Inventing Invention: New Tendencies in Capitalist Commodification', *Economy and Society*, 35 (2): 279–306.

— (2011) 'Lifeworld Inc – and What to Do About It', *Environment and Planning D: Society and Space*, 29 (1): 5–26.

Tompkins, E. (2005) *Review of Interdisciplinary Environmental Science Centres of Excellence*, report to MISTRA, Swedish Foundation for Environmental Research.

Turner, S. (2000) 'What are Disciplines? And How is Interdisciplinarity Different?', in P. Weingart and N. Stehr (eds.) *Practicising Interdisciplinarity* (pp. 41–65), Toronto: University of Toronto Press.

Turnpenny, J., Haxeltine, A., O'Riordan, T. and Lorenzoni, I. (2005) 'Mapping Actors Involved in Climate Change Policy Networks in the UK', *Tyndall Working Paper* 66, www.tyndall.ac.uk/content/mapping-actors-involved-climate-change-policy-networks-uk, (accessed September 2012).

Turnpenny, J. and O'Riordan, T. (2007) 'Putting Sustainability to Work: Assisting the East of England Region to Respond to the Challenges of Climate Change', *Trans Inst Transactions of the Institute of British Geographers* NS 32: 102–5.

UNECE (1998) 'Convention on Access to Information, Public Participation in Decision-making and Access to Justice on Environmental Matters', Aarhus, 25 June 1998, www.unece.org/env/pp/treatytext.html (accessed September 2012).

Wallerstein, I. (1996) *Open the Social Sciences: Report of the Gulbenkian Commission on the Restructuring of the Social Sciences*, Stanford, CA: Stanford University Press.

Weingart, P. (2010) 'A Short History of Knowledge Formations', in Frodeman et al (eds.) *The Oxford Handbook of Interdisciplinarity* (pp. 3–14) Oxford: Oxford University Press.

Weingart, P. and Stehr, N. (eds.) (2000) *Practising Interdisciplinarity*, Toronto: University of Toronto Press.

Whatmore, S. (1999) 'Hybrid Geographies: Rethinking the "Human" in Human Geography', in D. Massey, J. Allen and P. Sarre (eds.) *Human Geography Today* (pp. 22–39), Cambridge: Polity.

— (2009) 'Mapping Knowledge Controversies: Environmental Science, Democracy and the Redistribution of Expertise', *Progress in Human Geography*, 33 (5): 587–99.

Whitehead, A. N. (1920) *The Concept of Nature*, Cambridge: Cambridge University Press.

— (1926) *Science and the Modern World*, Cambridge: Cambridge University Press.

Wilson, S. (2002) *Information Arts: Intersections of Art, Science and Technology*, Cambridge, MA: MIT Press.

Wissenschaftsrat (2000) *Thesen Zur Künftigen Entwicklung Des Wissenschaftssystems in Deutschland*, Drs. 4594/00, Berlin.

Wynne, B. (1996) 'May the Sheep Graze Safely? A Reflexive View of the Expert–Lay Knowledge Divide', in Lash et al (eds.) Risk, Environment and Modernity: Toward a New Ecology (pp. 27–43), London: Sage.

2 How Disciplines Look

Simon Schaffer

Were it required to say, in one word, by what means these primary and essential requisites, attention and exertion, are to be called forth, that word were *discipline*, a word which at once conveys a happy illustration of the subject of inquiry. For, as its classical and original meaning is Learning, Education, Instruction, it has come, as often happens, to signify the Means by which this end is attained, whether it be the method, order and rule observed in teaching, or the punishment and correction employed for this purpose. In the last and common acceptation of the word it has often been termed the Panacea in tuition. . . . It embraces the chief means of education. It is in a school as in an army, discipline is the first, second, and third essential.

(Bell 1808: 10–11)

Indiscipline and Interdisciplines

Every discipline tells a story: where it comes from, what it is and where it is going. Disciples learn such parables as part of their induction. The story gives an account of the origin and course of disciplinary development. It provides a rationale and means for the pursuit of the disciplinary enterprise. So disciplines' stories are performative. They help make what they purport merely to announce. Across the sciences such stories pick out exemplary protagonists and passages of action whence disciples can implicitly acquire their sense of what counts as appropriate behaviour.[1] This is how a specific episode can be judged a disciplinarily significant discovery or that data count as being in what the discipline reckons to be reasonable agreement with its predictions.[2]

The relation between the normative and descriptive characters of these disciplinary narratives helps produce their uncanny quality. The common ambiguities of discipline, as account of the world and programme for action, give disciplinary histories their strength and strangeness. *Disciplina* referred both to the organisation of knowledge and the exercise of power, to cognition and to gymnastics (Shumway and Messer-Davidow 1991: 202; Lenoir 1993: 72; Kelley 1997: 16). Their stories' simultaneously mnemonic and monitory role depends on the genealogy of modern disciplines. This becomes peculiarly telling in the face of an expansive discourse of *interdisciplinarity*. Proclamations of the imminence and desirability of interdisciplinary inquiry also appeal to disciplinary histories.

This version of interdisciplinarity as ideology supports and relies on an image of long-standing disciplinarity in the process of welcome if painful transformation. This ideology, evidently if oddly, takes as accurate history the stories disciplines have told about themselves. This is how interdisciplinarity acquires its own disciplinary history.

The discourse of interdisciplinarity identifies itself with innovative and flexible responses to ever more complex realities. Under what our editors call an 'agonistic-antagonistic mode' of engagement with established disciplines, the discourse pictures disciplinarity as the inverse of this formation: formalised, strict and traditional (Barry et al 2008). One way of making this image work is to take seriously the histories that make disciplines look like well-institutionalised homogeneous systems of formal behaviour (Weingart 2000: 26, 31; cf. Petrie 1976, Heilbron 2003). Disciplinary histories do this. This is how a traditional map of disciplines is reinforced by a project that supposes the map should be and is being redrawn.

The claim that the established disciplinary order must now, at last, be overhauled is often accompanied by the touching remark that this claim is quite new and that, at last, some clarity can be introduced into the undisciplined project of interdisciplinarity. Its disciplinary histories often cite Alan Liu's remark, made two decades ago, that interdisciplinarity is 'the most seriously underthought critical, pedagogical and institutional concept in the modern academy' (Liu 1989: 743). One is regularly told this situation is now to be corrected. The *Oxford Handbook of Interdisciplinarity* will at last 'introduce a greater degree of order into the field of interdisciplinary research, education, and practice by creating a work that will become the bible for all future attempts at interdisciplinarity' (Centre for the Study of Interdisciplinarity nd).[3] Projects for interdisciplines produce histories that suppose prior disciplinary power and homogeneity. In his celebrated analysis of the movement of theories between sites of production and reinterpretation, Edward Said wrote that 'the distinction between one discipline and another has been blurred precisely because fields . . . are no longer considered to be as all-encompassing or as synoptic as, *until recently*, they once were' (Said 1982 in Bayoumi and Rubin (eds.) 2000: 197, my italics).

Interdisciplinary talk summons into existence a memory of a past disciplinary hegemony. Yet if, as the philosophers of the *fin-de-siècle* notoriously argued, truths are dead metaphors and scientific instruments are boxed experiments about which one has forgotten that this is what they are, then disciplines are interdisciplines about which the same kind of amnesia has occurred (Nietzsche 1873: 84; Duhem 1914: 182–3; Golinski 1998: 133–45).

Within astronomical sciences, Johannes Kepler's early seventeenth-century celestial physics, William Herschel's late eighteenth-century natural history of the heavens, or the late nineteenth-century astrophysics promoted by campaigners such as Samuel Langley and George Ellery Hale all provide cases of hybrid projects whose edgily oxymoronic character has been effaced. The first president of the National Research Council, Hale was certainly concerned with the character of subjects he saw set between 'the old established divisions of science' (Hale, cited in Frank 1988: 92).[4]

Interdisciplinarity's disciplinary history is a retrospective purification enterprise directed to the production of essential disciplines that can then somehow usefully be juxtaposed and recombined. There is a resemblance with more familiar stories of hybrids and individuals. Like Michel Foucault's political anatomy and Bruno Latour's ingenious moderns, these are enterprises that make embodied individuals out of multiple hybrids, then hold the purified individuals as the primordial category (Foucault 2007: 12; Latour 1993: 10–11). A mistake is to assume disciplines' inertia: their character is what requires labour by members and explanation by analysts. This argument challenges the strictly functionalist claim that the order of disciplines is simply the expression of a utilitarian division of intellectual labour set up in the early nineteenth century. This functionalism rests on a kind of forgetting of discipline's indisciplined history and a substitution by disciplinary histories.[5] Such oblivion is not a matter of the passage of time. It is not exactly that one has forgotten the ancestry of modern forms of knowledge. The question then arises: when exactly was this hegemonic moment and how did it look?

Several historians hold that one should only properly speak of disciplines from the nineteenth century. Robert Kohler has written that 'historically it seems evident that the institutional predominance of the scientific discipline was part of the massive restructuring of occupations of all kinds that accompanied and drove the expansion of educational systems in mid-nineteenth century Europe' (Kohler 1999: 330) and that disciplines 'first dominated the social organization of science' after 1840 (Kohler 1981: 104). The editors of a volume of *Historical and Critical Studies in Disciplinarity* state that 'knowledge has assumed a disciplinary form for only two centuries' (Messer-Davidow et al 1993: vii), while those of a volume on *Practising Interdisciplinarity* agree that 'the established order of knowledge . . . emerged with the modern universities in the nineteenth century' and that now 'the organizational matrix of disciplines is beginning to dissolve'. At long last, it is argued, 'science has been drawn out from its relative social isolation, its elite status, and moved closer to the mundane concerns of society' (Weingart and Stehr 2000: xi, xiv).[6]

Both Notker Hammerstein and Rudolf Stichweh have claimed influentially that scientific disciplines are inventions of the late eighteenth and early nineteenth centuries, since when 'scientists continue to believe in the cognitive rationality of an overarching disciplinary identity' (Stichweh 1992: 14; see also Hammerstein 1989: 173). Jan Golinski's lucid account of disciplinarity and its ambiguities states that it was in the period 1780–1850 that 'the boundaries of different disciplines became a more entrenched feature of the production of knowledge', accompanied by 'defining practices and regulated borders' (Golinski 1998: 67), while in their analysis of the new forms of discipline inaugurated in this period, Andrew Warwick and David Kaiser convincingly point to this 'major and unprecedented watershed in the history of the sciences' involving 'a profound relationship between the history of training and the level and scale of agreement achievable in a technical discipline' (Warwick and Kaiser 2005: 403).

Yet disciplines as systems of border maintenance and regulation of practice considerably predate the period of the so-called second Scientific Revolution. As

William Clark has well explained, to take this conjuncture as the moment of emergence of disciplinary knowledge is to write a disciplinary history centred on the figure of the 'charismatic Romantic bureaucrat' (Clark 2006: 446). Historians know, too, that mundane concerns and intense socio-political interaction have long characterised the forms of knowledge making. In a nuanced account of disciplinary formations across cultures, Geoffrey Lloyd shows that since Western traditions have involved many different, hybrid forms of disciplinary formation, it makes no sense to suppose that the current disciplinary orders practised by contemporary learned elites have universal scope nor, alternatively, to assume that any given discipline is exclusively to be found in the institutions set up in early nineteenth-century Europe (Lloyd 2009). In the classical tradition, disciplinarity governed the relation between the master *didaskolos* and the pupil, *mathetes*. As Donald Kelley has taught us, Renaissance, Reformation and Scientific Revolution seemed to alter these relations rather little (Kelley 1997: 22).

As an example, similar usages were commonplaces of the enterprises of Renaissance astronomy: 'the right to cross disciplinary lines', Robert Westman tells us, 'was not merely a matter of methodological manifestos, epistemological claims and humanist rhetoric.' The Astronomical Revolution took the course it did partly because 'any scientific innovation which bridges disciplines requires the adopters to negotiate the rules governing disciplinary behaviour' (Westman 1980: 134; Dear 1995). In the mid-seventeenth century, Robert Boyle systematically used the term *discipline* in order to explain the well-sanctioned boundaries between medicine and natural philosophy, then to describe how those boundaries had emerged in antiquity, and crucially to defend his risky entry into the disciplinary province of the physicians (Boyle 1660, 1663, 1685). Sorting out the geographical and chronological schemes of disciplinary power remains the analyst's task, since one cannot be sure exactly when there were disciplines to connect nor when they looked as they do now.

It is claimed that once upon a time there was 'a hegemony of disciplinary science, with its strong sense of an internal hierarchy between the disciplines and driven by the autonomy of scientists', now allegedly displaced by 'transdisciplinary' and 'multiply accountable' forms of knowledge (Nowotny et al 2006: 39). But this primeval world of disciplinary hegemony has not been easy to locate nor even to analyse.[7] The problem applies reflexively to the discipline of history of science. At a major international meeting at Oxford in 1961, a debate on 'history of science as an academic discipline' heard Asa Briggs 'confess that I have some initial difficulty in deciding what constitutes an academic discipline' and opine that the demand for a discipline of history of science came from 'vociferous' if 'untidy' student demands for 'an antidote to specialization' (Briggs and Cohen 1963: 765). Bernard Cohen grumbled that their discipline had already failed at this task: 'the slogan of the bridge still haunts us' (ibid.: 773).[8] The political vocabulary of interdisciplinarity is telling. The term 'interdisciplinary' entered Anglophone sociological vocabulary in the interwar period as part of debates on education policy (and by 1939 was already decried both as modish and passé) (Frank 1988: 94), while 'multidisciplinary' appeared in the years just after the Second World

War, especially in technocratic social science programmes (Klein 1990: 24–9). During the Cold War the virtues of interdisciplinarity were urged both by defence administrators and student radicals. Fields such as cybernetics and materials science were to be institutionalised as interdisciplines through mixtures of pragmatic military budgeting and visionary technocratic planning (for example, Bensaude-Vincent 2001). In response to such initiatives, the PCF philosopher Louis Althusser lectured sternly in autumn 1967 at the Ecole Normale Supérieure against interdisciplinarity as ideological slogan, denied that philosophers were 'artisans of interdisciplinarity' and mocked modish 'round tables' where research organisations summoned as many different specialists as possible to resolve salient problems: 'interdisciplinarity is the slogan and practice of specialists' spontaneous ideology, switching between a vague spiritualism and a technocratic positivism' (Althusser 1974: 20–1, 46–7).[9] Yet 'interdisciplinarité' also appeared on protesters' banners in May 1968 and it seemed, at least to some French scholars, that the very term was invented on Parisian streets. It quickly became a watchword for new university layouts and systems of thought (Dubreuil 2007).[10] In a celebrated if sybilline plan for a transdisciplinary university with cybernetics as 'organizing language', presented to the OECD at Nice in 1970 with Asa Briggs as auditor and editor, the Austrian astrophysicist Erich Jantsch juxtaposed student 'alienation' with the urgent needs of military technology as the joint prompts for his plans for a new academic order (Jantsch 1972: 111).

There is a need for nuanced political economic accounts of ways in which disciplinarity and interdisciplinarity function historically. Models of the belated displacement of disciplinary hegemony by transdisciplinarity, it has been acknowledged, have often neglected 'power relationships' (Nowotny et al 2006: 193). Dominique Pestre has argued that 'modern science, as an institution, has always been of the highest interest to political, economic and military powers', and, especially, that 'the discourse of pure science' which 'took on its definitive form in the nineteenth century' was itself the product of scientists' own ideological work and has 'helped position *western civilization* as superior' (Pestre 2003b: 18–21; 2003a my emphasis). Thus forms of disciplinary hegemony, hierarchy and autonomy are fragile and conflicted political achievements, not default conditions (Golinski 1998: 69–72). Robert Kohler argues that disciplines were simultaneously 'bodies of specialized knowledge and skills' and also 'political institutions' (Kohler 1981: 104). Lenoir concurred that disciplines are 'political institutions', their work 'essential to the functioning of the political economy and the system of power relations that actualize it' (Lenoir 1993: 72). For oddly familiar reasons, no doubt, the claim that disciplinary systems must be analysed as systems of power has not been easy to establish. In his 1999 review of Jan Golinski's account of discipline, for example, Kohler grumbled about linking scientific disciplines in Foucauldian style with nastily panoptic prisons, since 'initiation into disciplines was experienced as liberating, affording access to novel and interesting work' (Kohler 1999: 330, cf. Warner 1992). It's been hard to see just how disciplinary power can be productive and even harder to work out how disciplines look, to their members as well as their masters.

This is why the discourse of interdisciplinarity requires a close analysis of the vagaries of disciplinary vision: hence this chapter's ambiguous title. Critics have suggested that the entire Foucauldian enterprise of disciplines' genealogy rests on nothing but a comparably 'elaborate pun' (Walzer 1986: 64). One must ask how disciplines see and how they seem. Part of the inspiration is Dickensian, since a connexion is proposed between forms of imagery and forms of training. One of the greatest Victorian analyses of disciplinarity, *Hard Times* (1854), introduces the interlocking worlds of the schoolroom ('facts!'), the factory (where steam engines move back and forth like 'the head of an elephant in a state of melancholy madness'), the family home, the bank and the circus. In Coketown nothing is quite what it seems. One is shown how knowledge looks from many different sites. In Mr Gradgrind's 'charmed apartment the most complicated social questions were cast up, got into exact totals, and finally settled. As if an astronomical observatory should be made without any windows, and the astronomer within should arrange the starry universe solely by pen, ink and paper' (Dickens 1854: Book 1, Chapters 1, 5 and 15, cf. Malone 1989). Social questions, windowless observatories and paper technologies reach the heart of nineteenth-century reflexions on disciplines and their layout. Compare, for example, a widely-read Berlin lecture on the disciplinary systems of Britain in 1828 by the eminent physician and reformer Nikolaus Heinrich Julius:

> It is a fact worthy of the greatest interest, not only in the history of architecture but in that of the human mind in general, that in the remotest ages, I speak not only of classical antiquity but indeed of the Orient, genius imagined the idea of decorating with all the treasures of human magnificence buildings which had as their aim to make accessible to a great crowd of people the display and inspection of a small number of objects . . . while never, so it seems, did human imagination apply itself to provide a small number of people, or indeed one person alone, with the simultaneous view of a great crowd of people or objects . . . It was reserved to modern times, it was under the growing influence of the state, and through its ever deeper intervention in all the details and relations of social life, to increase and to perfect its guarantees by using and directing towards this great end the construction and distribution of buildings destined simultaneously to oversee a great crowd of people.
>
> (Julius 1831: Lecture 6, 1: 384)[11]

It was in reading texts such as Julius's lectures that Michel Foucault encountered panopticism, where the shifts between performance and surveillance were key (Foucault 1973: 71).[12] In his remarks on interdisciplinarity, the tone was often dismissive:

> the principle of intelligibility of relations between power and knowledge passes rather through the analysis of strategies than through that of ideologies. It seems to me it's this notion and its possible use which could allow not an

interdisciplinary encounter . . . but work in common by people who seek to *de-discipline* themselves.

(Foucault 1980: 39)

He notoriously drew attention to optical technologies, 'observatories of human multiplicity', as agents of a new kind of physics. 'Side by side with the major technology of the telescope, the lens and the light beam, an integral part of the new physics and cosmology, there were the minor techniques of multiple and intersecting observations, an obscure art of light and the visible' (Foucault 1977: 171). He thus explored what might be called the relation between *extramission* and *intramission* in disciplinary societies, between the systems that imagined the gaze as an active process that emerged from the subject and those that envisaged a passive subjection of discipline's inmates. These ambiguities are preserved in the language of looking, when we speak of meeting someone's eyes or of a penetrating gaze. We apply these ambiguities most when speaking of training (Jay 1993: 9–10, 408–16).

Like Julius and Dickens, Foucault made a great deal of the role of the school, at least as much as the prison, in the construction of disciplinary order. Indeed, as Keith Hoskin has argued, educational formation was crucial for Foucault's analysis (Hoskin 1990: 34–7; 1993: 276–80).[13] The monitorial systems of examination and schooling, espoused in the first decades of the nineteenth century in Britain by utilitarians and evangelicals, played important roles. New schools were described as 'a machine to intensify the use of time', the artful rearrangement of space and order designed to allow a play of visibility and oversight in order not to ban and expel dissidence but rather, as in workshops and laboratories, productively to extract and direct the powers immanent in its subjects. 'The techniques that make it possible to see induce effects of power, and conversely the means of coercion make those on whom they are applied clearly visible' (Foucault 1977: 145, 165, 170–1). This was what Julius' lectures implied and *Hard Times* satirised. The reflexion also included what remains a suggestive conjecture. In an interview in Japan Foucault was asked about the relation he saw between disciplinary society's meticulous organisation of knowledge-spaces and its mastery of the intensification of the timetable. Might it be the case that this new relation between spatial order and temporal application was related to the forms of colonial power that were developed in the late eighteenth and early nineteenth centuries? Foucault agreed: 'the object of my history is to some extent *imperial colonization inside the European space itself*' (Foucault 1978: 581, my italics).

So a genealogy of the fraught relation between disciplines and interdisciplines must at least address the period chosen by most historians as key for disciplinary society, roughly the late eighteenth through the mid-nineteenth century in Europe. An aim would be to show that the way disciplines looked was a critical problem and site of struggle, rather than a uniformly hegemonic system of domination. The schoolroom and the order of disciplines would be an appropriate focus, although by no means an exclusive one, for explorations of how these systems looked. Rather than concur with the tale that there was once (but when?) a vast, uniform, hierarchical system of scientific disciplines, one would explore how complex and entangled were the projects and appearances of disciplines. The genealogy would certainly attend to the histories of disciplines that agents of the period wrote and used rather than invent some abstract account of how disciplines must look. Furthermore, the conjectural linkage with colonial and imperial programmes, within and outwith Europe, seems especially telling.

A Disciplinary Interdiscipline: The Madras System

To exemplify interdisciplines from which disciplinary visibility emerged, an apt case of early nineteenth-century oversight and conflict is provided by the new projects in education and administration lauded by Julius and damned by Dickens. Subsequent commentaries have understood them as monolithic disciplinary programmes, thus reinforcing the most potent aspect of disciplinary histories. Less familiar is the mixed genealogy of these projects and the means through which interdisciplines were entangled in what might justly be described as 'colonisation inside European space'. Through its geopolitical deployment, the case considered here exemplifies both the remarkable hybridity of these disciplinary formations and the means through which that hybridity was systematically effaced. In an epoch of class struggle, imperial aggression and intense exploitation, projects of identifying classes preoccupied analysts of the imperial, social and scientific distribution of types. For romantics and utilitarians, positivists and radicals, the disciplinary order of head and hand was linked to the problem of the order of knowledge (Simon 1976; Barnes and Shapin 1976; Herzog 1998: 75–88). Dispositions of knowledge were politically charged. In 1817 Samuel Taylor Coleridge's visionary prospectus for the *Encyclopedia Metropolitana* treated the arrangements of chemical and electrical sciences as vital for spiritual faith and political order, and touted a hierarchical array of sciences:

> the political changes of the world have not been more wonderful than the scientific and moral revolutions that have occurred within the last few years . . . they affect the whole theory and consequent arrangement of the Arts and Sciences to which they belong.
>
> (Coleridge 1995: 586–7)[14]

In contrast, Richard Carlile's radical *An Address to the Men of Science* composed in jail in 1821 treated the same sciences as happily fatal to established religion and proposed an egalitarian form of politics and of disciplinary arrangement: 'our chemists have proved themselves the greatest of all revolutionists . . . Chemistry I deem to be the foundation of all other sciences and in a manner of speaking to comprise all other branches of science' (Carlile 1821: 5, 34). When Jeremy Bentham planned his portentous if abortive scheme of disciplinary order in education in 1814, he confessed that it was 'impossible to form any tolerably adequate judgement of the whole, without the means of carrying the eye with unlimited velocity over every part of the field' (Bentham 1983 [1817]: 15). Both enlightened encyclopedism and the theocratic universities were criticised because of how they made disciplines and classes look. The principle of 'the simultaneous view', as Julius put it, was thus applied not only to the topography of disciplinary systems, to the mechanics of what were called 'discipline mills', but also to the work of politics and publicity (Yeo 2001: 32; Ashworth 2000: 20; Clero 1999).

In Bentham's case, organisation of vision demanded the exploitation of an ambiguously secularised theology of light and illumination, a rationalised form of Gothic architectonics of the uncanny and, as needs emphasis here, models drawn from well outside the ambit of enlightened European knowledge systems (Himmelfarb 1968; Schaffer 1990: 233–41). For example, Simon Werrett has documented the ways in which the original panopticon, designed for Grigorii Potemkin's docks and woodyards in Russia in 1786 by Jeremy's brother, the engineer Samuel Bentham, impressively resembled the system of imperial absolutism and religious power and visibility embodied in the layout of the Russian Orthodox church. Werrett reminds us, too, that the first edition of *Panopticon Letters*, written on the Potemkin estate, was to have carried on its title page an epigraph from Psalm 139: 'Though art about my path, and about my bed: and spiest out all my ways./If I say, peradventure the darkness shall cover me, then shall my night be turned into day' (Werrett nd).

To construct its new illusion of an all-seeing gaze by hybridising discipline, religion and oversight, Bentham and his allies aimed at a generalised system of educational management at precisely the moment when, historians tell us, the modern system of scientific disciplines began to emerge. So, on the one hand, an exploration of the resources that this educational system used can indicate something of how scientific disciplines were in fact constructed at this decisive moment. On the other hand, because this educational system so evidently combined both senses of discipline, its formal mode of disposition of knowledges in classificatory order and its painstaking attention to the disposition of bodies in space, its construction and career can help indicate the entanglement of how disciplines seem and how they see. Most significantly, the obviously hybrid and heterogeneous character of Bentham's projects reinforces the claim that any story of primordial disciplinary unity and hegemony is entirely misleading.

The most important of these projects was *Chrestomathia*, which Bentham composed during 1814 in rural retreat at a former monastery leased with the cash he got from the government to compensate for their abandonment of the panopticon scheme. 'It has pleased the Almighty in his omnipotence', Bentham told one of his followers, 'to create for this special purpose a holy, most holy place called Ford Abbey. There shall we reign together, a sub-Trinity in Unity, Holy Ghost for the time being James Mill'. While the utilitarian colonial administrator Mill sat writing his vast *History of British India* and Bentham tried to build an icehouse in the Abbey grounds to preserve corpses for a projected National Anatomy Bank, most effort went into educational discipline.[15] The chrestomathic project was launched when a metropolitan alliance of philosophic radicals proposed a new London school based on up-to-date principles of utility, accountancy, economy, the division of labour, surveillance and a monitorial system in which more advanced children taught their juniors under the watchful scrutiny of overseers. Cash and enthusiasm ran out, but Bentham's manifesto survived the wreckage (Bentham 1817: xi–xvi). It laid out a detailed order of discipline, both in division of knowledge and management of the inmates.

> By the Panopticon Principle of construction, security, in this respect, is maximized, and rendered entire, viz., partly by minimizing the distance between the situation of the remotest Scholar and that of the Master's eye; partly by giving to the floor or floors that inclination, which, to a certain degree, prevents remoter objects from being eclipsed by nearer ones; partly by enabling the Master to see without being seen, whereby to those who, at the moment, are unseen by him, it cannot be known that they are in this case. In the Chrestomathic School this plan of construction is of course to be employed.
>
> (Bentham 1817: 106)[16]

The common principles of economy and of visualisation dictated that every square inch of free space be covered with charts, images and diagrams, setting out 'graphical imitations, or, in some instances, the things themselves' (Bentham 1817: 113).

Novel in *Chrestomathia*, and significant for the exploration of how scientific disciplines looked in the early nineteenth century, was the central role these reformers gave to sciences and technology. The project's title was a neologism, its literal sense derived from the Greek for useful knowledge. There were other contemporary pedagogical resonances: in 1806 the arch-conservative Antoine Silvestre de Sacy, eminent professor at the Parisian school of oriental languages, published his vast *Chrestomathie Arabe*, a magisterial collection of extracts of Arabic texts designed as the foundation for a newly institutionalised discipline. Edward Said, significantly, uses Sacy's *Chrestomathie* and associated projects to outline the relation of disciplinary formation with the politics of visibility: 'knowledge was essentially the making visible of material and the aim of a tableau was the construction of a sort of Benthamite Panopticon. Scholarly discipline was therefore a specific technology of power'.[17]

In the Benthamite Chrestomathia, tyros began with classificatory sciences; advanced through mechanics, chemistry, physics and, in particular, electricity; and culminated with technology and mathematics. All other disciplines were subordinated to these subjects. *Chrestomathia* was one of the very first texts in which the term *technology* began to acquire its modern sense, as 'the aggregate body of the several sorts of manual operations directed to the purposes of art'. The aim was to *show* the division of labour as well as to *impose* it, to illustrate the advance of what Bentham called *manufacture* as well as to follow its principles in the classroom:

> It will be necessary under the direction of the Logician to apply the Tactics (the art of arrangement) of the Naturalist to the contents of the field of the

Technologist . . . so far as concerns the middling classes, the most extensive the view thus obtained by the scholar of the field of Technology the more favourably will he thus find the field of his livelihood enlarged.

(Bentham 1817: 319, 86)

Chrestomathic projects were not limited to schooling, but were supposed to embrace an entire technology of discipline directed towards a series of crises that Bentham and his allies reckoned characterised modern society: punishment and cure, production and knowledge would all look like this.

But the location and source of the way this disciplinary society was supposed to look were by no means uniquely metropolitan. Some projects were drawn from Russian imperial and orthodox resources, then extended to naval dockyards and military schools. *Chrestomathia* also stressed its dependence on another set of religious and economic principles, those designed from the 1790s by the Scottish natural philosophy lecturer, minister and schoolteacher Andrew Bell (Miller 1973; Jones and Williamson 1979: 73–5). Bentham's praise for this predecessor was unstinting and significant. The economy of profit maximisation and expense minimisation, of the division of labour and of the monitorial principle, were all due to Bell: 'by Dr Bell that fiction of the gold age, which the boldest of prophets would never have dared to prophesy, has actually been accomplished' (Bentham 1817: 56). Bentham spent days at Ford Abbey indexing Bell's publications: 'I am all admiration at the genius and talent displayed in the work'. Bentham described his aim as 'the extension of the Bell Instruction system over the whole of art and science, language included'. He reckoned it 'the most useful of all the products of inventive genius, printing excepted, that this globe has ever witnessed, and that it may be applied to every the highest branch of useful learning'.[18]

From 1797 Bell released a stream of charts and models for his new system, culminating in the National Society for the Education of the Poor in the Principles of the Church of England in 1811 and spreading the model to the camp-followers of Wellington's army in Portugal and other garrison schools throughout the world (Bowyer-Bower 1954: 126–9). The way Bell's system looked was ingeniously machine-like, the principles of Scottish political economy to the fore. Resemblance to idealised models of the factory system was telling. Thus the Glaswegian chemist Andrew Ure, in his *Philosophy of Manufactures*, drew the contrast between the factory master under a system of formal subordination, 'entitled to nothing but *eye-service*', whose 'business is blasted as it were by an evil eye', and a new master of systems of real subordination in machinofacture, who would 'organize his moral machinery on equally sound principles with his mechanical, for otherwise he will never command the watchful eyes'. For Bell and Ure alike, 'the neglect of moral discipline may be readily detected in any establishment by a practised eye in the disorder of the general system' (Ure 1835: 416–18; Thompson 1968: 395–8).

Bell's wealthy patron Thomas Bernard, sponsor of the new Royal Institution, saw the link between this division of labour and Bell's classrooms: Adam Smith 'did not more essential service to mechanical than Dr Bell has done to intellectual operations . . . the principle in manufactories and in schools is the same'. Bell urged that 'like the steam engine or spinning machinery, it diminishes labour and multiplies work, but in a degree which does not admit of the same limits, and scarcely of the same calculations as they do' (Bernard, 1809: 35–6; Bell 1808: 36–7).[19] This was a machine utopia of a specific form, simultaneously showroom and classroom. Each school was to be divided into sets of classes, with more junior inmates subject to more advanced pupils; each stage was meticulously registered; each lesson divided into brief segments; under the 'place-capturing principle' each member of each class moved around the tightly disciplined space of the classroom; and the whole was under the surveillance of an inspector, 'whose scrutinizing eye must pervade the whole machine' under a 'never-ceasing vigilance' (Bell 1807: 2). The new term *classroom* to designate an educational space had emerged in Glasgow University under Adam Smith's aegis, thence was turned into a system of putatively scientific instruction and discipline readily adopted by Bell. It was claimed that the imposition of discipline through spatial, economic and optical organisation was not hazardous but the result of a *new science*: 'a series of consecutive laws, linked together in the closest union, and depending on a common principle, assimilates itself to a science, however humble that science may be' (Bell 1808: 50).[20]

The new alliances forged during world war and class struggle with the production utopias of the factory, the school, the prison and the military help explain the striking similarities in how these disciplinary machines looked. The innovation of the classroom was related to the sequential system of collective instruction and the moral principles of sympathy and emulation on which that system was held to depend. But the claim that the system was scientific helped and explained the work through which these models could be multiplied, built elsewhere and in principle everywhere. Like other fetishistic commodities of the period, the key lay in the system through which what worked in one place was replicated. In his 1816 *Statesman's Manual* Coleridge echoed the common sentiment that Bell's 'incomparable machine, this vast moral steam engine' must be 'adopted and in free motion throughout the Empire'. According to Bell, and allies such as his biographer Robert Southey and his admirers Coleridge and Bentham, the system would 'spread like any mechanical invention over the civilized world' and be 'the happy means of civilizing those regions, which are now barbarous and savage' (Coleridge 1816: 51; Bell 1808: 114; Richardson 1994: 91–7). Historians are now increasingly familiar with the pattern of colonial encounter and innovation in governmentality and discipline, then adopted and adapted in the metropolis: 'the colonization of Europe by extra-European interests', as Richard Drayton has put it. Disciplines such as cartography and criminology, literature and philology, all drew crucial resources from this hybrid imperial topography (Drayton 2000: xviii; Sengoopta 2003: 53–92; Raj 2006: 60–90; Trautmann 2006: 42–3). The Bell project of optical discipline is an example. It was universally known in Britain under the sobriquet of the *Madras System* and initially looked south Indian. Its colonial history teaches about the relation between the way these disciplines scrutinised their subjects and the way they appeared to their audiences.

Remarks about the imagined diffusion of this machine worldwide and its relation with the problems of civiliation and barbarism were indeed eloquent. After leaving St Andrews as a natural philosopher in 1774, the young Scotsman gained initial employment as a tutor on a Virginia tobacco plantation, then, after American independence, sought a post as an impoverished Episcopalian minister in Leith. At this point his patron, a radical Scottish MP, got him a place on an East India Company vessel. Bell's aim was to make himself a wealthy nabob. He equipped himself with a pricey cabinet of natural philosophical hardware with which to earn his living as an experimental demonstrator. From then, Bell's career stayed wedded to his work in Madras, which he reached in June 1787. Bell joined the prestigious Asiatic Society in Calcutta, corresponded with its president Sir William Jones on the 'theatre' for natural philosophy in India, and was encouraged by several Company men to learn Persian or Hindustani so as to be able to lecture 'the native gentlemen' on improving sciences. 'Such a diffusion of knowledge may extend to the best interests of a people blinded and enslaved by a stupid idolatry with all its intended evils'. He sought to draw in fee-paying audiences with shows of balloons and artificial ice, electrical sparks and air pumps. Rational theatrics, it was argued, could generate income and undermine false principles of vision (Southey 1844: 119–21).

Several groups in the European settlements seemed to offer Bell the best resources. He established close links with resident schoolmasters and missionaries, especially a group of German pietists from Halle, based in nearby Tranquebar under the sponsorship of the Society for the Propagation of Christian Knowledge. He showed them his philosophic experiments, subjected their awestruck children to electric shocks, and got hold of new scientific hardware and books shipped from Europe. The Halle programme, inaugurated there in 1706, matched his own fascination with object lessons, with the dramatic theatrics of experimental and astronomical knowledge, and with the relation the missionaries sought to establish between indigenous and European forms of knowledge. Heirs to the great tradition of pious Reformation discipline, the German missionaries set up their schools in Tanjore, Trichinopoly, Palamcottah and Madras. They attracted Brahmin and Vellalar students, established very close relations with the ruler of Tanjore, for whom they acted as counsellors, and won subsidies from the East India Company. The remarkable collections of naturalia, scientific instrumentation, printed works and curiosities accumulated by the Raja of Tanjore, Serfoji II, in south India from 1798 have sometimes been read simply as the result of his early contacts with these pietist German missionaries. However, as Savithri Preetha Nair argues, a better account would see the Raja's programme as an endeavour to forge a distinct centre of cultural accumulation, exploiting networks across India and Europe. Significantly for our concerns in this paper, the Tanjore project reveals the crucial role of local experts in Tamil and Marathi traditions: materials developed in south India were then linked in detail via the robust Tanjore networks with enterprises of European naturalists. These linkages are hard to recover unless and until historians do justice to the variable institutional forms in which a range of disciplinary practices was pursued in such sites as south India. The same principle applies to the Madras system. Bell's pietist allies praised his use of orreries and planetaria, 'by which we may give a proper idea of the motions of our terrestrial globe and the relative celestial bodies to the youth and remove a great part of the superstition among the natives'. In the event, Tamil scholars actively responded to and redirected these pietist and evangelical programmes throughout the region (Southey 1844: 200–4, 211; Frykenberg 1986: 40–2; Brunner 1993: 102–7, 114–18; Viswanath Peterson: 1999).[21]

Bell also worked closely with the young surveyors and astronomers based at the new Madras Observatory, built in 1786 at Egmore Redoubt. These military and territorial operations generated both the income and personnel to which the parson and teacher would most devote his attention. A year before he arrived, the Madras authorities had decided to use funds gained from recent conquests to build a school for the hundreds of young mixed-race orphans of British soldiers and their Indian wives. The Tranquebar missionaries had already launched such schemes with British military backing. Bell became head of this school, the Madras Military Asylum, in 1791. It was sited near the Observatory on the Egmore redoubt. This was where his eponymous Madras System was first developed and applied (Southey 1844: 139, 153, 176).

This was a dramatic test of hybridisation. Many of Bell's resources were intrinsically local, proper to the complexity of the demography, politics and cultures of southern India. The very term 'half-caste', the keyword for hybridity, was coined by the British administrators and commanders based in Madras in the 1790s. Bell was faced with the task of managing about 200 'half-caste children of this country, who reputedly shew an evident inferiority in the talents of the head, the qualities of the mind and virtues of the heart'. Their mothers, it was reported, imagined that once enrolled at the Asylum their sons would be 'sacrificed to some unknown god and went through all the ceremonies of mourning for them. Others fancied they were giving them up to slavery'.

It was certain that sacrifice and submission were basic principles of Bell's system. His claim was that the inmates' reputedly hybrid defects were environmental, not intrinsic, so corrigible by the systematic reorganisation of their milieu and their discipline. 'They are instruments in your hands, fitted for your hands, and no other, and can in no ways fail you'. The subservience of the Madras orphans was reckoned a positive resource for disciplinary management (Southey 1844: 168; see also Bell 1807: 50, 67).

However, it was equally the case that Tamil culture provided the most important resources for the Madras system. Bell reported that it was in the Tamil customary schools that he found some of the keys to his scheme. 'I had, at first sight of a Malabar school, adopted the idea of teaching the letters in sand spread over a board or bench before the scholars, as is always done on the ground in the schools of the natives of this country'. European travellers had long known that Tamil children were trained by writing in fine sand while 'all the rest sung and write down the same thing together' (Bell 1807: 53; Dharampal, 1983: 260). In the same fashion, through their 'Malabarick school', Bell's Tranquebar colleagues, the pietist missionaries, had exploited this indigenous pedagogical culture of ingenious mathematical and literary training, writing and learning. A 1715 London pamphlet on the Tranquebar mission schools reported that Tamil students there

> sit on the ground, writing with their fingers in sand, which is spread on the floor for that purpose, the lessons which every Child hath been taught in the Morning, chanting with an audible voice the names of the letters or words as they write them. *This is the common way of teaching young children to read in the East Indies.*
>
> (Ziegenbalg 1715: 7)[22]

Recent ethnohistorical studies of Tamil schools in the eighteenth century confirm and amplify these reports. Senthil Babu has shown how the indigenous *tinnai* schools met at temples, teachers' houses or those of local notables. These were designed for young members of upper and middle castes. A systematic monitorial system was used, with the senior student teaching younger children after receiving a lesson from the master. Literary, numerical and arithmetic mastery was inculcated through elegant and complex processes of recitation, chanting and mnemotechnics, checked by subsequently writing out numerical forms in sand, then on palm leaves. Some European observers named these 'multiplication schools'.

Babu remarks that 'writing seemed to add to the memory images, not in a simply abstract manner but as affective images. Writing in the *tinnai* mode made the student eligible for an occupational role, of a scribe, or at least for an apprenticeship with the local revenue official'. He explains how the local revenue bureaucracy depended on such roles as those of the village assistants who measured land and of the water regulators, the men charged with managing distribution of irrigation supply. 'The *tinnai* curriculum dealt with these occupational skills in the problem solving mode.' So in these schools, according to Babu, such fiscal, administrative, measurement and hydraulic practices became forms of authorised public knowledge and thus gained credibility. It was there, too, that men such as Bell encountered them through the networks of the Company officials, and whence they became in a highly hybridised form the principles of his notorious Madras system (Babu 2007: 30–1).

These Tamil sources of the Madras System were much discussed and signalled both in Britain and India itself. Thomas Bernard of the Royal Institution commented in 1809 that Bell's disciplinary project is 'no modern invention but an oriental practice of remote antiquity'. One East India Company commander pointed out that British fights for priority over the invention of the monitorial system were otiose, since 'the system was borrowed from the Bramans and brought from India to Europe. It has been made the foundation of National schools in every enlightened country'. Only now were British workmen in a position to enjoy the disciplinary benefits long cultivated in Malabar: according to the Company officer, in this case it was Europeans, not 'the natives of India', who had neglected a major innovative disciplinary opportunity (Bernard 1809: 32–3; Dharampal 1983: 259). When a new Charter Act was imposed on the East India Company in 1813 – abolishing its trade monopoly, licensing Christian missionaries throughout British dominions and ordering a large sum to be spent on 'the encouragement of the learned natives of India' and 'the introduction and promotion of a knowledge of the sciences' – orientalist authorities joined in praising indigenous education, which 'is represented to have withstood the shock of revolutions, and to its operation is ascribed the general intelligence of the natives as scribes and accountants'. The Company's directors noted the adoption of this native form of discipline in the guise of the Madras system by Bell: 'it has now become the mode by which education is conducted in our national establishments' (Zastoupil and Moir 1999: 91–5). They also ordered their Collectors to enquire into the existing state of education in India. A Carnatic officer reported that:

> the economy with which the children are taught to write in the native schools, and the system by which the more advanced scholars are caused to teach the less advanced, and at the same time to confirm their own knowledge is certainly admirable, and well deserved *the imitation it has received in England.*
>
> (Dharampal 1983: 182)

The Company's systems of fiscal and military surveys thus provided the mode through which Bell's appropriation of Tamil principles became fundamental for colonial governance. Bell's Asylum, the Revenue Survey, the Observatory and the hydraulic administration of the Presidency would be staffed by youngsters trained in a system of discipline adapted from Tamil schooling in calculation and accountancy, then applied systematically to the survey, mapping and administration of much of south India. Within a few years, Bell reported that graduates of his Madras System were working as clerks, surveyors, press couriers and cartographers. Company embassies to Persia were staffed by pupils of the Madras System, as were spectacular exercises in what might be called scientific diplomacy at the Mysore court of its great ruler Tipu Sahib.[23] It has been suggested that 'the origins of modern education in south India lay in northern Europe' and that 'Madras itself received few benefits from Bell'. Yet many observers noted the ways Bell's Madras System had exploited and adapted Tamil educational calculative discipline, and in other presidencies such as Bombay the system was recommended precisely because it matched 'the principles and rules on which education was conducted by the natives themselves'. The Company saw Bell's school as a crucial supplier of well-disciplined agents for its expanding domain and its military ambitions (Frykenberg 1986: 40, 42).[24]

Furthermore, while in *Chrestomathia* Bentham sought to turn the Madras system into a model of universal rational disciplines, his 'holy ghost' and Company administrator James Mill simultaneously composed a *History of British India* that violently condemned Indian scholarly achievements, denied any virtue in indigenous disciplines and demanded an entire overhaul of their institutions. Mill's analysis made Indian tradition into a sign of hegemony, rigidity and timelessness: thus producing a sclerotic discipline in need of transformation. As Bentham notoriously remarked, 'Mill will be the living executive – I shall be the dead legislative of British India'. These reforms were to involve complex forms of adaptation and reorganisation that both depended on and often effaced their local sources (Bowring 1838–43: 490).[25] In a directly comparable analysis of the development of a panoptic regime in the Bombay presidency in the 1820s, for example, Martha Kaplan has argued that such 'disciplinary practices' are of necessity highly variable, their cultural and historical uniformities only ever the result of partial and fragile attempts at stabilisation (Kaplan 1995: 94–5).[26]

The aim of this tale has been to highlight this hybrid character in systems of discipline established in the early nineteenth century. Consider what was co-present in the complex disciplines of education described here. A system of training had originally been adopted and adapted from Halle pietism and Tamil pedagogy. It was turned into a form of economic and scientific discipline for 'half-caste' Indo-European trainees destined for service in the East India Company's administration and surveys. Later, within the imperial metropolis, utilitarian and romantic writers then saw in this system powerful tools for securing social discipline, moral order and scientific advance. Terms such as 'technology' were developed to describe its effects. Eventually, it was changed from a complex mix of globally distributed and rather uneven components into something like a public system of training. Many British administrators and historians saw such disciplinary systems as the necessary means by which what they saw as Indian culture could at last be redirected and modernised. The so-called Anglicist-Orientalist debates of the early and mid-nineteenth century, which so intimately linked matters of imperial policy with those of discipline, have been widely understood as the consequence of these administrative and pedagogical polemics (Zastoupil and Moir 1999: 8–27; Dodson 2007: 78–86).

It has seemed apt to reflect on the politics of interdisciplinarity through these projects of colonial administration and educational formation in the decades around 1800. The current discourse of interdisciplinarity relies on a disciplinary history that claims that until recently knowledge systems were organised in formal, rigid, self-contained disciplinary fields and that somehow this organisation emerged alongside the European institutional and intellectual transformations of the Age of Revolutions. It is also claimed that such disciplinary organisation straightforwardly reflected the interests of its subjects both as the topics and as the inmates of disciplines. In scrutinising these claims, attention to the complex paths of imperial and colonial enterprises seems indispensable. Moments salient in this disciplinary history, institutionalisation around 1800 and interdisciplinary proliferation since the Cold War and the economic crises of the 1970s, match decisive conjunctures in the political economic development of imperialism and its forms of knowledge. One of the principal themes in recent models of a new mode of transdisciplinarity in science and technology, a mode allegedly emergent since the mid-1970s, has been the relation between multiply accountable, socially distributed, knowledges and the context of seemingly unprecedented globalisation (Nowotny et al 2003: 188–9). So it is important better to understand the genealogy of global networks and their entanglements throughout the histories of disciplinary formation.

A telling case of such genealogy is the career of orientalism as disciplinary form and critical topic, marked by intense attention to puzzles of interdisciplinarity. It has seemed as if such disciplinary systems should best be seen not only as tools of imperial rule but as imperial forms in their own right. Edward Said powerfully appealed for 'greater interventionism in cross-disciplinary activity' as part of 'a clarified political and methodological commitment to the dismantling of systems of domination'. His critic the imperial historian John Mackenzie responded with an artful comparison, redolent of Ibn Khaldun's cyclical historicism, between the career of academic projects like that of Said (which 'pass through the cycle of imitation, revision, subversion and rejection') and the career of imperial powers (which are 'asserted, modified, challenged, reasserted and transformed'). In his reflexions on the 'anxiety of interdisciplinarity' that he reckons are pervasive in post-colonial studies, the literature professor Graham Huggan has recently diagnosed post-colonialism's tendency to assault 'institutionally maintained "disciplinary imperialisms", in which the term "discipline" itself is held to have imperialistic connotations' (Said 1985: 107; Mackenzie 1995: 14; Huggan 2008: 6–7).

The frequency with which discipline as form of knowledge has thus been directly associated with the illegitimacies of colonial or imperial rule hints at how the discourse of interdisciplinarity urges its subversive or radical potency and, simultaneously, how disciplinary histories can be treated as simple accounts of the hegemonic exercise of power. This is what the agonistic-antagonistic mode of interdisciplinarity has come to mean in the past four decades (Barry et al 2008: 20–2). The stereotypes of disciplinary homogeneity and interdisciplinary critique need examination through attention to the ways hybrid systems are made and make up their subjects. As any optician knows, to see how such a system looks you have to start with an examination of its pupils.

Notes

1 The sociological literature on these topics is not new: see Lemaine et al (eds.) (1976) and Graham et al (eds.) (1983). For the case of social psychology see Klein (1993: 194–5); for the case of X-ray crystallography see Forman (1969).

2 For disciplinary histories and discovery stories, see Brannigan (1981: 89–119); for disciplinary histories and reasonable agreement see Kuhn (1961). These roles are discussed in Warwick and Kaiser (2005: 395–8).

3 Compare the remarks that 'the disciplinary framework is relatively new in the history of western science and teaching' but that interdisciplinarity 'has not yet been founded', in Apostel et al (1972: 23 and 72).

4 For Kepler: Martens (2000: 103–11) and Jardine (2009); for Herschel: Schaffer (1980: 211–39) and Williams (1983); for astrophysics: Lankford (1997: 35–74).

5 Compare Shumway and Messer-Davidow (1991: 218–19) and Fabiani (2006: 32) with Stichweh (1992).

6 The same chronology is set out in Swoboda (1979: 59–60); Klein (1990: 21); Lattuca (2001: 5); and Neuser (2007).
7 A slightly earlier version of this passage referred not to the 'hegemony of disciplinary science' but to 'the hegemony of theoretical or at any rate experimental science' (Nowotny et al 2003: 179).
8 For prior developments, see Mayer (2000: 667–8).
9 Thanks to Andrew Barry for this reference.
10 'Thanks to the May events, interdisciplinarity left its marginal place as a pious wish of certain critical academics and turned into a theoretical imperative for intellectuals whose audience grew after 1968' (Dubreuil 2007: 17–18). Dubreuil cites Michel de Certeau and Edgar Morin in this connexion. For a ferocious riposte to what were seen as Marxist and radical demands for interdisciplinarity, see Gozzer (1982). For an attempt to read Michel Foucault's interdisciplinarity, see Takács (2004: 878).
11 For these problems of disciplinary vision see Becker (2001); Jones and Williamson (1979).
12 Foucault introduced Julius' work in his course of 1972–1973: see Foucault (2000: 32).
13 See also Deacon (2005: 90–7).
14 This differs in important respects from the earlier version printed in Snyder (1940: 187).
15 Bentham to Dumont, 22 July 1817 in Conway (1988: 20). See Fuller (nd).
16 For Francis Place's architectural plan of the school see Markus (1993: 67–9).
17 For de Sacy as the scholar who 'more than any other created orientalism as a sustained discipline' see Irwin (2007: 146); for Said on de Sacy and the panopticon see Said (1978: 126–7).
18 Bentham to Koe, 20 December 1814 and to Gallatin, 28 January 1815, in Conway (1988: 441–2 and 446–7).
19 See Markus (1993: 56).
20 For Smith, Bell and the invention of the class-room see Hamilton (1980: 281–5).
21 For the Tanjore project see Nair (2005).
22 For Ziegenbalg's version of Tamil religious culture see Sweetnam (2004).
23 For Bell's pupils in Persia, see Phillimore (1945–58: 173, 176); for his pupils in Mysore, see Southey (1844: 472–83).
24 For the adoption of the Madras system in the Bombay presidency, see Parulekar (1955: 47–8, 52–3).
25 For the ambiguities in Mill's historiography of Indian sciences see Stokes (1959: 66–70); Majeed (1992); Dodson (2007: 63–71).
26 Compare Stokes (1959: 149–50).

References

Althusser, L. (1974) *Philosophie Et Philosophie Spontanée Des Savants.* Paris: Maspéro.
Apostel, L., Berger, G., Briggs, A. and Michaud, G. (eds.) (1972) *Interdisciplinarity: Problems of Teaching and Research in Universities.* Paris: OECD.
Ashworth, W. (2000) 'England and the Machinery of reason, 1780–1830', *Canadian Journal of History,* 35: 2–36.
Babu, S. (2007) 'Memory and Mathematics in the Tamil Tinnai Schools of South India in the Eighteenth and Nineteenth Centuries', *International Journal for the History of Mathematics Education,* 2: 15–37.
Barnes, B. and Shapin, S. (1976) 'Head and Hand: Rhetorical Resources in British Pedagogical Writing, 1770–1850', *Oxford Review of Education,* 2: 231–54.

Barry, A., Born, G. and Weszkalnys, G. (2008) 'Logics of Interdisciplinarity', *Economy and Society,* 37 (1): 20–49.

Bayoumi, M. and Rubin, A. (eds.) (2000) *The Edward Said Reader.* London: Granta Books.

Becker, P. (2001) 'Objective Distance and Intimate Knowledge: on the Structure of Criminalistic Observation and Description', in P. Becker and W. Clark (eds.) *Little Tools of Knowledge: Historical Essays on Academic and Bureaucratic Practices* (pp. 197–235). Ann Arbor: Michigan University Press.

Bell, A. (1807) *An Analysis of the Experiment in Education made at Egmore near Madras,* 3rd ed. London: Cadell and Davis.

— (1808) *The Madras School, or Elements of Tuition.* London: Bentley.

Bensaude-Vincent, B. (2001) 'The Construction of a Discipline: Materials Science in the United States', *Historical Studies in Physical and Biological Sciences,* 31: 223–48.

Bentham, J. (1983 [1817]) *Chrestomathia,* edited by M. J. Smith and W. H. Burston. Oxford: Clarendon Press.

Bernard, T. (1809) *Of the Education of the Poor.* London: Bulmer.

Bowring, J. (1838–43) 'Memoirs of Jeremy Bentham', in J. Bowring (ed.) *Works of Jeremy Bentham,* Vol. 10. Edinburgh: William Tait.

Bowyer-Bower, T. A. (1954) 'A Pioneer of Army Education: the Royal Military Asylum, Chelsea, 1801–1821', *British Journal of Educational Studies,* 2: 122–32.

Boyle, R. (1660) *New Experiments Physico-Mechanical.* Oxford: Henry Hall.

— (1663) *Some Considerations Touching the Usefulnesse of Experimental Naturall Philosophy.* Oxford: Henry Hall.

— (1685) *Of the Reconcileableness of Specifick Medicines to the Corpuscular Philosophy.* London: Samuel Smith.

Brannigan, A. (1981) *The Social Basis of Scientific Discoveries.* Cambridge: Cambridge University Press.

Briggs, A. and Cohen, I. B. (1963) in A. C. Crombie (ed.) *Scientific Change.* (pp. 765–780) London: Heinemann.

Brunner, D. (1993) *Halle Pietists in England.* Göttingen: Vandehoeck and Ruprecht.

Carlile, R. (1821) *An Address to the Men of Science.* London: R. Carlile.

Centre for the Study of Interdisciplinarity (nd) Frodeman, R., Klein, J. T., and Mitcham, C. (eds.) *Oxford Handbook of Interdisciplinarity,* www.csid.unt.edu/research/HOI (accessed October 2009).

Clark, W. (2006) *Academic Charisma and the Origins of the Research University.* Chicago, IL: University of Chicago Press.

Clero, J-P. (1999) 'Nomenclature et classification dans *Chrestomathia* de Jeremy Bentham: critique de l'*Encyclopédie* et image de la raison', *Kairos,* 14: 49–89.

Coleridge, S. T. (1816) *The Statesman's Manual.* London: Gale and Fenner.

— (1995) *Shorter Works and Fragments,* Vol. 1., ed. H. J. Jackson and J. R. de J. Jackson. Princeton, NJ: Princeton University Press.

Conway, S. (ed.) (1988) *Correspondence of Jeremy Bentham 1809–1816,* Vol. 8. Oxford: Clarendon Press.

— (2000) *Correspondence of Jeremy Bentham 1817–1820,* Vol. 9. Oxford: Clarendon Press.

Deacon, R. (2005) 'Moral Orthopedics: a Foucauldian Account of Schooling as Discipline', *Telos,* 130: 84–102.

Dear, P. (1995) *Discipline and Experience: The Mathematical Way in the Scientific Revolution*. Chicago, IL: University of Chicago Press.

Dharampal (1983) *The Beautiful Tree: Indigenous Education in the Eighteenth Century*. New Delhi: Biblia Impex.

Dickens, C. (1854) *Hard Times*. London: Bradbury and Evans.

Dodson, M. S. (2007) *Orientalism, Empire and National Culture: India 1770–1880*. Cambridge: Cambridge University Press.

Drayton, R. (2000) *Nature's Government: Science, Imperial Britain and the 'Improvement' of the World*. New Haven, CT: Yale University Press.

Dubreuil, L. (2007) 'Défauts de savoirs', *Labyrinthe*, 27: 13–26.

Duhem, P. (1914) *The Aim and Structure of Physical Theory*. Princeton: Princeton University Press.

Fabiani, J-L. (2006) 'À quoi sert la notion de discipline?', in J. Boutier, J. C. Passeron, and J. Revel (eds.) *Qu'Est-Ce Qu'une Discipline?* (pp. 11–34). Paris: Editions de l'EHESS.

Forman, P. (1969) 'The Discovery of the Diffraction of X-rays by Crystals: a Critique of the Myths', *Archive for History of Exact Sciences*, 5: 38–71.

Foucault, M. (1973) 'Truth and Juridical Forms', in J. Faubion (ed.) (2001) *Power* (pp. 1–89). London: Allen Lane.

— (1977) *Discipline and Punish: The Birth of the Prison*. Harmondsworth: Penguin.

— (1978) 'La scène de la philosophie', in (1994) *Dits et Écrits*, Vol 3 (pp. 571–95). Paris: Gallimard.

— (1980) 'La poussière et le nuage', in M. Perrot (ed.) *L'impossible Prison: Recherches Sur Le Système Pénitentiare Au XIXe Siècle*. Paris: Seuil.

— (2000) 'The Punitive Society', in P. Rabinow (ed.) *Ethics, Subjectivity and Truth*. London: Penguin.

— (2007) *Security, Territory, Population*, lectures of January 1978. Basingstoke: Palgrave Macmillan.

Frank, R. (1988) 'Interdisciplinarity: The First Half-Century', in E. G. Stanley and T. F. Hoad (eds.) *Words* (pp. 91–102). Cambridge: Brewer.

Frykenberg, R. E. (1986) 'Modern Education in South India 1784–1854', *American Historical Review*, 91: 37–65.

Fuller, C. (nd) '"It is the Theatre of Great Felicity to a Number of People": Bentham at Ford Abbey', www.ucl.ac.uk/Bentham-Project/journal/cfford.htm (accessed August 2009).

Golinski, J. (1998) *Making Natural Knowledge: Constructivism and the History of Science*. Cambridge: Cambridge University Press.

Gozzer, G. (1982) 'Interdisciplinarity: A Concept Still Unclear', *Prospects*, 12: 281–92.

Graham, L., Lepenies, W. and Weingart, P. (eds.) (1983) *Functions and Uses of Disciplinary Histories*. Dordrecht: D. Reidel.

Hamilton, D. (1980) 'Adam Smith and the Moral Economy of the Classroom System', *Curriculum Studies*, 12: 281–98.

Hammerstein, N. (1989) 'The Modern World, Sciences, Medicine and Universities', *History of Universities*, 8: 151–78.

Heilbron, J. (2003) 'A Regime of Disciplines: Towards a Historical Sociology of Disciplinary Knowledge', in C. Camic and H. Joas (eds.) *The Dialogical Turn: Roles for Sociology in the Postdisciplinary Age* (pp. 23–42). Lanham: Rowman and Littlefield.

Herzog, D. (1998) *Poisoning the Minds of the Lower Orders*. Princeton, NJ: Princeton University Press.

Himmelfarb, G. (1968) 'The Haunted House of Jeremy Bentham', in *Victorian Minds*. New York: Knopf.

Hoskin, K. (1990) 'Foucault Under Examination: The Crypto-Educationalist Unmasked', in S. J. Ball (ed.) *Foucault and Education: Disciplines and Knowledge* (pp. 29–53). London: Routledge.

—— (1993) 'Education and the Genesis of Disciplinarity: The Unexpected Reversal', in E. Messer-Davidow, D. Shumway and D. Sylvan (eds.) *Knowledges: Historical and Critical Studies in Disciplinarity* (pp. 272–304). Charlottesville and London University of Virginic Press.

Huggan, G. (2008) *Interdisciplinary Measures: Literature and the Future of Postcolonial Studies*. Liverpool: Liverpool University Press.

Irwin, R. (2007) *For Lust of Knowing: The Orientalists and Their Enemies*. London: Penguin.

Jantsch, E. (1972) 'Towards Interdisciplinarity and Transdisciplinarity in Education and Innovation', in L. Apostel, G. Berger, A. Briggs and G. Michaud (eds.) *Interdisciplinarity: Problems of Teaching and Research in Universities* (pp. 97–121). Paris: OECD.

Jardine, N. (2009) 'Kepler as Transgressor and Amalgamator of Disciplines', *Journal for the History of Astronomy*, 40: 375–80.

Jay, M. (1993) *Downcast Eyes: The Denigration of Vision in Twentieth Century French Thought*. Berkeley: University of California Press.

Jones, K. and Williamson, K. (1979) 'The Birth of the Schoolroom', *Ideology and Consciousness*, 6: 58–110.

Julius, N. H. (1831) *Leçons sur les prisons*, 2 Vols. Paris: Levrault.

Kaplan, M. (1995) 'Panopticon in Poona: an Essay in Foucault and Colonialism', *Cultural Anthropology*, 10: 85–98.

Kelley, D. R. (1997) 'The Problem of Knowledge and the Concept of Discipline', in D. R. Kelley (ed.) *History and the Disciplines: The Reclassification of Knowledge in Early Modern Europe*. Rochester: University of Rochester Press, translated as 'Le problème du savoir et le concept de discipline', in J. Boutier, J. C. Passeron, and J. Revel (eds.) (2006), *Qu'Est-Ce Qu'une Discipline?* Paris: Editions de l'EHESS.

Klein, J. T. (1990) *Interdisciplinarity: History, Theory, Practice*. Detroit, MI: Wayne State University Press.

—— (1993) 'Blurring, Cracking and Crossing: Permeation and the Fracturing of Discipline,' in Messer-Davidow, D. Shumway and D. Sylvan (eds.) *Knowledges: Historical and Critical Studies in Disciplinarity* (pp. 185–211). Charlottesville and London University of Virginic Press.

Kohler, R. (1981) 'Discipline History', in W. F. Bynum, E. J. Browne and R. Porter (eds.) *Dictionary of the History of Science* (p. 104). London: Macmillan.

—— (1999) 'The constructivists' toolkit', *Isis*, 90: 329–31.

Kuhn, T. S. (1961) 'The Function of Measurement in Modern Physical Sciences', in (1977) *The Essential Tension: Selected Studies in Scientific Tradition and Change* (pp. 178–224). Chicago, IL: Chicago University Press.

Lankford, J. (1997) *American Astronomy: Community, Careers and Power 1859–1940*. Chicago, IL: University of Chicago Press.

Latour, B. (1993) *We have Never been Modern*. Hemel Hempstead: Harvester Wheatsheaf.

Lattuca, L. (2001) *Creating Interdisciplinarity*. Nashville, TN: Vanderbilt University Press.

Lemaine, G., Macleod, R., Mulkay, M. and Weingart, P. (eds.) (1976) *Perspectives on the Emergence of Scientific Disciplines*. The Hague: Mouton.

Lenoir, T. (1993) 'The Discipline of Nature and the Nature of Disciplines', in E. Messer-Davidow, D. Shumway and D. Sylvan (eds.) *Knowledges: Historical and Critical Studies in Disciplinarity* (pp. 70–102). Charlottesville and London University of Virginic Press.

Liu, A. (1989) 'The power of formalism: the new historicism', *English Literary History*, 56: 721–77.

Lloyd, G. (2009) *Disciplines in the Making: Cross-Cultural Perspectives on Elites, Learning and Innovation*. Oxford: Oxford University Press.

Mackenzie, J. (1995) *Orientalism: History, Theory and the Arts*. Manchester: Manchester University Press.

Majeed, J. (1992) *Ungoverned Imaginings*. Oxford: Clarendon.

Malone, C. (1989) 'The Fixed Eye and the Rolling Eye: Surveillance and Discipline in *Hard Times*', *Studies in the Novel*, 21: 14–26.

Markus, T. (1993) *Buildings and Power: Freedom and Control in the Origins of Modern Building Types*. London: Routledge.

Martens, R. (2000) *Kepler's Philosophy and the New Astronomy*. Princeton, NJ: Princeton University Press.

Messer-Davidow, E., Shumway, D. R. and Sylvan, D. J. (eds.) (1993) *Knowledges: Historical and Critical Studies in Disciplinarity*. Charlottesville: University Press of Virginia.

Miller, P. J. (1973) 'Factories, Monitorial Schools and Jeremy Bentham', *Journal of Educational Administration and History*, 5 (2): 10–20.

Nair, S. P. (2005) 'Native Collecting and Natural Knowledge (1798–1832): Raja Serfoji II of Tanjore as Centre of Calculation', *Journal of the Royal Asiatic Society*, 15: 279–302.

Neuser, W. (2007) 'Science Between Disciplinarity and Transdisciplinarity', in J. L. N. Audy and M. C. Morosini (eds.) *Innovation and Interdisciplinarity in the University* (pp. 101–7). Porto Alegre: EDIPURCS.

Nietzsche, F. (1873) 'On Truth and Lies in a Non-Moral Sense' in D. Breazeale (ed.) (1979) *Philosophy and Truth* (pp. 79–97). Atlantic Highlands: Humanities Press.

Nowotny, H., Scott, P. and Gibbons, M. (2003) 'Mode 2 Revisited: the New Production of Knowledge', *Minerva*, 41: 179–94.

— (2006) 'Rethinking Science: Mode 2 in Societal Context' in E. G. Caryannis and D. F. J. Campbell (eds.) *Knowledge Creation, Diffusion and Use in Innovation Networks and Knowledge Clusters* (pp. 39–51). Westport: Praeger.

Parulekar, R. V. (ed.) (1955) *Selections from Educational Records (Bombay), 1815–1840*. Bombay: Asia Publishing House.

Pestre, D. (2003a) 'Regimes of Knowledge Production in Society: Towards a More Political and Social Reading', *Minerva*, 41: 245–61.

— (2003b) *Science, Argent Et Politique: Un Essai D'interpretation*. Paris: INRA.

Peterson, I. V. (1999) 'Science in the Tranquebar Mission Curriculum', in M. Bergunder (ed.) *Missionsberichte aus Indien im 19. Jahrhundert* (pp. 175–219). Halle: Franckeschen Stiftungen.

Petrie, H. G. (1976) 'Do You See What I see? The Epistemology of Interdisciplinary Enquiry', *Journal of Aesthetic Education*, 10: 29–43.

Phillimore, R. H. (1945–58) *Historical Records of the Survey of India*, Vol. 2. Dehra Dun: Surveyor General of India.

Raj, K. (2006) *Relocating Modern Science: Circulation and the Construction of Scientific Knowledge in South Asia and Europe*. Delhi: Permanent Black.

Richardson, A. (1994) *Literature, Education and Romanticism: Reading as Social Practice, 1780–1832*. Cambridge: Cambridge University Press.

Said, E. (1978) *Orientalism*. London: Routledge & Kegan Paul.

— (1982) 'Travelling Theory', in M. Bayoumi and A. Rubin (eds.) (2000) *The Edward Said Reader* (pp. 195–217). London: Granta Books.

— (1985) 'Orientalism Reconsidered', *Cultural Critique*, 1: 89–107.

Schaffer, S. (1980) 'Herschel in Bedlam: Natural History and Stellar Astronomy', *British Journal for the History of Science*, 13: 211–39.

— (1990) 'States of Mind: Enlightenment and Natural Philosophy', in G. S. Rousseau (ed.) *Languages of Psyche: Mind and Body in Enlightenment Thought* (pp. 233–290). Los Angeles: University of California Press.

Sengoopta, C. (2003) *Imprint of the Raj*. Basingstoke: Macmillan.

Shumway, D. R. and Messer-Davidow, E. (1991) 'Disciplinarity: an introduction', *Poetics Today*, 12: 201–25.

Simon, B. (1976) *The Two Nations and the Educational Structure, 1780–1870*. London: Lawrence and Wishart.

Snyder, A. D. (1940) 'Coleridge and the Encyclopedists', *Modern Philology*, 38: 173–91.

Southey, R. (1844) *Life of the Reverend Andrew Bell*, Vol.1. London: John Murray.

Stichweh, R. (1992) 'The Sociology of Scientific Disciplines: On the Genesis and Stability of the Disciplinary Structure of Modern Science', *Science in Context*, 5: 3–15.

Stokes, E. (1959) *The English Utilitarians and India*. Oxford: Clarendon.

Sweetnam, W. (2004) 'The Prehistory of Orientalism', *New Zealand Journal of Asian Studies*, 6: 2: 12–38.

Swoboda, W. (1979) 'Disciplines and Interdisciplinarity: An Historical Perspective', in J. Kockelmans (ed.) *Interdisciplinarity and Higher Education* (pp. 49–92). University Park: Pennsylvania State University Press.

Takács, A. (2004) 'Between Theory and History: On the Interdisciplinary Practice in Michel Foucault's Work', *MLN*, 119: 869–84.

Thompson, E. P. (1968) *The Making of the English Working Class*. Harmondsworth: Penguin.

Trautmann, T. (2006) *Languages and Nations: The Dravidian Proof in Colonial Madras*. Berkeley: University of California Press.

Ure, A. (1835) *Philosophy of Manufactures*. London: Charles Knight.

Walzer, M. (1986) 'The Politics of Michel Foucault', in D. C. Hoy (ed.) *Foucault: A Critical Reader* (pp. 51–68). Oxford: Blackwell.

Warner, D. J. (1992) 'Physics as a Moral Discipline: Undergraduate Laboratories in the Late Nineteenth Century', *Rittenhouse*, 6: 116–28.

Warwick, A. and Kaiser, D. (2005) 'Kuhn, Foucault, and the Power of Pedagogy', in D. Kaiser (ed.) *Pedagogy and the Practice of Science* (pp. 393–409). Cambridge, MA: MIT Press.

Weingart, P. (2000) 'Interdisciplinarity: the Paradoxical Discourse', in P. Weingart and N. Stehr (eds.) *Practicising Interdisciplinarity* (pp. 25–42). Toronto: University of Toronto Press.

Weingart, P. and Stehr, N. (eds.) (2000) *Practising Interdisciplinarity*. Toronto: University of Toronto Press.

Werrett, S. (nd) 'Potemkin and the Panopticon: Samuel Bentham and the Architecture of Absolutism in Eighteenth Century Russia', www.ucl.ac.uk/Bentham Project/journal/nlwerrett.htm (accessed September 2009).

Westman, R. S. (1980) 'The Astronomer's Role in the Sixteenth Century', *History of Science*, 18: 105–47.

Williams, M. (1983) 'Was There Such a Thing as Stellar Astronomy in the Eighteenth Century?', *History of Science*, 21: 369–88.

Yeo, R. (2001) *Encyclopaedic Visions: Scientific Dictionaries and Enlightenment Culture.* Cambridge: Cambridge University Press.

Zastoupil, L. and Moir, M. (eds.) (1999) *The Great Indian Education Debate: Documents Relating to the Orientalist–Anglicist Controversy 1781–1843.* Richmond: Curzon Press.

Ziegenbalg, B. (1715) *Letter to the Reverend Mr Geo. Lewis . . . Giving an Account of the Method of Instruction used in the Charity-Schools . . . in Tranquebar.* London: Downing.

3 Inter that Discipline!

Thomas Osborne

Of course, interdisciplinarity just has to be a good thing. But it's only a really striking and original idea when counterposed to something else, most usually and obviously to *disciplinarity*. However, the dichotomy is a completely misleading one. Far from being opposed to disciplinarity, interdisciplinarity assumes a certain consciousness of disciplinarity as a condition for its accomplishment. Disciplinarity and interdisciplinarity should not be seen as opposites. Hence the stark opposition conjured for instance by Moti Nissani – as if there were an array of rather miserable, bunkered, puritanical disciplinarians ranged against bright, progressive, brave-new-world interdisciplinarians – seems, to say the least, spurious (Nissani 1997). Samuel Beckett once declined an interview by claiming that, unfortunately, he had no 'views' to 'inter'. Interdisciplinarity is broadly analogous to that. If you lack a discipline to inter, you can't be interdisciplinary at all. Interdisciplinary research projects founder at the planning stages if prospective participants refuse to play the game by failing to own up to any recognisable disciplinary field of expertise, as any hapless 'post-positivist' – let alone any 'postmodern' – social scientist who has sat in on grant-application discussions with engineers or physicists or mathematicians will know. To qualify as a player in the interdisciplinarity game, you have to answer to some or other disciplinary identity.

Two Cultures?

The rubric of interdisciplinarity, when made too breathless, can serve to conceal a great divide that, in spite of the undoubted performative effects of that very rubric, simply refuses to disappear. Even within the prevalent managerially driven discourse of interdisciplinarity the well-worn problem of the two cultures lurks – if not necessarily between the practising arts and the natural sciences (see Born and Barry, this volume, and on which more later), then certainly between the natural sciences on the one hand and the social sciences and humanities on the other.

Part of the problem is that disciplines in the social sciences and humanities, like it or not, and with the possible exception of economics and parts of psychology, simply don't tend to have the more circumscribed epistemological profiles that are characteristic of the natural sciences. An epistemological profile is built upon a mixture of conceptual norms, research paradigms, procedures of formalisation and techno-conceptual 'implicature' – phenomenotechnics, as Gaston Bachelard labelled it. A strong epistemological profile would be one in which the rationalising elements and the technical elements meshed together particularly well. Generally speaking, the social sciences perform rather weakly on this score. They tend to be good, in some versions, at rationalism (grand theory for instance) and, in others, at application (empirical case-study research) – but very rarely at the composite 'applied rationalism' invoked by Bachelard (1949; although, for some variations, cf. Osborne and Rose 1999 and 2004). This is not necessarily because the natural sciences are better than the social sciences. But their cultures of inquiry are indeed broadly different, if not by nature – no deep epistemological claims about the status of naturalism or anti-naturalism are necessary on this score – then certainly by degree.

To paraphrase that well-known epistemologist Donald Rumsfeld, natural scientists tend to know what they don't know. They work with known unknowns. The same could not always be said of the social sciences and humanities, however hard they try. To restrict ourselves to the British context and some real examples, take a look at the kinds of topic funded by the Economic and Social Research Council as compared to those funded by the Engineering and Physical Sciences Research Council. In the latter, we have grant awards with titles such as 'Technologies and Techniques for Single Cell Proteomics and Lipidomics: Nanodigestion and Analysis of a Single Cell Plasma Membrane'. Here there is a known unknown; scientists know a lot about what kind of roles proteins play in the functionality of cells but not a lot about the role that lipids play, especially at the level of the cell membrane, although they know that the role that lipids play is controlled by the proteins. So there are things that they know and things that they don't know, but scientists know, roughly speaking, what these things that they don't know are.

Typically the natural science awards posit some kind of conjecture as to what they don't know – the famous hypothetical moment in natural science research. The social sciences, on the other hand, have grant awards with titles that are generally more straightforwardly descriptive (rather than discretely hypothetical), and which gesture more commonly not at known unknowns but either at unknown knowns or more interestingly, and more rarely, at unknown unknowns. So we have, on the one hand, titles such as 'Networks of Civic Organisations in Britain'. Social scientists know that there are networks of civic organisations in Britain but they don't know their extent, and nor do they have much of a sense of the role such organisations play in levels of political participation more generally. Civic organisations are not known unknowns: we know that they are there and we know more or less what they do. They are unknown knowns: we simply need to know more about them. On the other hand, there is the situation where social scientists investigate unknown unknowns. This, essentially, is what anthropologists do when they go and do their ethnographic research somewhere in a naturalistic setting, whether that is a tribal culture, a business, the European parliament or a science laboratory. Research into unknown unknowns can often be quite baffling to the objects of study (what on earth is that person doing here?), but that presumably is one of the attractions of it.

Now, after several decades of actor-network theory and its progeny, who would reveal themselves to be moronic enough to resurrect the idea of the two cultures? But it's not really about culture in a general sense; it's more as if the norms of disciplinary creativity and innovation are different across the natural and social science divide. Creativity in the natural sciences often lies precisely in having a nose for the next known unknown, even if this propensity can lead one into some quite random obsessions. Linus Pauling was a genius for sniffing out known unknowns in all sorts of places, constantly moving on from one thing to another but always being fairly sure of what he didn't know and what he wanted to know – although he perhaps paid a certain price for this ability in a rather deranged obsession with the benefits of vitamins (Goertzel 1995). Similar things could be said of other celebrated creative types in the natural sciences, such as Richard Feynman – his price, albeit perhaps paid more by others than himself, involving a famous obsession with the bongos (Gleick 1992).

Creativity in the social sciences, on the other hand, often proceeds in different ways that can look more random if no less obsessional. Great social scientists can simply be brilliant at description; deepening our knowledge of what we already know to such an extent that it begins to look different. When Erving Goffman investigated the asylum, he more or less took it for granted that he knew what an asylum was. But his ethnographic research led him to recategorise the asylum into something that was different from what we had previously thought of it; not just a therapeutic space but also an instrument of social control. For Goffman, this meant that the proper functions of the asylum had been skewed towards extraneous ends. It turned out that St Elizabeth's asylum wasn't just an asylum but also a prison (Goffman 1961).

Michel Foucault took this logic even further, or rather in a different direction. If you do a genealogy rather than an ethnography of the asylum you just about make it disappear altogether. It becomes something we didn't know at all. For Foucault, the asylum is not a skewed object, a prison rather than an asylum; it is not what we thought it was at all. It's a moral space where the moral homogeneity is actually what makes scientific – or at least psychiatric – inquiry possible rather than, as one might expect, getting in the way of it. The very idea of what an asylum *is* becomes problematic. Whereas Goffman's asylum is an unknown known in the sense that he showed there was more to it than we thought, Foucault showed that it is – or was – something of an unknown unknown. We might say that Goffman questions the asylum, but Foucault puts the asylum in question (Foucault 2006/1961). Neither of these types of inquiry, however, would make any sense at all within the natural sciences.

Now, sceptics of this backward brand of C. P. Snowism might profitably consider the different ethics of postgraduate training that divide the social from the natural sciences. Students in the natural sciences are typically informed what their topic of research is to be, and how this will fit into the wider programme of research of their supervisor. The supervisor provides the student with a pet known unknown.

In the social sciences, it is more typical that students will be told – even after they have received grant funding for a particular area of work – to go and feel their way into their topic. Supervisors in the social sciences who actually dictate what their students should study can sometimes be regarded as tyrannical monsters. The students begin by going off to rummage around in some kind of literature to see what they might come up with. Even when social scientists claim they know what they're doing, it's still fundamental to much even of the best social research that one has to feel one's way in, sometimes without knowing what one's research object, even one's actual field, is. Natural scientists are often visibly horrified at this way of proceeding in the social sciences and humanities; and yet the best work in the social sciences very often comes out of such marginal, localised, ambiguous beginnings. Those students in the social sciences who know exactly what they want to do and proceed according to the logic of known unknowns quite often produce just predictable – more often than not, ideological – research, the outcomes of which might easily have been predicted in advance.

But, actually, is this really the boring old two cultures at all? Perhaps not. It could be said that the basic problem is simply a matter of degree in terms of their objects; that the social sciences are much more difficult than the natural sciences. They research entities that are far more complex than those of the natural sciences. As Martin Rees has pointed out: 'The most commonplace objects can be the most complicated. An ant's internal structure is far more intricate than that of an atom or a star; humans are, of course, more complex still' (Rees 2010). In this sense, the natural sciences have it easy: they just deal with simple stuff like atoms, stars and planets. But what is it to understand a society, or to read a text?

The problem, in fact, is not so much with the idea that there are two (or more) cultures that are regrettably insulated from each other, but with the idea of disciplinary insulation itself, with the notion that disciplines are implicitly akin to monads – discrete entities of similar dimensions and formal attributes either in isolation or bouncing of one another. If the invocation of the great divide hasn't already disturbed this assumption, we certainly need to abandon any such monadism when it comes to thinking about disciplinarity (and, still more, interdisciplinarity).

For one thing, as Simon Schaffer shows (in this volume), disciplines, more often than not, emerge out of interdisciplinary contexts; it is a rare thing, either in the natural or the social sciences, to find a discipline that has ever been pristine or autarkic. Disciplines are always composites. In that, they are like the English in history – composites of Vikings, Celts and Normans and heaven knows what else. But that doesn't mean that there is no such thing as a discipline, any more than it means there's no such thing as an English person. For another thing, disciplines do not come with the same dimensions and attributes. Not all disciplines have discrete objects of inquiry that are clearly definable; they might, for instance, be more easily defined by their methodological protocols than by anything they focus upon by way of an object. Certainly, vulcanologists tend to be concerned with volcanoes, just as glaciologists are concerned with glaciers or virologists with viruses. But multi-level modellers do multi-level modelling all over the place; they don't have a specific object to model. Glaciologists are likely to be interdisciplinary in a different way from multi-level modellers; they are likely to call in different kinds of expertise to explain the effects of glaciation. Glaciologists may work with practitioners from mineralogy, oceanography, chemistry, water and atmospheric research and even space scientists (e.g. Petrenko et al 2008). Multi-level modellers are more likely to work with others who have called *them* in. So some disciplines typically import interdisciplinary expertise, and other disciplines export it. Mathematics is an interesting example in this context. Statistics is a discipline (or many) with a kind of object (relations of frequency), but it is also a formalising discipline that crosses boundaries across the sciences, natural and social. Yet when a biologist or a sociologist uses statistics, they are hardly being interdisciplinary; they are simply doing biology or sociology.

Parasites, Trespassers, Poachers

So disciplines are not monads. There is a basic transparency or porosity to disciplines, and some more so than others. They let in the light – or the water – in different ways. The social sciences, especially, seem to have an array of varying degrees of disciplinary porosity and varying degrees, one might say, even of promiscuity – the different ways in which they get themselves about. For the most part it would be difficult to say whether such porosity or promiscuity amounts to anything so grand as interdisciplinarity. In the social sciences, unlike for the most part in the natural sciences, it is often very difficult to distinguish disciplines from each other. Indeed there may be more differences *within* some disciplines than between others. A situation where sociologists are working with human geographers hardly amounts to interdisciplinarity in any strong sense; at least not in the way in which a molecular biologist working with a physicist (for instance, on problems in soft condensed matter) amounts to interdisciplinarity, but also – more surprisingly – not in the way that a human geographer might work with a physical geographer. Indeed, a human geographer working with a physical geographer would probably qualify as genuine interdisciplinarity – albeit interdisciplinarity, as it were, within one discipline.

On the other hand, although the mobility of some disciplines – mathematics, game theory etc. – across other disciplines is more or less normal to their very sense of disciplinarity, it is the case that some disciplines seem to be blessed with the habits of a kind of parasitic aptitude for cross-fertilizing with other areas of inquiry. Disciplines in the social sciences often tend to have this kind of parasitic quality, but this is part of their very style of being *disciplinary*, not something to do with interdisciplinarity as such.

Anthropology – or at least anthropology of the social and cultural kind – would be a good case in point, as would certain kinds of philosophy such as some versions of the philosophy of science. Anthropology, of course, has the ethnographic method. And what ethnography provides is a capability for a creative parasitism that is largely denied to other areas of the social sciences, such as sociology or political science. Anthropologists go out into the field ready, so to speak, to be absorbed into it. These days they study businesses, laboratories, just about anything. But this hardly makes anthropologists particularly interdisciplinary in a radical sense. Creative parasitism is not the same as interdisciplinarity; rather, it is just part of the logic precisely of the disciplinarity of anthropology, or certain kinds of philosophy, that they should be parasitic in this way. Nor, it should be said, if anthropology (like some branches of philosophy) can be described as a parasitic discipline by inclination is this meant in a negative sense. For one thing parasites tend to do well out of parasitism, and for another they can of course be of benefit to their hosts. Anthropologists, by virtue of their specific methodological expertise, can go into other domains and research the logics of those domains while leaving their own disciplinary core intact. Anthropologists exist as parasites on other domains, whether those are tribal cultures, scientific laboratories or IT businesses.

Of course, none of this is to say that the scope of a discipline such as anthropology has not been contentious. There are plenty of anthropologists who are sceptical of the ethnography of science for instance, just as there are those who have been sceptical of applying anthropological techniques to any other than non-Western cultures. And of course there are plenty of anthropologists who are indeed interdisciplinary in a stronger sense; for instance, those who work on environmental issues involving collaboration with the biosciences (German et al 2010). But, for all that, anthropologists engage as much in disciplinary as interdisciplinary research when they do the parasitic kinds of things that they tend to do with tribal cultures, science laboratories or businesses. And if there are well-known dangers of 'going native' involved here, then the very fact that going native is regarded precisely as a risk rather than an inherent virtue in anthropological research is indicative of the extent to which anthropology remains, precisely, a discipline.

The same is true of those philosophers of science or mathematics who parasite ideas from the fields of quantum mechanics or set theory. Parasitism, of course, demands an intimate knowledge of the terrain: philosophers of quantum mechanics tend to know a lot about quantum mechanics (see e.g. Ladyman et al 2007). The philosopher of science Georges Canguilhem trained as a doctor in order better to appreciate the rationalities proper to the medical and life sciences. This does not mean that Canguilhem was a better doctor for his knowledge of philosophy. It was not about interdisciplinarity between medicine and philosophy; it was simply a – disciplinary – matter of doing better philosophy. Likewise, the philosopher of quantum mechanics is not there to do better quantum mechanics but to take something of interest for philosophy from quantum mechanics. And of course the parasitism is supposed to be beneficial to all parties involved: IT businesses and quantum physicists can both benefit from the parasitic activity of anthropologists and philosophers. (Disciplines such as sociology, on the other hand, are not much good at parasitism in this respect.) But parasitism is still in fact just as much a feature of disciplinarity as it is of interdisciplinarity. What is involved is not necessarily a novel dynamism that comes from the confluence of disciplines but, more generally, the usage of one discipline for the purposes of another. But that is part of the more or less normal disciplinary ethos of those forms of inquiry just as much as it is of interdisciplinarity per se.

In fact, parasitism appears to be particularly a phenomenon that occurs within the social sciences. It's an example of what was referred to earlier as the disciplinary porosity-cum-promiscuity of so much social research. There also exist other phenomena, again especially within the social sciences, that perhaps look like interdisciplinarity, but which are really just part of a more or less unremarkable disciplinary ethos. Take, for instance, the activity of trespassing. In his early work, Bruno Latour used to invoke a nice image of knowledge as a form of transport or translation; someone with knowledge was basically someone who went somewhere and brought something back without transforming it in ways that were detrimental to knowing things about it. That image might fit the creative parasitism of the anthropologist's knowledge fairly well, as Latour's own examples showed (Latour 1987: 217, 220). But when you trespass you don't take something from somewhere else for your own purposes – although you certainly do this if you can – so much as attempt to impose your own view of the terrain on another disciplinary area. But, properly done, this is as much about bringing the other discipline into your own as it is of imposing yourself on another field. That at least is the understanding of disciplinary trespassing put forward by Albert Hirschman (1981). The trespasser passes into other domains and develops his or her own perspective.

Sometimes this can look like quite a reductive enterprise, but the reductiveness can be part of the creativity and usefulness of the endeavour itself. Economic perspectives within sociology and political science come to mind in this connection; for instance, in a work such as Hirschman's own *Exit, Voice and Loyalty* (1970), a work which trespasses into political science without, for all that, claiming an intellectually 'imperialist' role for economics. Here, Hirschman brought in an economic perspective to political science, but his book was of far less interest to his own constituency – the economists. Most of what Hirschman said was probably obvious to them. But for political scientists, or some of them, it added another dimension; it enabled them to become more like economists than they had been before. This was not an instance particularly of any radical kind of interdisciplinarity in action; adding another dimension to political science is not quite the same as being interdisciplinary, but just another way of doing political science.

Trespassing is something one can do largely on one's own. Just as we have had socialism in one country, we can invoke a tendency that looks a bit like interdisciplinarity in one person. Ian Hacking's example is Leibniz, who researched just about everything with equal brilliance (Hacking 2004). Often, in fact, when people say they are very interdisciplinary they mean they just do a lot of trespassing. Hacking points at himself in this connection. Having researched the history of probability and statistics, the history of physics, multiple personality disorder, child abuse and the philosophy of language, Hacking claims simply that he is doing analytic philosophy in all these areas. He is being disciplinary and interdisciplinary at the same time. And this sort of work requires a disciplinary outlook precisely in order to be interdisciplinary: 'I never seek help from an "interdisciplinary" person, but only from a "disciplined" one' (ibid: 2).

Such multifaceted individuals are one thing, but there is also the phenomenon of mass trespassing. Rational choice theorists in the social sciences would be a case in point. Rational choice theory is often presented as an 'approach' to the social sciences, by its proponents as the best approach and by its detractors as among the worst. A better way to think of rational choice is in terms of trespassing – it is more or less what happens when utilitarian economics trespasses on domains other than economics in the social sciences. So, arguably, the best work of this sort is not seeking to be the norm for the discipline as a whole but to retain its trespasser status; seeking, that is, to be critical and counterintuitive in relation to existing explanations. In other words, endeavours of this sort seem to work best with the least likely of cases. Jon Elster's work throughout his career has consisted, for instance, almost entirely of applying rational choice approaches specifically to nominally irrational phenomena; it is productive by being counterintuitive (e.g. Elster 1983). Elster eventually tired of rational choice theory, believing that it overstated its utilitarian assumptions about human behaviour. This is understandable if one considers that, for Elster himself, the project consisted of attempting to establish new – rational choice – norms for the social sciences. But, understood differently, rational choice theory was not unsuccessful. As an anthropology of human nature it scarcely stands up, but as an instrument for trespassing in fields outside its home domain of economics it was – and arguably remains – intensely interesting, as Elster's own work on apparently non-rational phenomena such as creative art clearly showed (Elster 2000: 175–269; Osborne 2011).

At least with regard to the social sciences, the key to successful trespassing seems to be that it should not veer into outright imperialism. Trespassing which becomes imperialism ceases to enlighten because the original object is lost. Gary Becker in economics is an imperialist in disciplinary terms, believing that everything can be reduced to the economic perspective (Becker 1976). Becker does not explain social phenomena in economic terms; rather, he turns social phenomena into economic phenomena and then proceeds, as an economist, to analyse them. That is imperialism. George Akerloff says of Gary Becker's project that it's the opposite of his own: 'You see I have gone the opposite way of Gary Becker. I have been trying to bring other things into economics; the other people have been trying to bring economics into the other social sciences' (in Swedberg 1990: 72). Imperialism is certainly not interdisciplinary; rather, it's simply reductive. Parallel points could be made about sociobiology and, latterly, cognitive psychology in relation to the social sciences. A more interesting trick than imperialism is to trespass by leaving things in their own domain and then to explain them in one's own way. That, then, with regard to economics, is what Hirschman or Akerloff or Thomas Schelling does, but it's not what Becker does. But nor is trespassing anything like a radical form of interdisciplinarity rather than just another mode of disciplinarity itself.

Economics appears to have a magnificent propensity for trespassing. In Britain, for instance, the Stern Report on the economics of climate change helped to change the terms of debate over the environment (Stern 2006). Climate change entails costs (mostly, it appears, financial) and potential benefits (an impetus towards technological development and hence growth). One might quibble over the ethics of reducing climate change to economic formulae derived from game theory, but on the other hand the Stern Report helped to transport the issue of the environment into political – as opposed to moral – terms by specifying as precisely as possible the temporality of the economic costs involved. Political discourse can work with the precision of economic language more easily than with the vagaries of well-meaning moral denunciation over the environment.

So much for economics. It should go without saying that other disciplines have other propensities. Some of these might be considered in quite negative ways. After parasitism and trespassing, we can invoke the phenomenon of poaching. This, again, might look a bit like a kind of interdisciplinarity. But in some ways that would be wrong. Poaching could be seen, in fact, as a sort of trespassing in reverse. The poacher ventures into another field, takes what he or she understands to be the key insights of that field, and then seeks to return these to his or her own area of research. Actually, poaching is almost invariably disastrous when it comes to interdisciplinarity, at least in the social sciences, and not much should be said about it. It's rife in the postmodern social sciences and especially the humanities, as when, to allude to some real examples, a famous cultural theorist tells us that he is preoccupied by quantum mechanics as a key to understanding modern ethics, or when various proponents of so-called 'security studies' attempt to apply Foucault's notion of liberal 'security' as a political rationality of social defence to something completely different – national and international territorial security. Poaching looks like interdisciplinarity, but it isn't; it's more like failed imperialism. It's not the Roman Empire, and more like the Scots in New Caledonia – basically, embarrassing. Poaching can have great pay-offs in terms of immediate cultural capital amongst one's own kind ('hey you're really reading up on quantum mechanics?'), but tends to go down less well amongst those who actually know something about things like quantum mechanics or liberal apparatuses of security. Poaching is an interesting example precisely because it isn't disciplinary enough. The poacher typically borrows metaphors or themes from some other discipline because they don't really know what they're doing in their own. Poaching is the product of a kind of disciplinary deficit.

Perhaps not all poaching is intrinsically a bad thing. Perhaps there are disciplines where it leads to productive possibilities that are novel. But perhaps, too, we need to distinguish between poaching proper and straightforward metaphorology. Poaching proper is genuine misunderstanding where the intention is to understand and to apply one concept to another field. It is difficult to see how this can ever be productive. Borrowing concepts in a metaphoric way seems broadly different and far more positive. When Ian Hacking develops insights from epidemiology using the language of vectors he is being metaphorical rather than being a poacher (Hacking 1998: 80–101; cf. Agassi and Laor 2000: 554–5). No doubt the language of epidemiology is not quite appropriate for analysing forms of transient mental illness (in so far as the kinds of parasites studied by epidemiologists themselves are not literally involved), but Hacking is clearly quite happily aware of that. The metaphor is itself an enlightening one which informs Hacking's argument concerning the varied surfaces of emergence, or 'niches', of various kinds of mental illness.

In any case, even with just our very broad brush and limited examples from the social sciences, two points should have hit home by now. First, that disciplines are not like equally-weighted monads circling around and joining together to make interdisciplinary super-monads (or something like that). Such a view both ignores the continued existence of the great divide but also underestimates the extent to which different disciplines simply have different ways of knowing and doing things that are more or less typical of them, that being a discipline is not a categorical form of identity like being a person or an animal. The label – 'discipline' – conceals differences. Different disciplines have different kinds of propensity for interaction, and it is generally part of the very 'disciplinarity' of disciplines that they should interact with other areas of inquiry in varying ways; these forms of interaction do not make these disciplines particularly interdisciplinary. If we don't think of disciplines as monads the fact that they can be porous or promiscuous should not come as much of a surprise; such tendencies are simply an aspect of their disciplinarity. This is the second point that should have hit home: that interdisciplinarity is not the opposite of disciplinarity at all.

Platonism and Emergence

In invoking the modalities of porosity and promiscuity that are differentially inherent within disciplines, not much has yet been said about the more commonly invoked notion of interdisciplinary research: where two or more separate disciplines get together and work on a particular problem or problems. This is a compulsory mantra of funding councils these days, not least because it suggests that disciplines exist not to service themselves but to answer particular problems that concern us all. Interdisciplinarity is not just fashionable, it's useful, and if disciplines are getting together then this has to be a good thing because, again, it suggests that research is oriented to actual problems and not the self-interests of researchers.

But this model, admirable as it is, scarcely represents a new epistemic order in itself. Interdisciplinarity is not über-disciplinarity or post-disciplinarity. We are not in a brave new epistemic world, but only, at most, a more intensive version of the old one. There is no seismic shift from Mode-1 to Mode-2, as some have claimed, but just an intensification of Mode-1 (cf. Gibbons et al 1994). What, if anything, is new in recent decades is not the fact of interdisciplinarity itself but, on the one hand, the pace of interdisciplinarity (egged on by new, more problem- and cost-sensitive funding regimes) and, on the other, an increase in initiatives for more interdisciplinary research specifically across the divides of the natural sciences and the social and human sciences, but especially across the art-science divide.

So, to reiterate, what is being claimed here is not that interdisciplinarity doesn't exist, but only that there is no emergent *sui generic* shift towards interdisciplinarity that makes it fundamentally different from an epistemic regime centred more on a narrower disciplinarity. If anything, the reverse is the case: more interdisciplinarity places greater demands on disciplines to be disciplinary. To prove this overall point, one would think it necessary to provide an exhaustive empirical account of interdisciplinary initiatives. That would be good, and certainly worthwhile. But actually one can also make the point deductively. What we would be looking for on the brave-new-world hypothesis would be cases not just of interdisciplinarity *per se*, but what might be called *emergent* interdisciplinarity in which the meeting of two or more disciplines produces a novel formation – in other words, a new *discipline*. But in that case, what we have is not just interdisciplinarity but more disciplinarity. Another discipline! No doubt a hybrid discipline, yes; but then all disciplines are hybrid. So, *QED*: even this kind of interdisciplinarity leads back to disciplinarity.

Of course, this deductive approach to things conceals the fact that there are different kinds of interdisciplinarity. Let's distinguish the Platonic sort from the emergent sort. The Platonic sort is where several disciplines get together and pool their resources without anything emergent or novel necessarily resulting. Platonic relationships don't involve the actual exchange of bodily fluids. The knowledge that comes out of Platonic research is summative of the different disciplines but is not emergent in the sense of being a novel kind of knowledge as such. In the UK the Severn Tidal Power Feasibility Study would be an excellent example of genuine interdisciplinary research, focused on a particular environmental issue, that appears to be basically Platonic. The Severn Estuary has a 14-metre tidal range, the second highest in the world, with potential to generate some 5 per cent of electricity needs in the UK, thus contributing fairly substantially to climate change and energy targets for 2020 (Sustainable Development Commission 2007). The feasibility study involved environmental research (for impacts on biodiversity and wildlife), geomorphological research (analysing the evolution and configuration of rocks and land forms), engineering research (assessing technical options, for instance between a tidal lagoon and a barrage), economic research (investigating financing options and energy market impacts), sociological research (on impacts on businesses and regional and economic impacts), legal research (inquiries into issues to do with regulatory compliance) and survey research (inquiring into stakeholder engagement and communication). But there's no indication that what's required here is emergent knowledge. What's going on is that disciplines are learning to work together and to pool results – not in the sense of merging them into something emergent, but in the sense of platonically laying them alongside each other in relation to an overall outcome.

Certainly, there have to be challenges in working alongside other disciplines in this way – as those who do interdisciplinary research often assert, usually with some (generally exasperated) humour – and no doubt such an experience can indeed destabilise disciplines in the sense of provoking new scales and ranges of objects and problems for them to confront. But what such challenges tend to effect is more likely to be a greater interrogation of one's own disciplinary identity than a stage towards something emergent and, in effect, post-disciplinary. On the contrary, it is more likely that the economists, the engineers and all the others are having to do a very disciplinary job precisely in order to be interdisciplinary.

And, remaining with the field of environmental research, where – as with the phenomenon of 'integrated assessment' – it does appear as if genuinely emergent results are the product of interdisciplinary endeavour, one quickly finds claims that although there is interdisciplinarity at stake, what has actually emerged is (unsurprisingly enough) a *new* discipline. That, in effect, is our deductive point again. Whether integrated assessment is in itself a new discipline or is a hybrid of disciplines may be a contentious matter. That it should be both disciplinary and hybrid should not, however, be surprising. Even Platonic disciplinarity still involves hybrids, of course. After all, disciplines – like children – have to have come from somewhere, and they are not carried in pristine and ready made by the stork. This means that, historically speaking, all disciplines are products of hybrid negotiations and compromises. Hybridity in itself is not something to be surprised about.

Actual emergence is another matter; that is, emergence as a norm that is beyond the disciplinary logic of any single discipline. We can briefly interrogate some of the claims made for this in the context of the art-science nexus; and this makes sense since, as mentioned earlier, it is specifically across the arts-science divide that many recent interdisciplinary initiatives have taken hold. Is there actually any evidence, however, that scientific knowledge in terms of its internal epistemological make-up – as opposed to its external perception of itself – has in any ontological way been transformed by the encounter with the arts? Important and influential encounters have happened, but actual epistemic emergence? Linear perspective in painting unquestionably had effects on the science of optics, and vice versa, but painting and optics remained separate enterprises (Edgerton 2009). And of course science can have aesthetic qualities. An equation can be beautiful (Ede 2005), but a beautiful equation is no less – or more – of a scientific phenomenon for being possible to appreciate in an aesthetic way.

Actual collaborations between artists and scientists – art-science proper – might seem to offer a better set of examples; but in fact such collaborations surely tend more often than not to be about different kinds of *art*, not novel kinds of science (Barry et al 2008: 38–40; cf. Wilson 2010) – which is not to say that scientists are not affected by the experience of working with artists. But art-science is surely just art, just as conceptual art was art and not philosophy. Conceptual artists may have read a lot of philosophy and philosophers may have philosophised over conceptual art, but they remained separate enterprises. When Marcel Duchamp displayed his urinal, this may have been subversive, but it was still art if it was anything and not the product of an innovative interdisciplinary collaboration between sculpture and sanitary engineering. Of course, artistic practice changes when confronted with scientific histories, technologies, objects and problematics, but then the practising arts are not themselves conceptual forms of knowledge at all, and so cannot be subsumed under any recognisable 'disciplinary' label – which is not to say that one doesn't need 'discipline' to do the arts. But the actual creative arts are engaged in a different cognitive game from the intellectual disciplines of the natural and social sciences and the humanities. Or rather, *qua* arts they are not engaged in a cognitive game at all. As Elster puts it with characteristic bluntness:

'if the artist only wants to convey a new cognition, he or she ought to use the medium that is tailor-made for this purpose, namely, that of logical argument and factual exposition' (Elster 2000: 205).

Of course, the practising arts involve discipline and are in that, particular, sense 'disciplinary', but the arts themselves do not partake, *qua* arts as opposed to anything else, of the epistemic (i.e. propositional knowledge-generating) logic of intellectual disciplines. At most, the parallel might be to claim that the arts are 'affective' disciplines, producing blocs of sensation and affect certainly; but those arts which seek to make intellectual points in the manner of intellectual disciplines are, in doing so, simply not part of the genre of art at all, nor of some 'destabilizing' art-science ontological hybrid but – were they actually to make substantive cognitive claims – then simply part of *science*. Part of what is at stake here is an ambiguity about what we mean by knowledge itself. Of course, it depends on how we define our terms. The arts are certainly productive of knowledge, but not of the propositional kinds of knowledge that are the staple of the sciences. When Milan Kundera argues that the history of the novel is a history of different kinds of knowledge, he adds that this applies in the context of different kinds of knowledge that are made available only by the novel (Kundera 1988). In supplying knowledge, the novel is producing something that only the novel can produce. It is specifically not aping the activities of science and the kinds of propositional knowledge found there. Likewise, when W. G. Sebald argues that only literature can provide a certain kind of knowledge of the trauma of the air war over Germany in the Second World War, his argument is not that this is a scientific kind of knowledge but that it is a specifically literary form of knowledge that is *sui generic* (Sebald 2003; cf. Osborne 2005).

So what is at stake is not so much whether the arts are capable of providing us with knowledge. For, after all, the entire apparatus of criticism – in the visual and the literary arts – is predicated on the presupposition that there is knowledge to be found in them there artistic hills. It is not the whether-or-not of knowledge that is at stake. Perhaps it is more than anything a question of the different institutional forms of knowledge and art. Nelson Goodman once insisted that the question should not be 'what is art?' but 'when is art?' (Goodman 1978). Perhaps we might say that the question should actually be 'where is art?' It is of course naïve and idiotic to say that art happens in art galleries and science happens in science journals. But it is not *that* idiotic. Science operates by promoting propositional forms of knowledge. Where the arts become propositional one is usually left simply with bad art, with ideological art. How would one institutionalise art-science? If it's in the form of a science journal then it's going to be science; if it's in an art gallery or in an aesthetic space like a sculpture garden it's going to be art. It might be bad science or bad art of course, and none of this is to preclude the arts and sciences having decisive influences on each other; only that they inhabit, for want of a better term, different domains of expression. Disciplines still matter, even here. One is reminded again of Hacking's point about disciplinarity. If one were a scientist wanting to collaborate in an interdisciplinary way with the arts, one is more likely to phone an artist than another scientist.

Conclusion

None of what has been claimed here has been aimed at debunking the idea of interdisciplinarity, of course. Far from it. But it is to claim that interdisciplinarity isn't necessarily new or particularly surprising. It can be exciting, however, and especially in those cases – the phenomenon of art-science being precisely a case in point – where one might least expect it. Interdisciplinarity is most exciting where most improbable; in other words, where the creative energies of its practitioners are most at stake in entering into the unknown. A sociologist collaborating with a human geographer is scarcely likely to generate as much excitement as an artist working with a scientist. Again, perhaps the question is not the what but the where. *That* interdisciplinarity happens is not particularly surprising; *where* it happens can be.

More generally, the point here has been to stress that interdisciplinary accountability is unquestionably a good idea, but that it is an idea contained or at least containable within the very idea of disciplinarity itself. Interdisciplinarity is what happens when disciplines collaborate and, hopefully, communicate, evolve, morph, synergise – whatever! But it's not, generally speaking, what happens when they stop being disciplines and become something else, whatever that may be.

All this has at least two fairly interesting consequences. The first is that it's not just empirically misguided but is actually doing a disservice to the idea of interdisciplinarity to aggrandize it as some kind of feisty brave new world where everything has changed from the boring old days of mundane, claustrophobic, curmudgeonly disciplinarity. That way only lies hubris, and ultimately disappointment. If you expect too much from something it risks being abandoned as last year's fad, whereas interdisciplinarity isn't – or shouldn't be – that. So to be nonchalant, blasé and de-dramatising about interdisciplinarity, or in any case less carried away by it than some, is to do a service to it not a disservice. The second consequence is that the main casualties of a more intensified interdisciplinary world will not so much be disciplines themselves as those areas of inquiry that don't really amount to much as disciplines at all – for instance, those disciplines that are weakly formed in the sense of being diffuse in their concerns, unsure of their object and (in other words) not disciplinary enough.

A good example of this would be sociology. Historically, sociology has been either a generalising discipline (Durkheim, Hobhouse) or one that is so parcellised as not to be a single discipline at all. Sociology has no distinct methodology to its name (having lost the social survey to other forms of enterprise, notably market research), and no distinct object of research. Even if there is such a thing as society, it's not something that sociologists have ever managed to turn into an object of inquiry. Sociology has had some success as an exporter discipline, in terms of training people in other areas of inquiry in the social sciences, and as a maverick discipline, in coming up with some interestingly counterintuitive themes and concepts (the whole sociology of science movement being an excellent example). But in an increasingly interdisciplinary world in terms of research, it is difficult to see what sociology can bring that is distinctive from other approaches easily available elsewhere, for instance from the marketing industry, social psychology, policy analysis or management science.

Unlike sociology, anthropology, with its basis in ethnographic fieldwork, is likely to thrive in an intensified interdisciplinary world. But that is because anthropology is more not less disciplinary than sociology. You might think that a discipline like sociology would be eminently interdisciplinary, mobile across all sorts of different domains. But that isn't the case at all. It's because sociology is so loosely disciplined that it can't make much headway in the interdisciplinarity stakes, unless it is either really boring sociology involving doing, say, a few opinion polls for engineers who want to build a bridge or, far more rarely, actually quite mobile and exciting sociology as with Bruno Latour's work on publics or Barry et al's own – basically, sociological – research on interdisciplinarity itself (Latour and Weibel 2005; Barry et al 2008).

But it can be difficult to be exciting all of the time. Certainly, a discipline cannot live off constant drama and counter-intuition. There are, in any case, diminishing returns on excitement when it becomes a norm. But disciplines – like sociology or certain kinds of philosophy – that aren't quite sure what they are about, that lurch from crisis to crisis, that lack stable epistemic norms, methods and conventions, that even lack basic points of agreement but which thrive by forms of opposition that are not just critique, surely have some place in the epistemic world order, if only as a counterweight to the logics of disciplinarity and interdisciplinarity that we have been invoking here. They at least open up a space to think, precisely because they let in a bit of air, if not always light. Philosophy used to be like that too, before it became an academic discipline with fixed methods and little branches of study. Nietzsche's claim that professional philosophers weren't philosophers at all was one of his most genuinely philosophical statements. Off-the-wall sociology and old-style philosophy were perhaps what might be called *idiot sciences* (cf. Deleuze and Guattari 1994: 61–3). They allowed for a certain creative idiocy, a certain kind of scepticism, of 'private thinking' as opposed to orthodox, sensible public knowledge – the kinds of stubbornness that are increasingly difficult to recapture the more we are dominated by disciplinarity and interdisciplinarity and, though such domination is not at all in itself a bad thing, they were the kinds of idiocy that are now perhaps all the more needed for it.

Acknowledgement

Thanks to Andrew Barry and Georgina Born for a great many comments, criticisms and corrections of an original version of this chapter.

References

Agassi, J. and Laor, N. (2000) 'How Ignoring Repeatability can Lead to Magic', *Philosophy of the Social Sciences*, 30, 4, 528–86.
Bachelard, G. (1949) *Le Rationalisme Appliqué*, Paris: PUF.

Barry, A., Born, G. and Weszkalnys, G. (2008) 'Logics of Interdisciplinarity', *Economy & Society*, 37, 1, 20–49.

Becker, G. (1976) *The Economic Approach to Human Behaviour*, Chicago: University of Chicago Press.

Deleuze, G. and Guattari, F. (1994) *What is Philosophy?* Trans. G. Burchell, New York: Columbia University Press.

Ede, S. (2005) *Art and Science*, London: I. B. Tauris.

Edgerton, S. (2009) *The Mirror, the Window and the Telescope*, Ithaca, NY: Cornell University Press.

Elster, J. (1983) *Sour Grapes: Studies in the Subversion of Rationality*, Cambridge: Cambridge University Press.

— (2000) *Ulysses Unbound: Studies in Rationality, Precommitment and Constraints*, Cambridge: Cambridge University Press.

Foucault, M. (2006 [1961]) *History of Madness*, trans. J. Khalfa, London: Routledge.

German, L., Ramish, J. and Verma, R. (2010) *Beyond the Bio-Physical: Knowledge, Culture and Politics in Natural Resource Management*, London: Springer.

Gibbons, M., Nowotny, H. and Limoges, C. (1994) *The New Production of Knowledge*, London: Sage.

Gleick, R. (1992) *Genius: The Life and Science of Richard Feynman*, New York: Pantheon.

Goertzel, T. (1995) *Linus Pauling: A Life in Science and Politics*, New York: Basic Books.

Goffman, E. (1961) *Asylums*, Harmondsworth: Penguin.

Goodman, N. (1978) *Ways of Worldmaking*, Indianapolis: Hackett.

Hacking, I. (1998) *Mad Travellers: Reflections on the Reality of Transient Mental Illness*, London: Free Association Books.

— (2004) 'The Complacent Disciplinarian', www.interdisciplines.org.medias/confs/archives/archive_3.pdf (accessed September 2012).

Hirschman, A. O. (1970) *Exit, Voice and Loyalty: Responses to Decline in Firms, Organisations and States*, Cambridge, MA: Harvard University Press.

— (1981) *Essays in Trespassing: Economics to Politics and Beyond*, Cambridge: Cambridge University Press.

Kundera, M. (1988) *The Art of the Novel*, Harmondsworth: Penguin.

Ladyman, J., Presnell, S., Short, A. and Groisman, B. (2007) 'The Connection between Logical and Thermodynamic Irreversibility', *Studies in History and Philosophy of Modern Physics*, 38, 58–79.

Latour, B. (1987) *Science in Action*, Cambridge, MA: Harvard University Press.

Latour, B. and Weibel, P. (eds.) (2005) *Making Things Public: Atmospheres of Democracy*, Cambridge, MA: MIT Press.

Nissani, M. (1997) 'Ten Cheers for Interdisciplinarity: The Case for Interdisciplinary Knowledge and Research', *The Social Science Journal*, 34, 2, 201–16.

Osborne, T. (2005) 'Literature in Ruins', *History of the Human Sciences*, 18, 3, 109–18.

— (2011) 'Rationality, Choice and Modernism: Notes on Jon Elster's Theory of Creativity', *Rationality and Society*, 23, 2, 175–97.

Osborne, T. and Rose, N. (1999) 'Do the Social Sciences Create Phenomena?', *British Journal of Sociology*, 50, 3, 367–96.

— (2004) 'Spatial Phenomenotechnics: Making Space with Charles Booth and Patrick Geddes', *Environment and Planning D: Society and Space*, 22, 209–28.

Petrenko, V. et al (2008) 'A Novel Method for Obtaining Very Large Air Samples from Ablating Glacial Ice for Analyses of Methane Radiocarbon', *Journal of Glaciology*, 54, 185, 233–44.

Rees, M. (2010) *Reith Lectures 2010*, London: BBC.

Sebald, W. G. (2003) *On the Natural History of Destruction*, trans. A. Bell, London: Hamish Hamilton.

Stern, N. (2006) *Stern Review on the Economics of Climate Change*, London: H. M. Treasury.

Sustainable Development Commission (2007) *Turning the Tide: Tidal Power in the UK*, www.sd-commission.org.uk/publications.php?id=607 (accessed September 2012).

Swedberg, R. (ed.) (1990) *Economics and Sociology: Redefining their Boundaries*, Princeton, NJ: Princeton University Press.

Wilson, S. (2010) *Art and Science Now: How Scientific Research and Technological Innovation are Becoming Key to 21st Century Aesthetics*, London: Thames & Hudson.

4   Fields and Fallows

A Political History of STS

Sheila Jasanoff

Interdisciplinarity is the new Canaan, the promised land where ailing scholarly traditions go to be reborn and academic creativity is set free. University administrators ceaselessly invoke interdisciplinarity as the solution to their institutions' ills: felt stagnation; drops in student enthusiasm; diminished research funds; reduced alumni support; and the perceived irrelevance of much academic scholarship to the crying problems of the times. Over and over claims are made that the most exciting problems, the best outlets for creativity, the greatest potential for making a positive difference in the world all lie in the territory defined as 'interdisciplinary'.

Here is one persuasive voice – that of Michael Crow, the energetic iconoclastic president of Arizona State University since 2002:

> Undergirding the strict disciplinary organization of knowledge is a social organization hidebound by behavioral norms of astonishing orthodoxy. Along with entrenchment in disciplinary silos has come a fixation on abstract knowledge for its own sake as well as the proliferation of increasingly specialized knowledge, which comes to produce diminishing returns on investment as its impact on the world is measured in smaller and smaller ratios. Rather than exploring new paradigms for inquiry, academic culture too often restricts its focus to existing models of academic organization.
>
> (Crow 2010: 52)

Contained in this brief extract are many of the themes and tropes that guide the search for interdisciplinarity. Disciplines are silos that promote orthodoxy, produce formal knowledge for its own sake, and carve up the universe of intellectual problems into minute and meaningless increments. By implication, it is in the zones that break out of disciplines – in ASU's case the schools and centers that have proliferated under Crow – that big problems such as planetary sustainability can be tackled and abstract learning be directed toward practical or commercial ends.

This analysis is in keeping with the familiar logics of top-down interdisciplinarity identified by Andrew Barry and Georgina Born in their introduction to this volume. Crow's criticism of the hidebound orthodoxy of disciplines (elsewhere he speaks more generally of the ossification of higher education) provides a springboard for demanding both more accountability and more innovation. By answering only to members of their disciplines, traditional academics are seen as having sacrificed more important forms of labor that matter in the world, including the duty to provide new products and services for society which was a key component of the US postwar social contract for science (Bush 1945, Jasanoff 2005, 2010b). Attempts by governments to rectify tendencies toward scientific irresponsibility, through research only for its own sake, help explain the turn toward what some European analysts have identified as Mode-2 of scientific production (Mukerji 1990, Gibbons et al. 1994, Nowotny et al. 2001). Implicit in the moves toward synthesis and problem solving is a diagnosis and prescription similar to Crow's: disciplines breed inwardness and idle navel-gazing; the solution, plainly, is to break the hegemony of disciplines in favor of other forms of accountability.

But interdisciplinarity, as this collection amply demonstrates, is not simply a matter of widening the zones of accountability from above or forcing academics to leave the safe havens of their disciplinary conversations. Sometimes interdisciplinarity grows from the bottom up: not because of external demands related to public funding or public problems, but because scholars, possibly at the margins of their own disciplinary enclaves, start asking questions that demand new modes of inquiry and challenge. Interdisciplinarity itself, in other words, can be curiosity-driven rather than instrumental, reflexive rather than mobilized by external circumstances. This comes closest to the agonistic-antagonistic mode of interdisciplinarity described by Barry and Born. The result of such uprisings from the periphery could be a field-internal revolution, producing the classic paradigm shift, which reorganizes but does not abandon disciplines (Kuhn 1962). More interestingly, interdisciplinarity can define new territories of intellectual creativity characterized by questions and answers not previously recognized as necessary or desirable. Eventually, a reconfiguration may occur, establishing a new pole of study distinguished by its own logics of production and justification.

Emerging in the latter half of the twentieth century and gaining definition over succeeding decades, Science and Technology Studies (STS) is such a field. It rings its own changes on the Kuhnian paradigm shift, showing that sometimes a 'shift' is more properly a struggle for independence. Motivating STS in part was a mounting, multi-dimensional concern with the adequacy of accounts of knowledge provided by traditional disciplines: history, philosophy, sociology, and the natural sciences themselves, to name the most salient. By aggregating these concerns, and by adopting the reliability of knowledge as the center of its inquiry, early work in STS made inroads into existing disciplinary formations. But the origins of contemporary STS lie in other histories as well, histories concerned more with the external accountability of science and technology to society than the internal accountability of theories of knowledge to scholars within particular disciplines. For that second branch of the nascent field of STS, the problems needing attention had centrally to do with governance. Who was in charge of steering scientific research and technological innovation? Was science education geared toward enhancing productivity? To what extent were publics involved in such decisions, and was their role well grounded in democratic theory? Were adequate institutions and procedures in place for supervising science and technology, especially in the aftermath of World War II when research came more and more to rely on the public purse?

To a great extent, advances in and contestations around STS are results of the sometimes uncomfortable meeting and merging of two intellectual traditions, each rooted in its own critical appraisal of the nature of science and technology. We can distinguish between these two streams of scholarship, as many have done, on several grounds: internal versus external; epistemic as opposed to political (Daston 2009); concerned with production, not reception (Jasanoff 2007); dealing with ideas rather than impacts; and so on. For purposes of understanding the interdisciplinarity of STS, however, commonalities are as important as contrasts. All STS work recognizes science and technology as human and social enterprises, separated from other domains of modern labor by boundaries that are in important ways socially constructed, and hence partaking to greater and lesser degrees in the dominant myths and imaginaries of particular times, places, and cultural conditions. Following the modes of interdisciplinarity proposed by Born and Barry, then, STS positions itself in agonistic-antagonistic fashion both within its own emerging boundaries and in relation to the intellectual territories occupied by other disciplines. These include the sciences and technologies, STS's particular topics of study, and the social sciences and humanities, the sources of some but not all of the methods that STS uses to build its distinctive representations of epistemic, material, and social realities.

Animating all of STS, moreover, is an implicit normative logic that is often neglected in discussions of interdisciplinarity. Many STS scholars think that the institutions, practices, and products of science and technology should be characterized in new ways not only for the sake of descriptive adequacy and analytic clarity, but also in order to reorder power relationships: for example, to make the exercise of power more reflexive, more responsible, more inclusive, and more equal. STS, in other words, undertakes its accounts of science and technology as part of a more or less self-conscious project of co-production, the simultaneous making, or remaking, of natural and social orders (Jasanoff 2004). Some of the dissensions and divisions within and around STS relate to these normative logics. To what extent should STS as a field or as a cluster of individual research trajectories seek to make its normative commitments explicit, open, and proactive? Is it important for STS scholars to intervene in ongoing social processes, and if so in what ways and on what authority? Is a field committed to the deconstruction of authoritative knowledge claims capable of asserting with confidence its own normativity? Is STS for or against science?

This chapter looks at the origins and gradual disciplining of STS through three phases of contestation, each shedding light on the field's foundational logics. The first is anchored in the 'science wars', the moment in the 1990s when a kind of trench warfare broke loose between science studies and the natural sciences, especially physics. The second involves two efforts to codify STS during the same decade and the divergent agendas and interests disclosed by those projects. The third reflects more recent soul-searching by some prominent players in the field, heralding an apparent retreat from STS's early, and radical, epistemic relativism. Each episode revolves, in effect, around a normatively loaded, boundary-defining struggle: who are (*should* be) STS's external interlocutors; whose work defines (*should* define) the field; and for whom does STS work have (*should* have) relevance? Together, these episodes bring into view the necessarily value-laden aspects of shaping a new domain of intellectual investigation, and the necessarily political struggles that surround interdisciplinarity when it stakes a claim on scarce academic resources. I conclude with reflections on STS's efforts to integrate its diverse internal logics and to serve as a valid source of authority on knowledge–power relations in what Ulrich Beck (2000) calls 'second modernity.'

Warfare in the Marches

It was perhaps inevitable that a field claiming the right to describe science and technology from without would run afoul of the denizens of the cultures it presumed to be describing. This is a difficulty that ethnographers encounter in 'studying up', or investigating those with greater power and social standing, which may account for the relative dearth of such inquiries in spite of calls for more (Nader 1972). Trouble could have been foreseen when the nascent field of STS apparently questioned science's central claim to supreme cognitive authority, namely, that science alone of all social institutions is capable of delivering the truth. Yet quarrels with science were not among the field's early preoccupations; and quarrels with technology, which had a longer history and potentially more social traction, got submerged by, or subsumed into, an unexpected confrontation over epistemic authority. Teasing apart the lines of disagreement helps sort out what STS claims to know, what it is agonistic about, and what it is antagonistic to. In turn, that inquiry is crucial to an understanding of STS's place among the disciplines.

Like all complex genealogies, the history of STS's confrontations with science, the so-called science wars, can be traced back to multiple starting points, but it has become conventional to name a few specific works by STS authors and a few specific attacks by or on behalf of scientists as crystallizing the debate. On the side of STS, the most notable names are David Bloor of Edinburgh and Bruno Latour of Paris; on the side of the critics are the Americans Paul Gross (biologist), the late Norman Levitt (mathematician), and above all Alan Sokal (physicist). Bloor, a philosopher of science and psychologist by training, positioned himself on the margins of disciplinary inquiry by taking aim against conventional philosophical accounts of science. In his now-classic work *Knowledge and Social Imagery*, Bloor (1991 [1976]) advocated for a 'sociology of scientific knowledge' that would look dispassionately at how scientific claims are generated, eschewing any preconceptions about nature's role in separating truthful knowledge claims from false ones. This 'strong programme,' he argued, should be committed to *causal* explanations, *impartial* in its treatment of successful and unsuccessful claims, *symmetrical* in explaining success and non-success, and *reflexive* in its application to sociological knowledge itself. Of the four attributes of the strong programme, symmetry proved the most controversial, as we will see below.

Where Bloor adopted philosophical skepticism as his methodological platform, the French philosopher Bruno Latour borrowed his early techniques for investigating science from cultural anthropology, his other formative field. His seminal work *Laboratory Life*, co-authored with Steve Woolgar, imported the estranging gaze of the observer of alien cultures into the laboratory of Roger Guillemin, a Nobel laureate endocrinologist at the Salk Institute, to explain how scientists established the facticity of the structure of a particular compound: thyrotropin-releasing factor (TRF) (Latour and Woolgar 1979). In a series of increasingly influential works, Latour (1987, 1988, 1990) developed in parallel with Edinburgh's strong programme an account of scientific production that eschewed references to external natural truths. In *Science in Action*, Latour propounded 'rules of method' that resembled those of the strong programme but were supported by different arguments. A key assertion, and later a cause of controversy, was that the conventional temporal relationship between external reality and its factual representations should be reversed. Thus, Rule 3, containing Latour's version of the symmetry principle, urged: 'Since the settlement of a controversy is the cause of Nature's representation, not its consequence, we can never use this consequence, Nature, to explain how and why a controversy has been settled' (Latour 1987: 258). What concerned Latour in such statements was relations between signifiers within a system of meanings, not as for Bloor the logical implications of assuming an unchangeable prior state of nature (see, for example, Bloor 2007).

The materiality of science matters far more in Latour's accounts, and in those of the French school of STS more generally, than in the Sociology of Scientific Knowledge (SSK). His work highlights the microprocessing of observation into material representations, often inscriptions on paper, that convey the meaning of scientific work in portable, exchangeable form (Latour 1986, 1987, 1990). This emphasis on the role of non-human objects in the social work of making science developed into the French school's elaboration of actor-network theory (ANT).[1] This framework views reality as the product of network building by powerful actors capable of holding together the heterogeneous, unruly agglomerates, both human and non-human, that sustain facts and other social formations. This insistence on the sociality of artifacts and objects, and of non-humans more broadly, put Latour's brand of STS more directly in conversation with other branches of the human and social sciences, in contrast to the more philosophically oriented Edinburgh school.

STS, as reflected in the work of these iconic figures and many colleagues, was neither aiming primarily at the sciences nor questioning the worth or validity of scientific knowledge. It was therefore something of a surprise for the field to get caught up in one of the uglier battles of the culture wars of the late twentieth century – an event that affirmed many observations that STS scholars were making about knowledge, while also underscoring the field's structural and organizational vulnerability. Hostilities began with the publication of *Higher Superstition*, a blunderbuss attack by Gross and Levitt (1994) upon what they termed the 'academic left' – a loose cluster of feminists, critical theorists, postmodern literary critics, and science studies scholars. All of them, the authors alleged, had joined forces in characterizing scientific knowledge as contaminated by social, political, and economic interests, as reflecting entrenched power structures, and hence as suspect in its claims to truth. These attacks, Gross and Levitt claimed, were as dangerous as they were frivolous, because they relativized science, denied its superiority to other modes of knowing, and thereby deprived society of its most reliable sources of evidence and reason.

Higher Superstition targeted specific individuals, and its attacks occasionally found their mark. A proposal to appoint Bruno Latour to the Princeton Institute for Advanced Study went down in flames (Berreby 1994). Nevertheless, that polemic might have entered history as just another episode in America's culture wars had it not been for the so-called Sokal hoax that followed it two years later. In August 1996, the cultural studies journal *Social Text* published a special issue on the 'science wars' – a term apparently coined by the editor Andrew Ross (1996), a sociologist and critical theorist at New York University. Prompted in part by the buzz around Gross and Levitt, the contributors were at pains to display that science was indeed a social process, affected by culture, politics, and money. The physicist Sokal submitted an article entitled 'Transgressing the Boundaries: Toward a Transformative Hermeneutics of Quantum Gravity' (1996). His piece, as he wrote in the journal *Lingua Franca* in the same month that 'Transgressing' appeared in *Social Text*, was a piece of made-up nonsense dressed up in the jargon of postmodern literary criticism and designed to expose the gullibility and ignorance of science's cultural critics. That sly send-up grabbed media attention in a way that Gross and Levitt had not and considerably raised the stakes for scholars wishing to comment on scientific practices from positions outside science.

The science wars of the mid-1990s tapped into two enduring wellsprings of American culture: resistance to modish intellectual discourse, especially when flavored with whiffs of France (see Sokal 1998: 7); and, more important for our purposes, the desire to hold science as a realm apart, a source of objective authority untouched by America's pluralist struggles for power, and hence available as a resource for all who wish to challenge any forms of social or cultural dominance (Ezrahi 1984, Jasanoff 2005). Beyond the tyranny of headlines, the Sokal affair's lasting legacy was to enable a kind of line-drawing that limited what other disciplines could properly say about science. A social text lampooning the language of transgressing boundaries took on minatory overtones, in effect cautioning other disciplines against transgressing the boundaries set by science. After the hoax, *any* questioning of science's basic product, the truthful representation of nature, was for a time ruled out of bounds in respectable academic discourse. Methodological symmetry, possibly the most important pillar of the strong programme (Barnes and Bloor 1982), became suspect since it appeared to put true and false claims on a par and to rule out explanations invoking nature as the supreme judge. As Sokal (1998: 12) put it:

> If the claim were merely that we should use the same principles of sociology and psychology to explain the causation of all beliefs irrespective of whether we evaluate them as true or false, rational or irrational, then I would have no particular objection. . . . But if the claim is that only social causes can enter into such an explanation – that the way the world is cannot enter – then I cannot disagree more strenuously.[2]

One could hardly ask for a purer illustration of Foucault's (1980) figure of power/ knowledge. In insisting on 'the way the world is,' Sokal implicitly reasserts that there is, and must be, a stopping point for sociological description and analysis, and that natural scientists have an exclusive right to declare what counts as closure around statements about the world. What began, arguably, as a conversation among disciplines about insights to be gained from looking at scientific knowledge-making from diverse perspectives is here reduced to a pure matter of relative authority over descriptions of reality. The science wars can be seen from this standpoint as emblematic of the politics of interdisciplinarity. Behind its parodic façade, Sokal's hoax was a deadly serious attempt to reconfigure the fluid, agonistic playing field on which Bloor, Latour, and others sought to position scientific knowledge-making into a territory of fixed monuments and markers, so designated at any given moment by an uncompromising science.

Struggles Within: A Tale of Two Handbooks

Making room for interdisciplinarity is, for all practical purposes, an act of remapping, whether by bringing new lands into view or by redescribing old ones so as to make visible new opportunities for colonization, mobility, and resource use. How existing disciplines will be represented in the worlds opened up by new initiatives is central. Is it a zero-sum game, and will they gain or lose representation? It is hardly surprising, then, that the dynamics of power/knowledge played out not only in STS's external relations with the natural sciences but also in ongoing debates within the field itself.

I have referred to this struggle before as a competition between two ideal-typical cartographic models: interstate highway construction, and charting the high seas (Jasanoff 2010a). Avoiding the tired and often confused debates around terms such as inter-, multi-, and trans-disciplinary, this way of representing interdisciplinarity problematizes the notion of a 'discipline' and stresses the political dimensions of challenging disciplinary configurations. Under the first model, old disciplinary hegemonies are allowed to remain largely intact while roads are built to connect interdisciplinary traffic across them. Under the second approach, interdisciplinarity is seen more as an exploratory endeavor, a project of discovering new territories and inventing or creolizing discourses in which to speak of them. To some degree, the agonistic play around defining STS can be seen as a struggle between these two approaches to reconceptualizing disciplinary space. The second *Handbook of STS* (Jasanoff et al. 1995) follows the exploratory model, whereas the *Science Studies Reader* compiled by Mario Biagioli (1999) adheres more closely to the model of continued disciplinary sovereignty.

Once again, a little historical background helps to position the analysis. Starting in the 1970s, there were attempts to codify the new social research on science and technology through collections of essays. Among the earliest was a volume edited by Ina Spiegel-Rösing and Derek de Solla Price (1977) that grew out of a desire to show the relevance of STS research to science policy. The book consisted of papers from a conference held five years earlier under the auspices of the International Council for Science Policy Studies, with support from the Ford Foundation. While the results did not convince experienced readers that knowledge of how science works is profoundly relevant to policymaking, John Maddox, the once and future editor of *Nature*, praised it as a contribution to STS studies (Maddox 1977). Steven Shapin (1979: 90) noted, in a perceptive and pointed review, that the study of science had entered what the philosopher Stephen Toulmin called the 'weaving' phase of scholarly development: the stage in which 'boundaries are blurred, and the password is "inter-disciplinarity."' The hyphen is instructive: it upholds boundaries while seeming to blur them. The two essays Shapin held up for special praise were both squarely grounded in known disciplinary traditions: Roy MacLeod's review of the social history of science, and Michael Mulkay's piece on the sociology of scientific practice.

By the late 1980s much had changed. A key development was the founding in 1976 of the Society for Social Studies of Science (4S), the flagship professional organization representing STS. Part of the new society's identity-building efforts was to acquire a journal (*Science, Technology & Human Values*), and to sponsor a new *Handbook of Science and Technology Studies* whose royalties would subsidize the administrative costs of running 4S. Quite fortuitously, I found myself drafted as one of the editors for the project, together with the Michigan State University sociologists Gerald Markle (who recruited me) and James Petersen, and York University's Trevor Pinch, whom I recruited simultaneously to serve as the *Handbook*'s fourth (and only European) editor and to apply for the tenured position in STS that had become available at Cornell. The selection of Pinch served two important purposes. As a scholar trained in the Edinburgh school of sociology of scientific knowledge, he was intimately familiar with transatlantic developments that had occurred largely apart from the evolution of studies of science, technology, and society in the United States (Dear and Jasanoff 2010; Jasanoff 2010a). He also brought invaluable editorial know-how as co-editor of an extremely successful although more focused collection of essays reviewing contemporary scholarship on technology and society (Bijker, Pinch and Hughes 1987).

Our charge as all four editors understood it was twofold: to represent science and technology studies as practiced in the early 1990s across its entire range, and to offer users a comprehensive but ordered guide to the literature that underpinned the field. As I recall, we were more intensely concerned with the problem of responsibly portraying a dynamic field of scholarship than with questions of audience or the politics of knowledge. In retrospect, this proved to be a posture of almost fatal innocence, but we were very conscious of performing an institutional mission, a service in the first instance to 4S and its membership, and we were not sufficiently attuned to the politics of interdisciplinarity to play strategically. As compilers of a handbook for a professional society, we felt answerable to the handbook committee that 4S created for oversight purposes, but we also felt accountable to the community of scholars the *Handbook* sought to represent. Accordingly, we believed we had complete editorial discretion to choose authors and reviewers, and to pass on the adequacy of individual chapters, once the guidelines for moving forward had been approved by the 4S committee.

Cartography, as a powerful technology of representation, is a popular metaphor in STS, and it nicely captured our editorial thinking. As we wrote in the *Handbook*'s introduction (Jasanoff et al. 1995: xi–xv), we created a territorial atlas of STS through a series of moves entailing varying degrees of 4S, editorial, and authorial involvement. The process began with a preliminary chapter outline approved by the Society's handbook committee, followed by a widely advertised call to 4S members and other interested parties to submit proposals based on that outline; we also solicited contributions from established authors in the field. Subsequently the editors met in borrowed space at the Yale School of Forestry and Environmental Studies in New Haven, Connecticut, where I was teaching in 1990–1991, to select a final list of authors from the 160 applications we received. Over an exhausting but exhilarating weekend we winnowed down the contributions to 28 chapters.[3] Authors were asked to refine their outlines and produce drafts, each reviewed by one of the editors and one or more external referees. The process proved laborious and time-consuming beyond even our most pessimistic predictions, lurching its way through several difficult years to eventual publication in 1995.

Unlike the Spiegel-Rösing and de Solla Price collection, the second *Handbook* had no pretensions to influence the worlds of policy and action, at least not directly. To the extent that we thought about such things, pedagogy was our primary objective. If a visitor from Mars had been knowledgable enough to ask 'what is this field that earthlings call science and technology studies?,' we wanted the book that could be put into its green and grasping hands. Our task, then, was enlightenment; we were encyclopedists of interdisciplinarity. The biggest challenge was to bring between covers the spectrum of works a well-read STS scholar should be aware of, but we wanted to hit a number of other high notes as well. The *Handbook* aimed to present the most promising theoretical and methodological orientations in the field (e.g., social constructivism, specific disciplinary approaches, new literary forms), review areas of well-articulated scholarship (e.g., science and politics, gender and science, environmental studies), highlight issues of current public and academic concern (e.g., biotechnology, computers, public understanding of science), and showcase younger as well as more established scholars.

As recounted elsewhere (see Daston 2009: 805), and possibly bespeaking disciplinary animosities smoldering beneath surface civility, we failed in our attempts to enroll a historian to review the considerable contributions of historical research to STS and vice versa. History was absent as a designated subfield in the *Handbook*'s terms, although many chapter authors drew liberally on historical studies. Interestingly, we also failed to attract authors willing to review earlier US contributions to the sociology of science, most notably the work and legacy of Robert K. Merton. It was clear that constructivist thought had gripped the self-identified sociologists in STS, and none seemed prepared to import older structur-alist approaches into the field's ballooning big tent. Sociology was extremely present as the disciplinary field of three of the four editors, and also as the field that most nearly characterized the disciplinary and departmental allegiances of the majority of authors. Yet the struggle over how to (or not to) represent older socio-logical traditions – those focused more on science's macro-institutional character-istics than its epistemology or its micro-practices – proved divisive. It left a trail of (fortunately temporary) rancor within 4S that we, the editors, had not foreseen.

A family quarrel, one may say, and perhaps so. A deeper division over the remit and boundaries of STS emerged with the publication of a second collection, the *Science Studies Reader* edited by Mario Biagioli (1999).[4] The first paragraph of the introduction employs map-making language, but beyond this surface similarity, the *Reader* fundamentally parts company from the *Handbook* in its strategy for representing the field. If the *Handbook* is a series of complex orchestral suites conducted by a lead author, the *Reader* is an album of greatest singles, a 'sampler' rather than a 'canonical text' (Biagioli 1999: xiv). It brings together 36 previously published essays, mostly sole-authored, including many by the best recognized writers in their respective fields. In cartographic terms, the *Handbook* was an exercise in political geography to map all of the major domains of STS; with these maps in hand, a newcomer, it was hoped, could navigate the field and locate herself in one or more of its principalities. The *Reader*, by contrast, offered a selection of milestones, 36 pieces that anyone aiming to be educated in STS should know, or know of, but without an intellectual apparatus to show the user how to think like an STS scholar or to generate distinctive pieces of her own.

Another striking difference between the two works is the *Reader*'s exclusion of materials dealing explicitly with technology. In her curiously misconceived attack on the coherence of science studies, Daston (2009: 800) remarks, 'Science studies is the mercifully short and clear abbreviation for a battery of disciplinary perspectives turned upon science and technology.' In his introduction to the *Reader*, however, Biagioli (1999: xvi) mentions that works on medicine and technology have been almost completely excluded, because those form such large fields of their own. The 'science' in 'science studies,' then, is not merely a merciful abbreviation; in Biagioli's conception it constitutes a defensible dividing line between literatures dealing with science and those focusing on its technological applications. This boundary is one that many STS authors have seen as problematic, as is implied by the popularity of the fusion term 'technoscience' in STS writing.[5] In accepting the division between science, technology, and medicine (and the literatures that study them) as given, the *Reader* takes the boundaries of science as unchallengeable in a way that is inconsistent with most STS scholarship.

The treatment of work on the political and social relations of science is another important axis of divergence between the two collections. The essays in the *Reader* deal almost exclusively with the production of knowledge in its considerable complexity; less evident by far is the circulation of science to communities beyond those of scientific practice, or its appropriation by users and actors who are not themselves scientists. Thus, in his brief 'instructions to the reader,' Biagioli (1999: xiv–xvi) flags the following centers of gravity in science studies: epistemological debates, especially the dichotomy between realism and relativism; cognitive styles; gender and science, with priority given to the gendering of science and to feminist epistemologies; scientific practices, including experiments and instrumentation; authorship and credit; and the differences between the sciences of the 'West' and the 'rest.' While all of these topics are also treated in the *Handbook*, sometimes in dedicated chapters (as in the case of gender and science), the focus there is on science and technology not only as social productions, but also as agents in society. In theoretical terms that did not have as much currency at the time these two collections were compiled, the *Handbook* is written in the idiom of co-production (Jasanoff 2004), showing science and technology as always already implicated in the ordering of society; whereas the *Reader*'s framing is more traditionally constructivist, displaying the social dynamics internal to scientific communities.

Not accidentally, then, the *Reader*'s contributions were drawn largely from fields associated with the observation of science as a self-demarcated sphere of activity or a self-contained culture: history, philosophy, anthropology, feminist critique. Biagioli (1999: xi) evidently saw the boundary problem as unproblematic: 'Unlike other academic fields, science studies does not have to define its subject matter in relation to its neighboring disciplines; over the years, the scientists have done much of that work.' And again (1999: xii): 'Science studies does not define its subject matter because, in some significant way, its subject matter comes prepackaged.' By contrast, how scientists of all stripes demarcate legitimate scientific activity from activities outside the pale of legitimacy has been a consistent concern of STS (cf., Gieryn 1995). Moreover, STS scholars have long recognized that demarcation poses important political challenges when science and technology intersect with public problems – as causes or solutions – in areas such as health and safety, environment, education, criminal justice, and financial markets. The struggles over power and authority that arise during such interactions are part and parcel of STS as defined by the *Handbook*. Accordingly, the disciplinary range of its authors is also significantly larger than in the *Reader*, including much greater representation of sociology,[6] as well as of political science, policy analysis, and law, which were virtually excluded from the *Reader*'s purview.

The different visions underlying these two representations of STS illustrate again the inevitability of politics in carving out spaces for interdisciplinarity. In this case, the two compilations highlight the topographic unevenness of the territories that pioneers have chosen to chart, for no intellectual ground imagined in the present ever comes empty of undulations, claims, and settlements. The *Reader* delineated the space of science studies through the lenses of exemplary works that could be located in identifiable disciplinary traditions, consistent with Daston's (2009: 800) characterization of the field as consisting of a 'battery of disciplinary perspectives turned upon science and technology.' In Toulmin's terms, quoted by Shapin (1979: 90), this was still a form of disciplinary marching, even if the marches led to relatively unfamiliar destinations. The *Handbook*, by contrast, sought to define the territory of STS in terms of questions, methods, and styles of work that did not sit comfortably within existing disciplines. The emphasis here was not on what the classic texts said, but how they might be mixed and matched to illuminate new areas of technoscientific endeavor and associated transformations in social thought. Interdisciplinarity, as conceived here, was distinctly a mode of weaving, to facilitate the creation of tents and tapestries that only new generations of scholars apprenticed in a field called STS would fully appreciate and, in their turn, extend.

Retreats and Advances

Travelers in new lands need ingenuity, resources, and agility to survive. Unexpectedness is the order of the day; that is both the seduction and the danger of seeking what lies beyond the known. STS's uncharted territory has proved to contain risks as well as rewards, as illustrated by the turf wars within and beyond its borders. Apart from questions about the accuracy and intellectual coherence of its accounts of science and technology, STS has also encountered questions concerning its utility. Such challenges are not unique to STS. Other branches of the human and social sciences have also confronted skepticism and have had to retrench or change their methods.[7] A field that stakes its authority on character-izing knowledge in new, boundary-crossing ways, however, exposes special vulnerabilities because it appears to gnaw at the roots of all science (in the encompassing sense of *Wissenschaft*, or systematic knowledge acquisition and learning). Developments within the field at the turn of the century testify to the difficulty of preserving identity and asserting a steady claim to resources in the interdisciplinary space occupied by STS.

Often unfair and unpardonably trivializing, the science wars and cross-disciplinary struggles of the 1990s nevertheless took their toll on STS. So did external events in the world in the first decade of the twenty-first century, most notably the September 11, 2001 terrorist attacks in the United States (hereafter 9/11), the mounting threat of global climate change, and the financial crisis of 2008. Coupled to these big events was the gradual penetration of electronic communications into politics and everyday life, increasing the speed, superficial-ity, and spatial range of communications among social actors – and altering the balance among visual, verbal, and mathematical modes of expression. In this world, the Israeli political scientist Yaron Ezrahi presciently predicted, knowledge itself would become depreciated as a thing of value, the place of information gradually overtaken by what he called 'outformations.' In contrast to information, outformations in Ezrahi's account constitute 'a much more diffused configuration of pictures, sounds, narratives, frames, etc.' They have the intensity, multidimensionality, and affective depth of wisdom, but they lack wisdom's connection to specific synthesizing and organizing intellects. Instead, 'outformations appear to be out there without specific relations to any visible agents.' Yet they also have an immediacy and a power to persuade that are lacking in the abstract, delocalized, formal, and logical constructs of scientific knowledge (Ezrahi 2004: 258).

The apparently decreasing role of scientific information in social and political life raises an analytic question of some significance for STS: to what extent does, or should, *scientific* knowledge and *science*-based technologies retain primacy as central objects of concern for the field? In demarcating itself from other disciplinary spaces, has STS in effect lost its meridians, because – after 9/11, global warming, and risky derivatives – it is society's uses of science and technology, rather than their disciplining impacts on society, that have gained in significance? If society, rather than science, regains centrality in the analytic frame, then do STS scholars have any special authority to provide insights into the science-technology-society complex? That question looms even larger if, as critics such as Daston have maintained, STS never has been more than a collection of loosely coupled disciplinary perspectives on science and technology – a marriage of convenience rather than of intellectual compatibility and coherence. Some intellectual retreats and numerous institutional advances of the turn of the century illustrate, on balance, moves toward answering the last question in the affirmative, thereby confirming the growing disciplinary autonomy of STS.

It is difficult to catch the history of a field in motion: each individual movement seems too contingent and local to add up to a bigger picture that carries a larger meaning; and a field's overall dynamics are heterogeneous, even contradictory, to the point of resisting generalities. 'Fields,' moreover, are represented by national communities that have followed different evolutionary paths, even if always engaging in transnational cross-talk. Nonetheless, there seems to be a dawning recognition that the version of STS represented by the 1995 *Handbook* mapped out a domain of inquiry at once capacious enough to facilitate systematic inquiry and bounded enough to provide definition for an expanding community. One sign is that the entanglement of science, power, and politics, which the *Handbook* explored and which American STS scholars had engaged with for decades, has moved closer to the center of European research agendas that previously took the lab or clinic as their primary domain. By the same token the vision espoused by the *Reader*, of a field driven principally by its focus on what Biagioli (1999: xii) termed a 'prepackaged' science, has proved constraining and theoretically ungenerative. Several moves by individual scholars and collectives support this reading.

Bruno Latour, perhaps the most visible of all the figures identified with STS, offers one instantiation – through actions as much as words. In 2006, Latour abandoned his almost 25-year association with the École des Mines, a prestigious engineering school, to join Sciences Po, France's premier training ground for public affairs, first as professor and then as research director. Around this time, too, his writings moved increasingly away from the inner workings of laboratories and other scientific workplaces to law and to politics in the large (e.g., Latour 2004a, 2010). At the same time, he diversified his activities from producing books and articles to the more spectacular genre of museum displays. His 2005 collaboration with Peter Weibel of the Center for Art and Media in Karlsruhe on technologies of political representation offers a notable example (Latour and Weibel 2005). In a much discussed article, Latour (2004b) seemed to abandon his earlier commitment to the construction of scientific facts, prompted by the reality and urgency of climate change (cf. Daston 2009: 799–800). More accurately, but also symptomatically, Latour here extended his constructivist imagination to the production of *political* facts or, as he called them, 'matters of concern.'[8] Michel Callon, Latour's longtime colleague and co-developer of the widely cited STS framework of actor-network theory, likewise turned his attention to politics, collaborating with two well-known French political scientists to explore anew the role of democracy in technical decision making (Callon et al. 2009).

In Britain, the shock of the mad cow epidemic and the resulting reexamination of the role of expertise in the British state catapulted the issue of public participation (or public engagement as it was more often called there) to the top of the STS research agenda. Contravening key elements of British civic epistemology, the mad cow case revealed the nation's government and its advisers as fallible, hostage to private interests, inadequately precautionary, and hence undeserving of the trust that had historically entitled small elites to see and speak for the people (Jasanoff 2005: 56, 256–8). Both the UK government and academic observers of its handling of technical controversies turned a critical eye on relations between experts and publics. A powerful line of critique blamed the British state for depreciating lay knowledge and constructing a 'deficit model' of an ignorant public continually in need of education and enlightenment by better informed experts (Irwin and Wynne 1996).[9] A House of Lords (2000) report on science and society echoed these concerns, in part because the authoring committee was advised by Brian Wynne, a leading STS scholar and coiner of the term 'deficit model.' Conducted in 2003, *GM Nation?*, Britain's unique if inconclusive experiment in consulting the public on its preferences with respect to genetically modified crops, offers another example. Old habits die hard, especially those durably rooted in a nation's political traditions. By the end of the first decade of the new century, British politics entered a period of oscillation between what Robert Doubleday and Brian Wynne (2011) have characterized as opening up and closing down the avenues of public engagement. For our purposes, however, this period of flux in Britain illustrates both the growing shift within STS to macro-scale political questions, and the gradual uptake of STS insights in the political realm.

Reactions in the United States were also colored by local political circumstances, which included the George W. Bush administration's widely criticized flight from science and reason, especially on the issue of anthropogenic climate change. Also relevant was the institutional history of STS in America – a history inflected with greater attention to graduate professional training than in Europe. The pervasive anti-intellectualism of the period's national politics underscored for some STS analysts the dangers of relativism and led them, like Latour, to distance themselves from constructivist accounts of scientific facts. Others, however, read the field's intellectual history in less reductionist terms, and neither the science wars nor the Bush era's anti-scientism prompted them to significantly change direction. In the continued institutionalization of advanced degree programs, STS in the United States and Canada seemed unconsciously to embrace the understanding of disciplines as constituted by training new generations in new habits of thought (Dear and Jasanoff 2010).

Symptomatic of the queasiness that some STS scholars apparently felt about being on the wrong side of public scientific controversies was a noticeable surge in works stressing the corruption of science through money or special interests.[10] Contributors to this genre, led prominently by historians, focused on the purchase of science to deny that smoking causes cancer (Brandt 2007), to contradict the hypothesis that carbon released through human activity causes climate change (Oreskes and Conway 2008), and to strategically manufacture ignorance when powerful actors did not want their interests prejudiced by uncomfortable facts (Proctor and Schiebinger 2008). Particularly noteworthy was a turn in some STS work toward accepting consensus in science as a sufficient marker of truth (Oreskes 2004). Applauded in some political circles, such analyses casually over-rode a generation of research on the complex social relations between boundary drawing, persuasion, and perceived facticity (Shapin 1994, see also Gieryn 1995, Jasanoff 1990). As a result, this whistle-blowing literature could not explain why a strong scientific consensus was not alone enough to persuade skeptical publics to turn matters of fact into matters of concern.

Fortunately for the field, these intellectual regressions were offset by institutional advances indicating an increased valorization of STS in academic settings. A striking feature of STS's turn-of-the-century development in the United States was a rise in new training programs, albeit often at levels short of the doctorate, and the continued mobility of STS-trained scholars into prestigious schools and departments, including business, public policy, communications, sociology, and anthropology. Patchy and unsystematic as they were, these movements testified to STS's growing ability to speak across disciplines while maintaining enough definition for the field's trainees to represent themselves, uniquely, as STS scholars.[11] Again, this is consistent with the expansive picture of STS presented by the *Handbook*: as a field conversant with the issues and problems confronting the social sciences in general, but possessing its own theories and idioms with which to address them.

Conclusion

The case of science and technology studies represents a very particular node and moment in the evolution of interdisciplinarity. STS was not the result of boundary-crossing conversations dictated by pressures to solve urgent social problems, as with sustainability studies or global health. It was not an instance of established disciplines borrowing tools and models from others to further their own core inquiries, as when political science seeks to learn from psychology or economics from neuroscience. Nor was it merely an example of interdisciplinarity arising through two or more disciplines questioning each other's methods in agonistic-antagonistic play, although the Edinburgh school's sociology of scientific knowledge did grow in part out of dissatisfaction with philosophical accounts of science. All of these modes of interaction begin with disciplinary lines already laid down; they see the challenge of interdisciplinarity as fostering collaboration across pre-existing divisions.

STS, by contrast, is a new island in the high seas of knowledge, coaxed into being through multiple, convergent, intellectual and social upheavals of the later twentieth century: postmodern skepticism about power structures and authoritative institutions; the rise of reflexivity and critical theory as frames of analysis; worries about the control of runaway technological systems; increasing use of scientific expertise to justify political choices; and of course the speed and penetration of discoveries in many areas of technoscience that transformed the world within one short century into a global village of genetically alike human beings.

STS's distinctive mission has not been only to speak across the boundaries of other fields, although that was and remains a problem. It has also, and even more, been to secure a place of its own in crowded academic waters that seem at times to leave no room for emergent territories and unknown languages. The story of STS's formation is therefore preeminently a political story, told in this chapter as a sequence of struggles: with science and scientists about the authoritativeness of STS's outsider representations; with established disciplines about the need for new questions and new methods and discourses with which to address them; and even among STS's own practitioners about how far to press the struggle for disciplinary independence.

Michael Crow (2010: 52) dismissed the disciplines as organizations 'hidebound by behavioral norms of astonishing orthodoxy.' Accurate as a descriptive statement, his indictment nevertheless misses a crucial feature of disciplinarity: its authorizing function. For as the history of the world attests, asking questions is a potentially risky business; to be on safe ground both the questions and the questioners need to come from somewhere recognizable. It has been the function of disciplines to provide that firm grounding, to signal to a potentially hostile world that an interrogator is coming from a known place, with kin or clan prepared to endorse her criticisms and join a fray on her behalf should one ensue. Disciplines warrant not only particular ways of examining the world but also the people conducting the investigation. It is hardly surprising, then, that the birth of a new discipline such as STS should have proved to be conflict-ridden. Yet, if modernity holds any lessons, it is that no source of power can remain forever insulated from questions about its assumptions. To the extent that STS serves that function with regard to science and technology, its moment has arrived – not a moment too soon.

Notes

1 Though Latour became by far the more visible exponent of the French school of science studies, a significant part of his early work was written in close collaboration with Michel Callon, his colleague at the École des Mines in Paris. In particular, ANT, the main analytic concept that emerged from French STS in the 1980s, was a joint intellectual product, and Callon should be credited with naming it.

2 In the preceding paragraphs, Sokal charges Barnes and Bloor (1982) with not clarifying the distinctions between ontology, epistemology, and the sociology of knowledge, though their text (quoted by Sokal) appears to draw just such distinctions.

3 We decided as a matter of editorial policy that none of the editors would contribute articles of our own.

4 Biagioli was the sole named editor, but it was produced 'in consultation with' Peter Galison and Everett Mendelsohn of the Department of History of Science at Harvard, as well as three significant women ethnographers of science, Donna J. Haraway, Emily Martin, and Sharon Traweek.

5 Bruno Latour (1987: 174), for example, has this to say on the subject: 'I will use the term **technoscience** from now on, to describe all the elements tied to the scientific contents no matter how dirty, unexpected or foreign they seem, and the expression **"science and technology"**, in quotation marks, to designate *what is kept of technoscience* once all the trials of responsibility have been settled' (emphases in original).

6 The relative dearth of sociologists among the *Reader*'s authors is striking given the centrality of sociology of science within STS. Bloor and Barnes were apparently excluded, along with figures such as Kuhn and Merton, as too 'classic' (though the *Reader* contains essays from the 1970s). It is harder to explain the exclusion of prominent American STS authors writing in a sociological tradition, except as reflecting the kind of boundary work described above.

7 Examples of challenges from outside the field include periodic assaults on social science funding at the National Science Foundation (cf. Mervis 2006), and the real or threatened closure or downsizing of some sociology departments in the United States in the 1990s and beyond. Internally, the social sciences are frequently under pressure to 'scientize' their methods through adoption of formal models (e.g., rational choice, game theory, social networks) or use of quantitative methods based on large empirical data sets.

8 Illustrating competing but complementary dynamics and tendencies within STS, American scholars also turned their attention to the co-production of knowledge and politics, but with significantly greater attention to the historical embeddedness and institutional complexity of such developments (Jasanoff 2004). Significantly, American scholarship in this vein did not focus only, or even primarily, on the agenda-setting moments when new 'matters of concern' emerge, but rather on the wide-ranging transformations in institutions, identities, discourses, and representations at moments of co-production in natural and social orders.

9 To be sure, not all STS scholars shifted toward the broad engagement with institutions other than those of science and technology contemplated in the 1995 *Handbook*. A notable example of continuing preoccupation with the philosophy of expertise, divorced from contexts of uptake and interpretation, can be found in the work of Harry Collins and Rob Evans (2007).

10 This surge was not limited to STS scholars, but included books, articles, and websites generated by regulators (e.g., David Michaels), legal scholars (e.g., Thomas McGarity and Wendy Wagner), journalists (e.g., Chris Mooney, Rick Weiss), and non-profit groups (e.g., Union of Concerned Scientists). This is not the place to discuss in detail the body of US work decrying the corruption of science in America produced during

and after the Bush administration. The important point is that some STS scholars, in contributing to this larger literature, were contributing in their own ways to the 'view from nowhere' characterization of science that holds dominion in US civic epistemology, and thereby were playing out underlying cultural scripts (Jasanoff 2005). This, of course, also marked an intellectual retreat from the constructivist and co-productionist accounts of knowledge generated within STS from the 1970s onward.

11 For example, when an STS-trained colleague recently came up for promotion at a public policy school at a major US research university, I was asked to write a letter explaining what it means to be trained in this field and how it contributes to the study of public policy.

References

Barnes, B. and Bloor, D. (1982) 'Relativism, Rationalism and the Sociology of Knowledge', in M. Hollis and S. Lukes (eds.) *Rationality and Relativism*, (pp. 21–4) Oxford: Blackwell.

Beck, U. (2000) 'The Cosmopolitan Perspective: Sociology of the Second Age of Modernity', *British Journal of Sociology*, 51(1): 79–105.

— (2006) *The Cosmopolitan Vision*, trans. C. Cronin, Cambridge: Polity Press.

Berreby, D. (1994) 'And Now, Overcoming All Binary Oppositions, It's . . . That Damned Elusive Bruno Latour', *Lingua Franca*, 4(6): 1.

Biagioli, M. (ed.) (1999) *The Science Studies Reader*, New York: Routledge.

Bijker, W., Pinch, T. and Hughes, T. (eds.) (1987) *The Social Construction of Technological Systems*, Cambridge, MA: MIT Press.

Bloor, D. (1991 [1976]) *Knowledge and Social Imagery*, Chicago, IL: University of Chicago Press.

— (2007) 'Epistemic Grace: Antirelativism as Theology in Disguise', *Common Knowledge*, 13(2–3): 250–80.

Brandt, A. M. (2007) *The Cigarette Century: The Rise, Fall, and Deadly Persistence of the Product that Defined America*, New York: Basic Books.

Bush, V. (1945) *Science – The Endless Frontier*, Washington, DC: US Government Printing Office.

Callon, M., Lascoumes, P. and Barthe, Y. (2009) *Acting in an Uncertain World: An Essay on Technical Democracy*, Cambridge, MA: MIT Press.

Collins, H. and Evans, R. (2007) *Rethinking Expertise*, Chicago, IL: University of Chicago Press.

Crow, M. M. (2010) 'Beyond the "new normal" in American Higher Education: Toward Perpetual Innovation', in D. W. Breneman and P. J. Yakoboski (eds.) *Smart Leadership for Higher Education in Difficult Times*, (pp. 50–69) Cheltenham: Edward Elgar.

Daston, L. (2009) 'Science Studies and the History of Science', *Critical Inquiry*, 35: 798–813.

Dear, P. and Jasanoff, S. (2010) 'Dismantling Boundaries in Science and Technology Studies', *Isis*, 101(4): 759–74.

Doubleday, R. and Wynne, B. (2011) 'Despotism and Democracy in the United Kingdom: Experiments in Reframing Citizenship', in S. Jasanoff (ed.) *Reframing Rights*, (pp. 239–62) Cambridge, MA: MIT Press.

Ezrahi, Y. (1984) 'Science and Utopia in Late 20th Century Pluralist Democracy', in E. Mendelsohn and H. Nowotny (eds.) *Nineteen Eighty-Four: Science Between Utopia and Dystopia*, (pp. 273–90) Dordrecht: Reidel.

— (2004) 'Science and the Political Imagination in Contemporary Democracies,' in S. Jasanoff (ed.) *States of Knowledge: The Co-Production of Science and Social Order* (pp. 254–73). New York: Routledge.

Foucault, M. (1980) *Power/Knowledge: Selected Interviews and Other Writings, 1972–1977*, New York: Vintage.

Gibbons, M., Limoges, C., Nowotny, H., Schwartzman, S., Scott, P. and Trow, M. (1994) *The New Production of Knowledge*, London: Sage Publications.

Gieryn, T. F. (1995) 'Boundaries of Science', in S. Jasanoff et al. (eds.) *Handbook of Science and Technology Studies*, (pp. 393–443). Thousand Oaks CA: Sage Publications.

Gross, P. R. and Levitt, N. (1994) *Higher Superstition: The Academic Left and its Quarrels with Science*, Baltimore, MD: Johns Hopkins University Press.

House of Lords Select Committee on Science and Technology (2000) *Third Report: Science and Society*, House of Lords papers 1999–2000, 38 HL, London: The Stationery Office.

Irwin, A. and Wynne, B. (eds.) (1996) *Misunderstanding Science? The Public Reconstruction of Science and Technology*, Cambridge: Cambridge University Press.

Jasanoff, S. (1990) *The Fifth Branch: Science Advisers as Policymakers*, Cambridge, MA: Harvard University Press.

— (ed.) (2004) *States of Knowledge: The Co-Production of Science and Social Order*, London: Routledge.

— (2005) *Designs on Nature: Science and Democracy in Europe and the United States*, Princeton, NJ: Princeton University Press.

— (2007) 'Making Order: Law and Science in Action', in E. Hackett et al. (eds.) *Handbook of Science and Technology Studies*, (pp. 761–86) 3rd edn., Cambridge, MA: MIT Press.

— (2010a) 'A Field of its Own: The Emergence of Science and Technology Studies', in R. Frodeman, J. T. Klein, and C. Mitcham (eds.) *Oxford Handbook of Interdisciplinarity*, (pp. 191–205) Oxford: Oxford University Press.

— (2010b) 'A Social Contract for the Life Sciences: The US Case', in S. Rodotà and M. Tallacchini (eds.) *Trattato di Biodiritto*, (pp. 103–124) Milan: Giuffré.

— (2011) *Reframing Rights: Bioconstitutionalism in the Genetic Age*, Cambridge, MA: MIT Press.

Jasanoff, S., Markle, G. E., Petersen, J. C. and Pinch, T. (eds.) (1995) *Handbook of Science and Technology Studies*, Thousand Oaks, CA: Sage Publications.

Kuhn, T. S. (1962) *The Structure of Scientific Revolutions*, Chicago, IL: University of Chicago Press.

Latour, B. (1986) 'Visualization and Cognition: Thinking with Eyes and Hands', in *Knowledge and Society: Studies in the Sociology of Culture Past and Present*, 6: 1–40.

— (1987) *Science in Action: How to Follow Scientists and Engineers through Society*, Cambridge, MA: Harvard University Press.

— (1988) *The Pasteurisation of France*, Cambridge, MA: Harvard University Press.

— (1990) 'Drawing Things Together,' in M. Lynch and S. Woolgar (eds.) *Representation in Scientific Practice*, (pp. 19–68) Cambridge, MA: MIT Press.

— (2004a) *Politics of Nature: How to Bring the Sciences into Democracy*, Cambridge, MA: Harvard University Press.

— (2004b) 'Why has Critique Run Out of Steam? From Matters of Fact to Matters of Concern', *Critical Inquiry*, 30: 225–48.

— (2010) *The Making of Law: An Ethnography of the Conseil d'Etat*, trans. M. Brilman and A. Pottage, Cambridge: Polity Press.

Latour, B. and Weibel, P. (eds.) (2005) *Making Things Public – Atmospheres of Democracy*, Cambridge, MA: MIT Press.

Latour, B. and Woolgar, S. (1979) *Laboratory Life: The Social Construction of Scientific Facts*, Beverley Hills: Sage Publications; republished as (1986) *Laboratory Life: The Construction of Scientific Facts*, Princeton, NJ: Princeton University Press.

Maddox, J. (1977) 'Review' of I. Spiegel-Rösing and D. de S. Price (eds.) *Science, Technology, and Society: A Cross-disciplinary Perspective* in *New Scientist*, October 27: 235.

Mervis, J. (2006) 'Senate Panel Chair Asks Why NSF Funds Social Sciences', *Science*, 312(5775): 829.

Mukerji, C. (1990) *A Fragile Power: Scientists and the State*, Princeton, NJ: Princeton University Press.

Nader, L. (1972) 'Up the Anthropologist – Perspectives Gained from Studying Up', in D. H. Hymes (ed.) *Reinventing Anthropology*, (pp. 284–311) New York: Pantheon Books.

Nowotny, H., Scott, P. and Gibbons, M. (2001) *Re-Thinking Science: Knowledge and the Public in an Age of Uncertainty*, Cambridge: Polity.

Oreskes, N. (2004) 'The Scientific Consensus on Climate Change', *Science*, 306(5702): 1686.

Oreskes, N. and Conway, E. M. (2009) *Merchants of Doubt: How a Handful of Scientists Obscured the Truth on Issues from Tobacco Smoke to Global Warming*, New York: Bloomsbury Press.

Proctor, R. and Schiebinger, L. (eds.) (2008) *Agnotology: The Making and Unmaking of Ignorance*, Palo Alto: Stanford University Press.

Ross, A. (1996) *Science Wars*, Durham: Duke University Press.

Shapin, S. (1979) 'Review' of I. Spiegel-Rösing and D. de S. Price (eds.) *Science, Technology, and Society: A Cross-Disciplinary Perspective*, in *British Journal for the History of Science*, 12(1): 90–1.

— (1994) *A Social History of Truth: Civility and Science in 17th Century England*, Chicago, IL: University of Chicago Press.

Sokal, A. D. (1996) 'Transgressing the Boundaries: Toward a Transformative Hermeneutics of Quantum Gravity', *Social Text*, 46/47: 217–52.

— (1998) 'What the *Social Text* Affair Does and Does Not Prove', *Critical Quarterly*, 40(2): 3–18.

Spiegel-Rösing, I. and Price, D. de S. (eds.) (1977) *Science, Technology, and Society: A Cross-Disciplinary Perspective*, Beverley Hills, CA: Sage.

5   Unexpected Consequences and an Unanticipated Outcome

Marilyn Strathern and
Elena Khlinovskaya Rockhill

In their introduction, Andrew Barry and Georgina Born place the Cambridge Genetics Knowledge Park (CGKP) at a rather undeveloped end of a spectrum of possibilities in interdisciplinary engagement. The study of its operations was also different in scope and ethnographic possibility from others in this volume. Instead of merging the analysis with what is presented elsewhere, we retain this dual singularity. We do so partly because we wish a certain outcome to emerge with its own plausibility. Stated in advance the outcome, which has to do with the way social science is valued and evaluated, might seem to come from a complaint or at the least from an agenda. But that was not anticipated by either of us. We do in retrospect think that the study of the Park has something to offer the apprehension of one of the persuasive contexts in which interdisciplinary becomes a public virtue, namely what is broadly collected under the rubric of 'science and society'.

Part of the interest of the CGKP lay in its development as a total social phenomenon: we see interdisciplinarity taking an institutional form. To appreciate the point, it will be necessary to spend some time on detail.

The Impetus

A series of conjunctions

An expressed interest in multi- or inter-disciplinarity has, for some years now, held centre stage in UK research policy. Among other things, it is taken as an index of engagement with the complexity of the 'real world' and the problems and issues it presents. At the same time, the formulation of what is called the relationship between science and society has shifted from a deficit model of public understanding never catching up with science to a proactive hope for public engagement with science. On occasion these two kinds of engagements have been joined together. This happened very specifically, over a period of five years between 2002 and 2007, in the social form of 'genetics knowledge parks' (GKPs). There was indeed much hope about the kind of public impact they would have.

When in 2001 the Department of Health (DH) and Department of Trade and Industry (DTI) sent out their tenders for the knowledge parks, two elements seemed axiomatic in the ideas to be developed. Explicitly, the first was that the parks would contribute to the new science and society debates that were making the public a significant reference point for scientific endeavour of all kinds. The second was that they would be multidisciplinary, this being invariably interpreted as bringing together different expertise from science – clinical and social science communities among others. Within the overall programme, one particular conjunction also appeared to stand for this larger conjunction. Emphasis was to be placed on ways to take into account the 'ethical, legal and social implications' of new genetic knowledge. Familiarly known as ELSI, an acronym originating in the United States,[1] this conjunction was to be addressed by all the parks, although it came to figure more prominently in some than in others. It was in its conception also at once multidisciplinary and oriented to the public.

Clearly ELSI signals engagement, minimally insofar as the public was thought to be the source of questions and problems that took genetic knowledge as having 'implications' for it; maximally (as the GKPs scheme envisaged) to facilitate the development of genetics knowledge for disease prevention and treatment pathways in socially acceptable and thus effective and deliverable terms.[2] Clearly, too, the very configuration of issues as a set (ethical, legal, social) indicated that multiple domains were being brought together. Now within ELSI itself, the same conjunction of ideas appeared again. For, within this configuration, a microcosm of the three components seemed to be epitomised by what lay in one of them: that labelled 'social'. 'Social implications' carried a stronger connotation of public involvement than did ethics or law, indeed pointed to 'society' in its largest sense; at the same time, in so far as expertise was concerned, it summoned more than a single domain. In contrast to the more narrowly defined law and ethics, within itself 'the social' embraced facets from various disciplines across the social sciences.

In terms of aims and ambitions, then, envisaged as a conjunction between multidisciplinarity on the one hand and public engagement on the other, there was an intriguing replication across different ideational levels – from ideas about the GKPs themselves, to ELSI as a component in the GKP programmes, and to 'the social' as a component of ELSI.

Could one discern any consequences to this nesting series of ambitions? In the way this particular conjunction worked itself out institutionally, as each of the GKP programmes was put into practice, was there any special relationship between the 'social' component of ELSI, the ELSI component of those parks where it was prominent and the GKPs themselves? We speak from the hindsight of knowing that ELSI figured prominently in the original proposal submitted by the Cambridge GKP.[3] We also speak from the hindsight of knowing something of the fate of the conjunction at these different levels in the Cambridge case, and of the GKPs overall.

There is one obvious set of issues in the Cambridge case in the way it was repeated across these different levels of activity: how they came to an end. The DH and DTI agreed that after the first five years the parks would not, as they might otherwise have done, continue to receive funding. The CGKP was the first for whom the termination of the scheme was made evident; it had highlighted ELSI among other things (other things including a strong public health orientation), rather than research projects with more clearly defined outputs for genetic knowledge. There is no necessary connection. However, we may note that within the CGKP the ELSI component was in fact the first to be redistributed, a process that had begun before the termination of all the parks was apparent. By redistributed we mean that the staff members recruited to the ELSI team were always somewhat at a remove from the CGKP core, and that what might have been the public outreach aspect of their interests was developed elsewhere in the CGKP – for example, through quite separate 'public involvement' arrangements. Other aspects of the CGKP's activities, especially those centred on the former Public Health Genetics Unit, proved more robust than ELSI. Finally, within ELSI itself, of all its components it was the social science ('social') component that was least supported and seemed the most 'marginal' – and the first to be abandoned. An early decision was made not to fill a vacant post, and by comparison with the more enduring ethics and law its contributions appeared least relevant and most ambiguous in relation to the CGKP programme overall.

Other parks will have had different configurations of emphasis in their activities. But the replication of *these* circumstances in *this* case leads us to ask whether there were particular pressures on the institutional conjunction of multidisciplinarity and public engagement that led to a ricochet effect.

An internalist account[4]

We propose to take advantage of the ethnographic opportunity afforded one of us (EKR) to construct an internalist account – that is, one that addresses the CGKP as an organisation largely from within its own parameters. While the commentary is intended to be critical, it derives its critical perspective from examining the abutment of different projects from inside the working of the organisation instead of creating them from a perspective purported to be from the (an) outside.[5] Of course all accounts, in being context bound, are internalist in some sense or other; it would be interesting, though it is not an interest pursued here, to see the extent to which changing the scale of analysis in this case would bring extra (different) rather than just additional (more of the same) information. Changing the scale, for instance, could mean enlarging the sphere of what is 'within' to embrace the workings of British politics or late twentieth-century management practices or international studies of science insights. Some of these particular issues nonetheless creep in, and it might indeed be objected that what follows is not 'internal' enough to the CGKP.

It will become evident that an internalist account is not the same as taking the natives' point of view, though it will work with their constructs. Nor does it bestow any ontological status to the organisation in question beyond the reality that the actors give it. It is of course explicit about its limitations from the perspective of other contexts, although before becoming too anxious about contextual limits it is worth being reminded of Schlecker and Hirch's (2001) discussion of the fallacy of intensifying 'contexts' to enrich understanding when changing scale alters the dimensions of the data. At the same time, one does not need to be ignorant of ('wider') issues elsewhere: indeed we offer the CGKP as, in many of its details, a microcosm of social processes that evidently bear on policymakers and the managers of research. Finally, an internalist account does not debar theoretical approaches that normally describe themselves otherwise – a political economy one, for example, that sees its perspective as always 'larger' than what is on the ground – and we write into the analysis of the CGKP an interest in complexity.

What we mean by this will unfold with the account. Here we note aspects of the CGKP discussed by the authors elsewhere. Khlinovskaya Rockhill (2007) puts the workings of the CGKP into the context of models of knowledge production, examining among other things the kinds of 'need' to which the British government, in supporting the DH/DTI genetics initiatives, thought it was responding. Strathern (2011) compares the goals which the CGKP set itself to the 'promissory' character of research proposals and the speculative synergy of what are imagined as collaborative enterprises. Both papers touch on the futuristic orientation of the CGKP's programme. Now, at about the time when the knowledge parks were being dreamed up, Rip and Shove (2000) pointed out the extent to which appeals to the public as users of research are, at the proposal stage, invariably unspecific – the very feature that also confers the advantage of allowing academics to link themselves to evidently significant, however distant, goals.[6] The observation would seem to hold for the imagined recipients of GKP benefit, who would be brought better information and enhanced knowledge. For a self-consciously knowledge-based society, the GKPs promised a great deal: in this (futuristic) regard, their hope was very much of its time.

The Study

Implementation

We have asked whether there were particular pressures on the institutional conjunction of multidisciplinarity and public engagement. The pressures we have in mind are those that would have taken shape and had effect on the working lives and policy decisions of employees and associates of the Park, and thus on the Park as an organisation or institution. We approach the question though considering some of the social consequences of implementing the aims and ambitions of the Cambridge GKP.[7]

The CGKP charged itself with developing public health genetics – an emerging concept hitherto – aiming to contribute to the development of policy in the application of genetics for health services (CGKP 2003: 2). In the words of the Director, the Knowledge Park was to be an inter-institutional 'knowledge broker' that brought together people and information in different combinations. This brokerage entailed management: knowledge management (creating, disseminating and exploiting knowledge) and organizational management (internal management of the Public Health Genetics Unit, the CGKP's predecessor and its core facility, as well as various expertise within and beyond the CGKP). In practice this 'bringing together' was embodied in various forms, where knowledge and organizational management often intertwined. Knowledge management included: genetics-related information being pulled together on the CGKP's website; seminars and forums bringing together experts from different disciplines and fields to deliver papers related to a particular topic; publications contributing to the overall knowledge pool; while reports provided evidence-based updated information on various topics. Institutionally, organizational management was required in coordinating the work of the five Public Health Genetics Unit's (PHGU's) teams: genetic epidemiology; ELSI; knowledge and dissemination (with a policy unit, science policy manager and information manager); public health (with education and public involvement officers); and business and administration (with an industry liaison officer and database and Web developers); as well as in conducting seminars, forums and public involvement activities outside PHGU (more on the work of the CGKP is in Khlinovskaya Rockhill 2007).

Across the country, the knowledge parks enjoyed greater or lesser realisation as social entities, in varying degrees of association with or autonomy from local universities. In any event, just as the organisation of knowledge was one of their remits, so the activities of people enrolled on the programmes required organisation. In the Cambridge case this took very obvious social forms through a building that offered office space, through work plans and calendars of events, interpersonal and institutional networks, and the intercollation of jobs and tasks, all under the eye of a central executive team. But while there was much that was thus organised in a strong sense ('managed' organisation), there was much that was not. (We do not imply that this should have been.) It is notable that both elements of the conjunction seemed to be as often below as above the managerial horizon.

The *multidisciplinary* composition of the Park's efforts was evident in public presentations, such as the annual forum, in conference and workshop programmes that ran to a multi-expertise formula, and in publications, many of which involved marshalling contributors from different backgrounds. However, any greater degree of managerial control here would have gone against the open ethos of the Cambridge Park as it flourished under the personal leadership of the Director. The principle was that people would work best according to their own agendas. There was thus no great pressure to convert the multi- into the inter-disciplinary. Indeed, it remained a moot point the extent to which the multidisciplinary strands of CGKP's endeavours achieved the kind of epistemic synergy between people's efforts always hoped for in interdisciplinarity.[8]

This doubt was the more remarkable given that such synergy was evidently achievable on an individual basis, as shown by the work of one of the ELSI team who wove together several strands of her different interests. Within the ELSI part of the programme there was more interaction and engagement between law and ethics than between either of those with sociology (the representative of social science), but overall the three components remained largely outside any central organising or managing of their efforts. Collaboration in multidisciplinary activities might have led to emergent organisation(s), but not much internal organisation emerged either. ELSI members did not have separate representation on the Executive Team (the Director nominally represented them), and between them they produced only one collaborative publication, put out by the CGKP itself.

What exactly *engagement with the public* could or should mean hovered perpetually at the edge of the CGKP agenda. Many of CGKP's outputs could be said to be geared to public information, including informing policy, and there were attempts to engage with specific audiences as local embodiments of a wider public. However, it should be said at once, there was never any intention to set up extensive outreach programmes as such, scepticism being expressed about the potential value of targeting a generic public. Instead, the initial proposal to the DH/DTI sought out health professionals as a segment of the population who were nonetheless, as far as genetics was concerned, 'lay persons' (not CGKP vocabulary) in a position to benefit from training. Training courses were certainly part of the programme, under an Education Officer. Attempts at workshops with persons coming from other segments of the population at large developed late in the programme, and were not fully integrated into the core activities.

Equally, what always remained a question found no single organisational form. On the contrary, the location of public engagement issues moved across the Park.[9] As early as 2004 the Director's intention to play down ELSI and focus on policy work elided public interest with useful policy recommendations, and in his eyes these could be found spread across the CGKP's agenda. A separate post concerned with 'public involvement' was established, but placed outside the ELSI group and alongside those of consultants and the Education Officer in the Public Health Team. If the post had always been envisaged as separate,[10] it was nonetheless something of a surprise to the post-holder that his work had so little to do with the ELSI team. Even more unexpected, on reflection, was the fact that when, after three years or so, this dedicated position fell vacant, like the sociology (social science) ELSI post, it was not filled.[11] It was almost as though public involvement, first marginalised as far as its operations were concerned and then dropping off the list of named jobs, repeated the fate of the 'social'.

Without making too much of the point, there were hints that this was happening *again* in the case of 'policy'. For even the policy experts felt that their work was at times seemingly not understood or taken seriously. Given that policy development was an evident and well-supported plank of the official CGKP programme there seems, then, to have been something unsettling about the very fact of having the public in one's sights. Indeed one might observe that the official strategy, to focus on health professionals, only served to keep the rest of 'the public' at a distance. It did not dispatch them, and it remained this way throughout the life of the Park; in other words, despite the efforts of the Public Involvement Officer, and the policy experts, this key 'distance' was never tackled as an issue.[12] Rather, not knowing when and what part of the public might become an 'audience' for CGKP output was a query that came back again and again.

Despite local surprises, overall there is nothing new here. What engagement with the public could or should mean hovers at the edge of many science and society agendas, and the difficulty of demonstrating epistemic transformation haunts many claims to interdisciplinarity. But might the CGKP experience throw any light on the way these issues continue to be perpetuated as problems?

Classification

Difficulties laid at the door of ELSI were frequently phrased in terms of the academic proclivity of the ELSI team, alleged to be removed from the kinds of practical aspirations that drove the rest of the GGKP. Indeed it is fascinating that the charge of being 'too academic', and its partner 'feet not on the ground', recurred throughout the system. At times policy work was thought by other CGKP members to be too academic, at times the whole CGKP setup was regarded (from a perspective outside) as an academic exercise.[13] It was said (by an outsider) that the CGKP belonged to a 'knowledge elite'. These classifications are worth spelling out.

The rhetoric of the 'practical' versus the 'academic' was an ideational axis that ran through the way the CGKP was modelled in much discussion, and informed the value that the core team put on different pieces of work. The practical was understood in a positive sense as pertaining to 'public service', taken to be a driving motivation founded quite differently from what drove academic work. So where the academic was a 'professional', the service providers were 'expert generalists'. The latter were able to react to real-life issues in a rapid response mode, and could take quick action as against the much slower research-based timetable of the former. Indeed it was because the latter were associated with the core mission of the CGKP, as seen from the centre, that it was possible in a negative sense to talk of work – for example, work holding up the programme – as *too* academic. (It was, on the other hand, impossible to have 'too much' service.) The notion of CGKP as a 'service' provider enabled it at one point to claim an interstitial position between the highly academic, on the one hand, and the very different practical concerns of the DH/DTI with their performance indicators, on the other. For the moment we stay with the simple dichotomy that put the CGKP's aspirations at the 'practical' end.

The dichotomy was also phrased as a contrast in the organisation of knowledge between 'management' and 'research'.[14] Management implied a 'pragmatic' approach to one's place in the organisation, whereas research looked to goals beyond (publications, reputation and so forth).[15] While links to research centres and the like, in the University and academia generally, were encouraged, the CGKP's daily operations did not themselves evince research behaviour, which might have involved them in setting up seminars, interrogating concepts or peer reviewing proposals. Instead, the divide between management and research informed perceptions of the 'usefulness' of knowledge, the demonstrably least useful (the social arm of ELSI) being ipso facto the most removed from core activities. In fact something of the negative way in which social science was perceived became an attribute of it; its research-derived habit of criticising and problematising what to others may have appeared 'common sense', while, crucially, not offering any usable 'solutions' to problems in hand, no doubt contributed to what constantly came over as 'negativity' (a CGKP term) on its part.

How did this happen? ELSI clearly began life as one of the 'communities' embraced within the overarching schema (depicted as an 'umbrella') of the CGKP. In its launching 2002 image, 'social' was firmly there with 'ethical' and 'legal' as one of the planetary-like globes orbiting the CGKP (the others with the epithets 'scientific', 'public health', 'commercial', 'clinical'). Towards the end of the road, in 2006, it was reported that the funders themselves had lost interest in financing academic research in the ethical, legal and social issues of genetics under the GKP scheme.[16] This was the point at which the Director made it evident that academic research in this area would in future have to be taken up by the University, or by dedicated research centres such as those fostered by the Economic and Social Research Council (ESRC) Genomics Network, with the rest of CGKP activity being assimilated by redeveloping the PHGU. This was a unit that the Director had been running before the CGKP took shape: supported by the NHS (National Health Service/Department of Health), it was attached to an NHS Trust teaching hospital, under whose auspices most of the CGKP activities were carried out. Somehow the CGKP would be returning to its original public-health oriented form (PHGU, see n. 32).

That was already in a sense foreshadowed. As soon as one asks what social shape ELSI took when the CGKP was set up, one realises that the split between 'practical' and 'academic' activities that drove the leadership was built in, structurally, from the start. It was embedded in the organisation itself, for the principal members of the ELSI team were all on joint appointments with the University, where they served as lecturers and had departmental and explicit disciplinary loyalties in addition to the other part of their commitment – involvement with CGKP. This was a different institutional arrangement from that of the core team and many other associates who were employees of the Hospital Trust.[17] The creation of ELSI as already 'academic' was there in its association with an academic institution (Cambridge University).[18] Or, to put it otherwise, if we take the way ELSI was institutionally configured, as a particular way of putting multi-/inter-disciplinarity into practice, we can see that the CGKP endorsed, as a social distinction, the ideational difference between academic and non-academic activities.

We come back to the CGKP's particular institutional conjunction of multidisciplinarity and engagement with the public. Did the implicit, or not so implicit, values here put it under pressure? We think they might have done. The argument will require introducing a new element: the nexus of accountability, measurement and evaluation.

Measurement

Now the term in the value-contrast between the practical and the academic that received the consistently higher value (the 'practical') implied laying knowledge open to scrutiny, disseminating it and thus showing it as communicable, applying it to difficult issues, and generally demonstrating engagement with the world and its complicated problems. In other words, practical effort somehow contained within it a gesture towards accountability. Potentially this could have been conceived as accountability *to* society, by virtue of addressing problems and issues that were felt to come *from* society. However the CGKP's service model pushed the idea of society as a sounding board to one side; its leadership was much more interested in imagining and thus anticipating what might be needed, including things society had not yet dreamed up. But whereas anticipating future uses of technology can become something of a discipline in itself (as in developing practices of technology assessment, Rip 2008), there seemed little that was systematic in the way that futures were being modelled.

In general public discourse in the UK over this period, 'accountability' offered a broad rubric under which sat all kinds of protocols about good practice, and it was a time of enthusiasm for formulating and formalising good practices. Here the public appears in a rather different guise, as arbiters or evaluators.[19] Among diverse good practices it was accepted that persons and projects drawing on the public purse needed to demonstrate value for money, of which a component in turn was demonstrating appropriate effort in aiming for (agreed upon or published) targets. Being able to measure outputs, as well as accounting for outcomes, was very much part of the process. However, putting into place procedures for evaluation, let alone deciding on the principles of measurement, was not at all straightforward in this case.

As already noted, it may be hard to show the impact of multidisciplinary but even more so of interdisciplinary effort. It may be equally hard to show the impact of attempts to engage the public. Demonstrating impact is at least assisted if specific outputs are planned in advance, if only because one can 'measure' along the way what seems to be leading to success or not. So an advance schedule of outputs ('performance indicators') would give targets against which to measure current effort. (And, in the interests of optimising work patterns and strategy, management audit procedures would allow a record to be kept of things still in development.) However, the view that was happy to anticipate future public needs was less happy about anticipating CGKP's own outputs. On the contrary, the CGKP directorate was frankly reluctant to close down options in this way, preferring to keep future directions 'open', and made no bones about resisting the wholesale application of performance indicators.[20] In this view, the downside of modelling the CGKP along (corporate/change) management rather than academic lines was precisely that 'some third party in managerialism [always] . . . imposes accountability on you'.

Perhaps it is not surprising, then, that an apparently firm contrast could be softened on occasion. What had been separated out as a contrast between academic and management orientations could also be refigured in such a way that the CGKP, especially as represented by the core facility, PHGU, appeared to belong to neither but to lie *in between* the two. Here its self-description as a 'service' organisation took on a connotation of distinctiveness. Neither scholarly nor public service standards were to be applied in an unmodified way (Khlinovskaya Rockhill 2007: 142). We add an observation of our own: that this qualification applied particularly to the two elements of the institutional conjunction.

Under a multi- or inter-disciplinary regime it is obvious that disciplinary protocols alone cannot verify how far from or close to specific validated approaches any one piece of work is. As in any such exercise, that critical context is frequently replaced by the appeal to communicability (Strathern 2006a). In addition, in the CGKP case, insistence on openness and flexibility meant that it saw topics for investigation on a far horizon, not a near one amenable to disciplinary scrutiny. Its deliberately unbounded conceptual framework was also a changing one, and 'genetics' expanded into a much wider consideration of issues that embraced numerous disciplines from an academic point of view. As for public engagement, and even when audiences can be specified, effective communication is inordinately hard to demonstrate; one can show that people have listened but not that they have heard. But at least the effort towards outreach indicates, in turn, a desire to grasp what people have to say. In the CGKP case the shift of emphasis from 'the social' to 'policy' meant that no such validation of CGKP work need be sought, even though public involvement retained its status as something of a stamp of approval.[21] The in-between mode, that is the sense that CGKP was an 'exceptional' organisation, also informed its stance to its funders – as we shall see.

The ostensible difficulty of validating the activities of an in-between organisa- tion is mirrored, we further suggest, in what we might ascertain about the two components of the Cambridge conjunction when they are taken together, that is, when both multidisciplinarity and engagement with the public are harnessed in tandem. For at times the two components seemed locked into one another in such a way that each had the potential of serving *as a reference point* for the other.[22] By way of example, in one case someone asked to prepare a contribution to a policy document felt he could ignore neither public attitudes nor information about the context that would have to come from several disciplines. Lack of internal collaboration across disciplines had an effect on the way engagement with the public would be seen. Certainly, in the CGKP's own formulation of its remit, it put understanding the social, economic and political influences on genetics side by side with seeking 'a patient and public perspective' that would put genetics knowledge into its ethical, legal and social context (CGKP 2004). More than that, the two components could be used to model one another. Let us explain what we mean.

Representation

Once the ideas behind the tender, proposal and the working schedule of CGKP began to take institutional shape, the social form was (so to speak) turned back again into an ideational one. The directorate produced a running series of diagrams and charts that presented and re-presented the Park in a schematic way. As they succeeded one another, each new depiction or rearrangement of boxes and arrows invariably showed up fresh facets in the relationship between the CGKP's various enterprises and the activities of its different parts. The terms linked in the diagrams had an epitomising function, offering general and abstract concepts to spotlight what the Park was doing. These were persuasive depictions – that is, they were intended to show the coherence and logical objectives of the enterprise. Above all they stressed interconnection.

The CGKP always claimed that the specific value it added to issues in relation to genetic knowledge and public concern was the way it brought together persons and interests that would not have otherwise been connected.[23] Network formation is an inevitable adjunct of mutidisciplinary collaboration, although the Park did not intend to have any specific organising role in the way networks grew up and it was not in the business of drawing network diagrams. But it did wish to offer a convincing image of a collaborative enterprise, the point being that this of itself would point to the synergy and potential for innovation that lay in the combination of effort. And here interdisciplinarity came in. In the context of reformulating models of the Park's scope, aspirations and operations, the term had a fresh appeal. The concept, in the abstract, *stood for* synergy and the potential for innovation through combination.[24] 'Our added value is coordination, bringing everybody together', said the Director on one occasion. A little later he put it, 'our added value is interdisciplinarity. Epidemiology, science, public health, all these expertises and languages – where else will you see it under one roof?'

It was not necessary for the CGKP to be explicit about interdisciplinarity all the time; it only had to show possible connections, for the audience for these diagrams (shown at workshops, conferences, CGKP presentations generally) would have understood the connotations. The diagrams had one interesting character. Such an oblique use of an interdisciplinary model implied that it was already successful (successfully implemented), that is, that power lay in the very connections as such, and even (in some cases it seemed) in the lines and arrows of the diagrams themselves. Now, if interdisciplinarity was used to model ways of thinking about connections, it appeared at once to validate those connections and to hold the position of a reference point for them. Rather than itself being subject to evaluation, it appeared to offer a (positive and self-evident) evaluation of the Park's self-depiction as 'bringing together' different communities. Questions about how successfully connections were pursued, or what might be expected of attempts at integration, were simply obviated.

In the same way, the idea of ELSI (and especially its 'social' element) *stood for* public engagement. Its presence in itself seemingly validated the CGKP's activities in this regard. For the very fact that this was a named component of the CGKP programme implied an orientation to science and society issues. Indeed this was in one sense so written into the CGKP's self-image that at times it appeared to require no extra investigation. With some exceptions,[25] everyone already knew the direction public opinion would take, or could guess it; or else had to conclude it was inscrutable. Either way, social enquiry was not thought to add anything. So the manner in which one went about addressing social issues did not have to be evaluated. Rather, (many) staff worked at their tasks with the public very much in mind, obviating the need to investigate what the public might have in mind.

Aside from the explicit visual models were other modellings, then, of relations between the CGKP's activities. We have taken the rhetorical use of multi-/interdisciplinarity and the presence of ELSI as themselves models of aspirations – in these examples the aspiration to connect everybody together and to be seen to be engaged with the public.[26] We can add here the value-laden binary divides encountered earlier, between academic and practical orientations or research and management practices.

Up to a point, EKR and MS have found this latter modelling a useful resource for analysis – and one of the issues for the present paper is the extent to which the observers' analyses follow the subjects' own. In brief, our strategy has been to work with the concepts and terms offered by our subjects, but to examine rather than reproduce the models themselves. It is clear, nonetheless, that our analysis is being carried out in a context where people reflect upon, depict and themselves 'analyse' what is going on. The study was allowed in as a contribution to internal evaluation procedures, and we hope we have already had face to face as well as written (Khlinovskaya Rockhill and Strathern 2005) input here. In other words, it fitted the Park's 'management' strategy. In so far as our eventual analysis might have taken its place alongside other analyses, however, we would have suspected a 'research' reaction on the part of CGKP too, and for the study to be in competition with these others. What follows is the briefest outline of the way some of the different parts of the CGKP replicated one another, and some of the consequences. We imagine that what was unexpected for us will also have been unexpected for the CGKP.

Outcome

The conjunction: a complex outcome

In summary, the term conjunction draws attention to the CGKP's attempt to do two things together: sustain multidisciplinarity (rhetorically conceived as interdis-ciplinarity) and engage with the public. This tandem formed a specific nexus of problems and issues for the ethos and practice of accountability. The same nexus seemingly appeared at three ideational levels of the CGKP's ambitions, to give the effect of an interlocking set of issues. When we looked further at the operation of the CGKP, taking it as a social entity, we found a series of incidents to do with the disposition of resources. The series (CGKP in relation to other parks; ELSI in relation to the rest of the CGKP's programme; the 'social' in relation to other ELSI components) is now to be understood not only as an ideational but as a social phenomenon. Similar events (in this case to do with termination of funding and diversion of resources elsewhere) seemingly cropped up at the different points, and thus appeared to cascade across these three levels. This must remain a particular set of observations, in so far as they depend on the initial observations about the fate of ELSI in the Cambridge example.[27] But what the rest of the paper has shown is that, particular as this was as a starting point, there was in the system we have been describing (the system comprising the CGKP, its effects, its social fields, its managed and emergent organisation) a similar ricochet effect over other parts of the same series.

These are not unrelated to the fact that the disposition of resources touched on accountability, that is, on the effectiveness of accountability procedures: decisions over funding were a judgment on what was (or was not) perceived to be value for money (see Miller 2005). We have been describing at least two further cascade effects connected to accountability issues. (There will have been others. We suspect a not dissimilar story could have been told of the public involvement portfolio or of some policy endeavours, even education – or commerce in the search for a sellable product.)[28]

The first cascade concerns evaluation rather directly. Frustration was expressed in the early days by the directorate at the inability of 'the social' end of ELSI investigations to point to the value they were adding to the general mix. It seemed hard to grasp the usefulness to which its findings could be put – even that there were findings. Aside from academic contributions, then, the potential outputs did not seem clear. This was a question of the communicability and applicability of the results of social science work, something that also affected the whole ELSI contribution as a coherent programme. As we have seen, an ELSI programme as such never emerged in a strong form. In a weak form, in terms of the works of its individual members, it had some very notable successes. Yet it seemed hard to demonstrate likely impact. Despite the public stance of the CGKP, that it did not want to tie up its activities with performance indicators, it was precisely in indicators of progress that there seemed a shortfall, that is, of deliverables in what the social end of the ELSI programme could document. One reason lay possibly in the way in which the ideas of exclusive 'academic' research kept encroaching on how ELSI activities were classified. This made it hard for their contributions to the public output of the CGKP, as opposed to disciplinary concerns, to be identified. As far as the CGKP as a whole went, the firmness of the principled objections of the directorate to performance indicators contributed to the sponsors' (DH, DTI) final evaluation. In the absence of such indicators, it was hard for its sponsors to document the extent to which it had met its targets.

In sum, in the context of seeking evidence of substantial, applicable, communicable outputs, the very issue of evaluation (how you measure performance) that seemed a deficit in relation to 'social'/ELSI activities within the Park was the same issue that created a credibility deficit for the Park as a whole. And it was not so only in the eyes of outside funders: there is evidence that CGKP staff would have liked to have been clearer about the value of what they were doing. They could have put up with much more guidance in their plans, targets to work towards, feedback on their activities and evaluation of the results.[29]

The second cascade concerns the split between 'practical'/'service' and 'academic' activities within the composition of the CGKP, for that internally reproduced (replicated) the Park's external relationship to the University as a whole (the Park's practical axis, the University's academic one). The same is true of the CGKP's relationship with the other GKPs. For despite being sometimes charged with being 'elitist' or not 'on the ground', the CGKP was also regarded as the least academic – in the sense of the least grounded in research or otherwise research-focused activities – of them all.

First conclusion

The conclusion is not one we were expecting: that the 'social' element of ELSI could be one of the keys to the CGKP's overall fate. Yet consider this. By contrast with the other parks, the way the open horizons of the CGKP were constantly stressed meant that, in its general orientation, it was actually quite close to and echoed the orientation of the academic/research/social end of its internal activities. Elsewhere we (Khlinovskaya Rockhill and Strathern 2005) have sketched the paradox of the research-like elements in the CGKP when it was service and non-research goals that were strongly emphasised by the centre.[30] For we know that this was the last thing that would have been overtly claimed to have been the case. On the contrary, the directorate explicitly put value on and strengthened other areas (such as public health) *at the expense of* ELSI/the social. Was it taking resources away from the very arena that might have been crucial to its success?

It could be that a fatal flaw was not taking the opportunity of its ELSI appointments, and even more so the 'social' dimension, seriously. This after all was its distinctive claim all along – one of its initial conditions. In the way the Park worked out, then, do we indeed see (drawing on complexity theory) 'a sensitivity to initial conditions'? As the Park's development unfolded, one of its own set of aspirations (the social/ELSI element) was being overlooked or downplayed as non-useful. The more other aspects of the Park were developed and the more usefulness was stressed, the more the social/ELSI element was neglected – or diverted elsewhere, with the same effect – and the more crucial the neglect of this area became. Having come to this conclusion, one might then hazard the suggestion that this is the very area to which the CGKP could have turned for the development of sensible indicators. For, above all, the CGKP had to work as a social entity. It could have looked to its social science academics for useful critique in this regard.[31] In a complex situation it is a fallacy to imagine that a selection of certain trajectories (on which to focus limited resources, for example) could have an outcome insulated from all the other factors that are in play. Given the manner in which the parks were set up, it is conceivable that diversion away from the 'social'/ELSI components was for the CGKP a negative choice that had significant forward consequences.

At the outset we said that other parks will have had different configurations of emphasis in their activities. Nonetheless, the replication of these specific circumstances in this particular case allows us to ask questions of it – that is, treat it (the replication) as a phenomenon. Whatever the initial conditions under which the parks developed their programmes, it is open to investigation the extent to which these were similarly repeated throughout the systems that emerged, regardless of the dimensions of any particular one, or of the effect that specific choices along the way will have had. The system described here for the CGKP is largely a social one, concerned with the CGKP as an organisation; it was the ideas that we have typified as Cambridge's conjunction of multidisciplinarity and engagement with the public that gave initial impetus to its social form. These ideas also, constantly, fed people's visions and aspirations, and were thus carried, repeated and reproduced through myriad encounters and documents. Perhaps they also fed the replication of similar phenomena at different levels: the kinds of priorities and values put on Cambridge's among the programmes of other parks, ELSI among other programmes within the CGKP, and the 'social' programme within other ELSI programmes. The failure of the CGKP to obtain from the outside the renewed funding it was expecting had already been acted out within.

Second conclusion

A larger and older issue behind all this is the relationship between the kinds of ideas, knowledge, aspirations and ambitions that get drawn up on paper and the urge to put the resulting templates, plans, schema and protocols into practice. In experimental (research oriented) mode, the failure of certain realisations will be positive information that spurs on fresh attempts; in institutional (management oriented) mode, it may mean in a much more negative sense the termination of contracts, policies and funding. The CGKP's self-described interstitial position, that of service provision, meant that some of the core team at least could see themselves continuing to provide the service they knew the public wanted even if it had to take on a different institutional form in the future. It was hoped that many of its practices could be carried over to the revamping of the unit that had provided CGKP with its administrative core.[32] The new institution need have no further recourse to ELSI as such, and certainly not to social science.

It seems too dramatic to ask if ELSI – or certain modes of its application – has had its day when in the UK it has only just begun to receive substantial public (governmental) credence. But that is precisely the question that Hayden asks of benefit sharing:

> benefit sharing is already, in many ways, a failed idiom [.] I say this with an eye on more than 10 years of bioprospecting experiments in which the promised sharing of benefits has proven a notably ineffectual facilitator of new kinds of 'downstream' redistributions.
>
> (Hayden 2007: 752)

It is not just an idiom that fails; institutions are dismantled. Thus she documents the termination of one apparently ideal relation between plant collection and benefits to the local population (US ethno-botanists and Mayan communities in the Chiapas): collaboration ended in disputes that led to the cancellation of the whole project by the funders. Another case, in Peru (Hayden cites Greene 2004), presented an exceptional example of local groups negotiating a 'know-how' license with the participating company (exceptional because benefits are invariably in assets other than property rights): it was short lived, the company refusing to renew on that basis.

There are certain substantive links between the aspirations of benefit sharing and ELSI, resting on an owner's or user's sense of responsibility towards a public who also (think they) have interests in the owner's property or knowledge. In the context of bioprospecting, benefit sharing creates a public out of research subjects – persons (in this case indigenous peoples) who have assisted the collection of genetic materials through their own knowledge or know-how. Extractive endeavours such as collecting plants as leads for new drugs could thus be refigured as a kind of ethical act in which drug-derived royalties would come back to source communities and nations in the form of compensation funds for economic development and technology transfer (Hayden 2007: 731). Hayden argues that such arrangements create certain kinds of publics, and asks what kinds of political or other socialities must be called into being in order to receive such benefits. She compares the US with Europe and its ethos of public participation in debate, consultation exercises preceding legislation and the need to take 'society' into account – the climate in which the idea of GKPs was born. In Europe this seemed the only way to socially 'robust' (ethical) research (Nowotny, Scott and Gibbons 2001).

Workers at the CGKP voiced concerns about whom they were honing their services for, but this was never translated into a systematic attempt to identify or define different publics as recipients of the knowledge it produced. Such an attempt could have started the CGKP down the road of investigating the impact of its activities. The inhibition is interesting: investigation would have required research, and it would have required social science. This might have involved, among other things, rooting the CGKP's work in voiced not just imagined or imaginable 'needs'. This in turn could have been used in the CGKP's relationship with the funders and *their* needs, for 'evidence' for example. Looking inwards, a social scientist might have provided an institutional critique contributing to an already developing foundation for self-knowledge. An interesting point here is what the directorate in fact chose to do, for going down this line would have inevitably brought in real-time connections with what seemingly remained an outside world, and would have meant taking into account others variously conceptualised as 'publics', 'audiences', 'funders' or 'partners'.

This brings one back to the boundary drawing, and in particular to the Park's rhetorical aversion to research. Here we benefit from insights proffered by Jean-Klein[33] in response to our development of the contrast between research- and management-oriented modes of knowledge creation.[34] She would emphasise the interdigitated, or cross-agentive, relationship between research and management. Each is entailed in the other; each can be thought of as the other's fractal dimension, and disciplines or projects or policy needs wink out of one mode into the other, oscillating between the two. This was apparent to both of us (EVR and MS) from our preliminary presentation to the CGKP. For all its protested aversion to research, there were many features of its open-horizons ideology and equal aversion to the micro-management of performance indicators that brought it closer to a research ethos than its directorate would have admitted. Jean-Klein adds that where these particular orientations appear to have a singular value, and we use her words, their singular value is only a momentary effect of (so to speak) punctuation. Perhaps the CGKP was an example of an institution trying against the odds to define itself along one of these two axes alone, freezing into one mould while freezing out the other, or eschewing oscillation altogether in the omnipotent concept of 'service'.

To put it another way, the hierarchisation of value and commitment that appeared to render some aspects of the CGKP's activities less important than others (shrink their size) concealed the complexity of interdependence (and the irrelevance of size). For all its diagrams about the overarching, 'bridging' functions of the CGKP, and the directorate's favourite early depiction of the CGKP as an umbrella under which many disciplines and activities sat, in the end the project was only as embracing as its pictures, words and publications were absorbed by others.[35] The efforts of individuals or of its diverse teams could be just as 'large' in their potential import as those of the overall institution.

It is hardly controversial to suggest that different parts of the CGKP's activities were inevitably bound up with one another. But the indigenous representations of scale and significance to which we have just referred did their concealing work to spectacular effect. The core team's constant attempts to purify and re-present its aims and objectives also meant cutting away parts of itself. This chapter has argued that ELSI, and especially the social in ELSI, can in retrospect be understood as initial conditions in the CGKP's formation that were ignored to its detriment. What was true of social science research was also true of performance indicators: nothing could prevent the ricochet effect of ignoring what one of the CGKP publics, the funders, wanted to know. Now (we have suggested), that did not begin with the meetings with the DTI and DH – it began with that aversion to research that deprived the CGKP of knowledge of its own social situation. Finally, the dismissive equation between social science and 'only research' meant that there was nothing in (the social end of) ELSI that needed managing either. The simplest recourse was to repeat statements also made by a government minister about its uselessness.

We emphasise that this is all in hindsight. But then it would be poor reflective practice that did not see anything of interest from such a position. Perhaps in turn that practice comes from our internalist account. It leads us to where we might not otherwise have gone, notably to the workings out of certain prejudices – in the literal sense of pre-judgings – over what social science research has to offer society.

Acknowledgements

This chapter is based on findings laid out in an unpublished and confidential report by Khlinovskaya Rockhill and Strathern in 2006, *An Ethnographic Study of the Cambridge Genetics Knowledge Park*. Almost all the information in this present account is drawn from that. Elena Khlinovskaya Rockill studied the CGKP over an 18-month period from 2004 to 2006, and our thanks are due to Dr Ron Zimmern and his team for the great courtesy and openness with which they welcomed the prospect. The project, 'Interdisciplinarity and Society', was undertaken jointly with Andrew Barry and Georgina Born (ESRC grant RES-151-25-00042) as part of the ESRC Science in Society Programme led by

Steve Rayner. We are particularly grateful to Don Brenneis for his close reading of the conference paper, and to Brian Wynne for his helpful criticism.

Notes

1 Implemented specifically in the US in tandem with the Human Genome Project (Nowotny et al. 2001: 239; HGDP: www.stanford.edu/group/morrinst/hgdp.html). The acronym may also be rendered 'Ethical, Legal and Social Issues'. They do not always need to be in concert. For an example of anthropological study with 'social' rather than legal or ethical issues in focus, undertaken as part of a project sponsored by the ELSI program of the US National Institutes of Health and the National Human Genome Research Institute, see Reddy (2007).

2 From *The Genetics Knowledge Parks Network-Overview*, 2002. An ELSI framework would have this facilitating role, it was understood though not in so many words stated, by addressing many of the existing impediments to public acceptance of scientific advance in this field.

3 The acronym ELSI was used from time to time in internal CGKP documents. In public presentations the phrase was usually spelled out: e.g. '[T]he Cambridge Knowledge Park will have a major role in the development of the ethical, legal and social basis of medical genetics through the involvement of the five lectureships [see below] and the work of the Centre for Medical Genetics and Policy' (DH 2002: 14).

4 We are grateful here to Brian Wynne for his critical characterisation of our project, but rather than overcome this trait exaggerate it.

5 After Weiner (2006). Weiner observes that ontologically one cannot distinguish between a difference that emerges within (for instance, a culture) from a difference that emerges from a contrast between inside and outside (between 'two' cultures).

6 On the contribution that technologically driven enterprises in particular make to the 'dynamics of expectations', structuring action before the fact, and inviting prospective technology analysis, see van Lente and Rip (1998); Rip (2008). We are grateful to Arie Rip for these references.

7 In what follows, the default perspective (observations about the CGKP in general or otherwise unattributed comments) is that of the centre, including official publications, statements and other documentation from the Executive Team or CGKP 'core' and the Director, collectively (our term) the directorate.

8 Let alone the synthesis of 'transdisciplinarity' (Nowotny et al. 2001). 'Multidisciplinary' was the term that was used most regularly in the documents, although the description of such collaborations was often accompanied, as in the original proposal (CGKP 2001), by the expectation that they would work 'synergistically'. Later in the programme the concept of 'knowledge integration', implying integration 'within and across disciplines', appeared. (It was evident, for example, in the 2005–2007 work plans.)

9 Although it was not regarded this way by CGKP's funders, we suspect that in the eyes of the CGKP executive 'policy' may have stood for a kind of public engagement (engagement with issues that are going to affect and assist the public). From other perspectives, of course, the devising of policy (top down) may be seen as about as removed as it could be from involving the public (bottom up).

10 Foreseen in the original plan but not filled till this moment.

11 The only two posts not renewed when vacancies occurred, although in the public involvement case there was an initial attempt to recruit to it.

12 The 'public' perpetually appeared amorphous, anonymous. These are of course characteristics created for it, whatever 'it' is. The social scientist might observe that the public loses its apparent inaccessible distance when it becomes a source of information, and thus is itself treated systematically and seriously. We return to this at the end. One consequence was that 'the public's' unexpected reactions to events or treatments,

inexplicable if one took a rational or common sense approach and tried to think things through on their behalf, remained inscrutable.

13 Echoed by a social scientist who thought that the rest of the CGKP was too removed from *practice*, and did not know what was happening *on the ground* (in relation to clinical practitioners and others); one cannot know in advance – one has to find out. A natural science view was that one cannot develop policy guidelines in the abstract, outside the *pragmatics* of the technological embeddedness of treatments and techniques, for they can only be valid as long as the techniques are valid.

14 Taking them as two models of knowledge creation, EVR and MS (Khlinovskaya Rockhill and Strathern 2005; Strathern 2006a, 2006b) picked them up to develop for analytical purposes.

15 For a number of staff, the CGKP promoted *too little* research, a view based on a personal pragmatism towards career prospects without academic publications to one's credit.

16 The funders were also said to have voiced disappointment in the public outreach side of CGKP and its interactions with 'the wider community'.

17 Who either were part of the base establishment of the PHGU, under the NHS, or were involved in projects without leaving their home disciplines at all. (The NHS Trust has the oversight of a major teaching hospital, with research strengths and an active clinical base. The hospital complex houses units and centres funded by the UK Medical Research Council and other bodies, as well as medical institutes and departments of Cambridge University.)

18 Under an umbrella managing committee in the University, CMGP (Centre for Medical Genetics and Policy), but otherwise allocated to different University departments.

19 Two examples from DTI publications of the time: 'in addition to highlighting the importance of public accountability and the involvement of the public in decision-making, the science and society agenda identifies an important role for the Research Councils . . . in helping to promote an awareness of science as part of the fabric of society and an understanding of science and new technologies' (DTI 2001a: 61). 'A modern democratic society is also one in which all citizens are expected to have opinions about major political, social and economic choices, and in which public participation in these choices and discussions is itself a major source of social responsiveness, and resilience' (DTI 2001b: 9). And on the rise of ethics committees (not committees of ethicists, but generally cross-disciplinary bodies, with representatives from the public), see Siegler (1999).

20 'Performance management' had to be part of the business plan. But the acceptance of the need for performance indicators was invariably accompanied by the caveat that, insofar as the GKP was a 'nascent organisation', systems for measuring its performance must be responsive to changing circumstances.

21 We know of a significant instance where it was a substantial public involvement element in a work programme that led to its endorsement by an outside body.

22 This was formulated as a hypothesis in Strathern (2004a) before we had identified Cambridge's conjunction as such.

23 The evaluation of network intervention is exceptionally teasing (see the case of the network manager in Strathern 2004b).

24 For some ELSI members it also stood for a responsible approach to social issues. Note that we use the term 'interdisciplinarity' in reference to the actors' model for synergistic combination, though as already observed it was moot the extent to which the multidisciplinary strands of the CGKP's activities were activated in a socially/conceptually interdisciplinary manner (cf. Rhoten 2003). The term was used in the CGKP business plan, but interchangeably with multidisciplinarity; the CGKP borrowed its meaning and connotations from our study as well.

25 And there were some critics of the prevalent view; others worried about not seeking out public opinion more actively.

26 Connectedness could be shown in other ways too, for example staff were encouraged to use the tea room. So, too, the Public Involvement Officer also signalled public engagement very clearly.
27 In fieldwork fashion, if this starting point began with the interest of the observers (social scientists), and specifically with their interest in the CGKP as a social phenomenon, that interest did not in any way anticipate the findings, which have come as a surprise. It should be evident that this paper is not intended to give a picture of all the CGKP's enterprises: it focuses on the Park as a social form.
28 And in relation to other themes. For example, the paradox that an organisation that was so much about bringing people together (in the abstract) did not provide regular meeting places, physical or intellectual, for its own staff outside a managerial milieu.
29 And in turn the directorate felt that the funders lacked clarity and specificity in what they were looking for, and claimed (for example) to have needed more guidance as to how to submit to a mid-term review. Note: these were the cultural idioms in which feelings about being undervalued were played out. The remedy would not necessarily have been more guidelines.
30 One partner organisation thought the CGKP was like a research unit ('but with a project management approach'), while another thought of it as an 'academic' organisation focused on ELSI.
31 This is not to say that the directorate/Executive Team did not welcome criticism; they did, and were (for example) most open in allowing this present study to proceed. Moreover they would have liked *this* study to have positioned itself as an evaluator, and referred to it as such. We need to ask why it seemed impossible (to us) to undertake evaluation and description (including analysis) at the same time.
32 Since then, however, another chapter altogether has opened. As of 2007, this unit morphed into an independent charity, which aims to provide news, information and knowledge to support the application of genome-based science and innovative technologies to issues of health and disease. It covers science, public health, policy and regulation, with links to a separate academic centre that attends to legal, philosophical and social issues under a science-in-society remit. The CGKP thus followed the sequence described by McGivern and Dopson (2010) for another GKP, where an NHS community and a university research centre successfully 'reincarnated' elements of the former GKP.
33 Dr Iris Jean-Klein (personal communication to MS). I adapt 'cross-agentive' from her 'cross-subjective' (Jean-Klein 2000).
34 Strathern (2006b); the contrast rose directly out of insights offered by EVR on the basis of her ethnographic observations at the CGKP.
35 Or not absorbed, as is evident from a comment regarding four presentations for a CGKP interdisciplinary forum: 'four pieces of a puzzle none of which fit together'. Similarly, one social scientist, when asked whether or not she found the complicated pictorial representations of the CGKP's work having explanatory power, replied that she did not try to penetrate those because she did not know what all the boxes and arrows actually *meant*.

References

CGKP (Cambridge Genetics Knowledge Park) (2003) 'Business Plan', November.
— (2004) *Annual Report, 2003–4.*
DH (Department of Health) (2002) *The Genetics Knowledge Parks Network – Overview*, London: DH.
DTI (Department of Trade and Industry) (2001a) *Quinquennial Review of the Grant-Awarding Research Councils*, Stage Two: Report by the Review Team, London: Parliamentary Office of Science and Technology.

— (2001b) *Report on the Arts and Humanities in Relation to Science and Technology*, London: Council for Science and Technology.

Greene, S. (2004) 'Indigenous Peoples, Incoporated? Culture as Politics, Culture as Property in Contemporary Bioprospecting Deals', *Current Anthropology*, 45: 211–37.

Hayden, C. (2002) *When Nature Goes Public: The Making and Unmaking of Bioprospecting in Mexico*, Princeton, NJ: Princeton University Press.

— (2007) 'Taking as Giving: Bioscience, Exchange, and the Politics of Benefit-Sharing', *Social Studies of Science*, 37: 729–58.

Jean-Klein, I. (2000) 'Mothercraft, Statecraft, and Subjectivity in the Palestinian Intifada', *American Ethnologist*, 27: 100–27.

Khlinovskaya Rockhill, E. (2007) 'On Interdisciplinarity and Models of Knowledge Production', *Social Analysis,* 51: 121–47.

Khlinovskaya Rockhill, E. and Strathern, M. (2005) *Interdisciplinarity and the Cambridge Genetics Knowledge Park*, paper prepared for the CGKP Annual Symposium, Hinxton. Unpublished.

McGivern, B. and Dopson, S. (2010) 'Inter-Epistemic Power and Transforming Knowledge Objects in a Biomedical Network', *Organization Studies*, 31(12): 1667–86.

Miller, D. (2005) 'What is Best "Value"? Bureaucracy, Virtualism and Local Governance', in P. Du Gay (ed.) *The Values of Bureaucracy*, (pp. 233–54) Oxford: Oxford University Press.

Nowotny, H., Scott, P. and Gibbons, M. (2001) *Re-Thinking Science: Knowledge and the Public in an Age of Uncertainty*, Cambridge: Polity.

Reddy, D. (2007) 'Good Gifts for the Common Good: Blood and Bioethics in the Market of Genetic Research', *Cultural Anthropology*, 22: 429–72.

Rhoten, D. (2003) 'A Multi-Method Analysis of the Social and Technical Conditions for Interdisciplinary Collaboration', *Hybrid Vigor*, Final Report. National Science Foundation (cited with permission). Abstract: www.ncar.ucar.edu/Director/survey/Rhoten_NSF-BCS.FINAL.pdf (accessed November 2012).

Rip, A. (2008) 'Nanoscience and Nanotechnologies: Bridging Gaps through Constructive Technology Assessment', in G. H. Hadorn et al. (eds.) *Handbook of Transdisciplinary Research* (pp. 145–58), Dordrecht: Springer.

Rip, A. and Shove, E. (2000) 'Users and Unicorns: A Discussion of Mythical Beasts', *Science and Public Policy*, 27(3): 175–82.

Schlecker, M. and Hirsch, E. (2001) 'Incomplete Knowledge: Ethnography and the Crisis of Context in Studies of Media, Science and Technology', *History of the Human Sciences*, 14: 69–87.

Siegler, M. (1999) 'Ethics Committees: Decisions by Bureaucracy', in H. Kuhse and P. Singer (eds.) *Bioethics: An Anthology*, Oxford: Blackwell Publishers.

Strathern, M. (2004a) 'Accountability across Disciplines', in M. Strathern, *Commons and Borderlands: Working Papers on Interdisciplinarity, Accountability and the Flow of Knowledge*, (pp. 68–86) Wantage: Sean Kingston Publishing.

— (2004b) 'Social Property: An Interdisciplinary Experiment', *PoLAR (Political and Legal Anthropology Review),* 27: 23–50.

— (2006a) 'A Community of Critics: Thoughts on New Knowledge', *Journal of the Royal Anthropological Institute,* (N.S.) 12: 191–209.

— (2006b) 'Useful Knowledge', Isaiah Berlin Lecture, British Academy. *Proceedings of the British Academy,* 139: 73–109.

— (2011) 'An Experiment in Interdisciplinarity: Proposals and Promises', in C. Camic, N. Gross and M. Lamont (eds.) *Social Knowledge in the Making*, (pp. 257–84) Chicago, IL: University of Chicago Press.

Van Lente, H. and Rip, A. (1998) 'Expectations in Technological Developments: An Example of Prospective Structures to be Filled in by Agency', in C. Disco and B. van der Meulen (eds.) *Getting New Technologies Together: Studies in Making Sociotechnical Order* (pp. 203–31). Berlin: Walter de Gruyter.

Weiner, J. (2006) 'Eliciting Customary Law', *The Asia Pacific Journal of Anthropology*, 7(1): 15–25.

6 Consuming Anthropology

Lucy Suchman

> Rather as existing 'cultures' get in the way of development, existing disciplines get in the way of interdisciplinarity.
>
> Marilyn Strathern 2006: 196

As a development project within the imaginaries of the 'knowledge economy', making useful knowledge seems to imply less interdisciplinarity than antidisciplinarity. Or to put it another way, the incorporation of academic disciplines into economic activity is assumed to require their appropriate transformation. Through a history traceable at least to the labour 'unrest' of the 1930s, American anthropologists along with others in the then emerging behavioural and social sciences have worked to legitimise themselves as relevant to industry (Eddy and Partridge 1987). My focus in this paper is on a recent chapter in this history: the incorporation of anthropology, as both figure and practice, within industrial research and development in the United States beginning in the 1970s.[1] More specifically, I examine the frames within which anthropology is imagined as valuable to contemporary industry, particularly in the area that I know best: the design of information and communications technologies. How is anthropology positioned both within these frames, and in relation to what Callon (1998a) has identified as their constitutive outsides or overflows?

My strategy for addressing these questions is to think about the embedding of anthropological research within corporate enterprises in relation to the turn to markets as a research object in the social sciences (Callon 1998b; du Gay and Pryke 2002; Barry and Slater 2005; Mackenzie 2006; Thrift 2006).[2] Thinking about these developments together helps me to articulate the imaginary within which anthropology in corporate settings has emerged, and to explore some of that imaginary's consequences for the forms of research and scholarship that are possible. A further disciplinary encounter in my story is that of anthropology (operating as icon for the social sciences) with the cognitive and computing sciences, the dominant disciplines within the sites of industrial research with which I am most familiar.

Contemporary theorising regarding relations of production and consumption emphasises the contingent, appropriative processes by which commodities simultaneously inflect the lives of their purchasers and are remade within the particular practices of their use (see for example Appadurai 1986; Slater 1997; Miller 1998a, 1998b; Cronin 2000, 2003; Lury 1996, 2004). This paper considers the implications of conceiving anthropology itself as an object of consumption within worlds of commercial research and development. Incorporated into this matrix over the past several decades, anthropological methods and imaginaries have been reconfigured at the same time that they have informed the discourses and material practices of their users. Drawing on 20 years as a researcher at Xerox's Palo Alto Research Center (PARC), an organisation identified as a centre of innovation and a founding site for interdisciplinary research and development in computing, I take a performative approach to the question of disciplinarity, asking when and how anthropology is enacted as a distinctive discipline with a particular value for industry. I close with a reflection on the messy contingencies of this interdisciplinary commerce, and their implications for more radical forms of inventive collaboration.[3]

Culture and the Making of Markets

Writing against the tradition of classical economics, particularly in its separation of 'the economy' from 'society' or 'culture', recent scholarship has developed the argument that economic and cultural activities are inseparably interrelated. This is so insofar as identifications of products, markets, competitors and the like fundamentally presuppose the mobilisation of cultural knowledge; that is, the persuasive assertion of qualities of sameness and difference between relevant objects (Slater 2002: 60). Taking advertising, design and marketing as his cases in point, Slater observes that 'the very notion of a market requires qualitative understandings of the place and meaning of objects/commodities in ways of life' (ibid.: 61):

> The supposedly 'economic' issues of 'what market are we in?' and 'who are our competitors?' are simply not economic in the conventional sense. Producers cannot know what market they are in without extensive cultural calculation; and they cannot understand the cultural form of their product and its use outside of a context of market competition. Moreover, the crucial question is not in fact 'what market are we in?' but rather 'what are the various interrelated definitions of product and competition that we can dream up, and how do we assess and choose between them as commercial strategies?' The answer to that question takes the form, eventually, of the identification of what we gloss as 'the market'.
>
> (ibid.: 63)

Figured as the expert on culture, it follows that the anthropologist would have an obvious currency in the making of markets. Indeed, in the service of making a space for workplace ethnography during the 1980s, my colleagues and I at PARC framed our arguments in terms of the relatively greater value of ethnographically based attention to practice over the kinds of decontextualised opinions and fragmented expressions of preference elicited through market research. And while Slater is critical of the failure of mainstream literatures to acknowledge the place of advertising as integral to business, we could also understand the value of activities related to 'culture' as located precisely in their promise to go beyond the reach of business as usual. The anthropologist promises to (re-) contextualise objects as entangled in meaningful social and material practice through ethnographic fieldwork, however much the results of those investigations must be translated back into commercially relevant terms in order to be useful for other actors such as designers, product managers, marketers and the like. Whatever might be lost in translation (and the loss of contingency is a requirement for translational efficacy), fieldwork's capture of the elusively cultural should afford insights and opportunities not available through any other means.

At the same time, du Gay and Pryke (2002) question the premise of the 'increasing culturalisation' of economies and organisations. As signs of the turn, Lash and Urry (1994) cite three developments: (1) the rise of what have come to be referred to as the 'culture industries'; (2) the argument that increasingly consumer goods and services across a range of sectors can be conceived of as 'cultural' in the sense that they are deliberately and instrumentally inscribed with particular meanings and associations in a conscious attempt to generate desire for them amongst end-users, as even banal products are 'aestheticised' and inserted into narratives about 'lifestyle' and 'experience'; and (3) the turn to 'organisational culture' within business and management discourses.

While du Gay and Pryke are critical of the epochal and often hyperbolic characterisation of these developments, they acknowledge the evidence for growing management interests in 'culture' as a means of improving organisational performance, and an associated concern with managing 'organisational culture' (2002: 1). The cultural turn, they observe, is tied to the premise that it is management's task to unleash workers' creativity and enterprise in order to compete within the new, knowledge-based economy (see also Salaman 1997; Marcus 1998; Thrift 2006). Culture is ambiguously the basis for *explaining* how people think, feel and act, and the means for *engineering* desired forms of behavioural change:

> [M]anagers are encouraged to view the most effective or 'excellent' organizations as those with the 'right' culture – that ensemble of norms and techniques of conduct that enables the self-actualizing capacities of individuals to become aligned with the goals and objectives of the organization for which they work.
>
> (du Gay and Pryke 2002:1)

I will suggest that it was in part these developments of the 1990s that worked to close down the space for difference that allowed a critical anthropology within Xerox PARC. For the moment, however, the point is simply that in thinking about the place of anthropology within these emerging market frames we need to attend to the ways in which, just as 'accounting tools . . . do not simply aid the measurement of economic activity, they shape the reality they measure' (du Gay and Pryke 2002: 12–13), so corporate anthropology is implicated not only in the introduction of new methods for 'knowing' but also in producing the realities of what we now identify as commercially relevant objects.

To say that anthropology is implicated is not to posit any singular accountability, nor any simple causal relationship between industrial anthropology and the turn to culture as a central trope in product design and marketing. The latter would overly simplify the disciplinary influences of anthropology among related fields within the social and behavioural sciences during this period, as well as the diffuse and contingent modes of circulation through which market imaginaries and their strategic enactments are constituted. It would, in other words, over-attribute both power and responsibility to the figure of a discipline. At the same time, we can trace some paths through which the figure of anthropology, and its identifying premises and practices, have conjoined with and helped to realise the market's 'cultural turn'.

Anthropology at Xerox PARC

Anthropological engagement at Xerox PARC began during the research centre's first decade, in the summer of 1976 on the initiative of Jeff Rulifson, a computer scientist and research manager of what was then the Office Research Group.[4] Rulifson was deeply dissatisfied with the office modelling on offer from consulting firms hired to advise the corporation on technology strategy. Searching for alternatives, he was inspired by his readings of Lévi-Strauss, from whom he took the lesson that 'we are our tools'. He turned to his academic networks in the San Francisco Bay Area in an effort to identify an anthropologist who might be interested in research on office work in the context of new technology development. Knocking on doors at the University of California at Berkeley he met Eleanor Wynn, then a graduate student in linguistic anthropology, who signed on for a summer contract.

The following summer, Rulifson sponsored a second round of studies, once again arranged through UC Berkeley. This time a team of three graduate students were placed in Xerox branch sales offices for six weeks, with the assignment to examine the informal procedures and social relations comprising the work of customer service (Browner and Chibnik 1979). In their account of the project in the journal *Central Issues in Anthropology*, Carole Browner and Michael Chibnik distinguish two aspects as unique at the time with respect to anthropological research: (1) adapting anthropological methods for use in a business setting, and (2) conducting research for a profit-making corporation. They report that the first proved relatively easy, the second more problematic. Observing that the 1970s was a time of decreasing opportunities in the academic job market for anthropology, they cite other publications by anthropologists engaged in non-academic research at the time (in government, non-profits and private consultancies), which reported a number of difficulties including political pressures, conflicting responsibilities to subjects and sponsors and the need to present findings 'of practical value' within short time-frames. In the context of corporate-sponsored research, they observe, practical value translates as relevance to profitability.

The research group to which they reported (given the pseudonym 'the Center for Office Studies')[5] was engaged in developing information systems designed to transform administrative work, and organisational communications more broadly, from paper to digital media. The field site for the study (the site of ongoing observations of office 'paper flow' by computer scientists in the research group as well) was a corporate branch office devoted to sales and customer service, also slated as the test site for the introduction of a prototype information system the following summer.[6] The justification for the anthropological initiative was framed with reference to problems that had arisen with the introduction of earlier computer-based office equipment (specifically word processors), and corporate concerns that these problems might repeat themselves. In a presentation to the anthropologists, Jeff Rulifson explained that he believed that these problems were due less to technical shortcomings of the equipment than to a flawed model of the work, focused only on the individual user's relations to the machine rather than the broader social relations of the office. 'The effect of installing new machines', he speculated, 'may be that they interfere with – or at least change – the way people work together' (Browner and Chibnik 1979: 64). Rulifson pointed out that while we know that 'work' goes on in offices, little is known about how it actually gets done; for example, the 'informal procedures' used to carry out tasks, the social relations necessary to carrying out procedures, or the effects that changes in routines might have on getting the work done. Social anthropologists seemed potentially able to provide information on these issues that would be relevant to the design of office information systems.[7] Moreover, as the champion of the project, Rulifson saw his engagement of anthropology as putting Xerox PARC on the cutting edge of social science research: Browner and Chibnik report that he announced to others regarding his employment of anthropologists that 'The best [our chief competitor] has done is an industrial psychologist!' (ibid.: 70). His main concern was to show that 'this crazy project', of placing anthropologists in the branch offices, could actually be done.

The research report produced from the project emphasises the necessity of autonomous decision-making to the conduct of clerical work, and the importance of interpersonal relations (for example, between customer service and sales representatives) for organisational effectiveness. The administration of the project proceeded less smoothly than the fieldwork, however, particularly with respect to project definition and direction (Browner and Chibnik 1979: 68). Negotiating access to the branch offices was difficult, given general scepticism on the part of branch management regarding what contributions anthropologists could make to questions of corporate interest. The productivity pressures on branch managers made them wary of the potential disruption, or at least distraction, that researchers might bring and, more specifically, of the possibility that researchers might report activities not sufficiently conforming to official procedures. In part as a consequence of this, access for the researchers was negotiated with upper-level managers, who then 'advised the branch managers of the desirability of cooperating' with research (ibid.: 69). While the branch managers could, in principle, decline they found it difficult to do so insofar as the suggestion came from those above them in the corporate hierarchy. Closer to home, computer scientists within the research group demonstrated some anxiety about the entanglement of their own procedural studies and those of the anthropologists. More generally, Browner and Chibnik report that the anthropologists faced unanticipated objections to their research from all sides (ibid.: 70).

With this origin story as background, I fast forward to the 1990s. The 'office of the future' (at least in its paperless imagining) is a thing of the past, while digital systems comprise an unremarkable, albeit continually changing, medium of administrative work. Fifteen years after the dissolution of the 'Center for Office Studies' (in 1980), the Systems Science Laboratory is now the Knowledge and Practices Laboratory, and the Work Practice and Technology (WPT) research area, established in 1989, is in place.[8]

Gradually achieving sufficient credibility to constitute a small research group comprising four anthropologists, including myself, and two computer scientists (over a decade after the 'first contact' described by Browner and Chibnik), we mobilised arguments about the value of ethnographically informed co-design of prototype technologies to industrial research and development.[9] Creating and iteratively refining these arguments was an integral aspect of our work. Along with concrete demonstrations of an associated research practice, these arguments opened a space for a range of collaborations: critical engagement with cognitive and computer scientists around questions of intelligence, knowledge, reasoning and related constructs; collaboration with system designers aimed at respecifying central issues for them, including the human–machine interface, usability and design expertise; extensive studies of work settings oriented to articulating tech-nologies as socio-material practice; engagement with an emerging international network of computer scientists and system designers committed to more partici-patory forms of system development with relevant workers/users; activism within relevant computer research networks to raise awareness of those alternatives;[10] and iterative enactment of an ethnographically informed, participatory design practice within the context of the research centre and the wider corporation.[11]

These efforts took advantage of the ways in which our position at Xerox PARC – in its identification as a centre for basic research and its members as aca-demically recognised 'scientists' – afforded us 'margins of manoeuvre' to sustain affiliations that exceeded the conventional market frame (Barry and Slater 2002: 303). In particular, we drew the model for our own practice from colleagues in Denmark, Norway and Sweden: academic computer scientists collaborating with Scandinavian trade unions to develop union-sponsored demonstration systems informed by values of quality of working life and workplace democracy. In our representations of the value of participatory design to the corporation, however, political values were minimised in favour of potentially superior design outcomes, producing information systems better suited to working practices. While this strategy, and the extended history of collaborative experimentation and engagement through which it was realised over two decades, was unquestionably fruitful it also raises a number of questions that have yet, in my reading, to be fully or clearly articulated in recent writings on interdisciplinarity. It is to those questions that I turn in the remainder of this paper.

Sponsorship and Accountabilities

In an interview published in 2002, Michel Callon reflects on the question of 'how social scientists can link themselves to social actors' (Barry and Slater 2002: 302). More specifically, Callon is concerned to articulate a conception of markets that 'overflow the frames' of conventional economic discourses, both theoretically and practically. The reference case for Callon is activists engaged in working for recognition of, and resources for, 'orphan' diseases such as muscular dystrophy, for which mass production medical and pharmaceutical research and development is not profitable. Callon urges social scientists to engage in collaborative partnerships with such groups:

> On the one hand, actors are interested in this form of co-operation because they can enhance their capacity to describe and analyse their own experience and, on the other hand, social scientists are also interested in co-operating because they can mobilise actors as colleagues who are as competent as academics or scientists.
>
> (ibid.: 302)

In response to this, Andrew Barry, Callon's interlocutor, asks the crucial question: 'which actors do you cooperate with, and with which do you not cooperate?'

One of the problems that Barry's question raises is that of sponsorship and associated accountabilities. Many writings on the virtues of social scientists' engagement with other 'social actors' (a category that I return to in a moment) assume either that researchers will be based in an academic institution, or that where researchers are based is not a critical question. I would like to suggest that this is perhaps *the* critical question. Without in any way diminishing the extraordinary creativity and commitment with which anthropologists working in industry have managed to open a space not only for constructive but even for critical and oppositional work within 'the engine rooms of technological production' (Wajcman 1991: 164), I focus here on the contradictions that frame that work and that are deeply woven into the everyday experience of doing it. Unless we explicate those contradictions, we are obscuring the conditions within which interdisciplinarity has emerged as a 'good' in contemporary discourses, and the realities of what it means to enact it, particularly in the constitution of markets.

I want to return, then, to Callon's urging that 'social scientists link themselves to social actors', to look more closely at the differences that are made in this statement, along with its call to connection. Most obviously, there is the implication that the social scientist is somehow not, herself, a 'social actor' at least in the sense that Callon has in mind. Presumably the latter are actors whose primary identifications and commitments are to something other than social science – to lobbying for recognition and resources for a disease that is invisible to the market, for example. The former, in turn, are actors whose identifications and commitments are to an ongoing engagement with the concerns of the academy, or at least of the historical disciplines from which they draw inspiration and to which they want their work to contribute. It is here in part, I would argue, that questions of sponsorship matter. That is to say, these distinctions become more complicated, slippery and problematic when the 'social scientist' is incorporated economically into an organisation committed to operating in the market, at the same time that she is committed to expanding and redrawing that frame. An example might help to make this clear.

Overflowing the Market

It is 1995, and the corporation has undergone a massive rebranding initiative aimed at establishing itself as The Document Company, imagining the document now as an object that moves seamlessly between paper and digital media facilitated by networks of 'multi-function' devices able to copy, print, scan and fax as needed. Four of us embark on a project that is the latest in a series, aimed at enacting an interdisciplinary design practice that mobilises ethnographically informed studies of work to create prototype document systems, designed cooperatively with their prospective users. These 'case-based prototypes' comprise the medium through which already existing work practices and materials can be reconfigured into systems incorporating both 'off the shelf' and emerging technologies, to create technologies that make sense and are useful (for multiple audiences), while also acting as demonstrations of new technological possibilities for the integration of paper and digital documents (Blomberg et al 1996; Trigg et al 1999; Suchman et al 2002).

Like the technology prototype that is its object, the project itself is designed to do multiple kinds of work. One aim is that this project should expand the boundaries of our last; more specifically, that we should go beyond a demonstration prototype (albeit one installed temporarily in the workplace of our collaborators; see Blomberg et al 1996), to a prototype that is fully usable and integrated into the wider infrastructure of our user/collaborators' workplace. A second is that we extend our growing understanding of document work practices, specifically in relation to what we are calling 'working document collections'; that is, corpora of documents that exist between the archive and the desktop (the filing cabinet being the canonical example). With high value now placed on strong endorsements from the corporation's product divisions, we have also designed the project to engage with the currently most politically salient of those, through our choice of workplace (a large state agency, considered an important market segment) and the positioning of the prototype (as part of a wider configuration that would incorporate the latest product line of multi-function machines).

While the project that unfolds is a complex and fascinating one, I focus here on the particular kinds of exchange relationships involved. Figured as a prominent customer, the California Department of Transportation (Caltrans) had long been a site for significant installations of company products. This formed the initial basis for its currency as a prospective site of our research engagement, a possibility that we pursued through the Sales Manager dedicated to the Caltrans account. This contact, along with the cultural capital afforded by our status as researchers at Xerox PARC, secured us a meeting with senior Caltrans management in District 4, the nearest Agency headquarters located in Oakland, California. While our identification with Xerox, and more specifically with PARC, was what made us legible to Caltrans management, that identification also framed the challenge for our first meeting. In contrast to the familiar relationship of technology vendor and customer, we placed a proposal for a different kind of relationship onto the table. Most notably, this would be a relationship in which no money would change hands, but rather (only) an exchange of time and labour. As salaried PARC researchers, we would require no payment from Caltrans, and would offer whatever expertise we could bring to bear for free. In exchange, we asked for an opportunity to work closely with a civil engineering team within the department over an extended time-frame (our subsequent engagement continued for two years), to identify some aspect of their document-related work that might benefit from translation between paper and digital media, and to collaborate with them to develop a demonstration system. The latter would not, we emphasised, be a working system in the sense of a purchasable product. But it would be developed sufficiently to be put into real use, in situ.

What we hoped Caltrans engineers and management would gain by the end of the project was, first, a deeper understanding of their 'requirements' for a document system that would be genuinely useful and usable within the context of an engineering team's daily work. And second, that they would gain a realistic appreciation of the state of the technological art, including relevant technologies already available, those currently in research and development, and others often promised but likely never to be realised. Taken together, we suggested, these would place the organisation in a stronger position from which to think about their technology strategy, and to assess the claims of future technology vendors who came along. In place of familiar relations of paid services or products for sale, in other words, we set up a kind of barter, exchanging labours for labours. Our exchange eventually included a small suite of gifted technologies (a scanner and dedicated personal computer plus requisite software) necessary for the prototype that emerged; procuring those technologies from Xerox without charges to Caltrans was among the more substantial of the practical challenges and achievements of our own labours on the project.

The form of our 'interdisciplinarity' by the time of this project was a collaboration within which studying the working practices of a team of civil engineers and designing a prototype system for managing their project documents were intertwined research objects. As researchers we all engaged in work practice studies and in design sessions, albeit that the technical work of writing code fell predominately to Randall Trigg, a gifted computer scientist. His work now was less to invent technologies *de novo* than to engage in extensive forms of configuration

work that drew upon software packages designed as generic toolkits for custom-
ised systems, or that at least made available application programmers interfaces
(APIs) that enabled him to do the necessary customisation and integration work.
The prototype that resulted was a mix of commercially available and bespoke
components, with the latter combining customisations required to make a system
that made sense for the work at hand, and other research technologies (for example,
for document image analysis) of interest to colleagues back at PARC (see Trigg
et al 1999).

While conscientiously aligned with the evident commercial interests and prevailing practices of the corporation, in sum, the project that unfolded overflowed
that frame as well. As a consequence, we found ourselves positioned at the interstices of received categories for economic exchange, both in our relation to the
site of our collaborative prototyping effort (some within Xerox management
believing that Caltrans should be paying us), and in the technologies created
(under what precedent could the hardware be donated? Should and could the software developed in the context of the prototype be patented and licensed as intellectual property? If so, what was the status of the prototype system installed at
Caltrans?). Our successful negotiation of these questions was a prerequisite for,
and an integral aspect of, the creation of a space (albeit a temporary and experimental one) for a different kind of market within the Market frame – a form of
exchange that didn't fit (Gibson-Graham 1996: ix), but that was necessary for the
kind of project to which we were committed.

Mediated Imaginaries

> The worldly authority of modern ethnography . . . may long outlive its credibility
> within the discipline.
>
>   Rosemary Coombe 1998: 35

With these fragments of a history of specific anthropological encounters in mind,
I turn back to the question of anthropology's value as a consumable within US
industry. Recent contributors to the cultural economy discussion argue for the
importance of documenting the performative naturalisation of economic objects,
as a basis for their contestation (Slater 2002). In Slater's analysis, product
definition, positioning, branding and marketing are all constitutive activities in the
stabilisation of commercial actors and organisations as well as their objects. How
does this apply to 'anthropology' itself?

On 24 February 1991 an article appeared in the business pages of the *New
York Times*, in the 'Managing' section, titled 'Coping with Cultural Polyglots'.
The article, by reporter Claudia Deutsch, told of a small (but by implication
increasing) number of anthropologists employed by major corporations. Twenty
years after its first sighting, the commercial market for anthropology is still
news. An article in *Business Week* published in 2006, with the title 'The Science
of Desire', drew the following account of anthropology's popularity: 'closely
observing people where they live and work, say executives, allows companies

to zero in on their customers' unarticulated desires . . . This makes anthropology far more valuable' (Ante 2006). The *New York Times* translated this added value as a matter of the difference between behavioural sciences of the individual versus the group, asserting that '[u]ntil recently, anthropologists – people trained to analyze group behavior – were spurned by corporations, which preferred to stress individuality and entrepreneurship' (Deutsch 1991). Along with the somewhat peculiar disciplinary characterisation and history on offer here, the proposition that anthropologists were actively spurned by the corporate world, rather than simply being invisible to it, is tied to the suggestion that anthropology's embrace is indicative of some new-found interest in the social, even some newly emergent sociality, in corporate affairs.

We have here, then, a resonance with the social sciences' own observation, discussed above, of the turn to a 'cultural economy'. As signalled by their common resort to colonialist cliché, it is the promise of access to territories beyond the boundaries of the familiar that most obviously dominates these media reports of anthropology's value. Anthropology is taken by business as emblematic of the capacity of the social sciences, specifically new methods of observation, to aid in the expansion and deeper penetration of the cultures of capitalism (Thrift 2006). Even more than the social it is the cultural that enters the picture, as the residual category left over after the psychologists and industrial sociologists are done with their work, the mysteries of which it is now the anthropologist's job to make accessible. The *New York Times* article explains that 'most anthropologists study exotic cultures in faraway places', and accounts for the interest in anthropologists on the part of management as a desire of those who want to expand their operations overseas to understand other cultures, while 'at home, the same companies want help dealing with work forces that are increasingly polyglots of cultures and behaviors' (Deutsch 1991). Globalisation, in sum, brings the exotic other into one's line of sight wherever it falls, whether far away or close to home, and the anthropologist is the logical choice to aid in the process of learning to deal with these new multicultural challenges.

While the promise of her unique expertise may provide the rationale for the anthropologist's employment, however, the fascination of that employment for the media lies in the unlikely juxtaposition of anthropologist as *investigator* of exotic other, with anthropologist *as* exotic other in the mundane, familiar halls of the corporate workplace (di Leonardo 1998). The interest in corporate anthropology involves the anthropologist herself in an identity marked as exotic other, in other words, within the context of familiar commercial and technological worlds: an other brought home to live inside and become part of the enterprise. My colleagues and I experienced this quite directly as we found ourselves, even after many years, being hailed by some of our computer science colleagues at PARC, if we happened to walk down the hall together, with the (only semi-ironic) warning, 'Here come the anthropologists!'. (We ultimately took this thinly veiled reference to the Jets to heart, donning satin gang jackets with our group name emblazoned on them.) As we have seen, this warning – half promise, half portent – is reflected clearly in the texts of the media reports as well as in their titles.

With this said, I want to suggest that the anthropologist's interest for the media derives not only from her promise of special access to the user/consumer, or even from her own unlikely appearance in the halls of corporate office buildings, but perhaps most importantly from the ways in which her traditional associations transform her objects of study from banal to exotic through her interests in them. That is to say, the anthropological gaze, insofar as it is defined by its traditional attention to the other, vicariously renders exotic those on whom it is turned. Factory floors, corporate offices and 'middle class' homes, assumed to be so transparently familiar as not to warrant anthropological attention, are turned into sites as foreign as the colonies once were by the mere fact of the anthropologist's presence: in her making of the familiar strange, the presence of the anthropologist in the 'tribal office' transforms what goes on there – the banal and ordinary activities of the working day – into something mysterious and correspondingly interesting. The anthropologist, in short, renders 'us', the reader addressed by these media stories, as exotic Other.

The appearance of these accounts in the 1990s makes clear that, however specific in their details, our peculiar histories were also part of some general trends, shifts in the rhetorics and practices of multinational corporate enterprise at the close of the twentieth century.[12] Naomi Klein suggests one way of understanding these shifts and their relevance to our experience when she proposes that

> [t]he astronomical growth in the wealth and cultural influence of multinational corporations over the last fifteen years can arguably be traced back to a single, seemingly innocuous idea developed by management theorists in the mid-1980s: that successful corporations must primarily produce brands, not products.
>
> (2000: 3)

It is this basic premise as well, Klein argues, that underwrites the rapid rise of the 'virtual' corporation, aimed at outsourcing production to various export processing zones around the globe, then attaching an image to the resulting assemblage of parts. Unlike their industrial ancestors, the in-house work of these companies is not manufacturing, but marketing. As Klein puts it:

> [s]ince many of today's best known manufacturers no longer produce products and advertise them, but rather buy products and 'brand' them, these companies are forever on the prowl for creative new ways to build and strengthen their brand images.
>
> (ibid.: 4–5)

A crucial element of brand building in an age of mass production and competitive marketing is the manufacture of difference, based less in products than in the packaging of products and their association with recognisable images. Starting in the 1940s, brand evolved from a mascot or catchphrase on a label to the identity of the corporation itself. By 1998, a UN Report found that the growth in spending on global advertising outpaced the growth of the world economy by one-third (cited in Klein 2000: 9).

It is here as well, in the early 1990s, that we find the rise of 'lifestyle' marketing, increasingly abstract 'high-concept' advertising and the first initiatives in the design of shopping 'experiences'. The search for 'brand essence', Klein proposes, moved companies progressively away from individual products and their attributes 'toward a psychological/anthropological examination of what brands mean to culture and to people's lives' (2000: 7). As Celia Lury sums up these developments, the market exchange is now a matter 'not merely of . . . calculation, but also of affect, intensivity, and the reintroduction of qualities' (2004: 7). The performativity of the brand, Lury observes, depends on the compulsory inclusion of consumers as information sources, insofar as 'information about consumers is used as a basis for multiplying the qualities or attributes of the product and managing relations between these multi-dimensional variables in time' (ibid.: 9). The brand under the sign of relationship marketing works to entangle the consumer in an exchange that extends beyond any specific object, or any given transaction.

It is surely no coincidence, then, that it is around this same time that the media began to proclaim the discovery by industry of the discipline of anthropology. The reinvention of the consumer as a social/cultural – rather than strictly rational – actor in contemporary economic and marketing imaginaries is both a condition of possibility, and the central charge, for the anthropologist figured as the medium through which the consumer can be known within, or translated into, sites of production. As at least a minor player in these developments, anthropology had a role both as brand (offering a human interest and public relations caché to corporate employers via the media) and as social science (promising new and appropriable insights into worker and customer 'culture' and 'experience'). The anthropologist as brand performs a kind of interface, at once connecting producer and consumer, and through her mediatory role helping to limit and make manageable their interaction. The anthropologist's relations to the making of brands is a reflexive one, insofar as her own brand efficacy operates through the promise of its contributions to this same process. Through its performativity the brand becomes a figure, an assemblage that operates in these ways through repetition, and through accretions of agency over time and within specific cultural imaginaries. While announced each time as an innovation, media sightings of the anthropologist in industry also work to fix the anthropologist's position as envoy of a discipline that, in Lury's words, if not a matter of certainty is at least an object of possibility. As a disciplinary identification that carries its own caché, the identity of anthropologist in turn doubles back to work as a novel contributor to what Lury identifies as the 'processes in which information about competitors and the consumer is fed back into production', making the brand itself dynamic (2004: 3).

Typically applied to an association of images and things, an interweaving of signs and commodity objects, I am suggesting that we consider the brand as taking persons, or more accurately disciplines, as its object. So what does this mean for those of us concerned about these appropriative translations of anthropology, but at the same time not wishing to be drawn into exercises of purification or the policing of disciplinary boundaries? Our work as anthropologists sits uncomfortably inside the close-knit interweaving of consumer experience understood as something prior, discovered through anthropological investigation and then addressed by design and marketing, and consumer experience understood as constituted *through* activities of design and marketing, in their contributions to the creation of desire and the crafting of cultural imaginaries. I do not believe that we can resolve this tension. But, as in our subject positions as employees or as consumers, our problem as anthropologists is to find the spaces that allow us to refigure the projects of those who purchase our services and from whom we buy, rather than merely to be incorporated passively within them.

Translations

> Knowledge grows through multiple layers of collaboration – as both empathy and betrayal.
>
> Tsing 2005: 155

I turn in closing to the tricky borderlands that differentiate two modes of collaboration across difference. The first assumes the existence of *a priori* truths, and the project of interdisciplinarity as an instrument for their discovery. The second, based on Helen Verran's construct of working disparate knowledges together (1998, 2002), assumes the irremediable multiplicity of the real, and reconciliation as too often the product of power-differentiated translations of one party's knowledges into the terms of another's. Rather than reconciliation, then, working knowledges together aims at possibilities for partial, practical connections (see also Strathern 1991). Translation has little tolerance for the persistence of differences that challenge the foundations of claims to universal knowledge; partial connection takes the negotiation of difference as an ongoing foundation for getting on together. Translation insists that politics should be suspended from the space of collaboration (and therefore must repress them); partial connection operates on careful attention to the politics of difference.

In the introduction to his book *Biocapital* (2006), Kaushik Sunder Rajan describes his discomfort at the lack of a legible story to tell about his dissertation project to the scientists in the laboratory that he was studying until he met Mark Boguski, a scientist at the National Center for Biotechnology Information, who provided him with one. Comparing Sunder Rajan to anthropologist Paul Rabinow, he exclaimed 'I think someone needs to write a contemporary history of genomics, and I think you should do it' (ibid.:1). Sunder Rajan goes on to describe the access that this provided him to the field of genomics (and by implication at least partial relief from his discomfort). But what are the implications of this recognition, the associated story of Sunder Rajan's project, and the expectations that it signals for what the anthropologist might do in researching this or any other field of technoscience? What, in particular, might Boguski have imagined, and what would become of the differences between that and the stories that Sunder Rajan himself, in his relations with anthropology and science studies, might go on to tell? Yes, recognition eases our discomfort at being illegible. But it also carries its own discomforts, insofar as the identification that it offers us limits our possibilities for difference.

In the case of Xerox PARC, and of collaborations between computer and social scientists more broadly during the 1980s and 1990s, two modes of interdisciplinarity were in tension: one general and programmatic, the other specific and practical. By the mid 1990s, programmatic debates over the relation of computer and social sciences held at major research conferences in the previous decade had largely been replaced by reports on practical experiments in working together computational, engineering and anthropological knowledges with those of practitioners in a range of sites in order to explore inventive configurations of relevant information technologies. Within Xerox PARC, the tropes of 'knowledge' and 'practice' were now conjoined in our laboratory's very name. On the face of it, then, it would seem that arguments reiterated over the preceding 15 years had been embraced fully.

My experience, in contrast, was that the space of interdisciplinarity in some significant respects closed down as the trope of 'practice' was embraced. As the latter became the general rubric for knowledge making, different – and in particular contested – readings of what research and scholarship on practice might entail were more threatening to what now should be an emerging consensus. Nigel Thrift (2006) helps to contextualise this experience for me in his analysis of what he names recent 'tendencies' in contemporary capitalism. The first, seemingly far removed from the enterprises of Silicon Valley (apart from the endless need of high technology for more materials – aluminum, coltan and so forth), comprises further intensification of resource extraction, involving 'force, dispossession and enclosure as part of a search for mass commodities like oil, gas, gems and timber using all the usual suspects: guns, barbed wire and the law' (ibid.:280). The second tendency he articulates as

> an obsession with knowledge and creativity and especially an obsession with fostering tacit knowledge and aptitudes through devices like the community of practice . . . [along with] a desire to rework consumption so as to draw consumers much more fully into the process, leaching out their knowledge of commodities and adding it back into the system as an added performative edge through an 'experience economy'. . . This stream of thought and practice has now blossomed into a set of fully fledged models of 'co-creation' which are changing corporate perceptions of what constitutes 'production,' 'consumption,' 'commodity,' 'the market' and indeed 'innovation'.
>
> (ibid.: 282)

This second tendency, clearly much closer to home, also includes projects of social engineering designed to accelerate creative collaboration including, of course, across disciplines.

It is within this nexus of designs and desires, during a time when profitable returns on investment among established technology manufacturers grew ever more difficult to achieve, that our work and the wider brand of corporate anthropology was formed. At the same time, our identification as anthropologists relied on continuing engagement with developments in the academic discipline of anthropology, where increasingly incisive critiques of contemporary capitalism, including the 'tendencies' that Thrift identifies, were under construction. So as the programme within the laboratory was in the process of developing its own orthodoxies – including the embrace of the social sciences – the space in which to question received assumptions regarding the politics of corporate anthropology seemed to diminish. Where before we had been enrolled in what was clearly an 'agonistic' form of interdisciplinarity (Barry et al 2008), we were now asked to contribute to an apparently cohesive undertaking. While the former could be negotiated based on partial connections, the latter demanded modes of loyalty that seemed to make our own differences increasingly indigestible.

Perhaps most obviously absent from the discourses of the research laboratory was any critical discussion of the political economies to which our work was increasingly accountable. As the corporation's performance on Wall Street (a topic of little or no interest to researchers when I arrived at PARC in the late 1970s) became a constant preoccupation (stock prices and business analyses being discussed at every lab meeting), there remained a deafening silence regarding any critical analysis of developments in the world economy and financial markets. To engage in such critique was treated as anachronistically naïve at best, 'biting that hand that feeds you' at worst. Yet in a more optimistic imagining of corporate anthropology, George Marcus writes, in his introduction to the collection *Corporate Futures* (1998: 2):

> in terms of their own highly specific idioms and purposes, the social actors who become, in conversation with us, our specific subjects of research may even provide more nuanced, deeper, and richer conceptualizations of contemporary change than the remade, distanced, and authoritative exposition typical of the social-scientist expert, cultural critic, or journalist-commentator.

My own critical reading of the position of the corporate anthropologist leads me to ask just what is at stake in this contrast of the actor-subject and ethnographer-analyst, including the privileging of the former. What if we were to abandon the ordering (even as an inversion), and ask instead what each brings to the project of theorising contemporary developments in science, technology, industry, capitalism or whatever? Unquestionably the actor deeply embedded in the sites of interest brings distinctive ways of knowing those sites, born of extended participation in and lived experience of relevant doings. But is it necessarily the case, as Marcus' formulation at least implies, that the social scientist's or cultural critic's account is any more 'remade', 'distanced', or 'authoritative' than the organisation member's? Certainly not inherently. I would argue that all accounts are equally 'remade', albeit with reference to different relevancies. Moreover, there are many forms of distance and authority evident within organisational actors' accounts of themselves, albeit different ones from that of the social scientist.

The differences between accounts made by organisation members and those of anthropologists is less about closeness *versus* distance, in other words, than about different frames of reference and audiences. It is even possible that social scientists and cultural critics have, at least potentially, additional resources to draw on, beyond those available to organisation members, in contextualising, theorising and conceptualising what it is that's going on. So what could it mean, rather than to order the accounts of organisation members and ethnographers, to work them together – and against each other: to treat the resonances and tensions as productive? In their discussion of the performative effects of categorisation (specifically of constructions of capitalism as a singularity, whether by enthusiasts or anti-capitalist critics), feminist economists J. K. Gibson-Graham observe that 'If there is no singular figure, there can be no singular other . . . Theorizing capitalism itself as different from itself – as having, in other words, no essential or coherent identity – multiplies (infinitely) the possibilities of alterity' (1996: 15). We might apply the same observation to the disciplines. Like other identity categories, the disciplines are over determined; that is, 'continually and differentially constituted rather than . . . pre-existing their contexts or . . . having an invariant core' (ibid.: 16). Like corporations and markets, disciplines are enacted and multiple. And practices – including economically relevant practices – invariably overflow the frames of any single account; they 'enact complex interferences between orders or discourses' (Law 2002: 22). Multiplying the possibilities requires articulating the frames that comprise markets, disciplines and the micro-politics of economies of knowledge, including close attention to their differential constitutions of value, or of the 'good'.

It is in this respect that I would argue that, however subject to creeping neoliberalism and corporatisation, the academy as an institution still affords frames of reference and accountability importantly different to those of industry. Most concretely, in the latter there are few bases for protesting growing corporatisation, demands for profitable entrepreneurship and the like: those are, rather, the primary social responsibility of corporate citizenship. Historical commitments of the academy – to education, understanding the human condition, the public good – can, commensurately, be invoked as grounds for resistance. These are differences in charter, I would argue, that make a difference in the forms of action that they at least potentially legitimise and underwrite. More substantively, commerce and politics get both entangled and obscured in contemporary calls for 'user' relevance in all things: we need to distinguish between calls for value in the sense of utility, and a recognition of values as inextricable from the conduct of research. There is a difference that matters between normative research enlisted in the service of agendas – public or private – in which the frame is not itself open to question, and research that affiliates with efforts to question the frames within which politics, markets or any other entities are disciplined. The history of anthropological research conducted under industry sponsorship makes evident both the possibilities for generative interference that come with anthropology's promise of reframing, as well as the tricky politics and frictions of its incorporation.

Notes

1 For a timely collection of writings on the types and extent of anthropological engagement in industry see Cefkin 2009.

2 I use the term 'embedding' here deliberately, despite the problems of its connotation of the corporation as some kind of containing entity, for its comparison to the situation of the 'embedded' reporter in the military. The controversy over embedded journalism turns, on one hand, on the argument that embedding provides unprecedented access to the daily activities and perspectives of military personnel and, on the other, on the question of whether and how the capacities of the journalist to raise critical questions are compromised. It is important to note in this analogy that the embedded reporter is not typically employed by the military: commentators generally treat military employment as something that must categorically affect the reporter's position, transforming her from an investigative journalist into a public relations representative. Without assuming that the latter is the fate of the anthropologist in industrial research, I come back to the further complications of her position in the discussion that follows. I take to heart as well the call to conceive of the market, or capitalism, not as a unity or as given in advance of its specific enactments (a form that we might refer to as the Market, or Capitalism), but as fractured and multiple; so I assume throughout that the performance of 'the corporation' as a singularity is itself a part of the everyday labours of its affiliated actors (Gibson-Graham 1996: 187; Sunder Rajan 2006: 7).

3 For a related argument developed through detailed ethnographic engagement with a high profile site of the musical 'avant garde', founded in the same year as Xerox PARC, see Born 1995.

4 Before coming to PARC, Rulifson had worked with Douglas Englebart on the 'Augment' project at the Stanford Research Institute, a source for many of the imaginaries and technologies that comprise the 'office of the future'. The founding of PARC in 1970 was itself symptomatic of Xerox's early concerns with its place in that future. The following account draws from an interview conducted by the author with Jeff Rulifson on 19 February 2003, as part of a project funded by the ESRC Science and Society Programme, Award/Grant Reference: L144250006.

5 While Browner and Chibnik felt it appropriate to adopt a pseudonym at the time of their writing, they have agreed that, with the consent of Jeff Rulifson, the group might be identified here.

6 The prototype configured PARC's Alto minicomputer into an administrative workstation running 'Officetalk', software created using the Smalltalk programming language also under development at PARC.

7 Much of this perspective was likely due to Rulifson's engagement with Eleanor Wynn, whose contract the previous summer resulted in subsequent support for her dissertation on the importance of informal office conversation in the communication of business-relevant information. See Wynn (1979).

8 Following a summer position in 1978 as a research assistant to Eleanor Wynn, I became a summer intern in the Office Research Group in 1979 and subsequently completed my own dissertation at PARC (Suchman 2007 [1987]).

9 Founding members of the group along with myself were Jeanette Blomberg, Brigitte Jordan, David Levy, Julian Orr and Randall Trigg.

10 In 1988, as Program Chair for the second conference on Computer-Supported Cooperative Work (CSCW), and in 1990 (as part of a working group of the educational non-profit Computer Professionals for Social Responsibility) as Program Chair for the first Participatory Design Conference (PDC), I found opportunities to help bring these ideas to academic computer scientists in the US. See Schuler and Namioka (1993).

11 For a partial overview see Suchman et al (1999).

12 See Reardon's discussion (2005: 91–2) of the enrolment of anthropologists in the Human Genome Diversity Project around this same time.

References

Ante, S. (2006) 'The Science of Desire', *Business Week*, 5 June.

Appadurai, A. (1986) 'Introduction: Commodities and the Politics of Value', in A. Appadurai (ed.) *The Social Life of Things: Commodities in Cultural Perspective* (pp. 3–63). Cambridge: Cambridge University Press.

Barry, A., Born, G. and Weszkalnys, G. (2008) 'Logics of Interdisciplinarity', *Economy and Society* 37: 20–49.

Barry, A. and Slater, D. (2002) 'Technology, Politics and the Market: An Interview with Michel Callon', *Economy and Society*, 31 (2): 285–306.

Barry, A. and Slater, D. (eds.) (2005) *The Technological Economy*, London: Routledge.

Blomberg, J., Suchman, L. and Trigg, R. (1996) 'Reflections on a Work-oriented Design Project', *Human–Computer Interaction* 11: 237–65.

Born, G. (1995) *Rationalizing Culture: IRCAM, Boulez, and the Institutionalization of the Musical Avant-Garde*, Berkeley, CA: University of California Press.

Browner, C. and Chibnik, M. (1979) 'Anthropological Research for a Computer Manufacturing Company', *Central Issues in Anthropology* 1: 63–76.

Buderi, R. (1998) 'Fieldwork in the Tribal Office', *Technology Review*, May/June.

Callon, M. (1998a) 'An Essay on Framing and Overflowing: Economic Externalities Revisited by Sociology', in M. Callon (ed.) *The Laws of the Markets* (pp. 244–69). Oxford: Basil Blackwell.

— (1998b) *The Laws of the Markets*, Oxford: Basil Blackwell.

Cefkin, M. (ed.) (2009) *Ethnography and the Corporate Encounter: Reflections on Research In and Of Corporations*, Oxford: Berghahn.

Coombe, R. (1998) *The Cultural Life of Intellectual Properties: Authorship, Appropriation, and the Law*, Durham and London: Duke University Press.

Cronin, A. (2000) *Advertising and Consumer Citizenship*, London and New York: Routledge.

— (2003) *Advertising Myths: The Strange Half-Lives of Images and Commodities*, London: Routledge.

Deutsch, C. (1991) 'Coping with Cultural Polyglots', *New York Times*, 24 February.

di Leonardo, M. (1998) *Exotics at Home: Anthropologies, Others, American Modernities*, Chicago, IL: University of Chicago Press.

du Gay, P. and Pryke, M. (2002) *Cultural Economy: Cultural Analysis and Commercial Life*, London: Sage.

Eddy, E. and Partridge, W. (1987) *Applied Anthropology in America*, 2nd edition, New York: Columbia University Press.

Garza, C. E. (1991) 'Studying the Natives on the Shop Floor', *Business Week*, 30 September.

Gibson-Graham, J. K. (1996) *The End of Capitalism (As We Knew It)*, Cambridge, MA: Blackwell.

Hafner, K. (1999) 'Coming of Age in Palo Alto', *New York Times*, 10 June.

Kane, K. (1996) 'Anthropologists Go Native in the Corporate Village', *Fast Company*, October/November.

Klein, N. (2000) *No Logo: Taking Aim at the Brand Bullies*, Toronto: Knopf

Knight, W. (2004) 'Anthropologists to Beat Gadget Rage', *New Scientist*, 18 December.

Koerner, B. (1998) 'Into the Wild Unknown of Workplace Culture', *U.S. News & World Report*, 10 August.

Lash, S. and Urry, J. (1994) *Economies of Signs and Space*, London: Sage.

Law, J. (2002) 'Economics as Interference', in P. Du Gay and M. Pryke (eds.) *Cultural Economy*, (pp. 21–38), London: Sage.

Lury, C. (1996) *Consumer Culture,* Cambridge: Polity Press.

— (2004) *Brands: The Logos of the Global Economy*, London: Routledge.

Mackenzie, D. (2006) *An Engine, Not a Camera: How Financial Models Shape Markets*, Cambridge, MA: MIT Press.

Marcus, G. (1998) *Corporate Futures: The Diffusion of the Culturally Sensitive Corporate Form*, Chicago, IL: University of Chicago Press.

Miller, D. (1998a) *A Theory of Shopping*, Ithaca, NY: Cornell University Press.

— (1998b) *Material Cultures*, Chicago, IL: University of Chicago Press.

Reardon, J. (2005) *Race to the Finish: Identity and Governance in an Age of Genomics*, Princeton, NJ: Princeton University Press.

Salaman, G. (1997) 'Culturing Production', in P. Du Gay (ed.) *Production of Culture/ Cultures of Production*, (pp. 235–284). London: Sage.

Schuler, D. and Namioka, A. (1993) *Participatory Design: Principles and Practices*. Hillsdale, NJ: Lawrence Erlbaum.

Slater, D. (1997) *Consumer Culture and Modernity*, Cambridge: Polity.

— (2002) 'Capturing Markets from the Economists', in P. Du Gay and M. Pryke (eds.) *Cultural Economy* (pp. 59–77), London: Sage.

Strathern, M. (1991) *Partial Connections*, Sabage, MD: Rowman & Littlefield.

— (2006) 'A Community of Critics? Thoughts on New Knowledge', *Journal of the Royal Anthropological Institute* 12: 191–209.

Suchman, L. (2007 [1987]) *Human–Machine Reconfigurations: Plans and Situated Actions*, revised edition, New York: Cambridge.

Suchman, L., Blomberg, J., Orr, J. and Trigg, R. (1999) 'Reconstructing Technologies as Social Practice', *American Behavioral Scientist* 43: 392–408.

Suchman, L., Trigg, R. and Blomberg, J. (2002) 'Working Artefacts: Ethnomethods of the Prototype', *British Journal of Sociology* 53: 163–79.

Sunder Rajan, K. (2006) *Biocapital: The Constitution of Postgenomic Life*. Durham and London: Duke University Press.

Thrift, N. (2006) 'Re-inventing Invention: New Tendencies in Capitalist Commodification', *Economy and Society* 35: 279–306.

Tischler, L. (2004) 'Every Move You Make', *Fast Company*, April.

Trigg, R., Blomberg, J. and Suchman, L. (1999) 'Moving Document Collections Online', *Proceedings of the Sixth European Conference on Computer-supported Cooperative Work (ECSCW)*: 331–50.

Tsing, A. (2005) *Friction: An Ethnography of Global Connection*, Princeton, NJ: Princeton University Press.

Verran, H. (1998) 'Re-Imagining Land Ownership in Australia', *Postcolonial Studies* 1: 237–54.

— (2002) 'A Postcolonial Moment in Science Studies: Alternative Firing Regimes of Environmental Scientists and Aboriginal Landowners', *Social Studies of Science* 32: 729–62.

Wajcman, J. (1991) *Feminism Confronts Technology*, University Park: Pennsylvania State University Press.

Walsh, S. (2001) 'Corporate Anthropology: Dirt-Free Research', *CNN.com*, 23 May.

Wynn, E. (1979) 'Office Conversation as an Information Medium', *unpublished PhD thesis*, Department of Anthropology, University of California, Berkeley.

7 Where Natural and Social Science Meet?

Reflections on an experiment in geographical practice

Sarah J. Whatmore

Earth/Life – An Old Path to Invention

The vital connections between the *geo* (earth) and the *bio* (life) are arguably the most enduring of geographical concerns. Although not always in fashion their durability bears the hallmark of geography's history which, like that of archaeology and anthropology, took shape before the now entrenched division between the social and natural sciences took hold. It is a division with which these disciplines have never been entirely comfortable and with which they continue to wrestle more self-consciously and, sometimes, productively than others. Some sense of the shared intellectual currents working against the grain of this settlement can be found in the persistence and renewal of such topics as landscape, ecology and material culture (e.g. Hicks and Beaudry, 2010). What these currents continue to freight is modern geography's investment in understanding the emergence and society of humankind with and through the fabrications of earth/life (e.g. Marsh, 1965 [1864]; Simmons, 1996; Whatmore, 2002; Clark, 2010).

As well as their association with the human sciences (see Anderson, 2007), all three disciplines owe much to what used to be called natural history (see Jardine *et al.*, 1996) and its peculiar commitment to an ethos of fieldwork. This mode of enquiry encourages researchers to engage bodily with the material world and to treat the situation (field) of knowledge production (work) as constitutive of, rather than incidental to, the research event and the evidence which it generates (see, for example, Gupta and Ferguson, 1997; Lucas, 2001; Pryke *et al.*, 2003). In consequence, these disciplines' practices of mapping into knowledge the life habits of various kinds, human and otherwise, have been implicated in/as technologies of empire building (see Driver, 2001) back into antiquity (Murphy, 2004). By the same token, it has sparked in them a subaltern concern with the politics of knowledge production and a more recent vein of methodological inventiveness with respect to the terms of research engagement.[1] In geography these genealogical tracks have exercised a keen disciplinary awareness of the complicity of knowledge and power. In consequence, geographers are more familiar than most with the burden of expectation attached to (re)combining the enterprises of natural and social science in the service of 'real world problems'. A burden that is now being vested in 'interdisciplinarity' by the policy regimes, funding bodies and knowledge industries amongst which academic research must make its way (Nowotny *et al.*, 2001).

Like archaeology and anthropology, the range of research and pedagogy undertaken in the name of geography spans subject matter and approaches to it found across the spectrum of the humanities, and the social and natural sciences. Suspended between the magnetic poles of 'human' and 'physical' geography, the diversity of the geographical project is a source of both strength and weakness. At its best, it equips scholars to tack between radically different knowledge practices, fostering an inventive interdisciplinarity rather than a prescribed path to some transcendent integration. However, geography's identity as an interdiscipline that works across the division of social and natural sciences can be argued to be realised more effectively today in the co-habitation of 'physical' and 'human' geographers in shared buildings and curricula,[2] than in research practice. As the contents of disciplinary journals and the publication habits of those working in the two wings of the discipline attest, both are commonly more conversant with work in cognate disciplines through common fields of interest (such as urban studies or glaciology) than with each other's. In this, as historians of geography have argued, geographical practice has always been exercised through different sites, techniques and materials which have kept it a heterogeneous and contested enterprise (see Livingstone, 1992; Withers, 2009). Yet these features might be unremarkable – heterogeneity and contestation is surely characteristic of all disciplines – were it not for the weight attached in the geographical tradition to integrating natural and social worlds.

Countervailing, and to some extent disguising, this divergent tendency has been the emergence in the later decades of the twentieth century of 'the environment' in general, and 'climate change' in particular, as archetypal imperatives for greater interdisciplinarity in the organisation and conduct of research. In the UK, for example, geography's institutional guardians such as the Royal Geographical Society and the Geographical Association have embraced this environmental bolster to its interdisciplinary claims and, thereby, its 'relevance' in terms of public policy agendas for science and education. University geography departments have been no less adept at repackaging themselves to suit the times, variously accentuating their 'environmental/science' credentials.[3] Any number of collaborations between human and physical geographers has been spawned in consequence to address designated 'multi-factorial' environmental problems. For the most part, such collaborations have been characterised by the adoption of common methodologies (e.g. modelling social and physical components of an environmental system) and/or the integration of data sets (e.g. social survey data and environmental field data). As such skill mixes become more commonplace in environmental research more widely so the stakes are raised for geography, prompting some to acclaim it now as 'the pre-eminent interdisciplinary environmental discipline' (Skole, 2004: 739).

That the resourcing of geographical research and teaching has benefitted as a result of this institutional embrace of 'the environment' is not in doubt, but at what intellectual cost? As Andrew Barry *et al.* (2008: 36) have observed of the kinds of interdisciplinary practice most in evidence in environmental research, it is an embrace that has incorporated too readily a normative rationale for Interdisciplinarity (with a capital 'I') in which research is positively allied to governmental and business agendas.[4] In so doing, geography is at risk of tripping over its own rhetoric. Its institutional compliance with this normative rationale, in the name of environmental 'problem solving', is at odds with one of its own most inventive interdisciplinary traditions – a practised attentiveness to the ontological demands of the complex artefacts and processes assembled in/as 'environmental problems' that calls the terms of every such problematisation into question. Where the first Interdisciplinary imperative takes for granted an *a priori* separation of 'human society' from 'the environment', the premise of efforts to measure and manage the impacts of the one on the other, the second insists on 'the ontological impossibility of sustaining the binary conception – human and environment' (Anderson and Braun, 2008: 1); an analytical and political imperative for intensifying the interrogation of just *what* is at issue. In this, geography's interdisciplinary practices can be seen to exemplify the tension characterised by Deleuze and Guattari as 'a perpetual field of interaction' between 'royal' (or machinic) and 'minor' (or nomadic) science (1988: 360–1).[5]

In this chapter I want to explore the tension between these two interdisciplinary imperatives at play in geographical practice by reflecting on my own experiences of a collaborative experiment in working 'across the human–physical divide' that involved tireless and, occasionally, tiresome negotiation of the differences between them. This collaboration was situated in that current of work still interrogating the earth/life nexus, the traditional pulse of geography's interdisciplinary inventiveness but now associated more narrowly with work in cultural geography (see Thrift and Whatmore, 2004). It is a source of inventiveness which has tended to be overlooked in debates about geography's 'relevance' (e.g. Martin, 2005; Ward 2007). The recent thrust of this work against the grain of any *a priori* distinction between 'societies' evacuated of everything except people and 'environments' untainted by their presence invites a different ontological disposition in which, as the political theorist Jane Bennett puts it, 'humans are always in composition with nonhumanity, never outside of a sticky web of connections or an ecology' (2004: 365). Figured thus, the fabrications of earth/life implicate all manner of artefacts and materials as well as organisms and elements and direct attention to the technoscientific practices of environmental 'problem solving' as ecologically constitutive themselves and, hence, as matters of crucial analytical (and political) concern (see Braun and Whatmore, 2010).

This redirection of an old path to invention invites interdisciplinary collaborations between human and physical geographers in which the production and contestation of environmental knowledge, particularly the practices of scientists and policymakers involved in the assemblage of environmental expertise, come into focus. There are growing numbers of such collaborative studies of environmental or field sciences at work.[6] However, the collaboration to which I refer here set out not only to study the environmental expertise of others but also to experiment with doing environmental science differently ourselves (see Lane *et al.*, 2011).

In this chapter I reflect first on the experience of winning funding under the Rural Economy and Land Use (RELU) programme for a project on 'Understanding knowledge controversies: the case of flood risk management' (knowledge-controversies.ouce.ox.ac.uk). In addition to examining the assemblage of flood risk management expertise in the UK, the project engaged in two local knowledge controversies through research collaborations with people affected by flooding. In the second part of the chapter, I outline the experimental apparatus of 'competency groups' that we trialled as an exercise in geography's interdisciplinary inventiveness designed to effect redistributions of environmental expertise (see Whatmore and Landström, 2011a).

From the beginning, however, such overtly intellectual intentions were entangled with much more pragmatic concerns. Would an application from human and physical geographers pass the interdisciplinarity test instituted by the RELU programme? If so, would we be able to hold on to the ontological imperatives of our own interdisciplinary experiment, or would these be subsumed by the normative demands of a programme strongly attuned to government Interdisciplinary agendas?

Working Across the 'Human'/'Physical' Divide: From Talk to Practice

The normative claims of Interdisciplinarity, to which geography has become institutionally aligned, have been elaborated most influentially by Helga Nowotny and her collaborators (2001) in their account of the rise of what they call 'mode 2 science'. They associate it with an ongoing shift in the relationship between scientific knowledge and democratic politics that is presented as both a 'new way of thinking about science' and a description of some 'empirically evident' attributes of scientific practice today.[7] This 'mode 2' regime is characterised by a replacement of discipline-driven academic research agendas with the interdisciplinary knowledge requirements of public policy and/or commerce.

In their critical interrogation of this apparently hegemonic Interdisciplinarity, Barry *et al.* (2008) associate it particularly with the twin logics of 'accountability' and 'innovation'. Accountability describes a logic in which publically funded science should service government policy priorities, not least engaging 'the public' more effectively in the understanding of science.[8] In contrast, the logic of innovation harnesses science to industry in the name of national economic competitiveness. To apply for research funding from any of the UK's research councils[9] today is to encounter these logics in the imperative tense through their incorporation into the guidance criteria and mandatory 'knowledge exchange' and 'impact' statements without which an online application is condemned to electronic purgatory as 'incomplete'.

One of the more notable initiatives in this 'mode 2' vein has been the effort of three of the research councils to institutionalise these interdisciplinary logics in environmental research through the Rural Economy and Land Use programme (www.relu.ac.uk).[10] Described by its directors as a programme providing 'insights into the challenges that interdisciplinarity and accountability present to established science institutions' (Lowe and Phillipson, 2006: 165), RELU was the first and largest programme in the UK to make collaboration between natural and social scientists a precondition of project funding. In the terms of the programme, such collaborations would necessitate research teams combining 'more than one discipline', and the roll-call of disciplines involved in funded research projects was to become totemic of the programme's brand (see Lowe and Phillipson, 2009). As an outgoing and internally diversified discipline, geography could be construed as both a 'natural' ally of RELU *and* at risk of disqualification if treated in applications as an interdiscipline in its own right.[11]

Perhaps this ambivalence explains my initial hesitation about engaging with the RELU programme, despite having become interested in putting geography's interdisciplinary inventiveness to the test through some kind of collaboration with physical geographers. This interest had been intensified by a conversation with the physical geographer Stuart Lane during one of the regular sessions at the annual conference gatherings of British geographers dedicated to 'bridging the human/physical divide' (see Harrison *et al.*, 2004). It was Neil Ward, an ex-colleague of mine and then colleague of Stuart's, who was to persuade us that the programme was more open to experimental approaches than had been obvious to me from the promotional materials. He also had the rural policy expertise that we both lacked, and brought on board another natural scientist to 'balance' the team. Buoyed by prior knowledge of each other and the complementarity of our intellectual concerns, we entered the vortex of the 'JeS system' for the electronic submission of research council funding applications.[12] We spent some eight months working up a research proposal under the auspices of a 'capacity building' award, a process that gathered momentum and direction from a constant negotia-tion of the tensions between the normative demands of the programme and our experimental motivations.

The 'specification' materials provided to applicants for RELU funding, stated the programme's rationale thus:

> A basic premise of RELU is that major challenges facing rural economy and land use cut across disciplinary boundaries. Interdisciplinarity is required in order to gain integrated perspectives on problems and to understand complex processes and issues involved in achieving sustainable rural development. A central challenge for innovation in project design and management is the requirement to pursue an approach that effectively combines research staff, methods and perspectives from social and natural science disciplines.
>
> (RELU 2004: 2)

The programme specification went on to identify three linked objectives. First, a 'science' objective 'to deliver integrative, interdisciplinary research of high quality that will advance understanding of the social, economic, environmental and technological challenges faced by rural areas and the relationship between them'. Second, a 'capacity building' objective 'to enhance and expand capabilities for integrative, interdisciplinary research on rural issues', which noted that 'attention will be given as much to promoting novel cross-disciplinary couplings as to further refinement of established interdisciplinary methods and techniques'. The third objective related to 'knowledge transfer' and aimed 'to enhance the impact of research on rural policy and practice by involving stakeholders in all stages of RELU, including programme development, research activities and communication of outcomes' (ibid.: 2). Searching for some point of purchase amidst these smooth 'mode 2' formulations, the invitation to 'novel cross-disciplinary couplings' looked like the most promising opening for our experimental project even as we were doubtful whether our status as human and physical geographers would meet the 'cross-disciplinary' criteria.

In addition to the usual information requirements stipulated by research council application pro-forma (including 'user engagement and communication plans'), those for the RELU programme had two additional sections – M and N. Section M (i) required 'the primary discipline for each investigator' to be identified in terms of 'a person's fundamental scientific training and disciplinary orientation', and restricted this identification to the selection of 'just one primary discipline' from an annexed list. Working with what elasticity these definitional parameters permitted, we identified both social science applicants as 'human geographers' but the natural scientists (both of whom had received doctoral training, in part at least, in geography departments) by their specialist field of environmental expertise.[13] Our efforts to address this requirement emphasised too that at the time of application only one of us was employed in a department of geography. Two of us were located in multidisciplinary research institutes, and my own department had been newly redesignated as a 'Centre for the Environment'. Section M (ii) asked for a description of, and justification for, 'your approach to interdisciplinarity' (in a maximum of 750 words), including 'the reasons for your choice of disciplines and how you will ensure effective integration of the social and natural sciences'.

Our response sought to reconcile the experimental nature of our approach with the specifications of the programme by distinguishing it from the more usual 'mixed skills' rationale for interdisciplinarity. In this way, our anxieties about whether or not human and physical geographers qualified as a 'novel cross-disciplinary coupling' became bound up with an implicit critique of the programme's 'mode 2' presuppositions:

> Our project design has the challenge of interdisciplinary working at its core. We identify three 'levels' of interdisciplinary engagement. First, *superficial interdisciplinarity* involves scientists from different disciplines working in compartmentalized work packages that are subsequently stitched together with little cross-disciplinary engagement. Second, *functional interdisciplinarity* involves data exchanges and common epistemological approaches linking different disciplines and framing integrated research projects but with little or no reevaluation or development of research practice. Third, *radical interdisciplinarity* involves the sustained interrogation of, and engagement with, the different research approaches and practices of collaborating

researchers to generate new collective modes of working. Here, implicit philosophical assumptions and methodological conventions are subject to scrutiny, along with the taken-for-granted scientific cultures and working practices of different disciplines. (Section M (ii) Full proposal (version 1) submitted by Whatmore *et al.*, February 2005)

The rest of the permissible word limit in this section was used to highlight features of the project design that would support the 'delivery' of this third approach – *radical interdisciplinarity*. The most important of these was an intensive induction and training programme for the whole project team (elaborated in Section N 'training provision') in the working methods of the proposed research activities. These included (i) the ethnographic methods of science and technology studies (STS) being used to interrogate the modelling practices which inform flood management in the UK (Work Package One); (ii) the hydraulic modelling practices of the project team's 'in-house' flood scientists (Work Package Two);[14] and (iii) the philosophy of science informing the design of 'competency groups' (CGs), a methodological experiment involving extended research collaborations between the whole project team (social and natural scientists) and people affected by flooding in two localities in the UK. In addition, we indicated that a reflexive analysis of the interdisciplinary dynamics of the project team would be led by an 'affiliated' researcher, informed by video/audio recordings of CG activities and interviews with project team members at different points through the course of the project.

In the 'case for support', a narrative 'free entry' supplement to the electronic pro-forma, we elaborated further on the conduct and evaluation of the experimental CG methodology as the primary vehicle for our 'approach to doing interdisciplinary public science differently. . . . [by] combining a radical kind of interdisciplinarity between social and natural scientists and a collaborative form of public engagement, such that non-scientists are involved in the knowledge production process from the outset' (full proposal, (versions 1 and 2) submitted by Whatmore *et al.*, February and November 2005, respectively). The text was illustrated by the diagram reproduced in Figure 7.1.

As it turned out, the peer review process was to be the least of our problems. The first set of comments from reviewers across the natural/social science spectrum was uniformly supportive of funding the project. Not one of them mentioned the issue of our disciplinary affiliations. Indeed, our proposal was scored particularly highly for its 'interdisciplinary integration [which is] without doubt a very strong and innovative part of the project' (assessor comments appended to decision letter of 14 July 2005).

However, our initial delight was rapidly overtaken by the decision of the programme's 'Assessment Panel' to grant the award subject to a 25 per cent cut to the proposed budget.[15] The Panel directed our attention to the staffing and fieldwork costs of 'data acquisition' required to support the natural science, particularly that associated with one of our two proposed knowledge controversies. In vain, we contested the justification for these cuts and the natural science co-applicant whose work they most affected withdrew from the project. For the three of us

		Modes of Scientific Interdisciplinarity		
		Multi-disciplinary	Functional Interdisciplinary	Radical Interdisciplinary
Modes of Public Involvement	Public Understanding			↑ ↑
	Binary			↑ ↑
	Integrated	← ← ←	← ← ←	Competency Groups

Figure 7.1

remaining, the process then became increasingly Kafkaesque. We were presented with various options by another RELU body – the 'Programme Management Group' – consisting principally, so far as we were able to ascertain, of senior officers from relevant research councils and key policy stakeholders.[16] The option that we elected was to submit a revised proposal focusing on one rather than two controversies (flooding), with the stipulation that any such resubmission would be subject to further peer-review. To cut a very long and frustrating story short, it was this revised project for which funding was eventually approved some 20 months after making the original application.

In some ways, our initial hesitation about the compatibility of an application from human and physical geographers with the interdisciplinary agenda of the RELU programme continued to haunt us. The programme's normative presuppositions and the ontological logic of our experimental ambitions were in constant tension through what turned out to be a fraught but, ultimately, successful process. While our sense of working against the grain of the programme intensified with each setback so too did our appreciation of what made the project intellectually worthwhile and, hence, on which elements of the proposal we were and were not willing to compromise.

What also became clearer to us along the way was that rather than institutionalising a 'mode 2' rationale, the RELU programme was itself a large and very public experiment in promoting interdisciplinary research in which this normative agenda served to secure the financial investment and policy buy-in required to get it off the ground. The programme's academic directors and peer reviewers proved more open to experimentation than we had presumed. However, as we were to learn the hard way, their academic judgements too were subject to the budgetary and bureaucratic machinations of the funding institutions. Having eventually won the resources to put geography's interdisciplinary inventiveness to the test, what of the Competency Group experiment for which we had held out?

A Collaborative Experiment in 'Ontological' Interdisciplinarity

In their critique of the normative logics of 'accountability' and 'innovation' that dominate interdisciplinary practice, Barry *et al.* (2008) argue that interdisciplinarity is neither historically novel nor just an orchestrated response to the demands of science policy (and funding). They discern more inventive potential in those currents that 'lead to the production of new objects and practices of knowledge' (ibid.: 42), and which they associate with a third logic – that of ontology. Among their three ethnographic case studies of interdisciplinary practice, this third logic is least developed in the environmental research case. Here, they point to the emergence of a 'more encompassing ontological rationale' in which the

> development of environmental policy and politics has implications for the relations between the natural and social sciences not because the environment is a complex system of natural and social elements, but because environmental issues raise fundamental questions concerning the very distinction between the natural and the social.
>
> (ibid.: 37)

It is an argument, they contend, that 'has been made intellectually in the social sciences' but the implications of which 'for the conduct of interdisciplinary environmental research and for policy remain contested and in development' (ibid.: 37). This is as good a description as any of the experimental pitch of our 'knowledge controversies' research project (2007–2010).

Environmental knowledge controversies refer to those events in which an environmental disturbance of some kind forces people to notice the unexamined stuff on which they rely as the material fabric of their everyday lives, and attend to its powers and effects. In such moments, the ontological settlement that divides the social from the natural, and which expert environmental management practices assume and perpetuate, loses its grip. In these conditions, such expertise and its various socio-technical intermediaries come under intensified scrutiny by those sufficiently affected by the matter at issue to want to participate in mapping it into knowledge and, thus, in its social ordering.

In the work of STS scholars such knowledge controversies are associated with the emergence of new political capabilities and formations, picking up on the political implications of Deleuze and Guattari's notion of the powers of 'minorities' (see Patton, 2000). Michel Callon's 'hot situations' (1998); Bruno Latour's 'matters of concern' (2004) and Isabelle Stengers' 'things that force thought' (2005) all provide vocabularies for addressing knowledge controversies as generative events. Generative that is in their potential to foster the disordering conditions in which expert reasoning is forced to 'slow down' and opportunities are created to arouse 'a different awareness of the problems and situations that mobilise us' (Stengers, 2005: 994). Taking the event of flooding as our test case, the project built on this work to investigate the conditions in which controversies take hold and with what consequences for the problematisation of flood risk.

The project explored the particular reliance of flood risk estimation and management on mathematical/computer modelling. Working with practitioners in academic, consultancy and public agency settings we were able to show how and why scientific assumptions about the uncertainties and conditions attached to the production of model projections become dulled in the hardwiring of these projections into flood management policy and practice (Landström *et al.*, 2011). In the UK, the public face of this complex mesh of flood management science/ policy expertise is the Environment Agency (EA). Those moved by the experience of flooding to interrogate this expertise are confronted with 'scientific and technical knowledge presented in its final form' in which 'its certitude has been achieved' (MACOSPOL, 2008), little trace remaining of all the careful provisos attached to its production. It is in this opaque interval between 'conditional propositions' and 'hardwired facts' that controversies thrive. 'Why do they keep saying it's a one in a hundred year event when we've been flooded twice in five years?' 'Wouldn't proper maintenance of the river channels be more effective than building flood walls?' 'We're the ones with experience of flooding, why aren't the "experts" interested in what we know?' These were the kinds of questions around which we found political concerns and attachments already gathering when we began our research.

Such questions articulate a profound disconnect between the first-hand experience of flood events and the vernacular knowledge accumulated in affected localities, and the modelling practices and devices on which flood risk management expertise relies. A major focus of our efforts in the RELU project to 'do environmental science differently' was to effect redistributions of expertise by trying both to render the interval between 'conditional proposition' and 'hardwired fact' more transparent, and to make connections between vernacular knowledge and modelling practice. In this, our approach involved a conscious attempt to translate key features of Stengers' philosophical project of 'experimental constructivism' into research practice. We set out to invent a research apparatus capable of harnessing the ontological force of events such as flooding to the 'slowing down' of expert reasoning and the creation of opportunities to reason differently (see Whatmore and Landström, 2011a). We called this experimental apparatus a 'competency group' (CG).[17] It was experimental both in the sense that our designs for it had more to do with the staging and ethos of the intended research collaborations than with anticipating their direction of travel or the kinds of knowledge they might produce, and that the project had been funded in part to trial this apparatus.

In practice, our CGs involved the natural and social scientists in the project team[18] ('university' members) collaborating with volunteer residents ('local' members) in localities in which flood risk management was already a matter of public controversy. Their modus operandi of 'slowing down' reasoning was achieved by working closely with some of the materials that mediate the scientific and policy practices of flood risk management and in which its composite expertise becomes 'objectified' (ibid.). In this way, the interval between rainfall/slope/ channel capacity (etc.) and the inexorable rise of floodwaters in streets and homes becomes legible through the constitutive transactions of rain gauges/modelling software/Manning's n values (etc.) (Whatmore and Landström 2011b). Attention to the role of intermediary objects in mapping flood risk into knowledge extended to the production of intermediaries of our own, with which we were able to try out alternative knowledge claims and propositions and, subsequently, to convey them to others. Because of their central role in the assemblage of flood risk management expertise, flood models became the primary intermediaries with which the CGs worked, informed by any number of other materials (see below) generated in the course of our collaborations. This emphasis on practical reasoning or 'thinking with things' also helped CG members to negotiate each other's different ways of apprehending the problem of flooding and to appreciate the different insights each other's situated experiences brought to the process of producing knowledge together.

The project involved two such collaborations, each of some 12 months' duration. The first was in Ryedale in North Yorkshire, based in the town of Pickering, and the second in the Ouse/Uck catchment in East Sussex, based in Uckfield. Knowledge controversies of differing intensity centred in both cases on the inadequacy of existing flood defences and disputation of the evidence and reasoning on which the flood risk management decisions of the responsible statutory authorities relied. In each case, CG membership comprised 5–6 'university' members and 5–8 'local' members. Activities centred on bimonthly meetings in which hands-on modelling became a key practice through which we collectively put different knowledge claims about the local flooding problem to the test.

To the usual modelling ingredients of data (official rainfall and flow records and topographic readings) and theory (Newtonian physics), the CGs added the vernacular knowledge associated with members' differently situated experiences of flooding in the locality (see Lane *et al.*, 2011). Meetings were supplemented by a variety of other activities which emerged in the course of the CGs' work (e.g. field visits, video recording and photographic analysis). Audio transcripts and video recordings were made of CG meetings. Each CG was supported by a password-restricted website hosting a resource depository for materials generated by group members (e.g. maps, transcripts, photos/videos, newspaper cuttings, policy documents etc.) and a group blog. In both localities, the knowledge claims and management options arrived at by the CGs were themselves subjected to public scrutiny through the organisation of local exhibitions and meetings (see Whatmore and Landström, 2011a).

The experimental apparatus of the CG exercised a shift in the rationale of interdisciplinary research from a technical question of solving designated multifactorial environmental problems, to an ontological question of de/reconstructing their assemblage. In the event of flooding, the fusion of geophysical forces and hardwired expertise encountered in the edifice of flood risk management baffles effective public scrutiny or engagement. These are the conditions in which knowledge controversies flourish, opening up 'fundamental questions about the very distinction between the natural and the social' (Barry *et al.*, 2008: 37) in which the expertise that designates the problem becomes apprehended as integral to it. In this context, research informed by the normative logics of 'mode 2' Interdisciplinarity might be expected to be aligned with the efforts of statutory authorities to manage the consequences of a pre-existing *public* disagreeing with established *experts* about how to ameliorate an already defined *problem*. By contrast, the ontological logic of our experiment in geography's interdisciplinary inventiveness allies research with the potential for knowledge controversies to act as democratic force-fields in which any, or all, of these terms might be unsettled and reconfigured.

Negotiating the tensions between these approaches has been an ongoing challenge for the 'knowledge controversies' project team. As part of the RELU programme we have found ourselves handling recurrent requests from its policy 'stakeholders' (and other projects) to explain our interdisciplinary practice through the prism of public 'accountability'. How had our research engaged with local 'stakeholders' (organisations and statutory authorities with recognised stakes in flood risk management)? What methods of 'knowledge exchange' were we using to enable such stakeholders to conduct CGs for themselves?

While we did our best to engage in a process of simultaneous translation, over time we became more confident about articulating how and why this research apparatus was allied to a very different understanding and practice of 'public' engagement. The difference could be illustrated most starkly by pointing out that had our project been funded by, or otherwise 'accountable' to, the statutory authorities responsible for flood risk management in the localities in which we recruited CGs it is highly questionable whether they would have got off the ground at all. In this, the experimental ethos of CGs aligns geography's interdisciplinary inventiveness with minority currents in the now familiar question of how to strengthen the relationship between science and democracy: the right of citizens to disagree with government/policy over matters that concern them, and the generative potential of such matters to exercise new knowledge polities in which expertise is redistributed.

Conclusions

In this chapter I have argued that it is in geography's insistence on working against the grain of *a priori* distinctions between social and natural worlds that its most inventive interdisciplinary tradition is to be found. Yet this insistence sits awkwardly with the discipline's strategic embrace of 'environmental problem-solving' and the normative Interdisciplinary rationales that it entails, and which ally research to governmental and business agendas. The 'knowledge controversies' project represents one attempt to address this minority tradition to the complex assemblage of 'environmental problems', problems in which scientific and policy practices are themselves implicated. In this, it keeps company with wider efforts by cultural geographers, working in collaboration with natural scientists of various kinds, to recharge this tradition with intellectual resources generated in conversations with political theory and science and technology studies over the last ten years or so (see Braun and Whatmore, 2010).

Such efforts have articulated different ways of putting what Annemarie Mol has called ontological politics (1999) – the close and multidimensional interrogation of *what* is at issue – into research practice (e.g. Hinchliffe *et al.*, 2005; Davies, 2010). My argument has been not that there is a single, or ready-made formula for realising the potential of geography's interdisciplinary inventiveness, but rather that the earth/life nexus is a generative site in which to stage experimental practices to this end. In this, the geographical habit of negotiating different kinds of knowledge and modes of producing it remains a more important touchstone than any prescribed method or approach.

However, it is curious that more of the research effort in this vein has been directed at the *bio*sciences than the *geo*sciences or environmental sciences despite, as Nigel Clark (2010: 38) has observed, the latter having no less palpable effects on the phenomena and problems that they study than the former. Perhaps part of the explanation lies in the rhetorical power of 'environmental problem-solving' as justification enough for institutionalising the normative 'mode 2' rationales for Interdisciplinarity. That siren urgency with which environmental problems are cast as so universal/catastrophic and science as our last/best hope, carries with it the dangerous implication that being concerned about how such problems are constructed, by whom and with what consequences, is a trivial/unaffordable nicety.

The institutional promotion of geography's 'relevance' as an exemplary 'environmental interdiscipline' implies as much, and the more overtly, as the competitive clamour of other disciplinary collaborations working at the interface between environmental science and public policy grows. On these terms, geographers' success at winning funding to produce high quality 'mixed skills' and 'stakeholder endorsed' interdisciplinary environmental research should come as no surprise. It would be naïve to imagine geography would or should do otherwise, and only a dogmatist would want to deny that work in this dominant Interdisciplinary vein can be inventive in its own terms. However, it would be equally misguided to imagine that the contribution of geography's minority interdisciplinary tradition amounts only to so much distraction.

The lesson I would draw from our CG experiment and the knowledge controversies that we studied is that minority practices, in scientific research as in democratic politics, are vital sites in the invention of more effective ways of handling the scientific uncertainties inherent in the designation and management of environmental problems. Put another way, strengthening the relationship between environmental science and politics lies not in homogenising research/policy, government/governed, Interdisciplinarity/interdisciplinarity, but in harnessing the frictions between them.

In this, it is not enough for geography's minority interdisciplinary tradition to address its insistence on the 'impossibility of sustaining the human and environment binary' (ibid.) to interrogating the practices of 'environmental problem solving' in which others (including other geographers) are engaged. Such interrogation can usefully *de*construct the assemblage of environmental problems/ expertise but, however necessary, critique alone is not sufficient to either the political or scientific demands of such problems. Perhaps uniquely, geography's habitual and diverse interdisciplinary disposition harbours within it the possibility of *re*constructing how environmental research is done. This cannot be by allying its interdisciplinary energies exclusively with institutionalised power – statutory bodies, corporations, interest groups and stakeholders, but only by addressing them also to those whose power comes from being moved to interrogate expert knowledge claims by matters that 'force thought' and come to concern them. Among other things, this means using research funds, skills and energies to generate opportunities and invent apparatuses in which those whose experience makes them sensible of and knowledgeable about *what* is at issue are enjoined in the exercise of more effective public environmental reasoning.

Acknowledgements

I am grateful to Andrew Barry for constructive comments on this essay. I should also like to thank my collaborators on the RELU project, particularly my co-applicants Stuart Lane and Neil Ward, but absolve them of any responsibility for the account given here of the application process which is based on my own recollections and rereading of documentary materials associated with it.

Notes

1 I am thinking, for example, of Jacquie Burgess's pioneering work on the research applications of group-analytic psychotherapeutic focus groups in the late 1980s (Burgess *et al.*, 1988) and that of Gail Davies and colleagues on 'deliberative mapping' (Davies, 2006).
2 Although this institutional arrangement is either under threat, never took hold or has been abandoned in different national contexts (see Holt-Jensen, 2009).
3 For example, some have associated the recent resurgence of 'geography' in university programmes in the US with the rise of 'environmental monitoring and management techniques' as marketable devices and skills. Such arguments were well exercised in a 'Centennial Forum: Where We Have Come From and Where We Are Going' at the annual conference of the Association of American Geographers in Philadelphia in 2004, and published later that year in the *Annals of the Association of American Geographers* (volume 94, issue 4).
4 The case study that informs Barry *et al.*'s analysis (2008) of this 'problem-solving' approach to environmental interdisciplinarity is the Tyndall Centre for Climate Change Research (www.tyndall.ac.uk). A more directly relevant example of the same approach for the purposes of this chapter is the Flood Risk Management Research Consortium (www.floodrisk.org.uk/).
5 Coincidentally, Deleuze and Guattari's proposition iii about 'the existence and perpetua- tion of a "minor science"' characterises it (after Michel Serres) as using 'a hydraulic model' which 'rather than being a theory of solids treating fluids as a special case; . . . [treats] flux [as] reality itself' (1988: 361). For recent discussion see the special issue of *Paragraph* (26/2) on 'Deleuze and science', edited by John Marks (2006).

6 Examples include collaborations informed by science and technology studies (e.g. Naylor *et al.*, 2008) and the history of science (e.g. Bravo, 2006).

7 The term was first coined by Michael Gibbons and others in *The New Production of Knowledge* (1994), a report commissioned by the Swedish Council for Research and Planning and initially led by Roger Svensson. I am grateful to Catharina Landström for drawing my attention to this provenance.

8 A leading example of the translation of STS work on this topic into policy practice can be found in the Report of the Expert Group on Science and Governance (chaired by Brian Wynne) *Taking European Knowledge Society Seriously* (2006), Science, Economy and Society Directorate, European Commission.

9 The seven research councils are quasi-governmental bodies responsible for allocating a good part of public research funding in the UK (www.rcuk.ac.uk), alongside monies allocated directly to universities on the basis of their performance in a national research assessment exercise conducted once every five or so years. Both funding mechanisms are heavily weighted towards the sciences.

10 The RELU programme was funded by the Economic and Social Research Council, the Natural Environment Research Council and the Biotechnology and Biological Sciences Research Council. Between 2004 and 2011 it funded some 85 projects

11 By the end of the RELU Programme it had tallied the involvement of some 40 disciplines, with 'human geography' having one of the highest frequencies in the disciplinary mix of funded projects, most commonly as a partner in cross-disciplinary project teams.

12 Je-S is the electronic system used by all the UK research councils to 'provide their communities with electronic grant services' (je-s.rcuk.ac.uk). The applicant experience of this 'service' is somewhat akin to that of a 'user' of 'parking services', i.e. a euphemism for automated and inflexible systems that require the 'service user' to conform to the pre-programmed demands of the 'service provider'.

13 The abbreviated account presented here seeks to preserve the confidentiality of parties other than those involved in the project which eventually received funding.

14 In addition to this training in flood modelling from the project team's 'in-house' modellers, team members associated with Work Package 1 based at Oxford also undertook a professional flood modelling course run by one of the UK's leading engineering consultancies – JBA (Jeremy Benn Associates).

15 We subsequently learnt from the RELU Programme Director that of the 11 projects funded (out of 28 submitted under this round) five had been conditional on substantial budget cuts. These cuts were not driven by peer-review assessment but by a withdrawal of funds from the Programme by one of the partner councils.

16 These included, for example, representatives from the Department of Environment, Food and Rural Affairs (DEFRA) and the Environment Agency.

17 To the best of my knowledge, the term 'competency group' was coined in a small office in the centre of Brussels in 2001 by Pierre Stassart and Sarah Whatmore in the process of trying to derive a research practice for a collaborative project on novel foods from the notion of 'competent publics' in a web-essay by Stengers on 'sustainable development'. In this, it differs from the usage we later came across in medical and legal circles in which competency groups refer to gatherings of practitioners of specialist branches of medicine or law.

18 Other members of the project team included Catharina Landström, Anders Munk and Gillian Willis at the University of Oxford, Stuart Lane, Nick Odoni and Geoff Whitman at Durham University, Neil Ward at the University of East Anglia, and Sue Bradley and Andrew Donaldson at Newcastle University. Different but complementary perspectives on Competency Group practice can be found in Lane *et al.* (2011) and Whatmore and Landström (2011a).

References

Anderson, K. (2007) *Race and the Crisis of Humanism*. London: Routledge.

Anderson, K. and Braun, B. (eds.) (2008) 'Introduction' to *Environment: Critical Essays in Human Geography*. Aldershot: Ashgate, xi–xx.

Barry, A., Born, G. and Weszkalnys, G. (2008) 'Logics of interdisciplinarity', *Economy and Society*, 37: 20–49.

Bennett, J. (2004) 'The force of things: steps to an ecology of matter', *Political Theory*, 32/3: 347–72.

Braun, B. and Whatmore, S. (eds.) (2010) *Political Matter: Technoscience, Democracy and Public Life*. Minneapolis, MN: University of Minnesota Press.

Bravo, M. (2006) 'Science for the people: northern field stations and governmentality', *British Journal for Canadian Studies*, 19/2: 78–102.

Burgess, J., Limb, M. and Harrison, C. (1988) 'Exploring environmental values through the medium of small groups: 1. theory and practice', *Environment and Planning A*, 20: 309–26.

Callon, M. (1998) 'An essay on framing and overflowing', in M. Callon (ed.) *The Laws of Markets*. Oxford: Blackwell, 244–69.

Clark, N. (2010) *Inhuman Nature: Sociable Life on a Dynamic Planet*. London: Sage.

Davies, G. (2006) 'Mapping deliberation: calculation, articulation and intervention in the politics of organ transplantation', *Economy and Society*, 35: 232–58.

— (2010) 'Captivating behaviour: mouse models, experimental genetics and reductionist returns in the neurosciences', *Sociological Review Monographs*, 58: 53–72.

Deleuze, G. and Guattari, F. (1988) *A Thousand Plateaus: Capitalism and Schizophrenia*, trans. B. Massumi. London: Athlone Press

Driver, F. (ed.) (2001) *Geography Militant: Cultures of Exploration and Empire*. Oxford: Basil Blackwell.

Gibbons, M., Limoges, C., Nowotny, H., Schwartzman S., Scott, P. and Trow, M. (1994) *The New Production of Knowledge: The Dynamics of Science and Research in Contemporary Societies*. London: Sage.

Gupta, A. and Ferguson, J. (eds.) (1997) *Anthropological Locations: Boundaries and Grounds of a Field Science*. Berkeley: University of California Press.

Harrison, S., Massey, D., Richards, K., Magilligan, F., Thrift, N. and Bender, B. (2004) 'Thinking across the divide: perspectives on the conversations between physical and human geography', *Area*, 36: 435–42.

Hicks, D. and Beaudry, M. (eds.) (2010) *The Oxford Handbook of Material Culture Studies*. Oxford: Oxford University Press.

Hinchliffe, S., Kearnes, M., Degen, M. and Whatmore, S. (2005) 'Urban wild things: a cosmopolitical experiment', *Environment and Planning D*, 23/4: 643–58.

Holt-Jensen, A. 2009 *Geography: History and Concepts*, 4th edition. London: Sage.

Jardine, N., Secord, A. and Spary, E. (eds.) (1996) *Cultures of Natural History*. Cambridge: Cambridge University Press.

Landström, C., Whatmore, S. and Lane, S. (2011) 'Virtual engineering: computer simulation modelling for UK flood risk management', *Science Studies*, 24/4: 3–22.

Lane, S., Odoni, N., Landström, C., Whatmore, S., Ward, N. and Bradley, S. (2011) 'Doing flood risk science differently: an experiment in radical scientific method', *Transactions of the Institute of British Geographers*, 36/1: 15–36.

Latour, B. (2004) *Politics of Nature: How to Bring the Sciences into Democracy*. Cambridge, MA: Harvard University Press.

Livingstone, D. (1992) *The Geographical Tradition: Episodes in the History of a Contested Enterprise.* Oxford: Basil Blackwell.

Lowe, P. and Phillipson, J. (2006) 'Reflexive interdisciplinary research: the making of an interdisciplinary research programme on the rural economy and land use', *Journal of Agricultural Economics*, 57: 165–84.

— (2009) 'Barriers to research collaboration across disciplines: scientific paradigms and institutional practices', *Environment and Planning A*, 41: 1171–84.

Lucas, G. (2001) *Critical Approaches to Fieldwork: Contemporary and Historical Archaeological Practice*. London: Routledge.

Marsh, G. P. (1965 [1864]) *Man and Nature. Or, Physical Geography as Modified by Human Action*, D. Lowenthal (ed.). Cambridge, MA: Harvard University Press.

Martin, R. (2005) 'Geography and public policy: the case of the missing agenda', *Progress in Human Geography*, 25: 189–210.

MACOSPOL (2008) 'Mapping Controversies', www.demoscience.org/controversies/description.php, (accessed November 2012).

Mol, A. (1999) 'Ontological politics: a word and some questions', in J. Law and J. Hassard (eds.) *Actor Network Theory and After*, (pp. 74–89) Oxford: Blackwell.

Murphy, T. (2004) *Pliny the Elder's Natural History: The Empire in the Encyclopedia*. Oxford: Oxford University Press.

Naylor, S., Dean, K. and Siegert, M. (2008) 'The IGY and the ice sheet: surveying Antarctica', *Journal of Historical Geography*, 34/4: 574–95.

Nowotny, H., Scott, P. and Gibbons, M. (2001) *Re-Thinking Science: Knowledge and the Public in an Age of Uncertainty*. Cambridge: Polity Press.

Patton, P. (2000) *Deleuze and the Political*. London: Routledge.

Pryke, M., Rose, G. and Whatmore, S. (eds.) (2003) *Using Social Theory: Thinking Through Research* (part II: investigating the field). London: Sage.

RELU (2004) Rural economy and land Use Programme: Specification for the Second call for Proposals. www.relu.rures.net/documents/specification2.pdf (accessed February 2013).

Simmons, I. (1996) *Changing the Face of the Earth*. Oxford: Basil Blackwell.

Skole, D. (2004) 'Geography as a great intellectual melting pot and the preeminent interdisciplinary environmental discipline', *Annals of the Association of American Geographers*, 94/4: 739–43.

Stengers, I. (1997) *Power and Invention: Situating Science*. Minneapolis: University of Minnesota Press.

— (2005) 'The cosmopolitical proposal', in B. Latour and P. Weibel (eds.) *Making Things Public*: *Atmospheres of Democracy*, (pp. 994–1003) Cambridge, MA: MIT Press.

Thrift, N. and Whatmore, S. (eds.) (2004) *Cultural Geography: Critical Concepts*, (2 volumes). London: Routledge.

Ward, K. (2007) 'Geography and public policy: activist, participatory, and policy geographies', *Progress in Human Geography*, 31: 695–705.

Whatmore, S. (2002) *Hybrid Geographies: Natures Cultures Spaces*. London: Sage.

Whatmore, S. and Landström, C. (2011a) 'Flood apprentices: an exercise in making things public', *Economy and Society*, 40/4: 582–610.

— (2011b) 'Manning's *N*: putting roughness to work', in P. Howlett and M. Morgan (eds.) *How Well Do Facts Travel? The Dissemination of Reliable Knowledge*. Cambridge: Cambridge University Press, 111–35.

Withers, C. (2009) 'Place and the "spatial turn" in geography and in history', *Journal for the History of Ideas*, 70/4: 637–58.

8 Multiple Environments

Accountability, integration and ontology

Gisa Weszkalnys and Andrew Barry

In their book *Re-Thinking Science*, Helga Nowotny and her colleagues note that the environmental sciences, 'which burst upon the research scene in the wake of the influential environmental movement of the 1970s', are exemplary of what they term a 'strongly contextualized' field (Nowotny et al. 2001: 131). In such a field, research is not directed by government policy (or 'weakly contextualized' in their terms); rather, 'researchers have the opportunity, and are willing, to respond to signals from society' (ibid.). In what follows, although we question whether environmental research is necessarily 'strongly contextualized' in the manner described by Nowotny et al., their thesis does point to one key feature of the environment as an object of scientific research. Namely, that the concept of environment does not clearly refer to a specific empirical object or a series of 'well-defined entities' (Anderson and Braun 2008: xiii) but rather to a field of problems whose existence and importance is regarded as self-evident.[1]

Despite what they see as the exemplary character of the environmental sciences, it is striking that Nowotny et al., writing in 2001, found it difficult to come up with a specific example of environmental research that is 'strongly contextualized': 'it is not easy to identify unequivocal examples of strong contextualization, when such examples should also demonstrate what a difference strong contextualization makes' (ibid.: 134). In this chapter, we address this empirical lack, focusing on the work of research institutions that have explicitly addressed the relation between environmental research and 'society' – although this has not necessarily implied, as we shall see, that researchers have directly responded to 'signals from society'.

Our analysis of the different, and often competing, motivations and purposes of interdisciplinarity in this field draws on research conducted in 2006 in three different research institutions: the German Öko Institut, the Tyndall Centre for Climate Change Research in the UK, and the Earth Institute located at Columbia University, New York.[2] In these institutions, along with others, we argue that the growth of environmental research manifests, first, what we have termed a logic of accountability (Barry et al. 2008; Barry and Born, this volume) that is enacted in diverse forms, and in which the question of which 'society' should be addressed or responded to is itself at issue.[3] Nonetheless, we argue that we cannot assume that there has been a movement from less to more 'strongly contextualized' research over recent decades. Some research institutions that in the past pursued a self-conscious critique of disciplinary forms of knowledge production have now to some extent been rendered accountable by more conventional forms of academic assessment.

But if the conduct of environmental research has been guided in part by a logic of accountability, it is also thought by many researchers to have been driven by the challenge of the complexity of the environment as an object of research. Viewed in this light it is the environment itself – on account of its complexity, heterogeneity, or the range of its impacts – and not just society or the growing social concern with the environment that is thought to require what is referred to as the integration of different methods and concepts, seemingly forcing researchers to move beyond their normative disciplinary commitments. Indeed, for some researchers, the environment has come to be understood not merely as an interface or zone of interaction between the natural and the social, but as a domain that problematises the distinction between nature and society (Strathern 1992; Halewood 2011). In short, we will argue that some instances of environmental research have been oriented by incipient manifestations of what we have termed a logic of ontology as well as a logic of accountability. In this chapter we point to connections between accountability and a transformation of the objects and relations of research; but we also argue that analytically these logics should not be collapsed. Rather than identifying a movement from one mode of knowledge production to another, the chapter offers an analysis of the politics of differences in interdisciplinary forms.

The argument is organised in three parts. In the first part, we consider the genealogy of the three institutions, stressing their relation to specific national contexts as well as to wider movements in the environmental sciences. In the second part, we consider the ways in which the logic of accountability is performed in the research practices and strategies of interdisciplinary institutions. In the third part, we identify the critical importance of the idea and practice of integration to interdisciplinary environmental research, highlighting the relations between some forms of integration and the logic of ontology.

Genealogies

The concern with the 'society–nature interface' (Castree 2001: 1) implied in contemporary environmental research is not new. It was critical, for example, to the constitution of geography as a discipline which, in Halford Mackinder's famous formulation, was understood 'as the science whose main function is to trace the interaction of man in society and so much of his environment as varies locally' (Mackinder 1962 [1887]).[4] But if geographers have tended to conceive of the question of the relation between nature and society as internal to the discipline, it seems fair to say that there is something distinctive about the current concern with the necessarily interdisciplinary character of environmental research more generally.

In recent decades environmental research has come to straddle an expanding range of interdisciplinary fields and sub-fields including earth system science (Wainwright 2009), sustainability science (Komiyama and Takeuchi 2006; Turnpenny and O'Riordan 2007), ecological humanities (Bird Rose and

Robin 2004), integrated assessment (Rotmans 1998), environmental health, human ecology and conservation biology (Callicott 2010), political ecology (Watts and Peet 2004), science and technology studies (Jasanoff and Wynne 1998; Jasanoff, this volume) and 'human dimensions of global environmental change' (Rayner 1992; Liverman 1999: 110).[5] The research domains affected by these developments include academy-wide scientific sub-fields, but also specifically national trajectories of thought such as the 'social ecology' tradition based at the Institute for Social-Ecological Research (ISOE) in Frankfurt/Main (e.g., Becker 2003; Becker and Jahn 2005). In addition, geographers themselves have sought to (re) claim the field of environment for a discipline that during the second half of the twentieth century was thought to be increasingly divided between its 'human' and 'physical' halves (Harrison et al. 2004; Castree 2005; Hinchliffe 2007; Demeritt 2009).[6] For some environmental researchers, including environmental geographers, it is the inherent relationality of the new 'socialized nature'[7] – where the environment is understood to be simultaneously 'natural' and 'social' – that should be mirrored in research outputs which embody these relations (Hulme 2008).[8]

These disciplinary and interdisciplinary movements both followed and existed in conjunction with the emergence of an environmental consciousness, with both scientific and popular expression. It was catalysed by what were widely experienced as a series of environmental and socio-economic crises throughout the 1960s, 1970s and 1980s (Agar 2008). These crises were associated variously with the threat of resource depletion and the belief that there were 'limits to growth' (Harvey 2011: 72), the 1973 'oil crisis' (Mitchell 2011: 173–99), the occurrence of El Niño and associated droughts (Cane 1986; Zebiak and Cane 1987), a burgeoning awareness of air pollution, pesticides and acid rain, and the risk of nuclear accidents (Nowotny 1976; Beck 1992). The growing sense of an interconnected and vulnerable global environment reverberated in a number of key political and scientific gatherings, such as the UN Conference on the Human Environment in Stockholm in 1972 (Liverman 1999: 107), and led to the development of the UN Environment Program as well the establishment of new research institutes including, in the UK, the School of Environmental Sciences at the University of East Anglia and the independent International Institute for Environment and Development (IIED) and, in Austria, the International Institute for Applied Systems Analysis (IIASA). At the same time, citizens, institutions and states were increasingly expected to recognise their responsibility for the generation and the solution of environmental problems (Grove 1995; Agrawal 2005; Luke 2006), as well as the need to be informed (Strathern 1999: 68; Barry 2001). In other words, society was conceived both as a cause of environmental crises and as a domain in which environmental problems must be considered and solved.

The three environmental research institutions examined in this chapter emerged out of different historical and political circumstances and research traditions, and in each case interdisciplinarity presents a different arrangement of research agendas, objects and actors. One, the Öko Institut, was conceived in the late 1970s as the 'scientific arm' of German environmental citizen groups, and by the early 2000s it had grown into an important independent advisory centre with about

100 employees. The second case study, the Tyndall Centre for Climate Change Research, was established in 2000 as a self-consciously interdisciplinary endeavour, backed by public funding and distributed across a number of major British universities.[9] However, it also built on a history of interdisciplinarity at the University of East Anglia (UEA) dating back to its founding in the 1960s. Our third case study, the Earth Institute at Columbia University, involved yet another kind of experiment. It was set up in the mid 1990s by Michael Crow, then the university's Vice Provost, as an experiment in institutional innovation, and it aimed to configure a new kind of knowledge for the twenty-first century, drawing together existing research centres at Columbia.[10] This institutional experiment apparently faltered after only a few years of existence, and was given new life with the arrival in 2000 of the current director, Jeffrey Sachs, who gave the institute a distinct new vision, linking environmental to developmental concerns (e.g. Sachs et al. 2009). While at the Earth Institute interdisciplinarity has come to be considered a tool for solving so-called 'real world' problems, and at the Tyndall Centre interdisciplinarity is associated with a concern to move beyond a largely natural scientific understanding of climate change, the Öko Institut is portrayed by its staff as having pioneered the future-oriented mode of transdisciplinarity – a concept that subsequently became central to the work of Nowotny and others.[11]

The first of our case studies, the German Öko Institut, has its origins in a political situation that also saw a proliferation of environmental and related protest movements across Europe (Doherty 2002). The institute was founded in 1977 in conjunction with a conference entitled 'The Role of the Scientist in Society'. At this time it was conceived, drawing on a self-consciously ethical and bottom-up agenda, as a kind of service provider, delivering scientific evidence to buttress the environmental protests led by several civic action groups in south-western Germany (Roose 2002: 17–18). These groups were involved in anti-nuclear protests focused on sites such as Wyhl in southern Germany and Biblis near Frankfurt. They brought together concerned citizens and students keen to bolster civic protest with scientific argument. The notion of a potential relation – or, rather, criticism of the perceived *lack* of a relation – between science and society was key. The aim was to develop a 'counter-science' or 'counter-expertise' (*Gegen-Wissenschaft*) (see also Nowotny 1976: 3; 1979).[12] These groups denounced the apparent complicity of renowned scientists in both the troubling practices of large chemical-industrial corporations and the establishment of the nuclear energy industry in Germany, while recognising – as Ulrich Beck came to argue – that 'the diagnosis of [ecological] threats and the struggle against their causes is often possible only with the aid of the entire arsenal of scientific measurement, experimental and argumentative instruments' (Beck 1992 [1986]: 162–3; see also Berglund 1998).

The American Union of Concerned Scientists in the US may have been an early role model for these developments; but in the German context the actors involved, some of whom are today researchers at the Öko Institut, perceived themselves very much as pioneers.[13] In 1970s Germany, the practice of popular participation – that is, the inclusion of a variety of (conflicting) views in policy and planning – was still in its infancy. In these circumstances, Öko Institut researchers and their allies demanded a new type of accountability and responsiveness to society on the part of the state. By implication, they saw themselves as using their scientific expertise in the name of society. During the Chernobyl crisis of 1986, for example, institute researchers, who had already established themselves as outspoken critics of nuclear energy, offered much-needed advice from a single telephone line in a small office in Darmstadt, a mid-sized German town, to a panicked and largely ill-informed population. Today, this intervention is invoked as a highly significant moment: it resulted in the establishment of a German environmental ministry and underscored the institute's raison d'être.

In this evolving situation a new interdisciplinary space was constituted, existing outside and alongside academic infrastructures and conventions. In a double sense, the interdisciplinary research practices opened up by the Öko Institut were conceived antagonistically to dominant forms. First, they were at odds with disciplinary scientific practice, bringing together the natural and social sciences around redefined research objects and questions. Second, they were understood as standing in self-conscious and vocal opposition to the conservatism, hierarchies, political networks and persistent links to industry that were thought to corrupt German academia. In short, the institute was expected to embody an important shift towards non-academic, although not necessarily commercial, forms of knowledge production in which the production and circulation of interdisciplinary knowledge could flourish freely.

In addition, a number of new institutions embodying altered research models began to spring up. For example, in 1991 the government of North Rhine Westphalia added a new part to its Science Centre named the Wuppertal Institute for Environment, Climate and Energy Research. This interdisciplinary institute can be seen as a kind of imitation of the template provided by the Öko Institut, albeit under improved conditions, notably continuous public funding. The Wuppertal Institut was given added conceptual direction by its founding director, Ernst Ulrich von Weizsäcker, who in 1989 laid out his thoughts regarding the necessity for a new type of politics coupled with a new type of research in an influential publication: *Erdpolitik (Earth Politics)*. The ideas contained in this book reflected a broader shift in German environmental politics: significantly, it included a call for interdisciplinary research that would bring together the 'two cultures' characteristic of academia around new themes, in an effort to shape twenty-first-century politics and culture (von Weizsäcker 1997: 245). In the UK, wider debates about the problems resulting from the two cultures had been prevalent since the 1960s, and influenced the pedagogic practice and institutional form of new universities established in the period, such as UEA and Sussex. However, there was no UK equivalent to the Öko Institut, which had been established outside of the university system.

In the 1980s, the emerging concern with ozone depletion, global warming and the decrease of tropical forest cover rendered 'climate' – an area of research previously subsumed under the heading of meteorology (Bray and von Storch 1999: 439; Miller and Edwards 2001; Edwards 2010)[14] – an object of study in its own right (Liverman 1999: 108). This shift was buttressed by several landmark conferences, including the first international conference on the 'greenhouse effect' held at Villach, Austria in 1985,[15] the subsequent meeting of climate scientists in Toronto in 1988, and the creation of an Intergovernmental Panel on Climate Change (IPCC) which delivered its first report in 1990 (Schröder 2010).[16] In Britain, the establishment in 1990 of the government-funded Hadley Centre can be seen both as a direct result of these developments and as a manifestation of the government's increasing recognition of the importance of environmental issues, particularly following an influential speech by Prime Minister Margaret Thatcher to the Royal Society in 1988 (Whitehead et al. 2007: 138).[17]

However, in the late 1980s and early 1990s, the notion of interdisciplinarity as a means of integrating the social aspects of the emergent problems with natural scientific data was marginal to the agenda of climate change research in the UK and elsewhere. In our interviews, researchers at the Center for International Earth Science Information Network at Columbia, who had been involved in the 1980s in a rethinking of the US Geosphere-Biosphere Program, commented on the reluctance on the part of natural scientists to embrace the social sciences, which were considered to be relatively imprecise and messy. Significantly, 'human factors' were quite literally represented as a black box in the diagrams visualising the interrelations between the different spheres in the context of the Global Change programme (Rayner and Malone 1998c: 35) and in the early formulations of earth-system science (Wainwright 2009: 153). Nonetheless, the view that climate change represented a considerably more complex research challenge than what had previously been encountered as environmental problems – such as nuclear power or acid rain – was quick to gain hold. Increasingly, through the 1990s and early 2000s, it became apparent to many researchers that climate change would require not just a global and longer-term research response, but that it would have to draw together in some way the contributions of both the natural sciences and social sciences (Rayner and Malone 1998a; Aspinall 2010).

In the UK, the formation of the Tyndall Centre in 2000 was the most visible expression of the increasing conviction that the social sciences, as well as the natural sciences, were needed in order to make progressive inroads into the study of climate change. Yet the institutional development of the Tyndall Centre also reflected the longer history of interdisciplinary work on the environment at UEA in Norwich. In particular the zoologist Solly Zuckerman, Chief Scientific Advisor to the Labour government of Harold Wilson, played a key role in promoting the formation of an interdisciplinary research agenda in the environmental sciences at UEA. Zuckerman wrote in a letter:

[I]f one had it in mind to do something absolutely new and fresh in science I am wondering whether Norwich could not embark in its faculty of Science, on a Division of Environmental Sciences – meteorology, oceanography, geology, conservation etc. If it were, I am quite certain that nobody would ever be able to say that scientists were trained in a narrow way. Conservation would lead to the social sciences, population studies etc. and so over into the preoccupations of at any rate one sector of those who teach the humanities.[18]

Reflecting Zuckerman's vision for the environmental sciences, the first Director of the University's Climate Research Unit, Hubert Lamb, drew on historical sources such as grain price records and diaries as well as more conventional forms of scientific data in developing an analysis of climate change in the modern world (Lamb 1982: 89). While the development of the Tyndall Centre can be understood as a manifestation of the long-standing interest in the environmental sciences at UEA, it also coincided with a period in which the UK research councils and policymakers came to stress both the value of interdisciplinary research and the importance of attending to the needs of users and stakeholders more generally (HM Treasury 2006: 6; see also Doubleday 2007; Lowe and Phillipson 2009). In these circumstances the constitution of the Centre embodied an agonistic relation to existing natural scientific approaches to climate change research, while also resonating with broader trends in UK science and technology policy.

If the Tyndall Centre placed explicit emphasis on the value of interdisciplinarity and transdisciplinarity,[19] notions of interdisciplinarity and transdisciplinarity were of much less significance to the public identity of the Earth Institute, which defined itself largely in terms of the range of global policy problems that its research was intended to address. When accepting the directorship of the Earth Institute, Jeffrey Sachs could build on Columbia's expertise in earth and climate sciences at the Lamont Doherty Observatory, and on a series of existing cross-disciplinary research centres. These centres had developed progressively through-out the 1980s and 1990s, and were now brought under the Institute's umbrella. They included, for example, the Center for International Earth Science Information Network (CIESIN), which was originally established at the University of Michigan in 1989 and became a centre within the Earth Institute in 1998, and the International Research Institute for Climate and Society (IRI) – previously the International Institute of Climate Prediction – which succeeded in attracting substantial funding from the National Oceanic and Atmospheric Administration. Under Sachs's direc-torship, problem-oriented research became prioritised. No longer an experiment in institutional organisation, as it had been under its founding director Michael Crow, the Institute now aims to respond to global policy problems, linking the environment to broader development concerns, particularly in low-income coun-tries. The shift in focus is also observable in Sachs's own research and policy contributions, which over the last decade have steadily placed greater emphasis on the close connections between apparently geographic, environmental and climate-related problems, such as malaria, and prospects for economic growth and poverty alleviation (Sachs 2000; 2003).

The growing importance accorded to interdisciplinary research on the environ-ment has come not just with organisational and institutional implications, but also with implications for the identity of researchers. At the Öko Institut, the Earth Institute and the Tyndall Centre, the institutionalisation of interdiscip-linarity was accompanied by explicit efforts to create a new type of researcher. The developments outlined above suggest that the ability to integrate the insights of the natural and social sciences and to think across disciplinary boundaries was increasingly seen as desirable on the part of environmental researchers. The

Earth Institute, for example, runs a fellowship programme aimed at equipping postdoctoral researchers in the natural or social sciences with broad skills gained through working within multidisciplinary research teams. Similarly, participants at the annual Tyndall Centre conference in November 2005 were expected to place themselves somewhere in an interdisciplinary space represented by a triangular diagram, the three vertices of which were associated with engineering, the natural sciences and the social sciences. In principle, a true 'interdisciplinarian', it was suggested, might find themselves somewhere at the centre of this figure, although in practice a capacity to be more interdisciplinary was something that could be acquired over time. As Simon Schaffer (this volume) reminds us, the association is often made between the constitution of (academic) disciplines and the cultivation of discipline. The burgeoning interdisciplinary centres of environmental research embodied the belief that the capacity to be interdisciplinary might require cultivation too (Tompkins 2005).

Accountability and Innovation: Useful Science

As noted in the introduction to this volume, calls for greater interdisciplinarity or transdisciplinarity in recent decades have often been linked to a heightened concern with the accountability of scientific research (Nowotny et al. 2001; Strathern 2004, 2005). In this sense, accountability towards varied constituencies was felt to matter in all the institutions that we examined. In this section, we stress the centrality of the logic of accountability, while indicating the multiplicity of ways in which it is empractised.

At the Öko Institut, the prevalent mode of interdisciplinarity – or transdisciplinarity, in the researchers' preferred terminology – was understood as a kind of pragmatic response, one that was in line with the critique of 'mainstream science' and the reconceptualisation of the environment as an inherently politicised realm outlined earlier. For Nowotny and her collaborators, the development of Mode-2 knowledge production entails a new 'social contract' for science. Interdisciplinarity and transdisciplinarity are crucial, in this view, because they are reckoned to be capable of dealing with the increased uncertainty characteristic of our times and with meeting the need for a more open, inclusive and 'contextualized' science. The authors sketch an evolution from the closed science lab to the open knowledge agora, such that the latter is conceived as a 'space where science meets and interacts with' the public, government institutions and other important agents (2001: 260; see also Funtowicz and Ravetz 1993; Callon et al. 2001). Öko Institut researchers largely recognised themselves in this definition of transdisciplinarity, which they claimed to have anticipated in their own practice, and which they achieved through the involvement of policymakers, citizens and industry in the production of knowledge, or through their mediation of already ongoing discussions between stakeholders (cf. Bergmann et al. 2005). The Öko Institut did not invent the term, but the institute was seen by its researcher members as one of the examples on which Nowotny and her colleagues may have based their analysis of Mode-2 knowledge production.

At the Earth Institute, in contrast, the relations between interdisciplinary environmental research and society were less explicitly politicised than at the Öko Institut. They were also understood in a variety of different ways, ranging from an instrumentalist view of the social sciences as a bridge to key stakeholders, to attempts to develop possibilities for integrating environmental and socio-economic data, for example through the use of geographic information systems (GIS). More critical viewpoints urging a rethinking of the theoretical underpinnings of environmental studies, however, have tended to be marginalised at the Earth Institute.[20] Indeed the institute's primary mission in forging new links between science and society is not to rethink the distinction between science and nonscience in general, nor to develop a form of counter-expertise (Beck 1992), but to make science useful to the concerns of policymakers and interested publics. In effect, the Earth Institute is expected to engage not just in the production but also in the mediation of knowledge (Osborne 2004).[21] At the International Research Institute for Climate and Society (IRI), for example, founded in the mid 1990s and now part of the Earth Institute, it is claimed that the usefulness of scientific research is achieved through the forming of partnerships with local people, decision makers and experts. As one researcher observed: 'one of the things that drives the multidisciplinarity of this institution [IRI] is the idea that if you have an innovative technology it's not enough to just have the technology, it's to get it out there and make it useful'.[22] The aim was to turn scientific knowledge into information that would be directly useable in the specific locations where it is needed, creating 'solutions for problems in public health, poverty, energy, ecosystems, climate, natural hazards and urbanization'.[23] The partnerships envisaged were thought to enable an immersion of the scientific research institute in local problems. The assumption was that scientific knowledge and technology were rarely useful in themselves, as evinced by high non-take-up rates. In this context, the interpretation and communication of scientific research by social scientists were expected to enhance society's capacity to act upon climate fluctuations.

Making science 'truly useful' was also an explicit goal at the Tyndall Centre (Hulme and Minns 2006). In practice this goal was addressed in diverse and contrasting ways, depending both upon the research problem and the research group. In some instances, the aim of Tyndall research was to inform (global) policy institutions through the development of rigorous interdisciplinary climate change research that incorporated the work of both social and natural scientists. For example, when addressing the question of the constitution of 'dangerous' climate change it was thought necessary to consider it both from an 'external' scientific viewpoint and from an 'internal' analysis of individual or collective human experience. For Tyndall researchers concerned with this problem, both forms of analysis should contribute to public policy, for 'public policy institutions need to make this decision [about what constitutes dangerous climate change] on behalf of global society and act on its implications' (Dessai et al. 2004: 11).

However, Tyndall researchers also sought to develop closer relations with political institutions, stakeholders and civil society. One researcher, for example, described his approach as involving a 'civil-society peer review process' specifically tailored for each project, rather than relying on a single overarching advisory group in its initial phase. Another Tyndall researcher concerned with problems of climate change adaptation and mitigation emphasised the value of engaging not just with policymakers and governments but with a wide range of social groups, including civic associations and local populations (O'Riordan 2004). In this respect, the Tyndall Centre's approach to research reflected wider trends in the conduct of environmental governance. For while the environment was increasingly understood as an object of interdisciplinary research, this development occurred in conjunction with a greater presence of NGOs and other non-state actors in the development of environmental policy, which became increasingly apparent following the 1992 Rio Earth Summit (Liverman 1999: 111).

Nowotny et al. capture something of this diversity of forms of 'contextualization': from a political notion of the accountability of science, prompted by a kind of democratic impulse and by movements such as those that fuelled the founding of the Öko Institut, to the problem-oriented conception of the utility of scientific knowledge embodied in the Earth Institute (Nowotny et al. 2001: 97). But although Nowotny and her co-authors identify and promote values of accountability, contextualisation and transdisciplinarity, they have had less to say about the difficulties confronting institutions and researchers that, in adopting these practices, have been expected to demonstrate the worth and the rigour of their research to others. In this respect, the cases of the Öko Institut, the Tyndall Centre and the Earth Institute are all instructive.

In our research we found that while the Earth Institute and the Tyndall Centre needed to be explicit about their efforts to ensure usefulness and accountability, at the Öko Institut this seemed to be a less pressing concern. In a sense, however, this is unsurprising, for the Öko Institut had already built 'society' into its organisational design. The institute was set up as a *civic* association – a *Verein* – with about 3,000 members, 230 of which were active members with voting rights, including the institute's staff. For many years, the assumption was made that this organisational form provided a 'societal anchoring' to the research conducted by the institute. Legally, a *Verein* is required to bring public benefits; and there is a strong sense that all research at the institute is conducted in and for 'society', as represented by the members. However, this 'embodiment' of society by the institute may seem less obvious today. During the period of our research, the *Verein* members still met regularly to develop suggestions for the institute's research direction. But partly due to the recognition that *Verein* membership was comprised only of a small segment of society, partly due to a stagnation of membership numbers since the mid-1990s, and partly because the institute is no longer financially dependent on membership fees,[24] there were tentative calls for a revision of its organisational form.

The Öko Institut had also conducted a long drawn out internal participatory process to formulate a *Leitbild*, a mission statement, for its operations. It emphasised that the significance of their research and science was decidedly not value-free. The institute's science was deemed to embody values of independence, transparency and creativity, as well as respect for each other and for collaborators, without foregoing objectivity.[25] In addition, new concepts were invoked to convey the sense of society being folded into Öko Institut research. The concept of transdisciplinarity, for example, as indicated above, is defined by the institute as a type of research that involves a meaningful connection to relevant political, economic and social actors. While there was little sustained theoretical debate on transdisciplinarity at the Öko Institut during our fieldwork, the presence of an ethnographer (Weszkalnys) had the effect of prompting animated discussions over lunch about the content and definition of the term. Transdisciplinarity had become a deliberate strategy with which to ensure innovative and accountable science. The adoption of the term in the institute's self-descriptions indicated a new phase in its development, in which the relation to 'society' or the 'public' had become increasingly formalised. However this formalisation, in turn, brought its own problems. First, a major 'user' of knowledge, identified directly and indirectly in the writings of public funding bodies and government strategy papers, is industry. In Germany as elsewhere, forging links with industry is widely considered to be a way to foster innovation and to cut public spending. Nowotny et al. similarly suggest that closer links between academia and the market are part of the move towards Mode-2 science. This assessment, however, overlooks important moral ambiguities and worries about the potential loss of scientific autonomy.

Moral ambivalence regarding the encroachment of commercial and political interests into the Öko Institut's independent research was pronounced at the time of our study. Such ambivalence could be discerned where close relationships to industry – in the form of clients commissioning new projects – are part of the everyday operations and, as such, considered valuable and indispensable. As one of the founding members explained, at the initial stage of the institute's operations, some researchers got involved less for environmental concerns than out of an anti-statist impulse. This was at a time when the so-called 'phalanx of state and industry',[26] whose interests were seen as inextricably entwined, formed a key target of the civic protest movements that also motivated the institute's creation. Thus, although the environmental movement and the civic movement of 1968 with its neo-Marxist ideas developed largely separately in Germany, in the context of the institute and its individual actors they could not readily be kept apart. A more differentiated view of the institute's major 'antagonists', including industry and state, has gradually developed.[27] Today, providing advice and preparing reports for chemical companies is a regular occurrence, but it still invites comment (Ewen et al. 1997). In May 2006, for example, at the time of fieldwork for this study, a former economist for the large chemical manufacturer Hoechst, a one-time 'enemy', was elected into the *Verein*'s council. There is a sense of having 'arrived in the mainstream', as one researcher put it, emphasising that this was a welcome transformation that the Öko Institut itself has helped to bring about.

While funding by business and industry has become significant, and is generally accepted and seen as desirable in the institute, the entanglements of market, politics and academy, private interests and the public good, are experienced ambivalently.[28] Assertions of autonomy and independence could lack credibility where specific 'societal interests' enter in the form of grants, or governance, and accompanying expectations. In the minds of some researchers and commentators, the line between strongly contextualised outputs and partisanship or bias may be very fine indeed. By becoming more useful, research also risks becoming more open to the political agendas of funding bodies, whether they are companies, NGOs or governments (Monbiot 2006).

Evaluation and Assessment

More generally, the researchers that we interviewed across the different institutions recognised assessment as a major challenge for present-day interdisciplinarity; for if the research processes and outputs are so innovative and different from established and canonic science, then who is able to evaluate them? And what are the appropriate means to measure and compare efforts to engage with 'society'? These questions were posed particularly acutely by researchers at the Earth Institute who, if their positions were not funded by 'soft' money, usually held positions within Columbia University departments and were therefore subject to the tenure track system of review. Like the formal research assessment procedures carried out periodically in British universities, the tenure track system is considered to revolve around disciplinary categories of evaluation compounded, as several interviewees noted, by Columbia's 'Ivy League' status. Junior and untenured interdisciplinary researchers were seen to face especially difficult predicaments in this context, where strong disciplinary traditions are characteristically upheld and interdisciplinary ventures devalued (Lamont 2009).

The Tyndall Centre experienced parallel but wider problems of evaluation and legitimation. Tyndall staff found that their efforts at establishing interdisciplinary practice risked being disregarded at the end of the Centre's first five-year phase of operation. Although the Centre received a glowing assessment by its external reviewers, who applauded its successful interdisciplinary accomplishments, a bid for continued funding to the UK research councils resulted in a drawn-out process of writing, review, attempted justifications and interviews. The outcome of this process was that Tyndall was funded only for a further three years, at a lower level than had previously been assumed and than the Centre thought appropriate (House of Commons 2006a: question 253; 2006b). Some Centre staff were perplexed and dissatisfied with the way the councils handled the review process, perceiving the outcome as an attack on interdisciplinarity despite the rhetoric regarding its value.[29] They also felt that there had been no identifiable criteria to assess the new bid, or that the criteria applied were inappropriate or simplistic – such as the number of peer-reviewed journal articles. The range of knowledge-transfer activities in which the Centre had successfully engaged, they argued, was not captured in this process (House of Commons 2006b: 3.3). In a memorandum to the House of Commons Select Committee on Science and Technology, the Centre noted the difficulty of finding suitable performance indicators for interdisciplinary research:

> Interdisciplinary research in policy sensitive areas is difficult to fund, difficult to do and difficult to evaluate. It raises issues of learning and interactivity, of

capacity building, of working within conventional academic and funding structures designed for a different era, and of finding powerful and appropriate performance measures (for purposes of accountability). Yet the potential contribution of interdisciplinary research to the development of evidence based policy surely requires that these difficulties are overcome.

(ibid.: 1.2)

During the early years of the Centre's development, Tyndall researchers had stressed the importance and value of interdisciplinarity, but in the context of the existing organisation of British university research funding, this value was not always easy to recognise. The research councils, in particular, embody a commitment to peer review, which tends to lead to the dominance of disciplinary modes of evaluation. As Mike Hulme, the former Director, articulated:

There is an instinct within research councils in Swindon and also an instinct amongst the professional academics who advise research councils, do peer review, that is still innately disciplinary. There are some individuals who are exceptions to that but there is a natural instinct still, I feel, both organisationally and individually within the academic community, and that makes it hard, sometimes, for the value and the benefit of interdisciplinary research to be properly recognised.

(Hulme in House of Commons 2006a: question 254)

In contrast, as an environmental consultancy, the Öko Institut operated largely on terms independent of those applied to university-based research (see also Guggenheim 2006). However, there were important exceptions. In a bid to receive additional funding, the institute applied to the German Federal Ministry for Education and Research to fund certain projects, in competition with university-based research outfits. A concept of transdisciplinarity was part of these funding programmes. Öko Institut researchers thus found themselves in a position of having to meet the Ministry's stipulations about transdisciplinarity, a practice which – as we have mentioned – they themselves claim to have pioneered.

Indeed in Germany, Nowotny et al.'s account is woven into research programmes via its consumption in the research and policy sectors. For example, the social-ecology research programme of the ISOE, now taken up by the Federal Ministry for Education and Research, is self-reflexively described as indicative of a 'mode-2 knowledge production' which aims to offer problem-oriented, transdisciplinary research situated at the interface of science, politics, the market and the public (see also Becker 2003; Jahn 2003; Becker and Jahn 2005; Bergmann and Jahn 2008). As transdisciplinarity is transformed from a 'mere' descriptor of research practice into a prescriptive research model, Öko Institut researchers have had to change their practice partly to respond to evolving expectations.[30] Instead of bringing about 'societal change', the researchers funded by such public research programmes are increasingly under pressure to publish the results of their work in relevant academic journals and other publications in order to attain academic recognition.[31] As with the Tyndall Centre, and ironically, traditional academic outputs are gaining a growing importance in rendering the institute 'accountable'.

Integration, Participation and Ontology

Despite the foregoing, it would be a mistake to think that interdisciplinarity in environmental research has been driven primarily by a desire to make research more accountable and/or useful. For at the same time, and sometimes in tension with this logic, environmental researchers have argued that it is the nature of their research object, the environment, that requires the development of an interdisciplinary practice: the environment is seen as a hybrid research object containing both nature and society (e.g. Acutt et al. 2000). Yet while this is so, the question of how it is possible to research such a hybrid object was far from settled in the three institutions.

For many environmental researchers, the problems posed by the hybridity of the environment were primarily organisational and methodological, requiring contributions from both natural and social scientists. For others, however, the conduct of environmental research potentially posed more profound challenges, challenges that we will argue are ontological as much as they are technical or organisational. In making this argument, we recognise that generally, environmental researchers would not themselves consider the problems they address to be ontological. Nonetheless, in what follows we analyse the variety of existences of a key term – 'integration' – used by the research organisations that we studied to reflect what they saw as a hybrid research object and to work across disciplinary divides (Tansey 2009). In so doing, we point to the incipient manifestation in some of these practices of what we have called a logic of ontology.

While the notion of integration is widely used in the field of environmental research, it refers to a remarkably broad array of practices, ranging from the analysis of causal chains leading to environmental problems, to the spatial integration of social and environmental data, to the involvement of lay experts in the research process. In this section we outline a number of prevalent integration practices. Our discussion shows that instead of bringing nature and society together into a neat and coherent whole, integration offers a number of pragmatic solutions to researching the problem of the complexity and heterogeneity of the environment and the uncertainty of its future development. At the same time, in its diverse forms, integration is best understood as a practice or process rather than an end result. In the institutions that were the focus of our analysis we identify five broad forms of integration practice, which are not necessarily mutually exclusive and which evolved progressively over time: problem-oriented research, data integration, modelling, user involvement and scenario building.

The first form is evident in those research activities that proposed interdisciplinary integration as an appropriate method to respond to certain kinds of complex, multidimensional research problems. In order to provide an in-depth and comprehensive investigation of the problem of arsenic groundwater contamination in Bangladesh, for example, researchers at the Earth Institute set up interdisciplinary research groups capable of studying both the scientific nature of the problem and its environmental impacts and associated socio-cultural factors and consequences (e.g. Argos et al. 2007). This integration practice can be equated with a problem-oriented and pragmatic approach to interdisciplinarity. In this case, earth scientists and public health experts brought together their scientific data and social knowledge in what was described by Institute staff as an exemplary case of interdisciplinary collaboration.

Yet instead of overcoming the perceived limitations of disciplinary approaches, integration practices of this kind may also result in unanticipated tensions and questions, thus opening up additional (and not always welcome) avenues for research. The interdisciplinary encounter, and attempts at integration, may even generate acute 'perspectival disparities' (Weszkalnys 2010: 154) that can threaten a unified understanding of the research problem. The increase in 'complexity' that is effected by adding social scientific insights may be perceived to hinder the accessibility of research outputs, as discussed above, to broader constituencies of potential stakeholders or users (Strang 2009: 7–11). It may also cause tensions within the research group; thus, a geographer interviewed for this research observed: 'where I see the collisions is when people really sit down to share theory and methods. The scientists suddenly realize that many social scientists think that human behaviour isn't predictable. That, to me, is one of the biggest collisions in interdisciplinary work'.[32] A further problem with attempted integration turns on differences and tensions between social scientific perspectives. When stressing the importance of social scientific research on climate change, Rayner and Malone, in *Human Choice and Climate Change* (1998a), broadly distinguish between two schools: a quantitative-descriptive school, on the one hand, and a qualitative-interpretive school, on the other. Wolfgang Sachs, sociologist and senior researcher at the German Wuppertal Institut, invoked a comparable distinction when interviewed for our study. He noted that in interdisciplinary projects the divisions between the quantitative and qualitative schools, or what he termed the 'counting' and 'narrating' approaches to social science, may seem more significant even than those between the natural and social sciences (see also Sachs 1995).

Arguably, there has been a tendency to consider quantitative social science data to be more tractable and valuable as it appears to be more readily integrated with natural scientific data (Adger et al. 2005: 2). And indeed, preconceptions regarding the imprecision or lack of scientificity of the qualitative social sciences are not uncommon. Yet while in the majority of cases interdisciplinary integration privileges the 'hard sciences', occasionally collaboration may be such that social scientists define the nature of the research problems. In the case of the International Research Institute for Climate and Society (IRI) at Columbia, for example, climate scientists felt that the social scientists' delineations of what kinds of knowledge about climate change would be useful for people had begun to dictate the direction of their scientific enquiries. On the other hand, other Earth Institute researchers claimed that the anthropocentrism of the social sciences functioned as an obstacle to their interdisciplinary endeavour. Certain social theoretical approaches, occasionally labelled 'constructivism', were rejected as incompatible with the applied aims of interdisciplinary environmental research. In this light, the narrative of interdisciplinarity as the harmonious integration of disciplinary approaches – one that we frequently encountered – ignores long-standing preconceptions, conflicting epistemologies and lines of division existing across and within disciplines, making for seemingly incompatible 'epistemic cultures' (Knorr-Cetina 1999; see also Bensaude-Vincent and Stengers 1996). As Strathern notes, there may be insensitivity to intra-disciplinary differences and divisions in encounters where 'each expert becomes a representative of his or her discipline' (Strathern 2004: 5). Thus, it would be wrong to think that what is termed integration in environmental research is necessarily associated either in aspiration or in practice with the 'integrative-synthesis' mode of interdisciplinary research observed in other contexts; for it can equally be associated with what we have termed the subordination-service or agonistic-antagonistic modes of interdisciplinarity (Barry et al. 2008; Barry and Born, introduction).

A second, quite different form of integration has been pursued at the Center for International Earth Science Information Network (CIESIN), one of the sub-centres of the Earth Institute. CIESIN's work pivots on data integration, employing geospatial information systems (GIS) to capture, store, edit, manage and share geographically referenced information and associated attributes. This methodological use of spatiality makes it possible, as CIESIN researchers explained, to render commensurate disparate sets of data, including environmental information and social research, providing the basis for discovering correlations between them that would otherwise go unnoticed. As a corollary, climate change researchers at CIESIN and elsewhere have to confront the problem of how to make data comparable, given the geographical unevenness and path-dependency of different national and local systems of measurement. The development of these practices has therefore been bound up with the necessary but uneven development of a global metrological zone, one that informs the construction of global climate change models (Barry 2006; Edwards 2010).

A third practice of integration centres on the pursuit of mathematical models, particularly in the context of the development of the interdisciplinary fields of climate and earth system science (Edwards 2001; 2010; Wainwright 2009). This approach was particularly apparent at the Tyndall Centre. Tyndall's first director, John Schellnhuber, who came to the Centre from the Potsdam Institute for Climate Impact Research (PIK) in Germany, promoted a strong systems model approach in which society was conceived in terms of a combination of what Schellnhuber called the 'anthroposphere' and the 'global subject':

At the highest level of abstraction, the makeup of the Earth system E can be represented by the following 'equation': $E = (N, H)$ (1) where $N = (a, b, c, \dots)$; $H = (A, S)$. This formula expresses the elementary insight that the overall system contains two main components, namely the ecosphere N and the human factor H. N consists of an alphabet of intricately linked planetary sub-spheres: a (atmosphere), b (biosphere), c (cryosphere; that is, all the frozen water of Earth), and so on. The human factor is even more subtle: H embraces the 'physical' sub-component *A* ('anthroposphere' as the aggregate of all individual human lives, actions and products) and the 'metaphysical' sub-component *S* reflecting the emergence of a 'global subject'.

(Schellnhuber 1999: C20)

In practice, however, integration and modelling both served at the Tyndall Centre as boundary objects (Star and Griesemer 1989): ideas shared by different communities of practice but enacted differently across the Centre. While the notion of integration was commonly used by Tyndall Centre researchers, the Centre's different research groups adopted a variety of integration practices, mathematical modelling among them, but also forms of integration involving the participation of users and non-experts.

We associate a fourth practice of integration with these softer forms, which entailed the use of focus groups and interviews as well as modelling techniques. Indeed, within the Tyndall Centre there was a reflexive debate about what was meant by 'integration' and what it might entail in practice. One researcher, for example, drew a contrast between two broad approaches to the integrated assessment of climate change (Rotmans 1998: 155; Tansey 2009). In the first, an interdisciplinary research team would seek to simulate the climate system as a whole, and subsequently report the results of their research to policymakers. In the second approach, however, which he favoured, a research team would develop policy options in conjunction with policymakers and stakeholders using participatory methods such as focus groups. The advantage of this latter approach was that, in principle, through the use of participatory methods, climate change models would be more closely attuned to the needs and concerns of policymakers as they evolved over time. But the different practices of integration could also exist in agonistic tension with one another, as shown by the contrast drawn by these Tyndall Centre researchers between their approach and one associated with mathematical modelling:

[Integration] does have a formal definition within mathematical physics and computing; but here we use it in a more general sense of bringing together knowledge from diverse sources. Users' own integration of information may be either implicit (e.g. by ignoring or prioritising certain information), or it may be explicit, ranging from a lone policy analyst being asked to perform an analysis of literature on a certain issue to a policy-making organisation actually having its own in-house team of modellers. Integration may hence happen within the user organisation/network or through the interactions between the researcher and user, the processes interacting in complicated ways.

(Haxeltine et al. 2005: 19)

A fifth practice of integration evident in our institutional case studies was scenario building. Scenarios first emerged in the military domain, were subsequently applied in the corporate sector, and are now widely drawn upon as a method in academic research (van der Heijden 2005). In the institutions that we researched, scenarios tended to be valued on two grounds. On the one hand, it was claimed, they allow researchers and society 'to plan under uncertainty', by combining predictable and unpredictable elements (Anderson and Bows 2008). Indeed, uncertainty is generally held to be 'perhaps the most pervasive feature of climate scenarios' (Hulme and Dessai 2008). Scenarios were not intended to predict the future, but to raise questions about a range of possible futures (Robinson 1982; Anderson 2001). On the other hand, they gave quantitative data a kind of qualitative sheen through the 'narratives' and 'stories' generated by the scenario exercises (Arnell et al. 2004). In this way, scenario work was considered useful in so far as it generated workshops and discussions that brought together experts, stakeholders and various other publics (Funtowicz and Ravetz 1993; Owens 2000). This was necessary, it was reasoned, not only in order to render climate science accountable to society, but also in recognition of the way that human decisions, interests and judgments, including the conclusions of natural scientific research, enter into and affect the evolving phenomenon of climate change.

For many environmental researchers integration appears to be demanded by the nature of the environment in itself. For the environment presents itself to researchers as a series of multidimensional problems, or as a complex system containing many distinct elements stretched across time and space. In this account, integration refers to the process through which the contributions of many different experts and non-experts as well as other sources of data are brought together. However, for other researchers, including some of our informants, research on the environment poses more profound challenges. We contend that these challenges can be understood as ontological rather than primarily epistemological, organisational or technical. They are manifested in two ways.

First, some environmental researchers have come to be concerned with the ways in which environmental problems and objects are constituted (Castree 2005: 35). In our study, this concern was particularly evident at the Tyndall Centre. As we have seen, certain researchers at the Centre explicitly argued that knowledge of environmental problems should be generated through the integrated involvement of both researchers and stakeholders (O'Riordan 2004; Haxeltine et al. 2005). This stance was captured, for example, in what some Centre researchers came to term the Interactive Integrated Assessment Process (IIAP):

> The IIAP approach indicates that 'knowledge' of what causes climate change, or how a given policy measure may affect future economies, societies and emissions of greenhouse gases, is a joint product of how the stakeholder judges the 'worth' of the assessment models, or scenarios, and how the researcher judges what form of presentation of predictive outcomes will be most clear or helpful to the stakeholder.
>
> (Turnpenny et al. 2005: 3)

The commitment to IIAP was explicitly guided by a desire to ensure that research had real implications for policy, and was based on the recognition that the concerns of policy makers were themselves situated within a political and organisational context, ensuring 'the acceptability and applicability of IAM [Integrated Assessment Methodology] in the policy arena' (Holman et al. 2005).

However, the idea of IIAP also conveys a sense that knowledge of climate change is more than a representation of a problem, highlighting instead how that problem is formed through a series of relations with others, including stakeholders. In this way, IIAP points towards the more general proposition that environmental problems do not exist independently of their problematisation. When viewed in this way, environmental research can be understood in the terms of what Lorraine Daston (2000) has called an 'applied metaphysics', one that – as noted in the introduction to this book – contributes to and forms part of, as well as analysing, the world that it envisages. In coining the term applied metaphysics, Daston notes how phenomena such as 'dreams, atoms, monsters, culture, mortality, value, cytoplasmic particles, the self, tuberculosis can come into being and pass away' (2000: 1; see also Latour 1999). Daston's argument is a general one. In her account all scientific objects have a history: 'they grow more richly real as they become entangled in webs of cultural significance, material practices, and theoretical derivations' (2000: 13).[33] Our argument is more specific: it is that environmental research has come explicitly to interrogate its own entanglement in the world that it analyses, concerning itself with the ways in which it needs to become 'more richly real' (Braun and Anderson 2008). The notion of IIAP proposed by Tyndall researchers can thus be understood as a novel way both of addressing and of managing this entanglement. But a similar 'applied metaphysics' underlay the use of scenarios by Tyndall researchers; for this in turn was based on a recognition of the difficulty of predicting the impacts of climate change due to the complex feedback between impacts, the production of knowledge about impacts, and the generation of policy responses that affected impacts. In effect, the task of the scenario builder was not so much to predict impacts, but to address the ways in which future impacts are affected by the outcome of a political process, within which the elaboration of scenarios plays a critical part.

A second manifestation of an incipient logic of ontology in our study of interdisciplinary environmental research turns on calls for the involvement of affected populations in research on environmental problems, including climate change (Thompson and Rayner 1998; Adger et al. 2005). Such developments have been driven by a sense of the potential contribution of non-experts to the production of scientific knowledge, as well as by demands for greater accountability. However, they may also derive from a conviction that environmental problems are not objectively given in nature, independently of the multiple ways in which they are encountered, created, experienced and valued (Hinchliffe 2001; Latour 2004; Whatmore, this volume). According to one Tyndall researcher involved in scenario development, for example, his approach 'is built on an explicitly value-driven assessment of future goals that leads to the reduction in the authority of professional elites and wider participation in planning process' (Anderson 2001: 611). While for Mike Hulme, former Director of the Centre, 'our sensual experiences and scientific depictions of physical climates have historically been inexorably entangled with meanings reflecting broad cultural and ideological movements' (Hulme 2009: 355). In this account, the environment is recognised not only as a material formation but as one that is aesthetically and affectively experienced;[34] the importance of engaging non-experts in the research process may therefore arise from a conviction that their experience and knowledge forms part of what we mean by the environment (Whitehead 1920: 27–31; Halewood 2011). As Isabelle Stengers argues, 'It is not an objective definition of a virus or of a flood that we need, a detached definition everybody should accept, but the active participation of all those whose practice is engaged in multiple modes with the virus or with the river' (Stengers 2005: 1002; see also Gabrys and Yusoff 2012).

Whatever the significance of these incipient developments, it has to be said that an explicit concern with the realm of the experiential and the affective was quite marginal to the work of the research institutions at the centre of our study, even though it has increasingly become a focus for research in human and environmental geography (Lorimer 2007). Nonetheless, in the context of a concern with experience, the object of environmental research could be understood as a different kind of object from those typically encountered in the natural sciences – 'in fact, one that can no longer be characterized as an object at all' (Greco, this volume).

In light of these observations, the history of the Öko Institut is also instructive; for our research at the institute showed that the question of ontological transformation need not be understood as arising from scientific reflection, but resulted at least in part from an engaged ethical practice that was defined not in the first place through science. When the proto-Öko Institut researchers originally opted to turn against the 'phalanx of state and industry' to pursue a counter-science, they came to be embodiments not just of what science ought to be, but also of what one's relation to the environment – as one's living environment and one's object of research – ought to be. At least some of them were primarily extending their critical personal ethics and ongoing environmental practice to their professional activities, rather than vice versa. The institute's founding moment may be seen to have entailed two things. First, a sudden eruption of a multiplicity of sciences, aligned with a variety of conflicting points of reference, including both the state and society; and second, a relational reformulation of the research object that also includes the scientist him/herself in the relations it contains. In this light, as we argued earlier, the environment should be seen not only as an object of the institute's research, but as a contested and inherently relational field of problems.

Conclusion

Nowotny et al.'s notion that environmental research is 'strongly contextualized' and responsive to demands and signals from society is a provocative one. Indeed, for at least some of the researchers that we interviewed and observed, this analysis has been influential, whether as a public statement of a practice that they had themselves already developed, or as a guide to and a catalyst of their own emerging practice. Moreover, as we have seen, interdisciplinarity and transdisciplinarity have come to be qualities that are expected to be performed to research funders and policymakers. In short, in environmental research, the social scientific analysis of interdisciplinarity and transdisciplinarity has rapidly come to enter into and inform the reality that it describes.

Yet if the problem of how to incorporate 'society' into research practice is critical to the interdisciplinary identity of some environmental research, there is no universal or general way in which this has been accomplished. Our study points to two conclusions. First, there has not been a straightforward movement towards greater 'contextualization' or engagement with society. In practice, 'society' has been summoned into existence in multiple forms in different research contexts. While some social scientists have called for greater public participation in the environmental research process, in practice many interdisciplinary projects have engaged with society mainly through the mediation of its political representatives or through established regulatory institutions. Indeed, in so far as it is oriented towards the solution of problems in environmental policy, interdisciplinary research may be particularly well attuned to the needs and concerns of policymakers. At the same time, there has been some movement towards the (re)-introduction of academic forms of evaluation as a way of rendering research accountable to government. One crucial question arising is therefore the extent to which relations with government and policy can really be equated with an engagement with 'society'.

Second, while environmental research appears to be a highly instrumental 'problem-focused' or applied field of research, it has also come to raise ontological questions. Given the proximity of academic environmental research to the much broader, extra-academic rethinking and re-practising of the environment, some researchers have been compelled to confront how their practice is woven into the constitution and evolution of the object of their research. In this sense, the environment does not exist as a given set of problems, but as a domain whose existence is bound up with shifting and conflicting engagements with it. As we have shown, environmental research has also begun to address the environment as something more than an object of natural scientific inquiry: as a domain of problems and processes that do not exist independently of the multiple ways in which they are known, valued and experienced.[35]

Notes

1 In Foucault's terms, the critical importance of the idea of the environment to research in the late twentieth and early twenty-first century can be understood as an event: for a multitude of reasons 'the environment' has come to be regarded as something that 'counts as being self-evident, universal, and necessary' (Foucault 2000: 227).
2 The case studies were selected because they exemplify quite different forms of interdisciplinarity, rather than because they correspond to any generalised type of institution. The field research included about 60 interviews with researchers and, where feasible, observations of meetings, project discussions and similar instances of research

in practice. The range of material gathered and the comparison across institutions allowed for rich insights regarding interdisciplinary practices in each institution, as well as the wider context in which these prevailed. Additional interviews were conducted with researchers at the Wuppertal Institut in Germany and at the Oxford Environmental Change Institute. We would like to express our appreciation and gratitude to the staff across all the institutions for having made time in their busy and demanding professional lives to be interviewed and observed for this project.

3 An analysis of the nature and feasibility of interdisciplinary environmental research in Australia is provided by Strang (2009), stressing the need for greater openness to and integration of critical social analysis.

4 On Mackinder's significance to the formation of the discipline of geography in the UK, see Livingstone (1992).

5 The contribution on 'the environment' in the *Oxford Handbook of Interdisciplinarity* (Frodeman et al., 2010) points to the difficulty of describing this heterogeneous series of fields, noting that 'to keep this chapter within reasonable limits the discussion of interdisciplinarity will be confined to one self-consciously interdisciplinary trans- (or better meta-) discipline, conservation biology' (Callicott 2010: 495).

6 In the introduction to a recently published *Companion to Environmental Geography*, Castree et al. observe that 'the book is not beholden to the now conventional view – among geographers at least – that geography comprises two "halves" and only a vanishing centre' (2009: 2).

7 The changes that we describe stem from critiques of conventional Western conceptions of 'nature' as the opposite of 'culture' and as devoid of human traces (Strathern 1992; Descola and Pálsson 1996; Berglund 1998; Whatmore 2002; Latour 2004).

8 A similar interrogation of the divide between nature and culture and thus a reclaiming of the environment or, rather, 'natureculture' (Haraway 1991) as proper research objects can also be observed in anthropology (e.g. Descola and Pálsson 1996; Viveiros de Castro 1998; SCA 2010).

9 Notably, the Tyndall Centre drew support from three different UK Research Councils spanning the natural and social sciences: the EPSRC (Engineering and Physical Sciences Research Council), the ESRC (Economic and Social Research Council) and the NERC (Nature and Environment Research Council). The Tyndall Centre brought together research groups and centres at the University of East Anglia and Southampton, Manchester, Cranfield, Sussex and Cambridge Universities, together with the Rutherford Appleton Laboratory and the NERC Centre for Ecology and Hydrology.

10 Michael Crow had conducted extensive research on organisational structures and innovation processes in the US (Crow and Bozeman 1998). Following his directorship of the Earth Institute he became President of Arizona State University, where he sought to implement his vision of post-disciplinary research on a larger scale (Crow 2010; cf. Frodeman et al. 2010; Jasanoff, this volume).

11 Something of the intensive circulation of discourses among our research sites is indicated by the fact that the idea of Mode-2 knowledge production was also explicitly referred to by informants at the Tyndall Centre. Nonetheless, the term transdisciplinarity is seldom used in policy circles in the UK, while it is widely used in the German-speaking world, including by the German government.

12 Close relations existed between these groups and the wider German anti-nuclear movement, specifically the protests around Wyhl which centred on the occupation of the site of a planned nuclear power plant. An important element in this occupation was the construction of a building for a variety of events including what was called a 'people's university' (*Volksuniversität*).

13 Guggenheim (2006) suggests a similar trajectory of environmental consultancies in Switzerland.

14 In the area of interdisciplinary thinking about climate change, an important publication was the edited collection, 'Climate Impact Assessment' (Kates et al. 1985),

assembled by the international Scientific Committee on the Problems of the Environment (SCOPE).

15 This conference 'established the hegemony of the natural sciences in the way climate change would subsequently be presented to the world' (Hulme 2008: 6).

16 A number of environmental research institutions were founded at this time, including The Beijer Institute, Sweden (1977/1991); the Norwegian Institute for Nature Research (NINA, 1988); the Stockholm Environment Institute (SEI, 1989); the Frankfurt Institute for Social-Ecological Research (ISOE, 1989); and the Regional Environmental Centre for Central and Eastern Europe (1990). The ISOE now describes itself as 'an innovative scientific think tank [that] undertake[s] *transdisciplinary* research for society, policy makers and industry' (emphasis added), www.isoe.de/en/isoe/ (accessed January 2012).

17 The Prime Minister formulated the problem in natural scientific terms: 'In studying the system of the earth and its atmosphere we have no laboratory in which to carry out controlled experiments. . . . We must ensure that what we do is founded on good science to establish cause and effect', www.margaretthatcher.org/document/107346 (accessed January 2012).

18 Letter to Sir Christopher Ingold (nd), quoted in Krohn (1995: 591).

19 In the original proposal for funding, it was argued that: 'The Tyndall Centre Research Programmes have been deliberately chosen to *require* the integrated, interdisciplinary approach that the climate change problem demands' (Tyndall Centre 2000: 44, emphasis in original). More recently the Tyndall Centre has come to define its objectives as: 'To *research*, *assess* and *communicate* from a distinct trans-disciplinary perspective, the options to mitigate, and the necessities to adapt to, climate change, and to integrate these into the global, UK and local contexts of sustainable development' (emphasis in original), www.tyndall.ac.uk/about/objectives (accessed January 2012).

20 Interview, New York, June 2006.

21 The Director of the Earth Institute, Jeffrey Sachs, has called for 'A global network of respected ecologists, economists, and social scientists working to bring scientific knowledge to decision-makers and to the public [that] can clarify the state of scientific knowledge, help to mobilise needed research, and defeat the obfuscation led by vested interests' (Sachs and Reid 2006: 1002).

22 Interview, New York, June 2006.

23 See www.earth.columbia.edu/articles/view/1791 (accessed July 2011).

24 Membership fees in 2005 represented only around €140,000 of the Öko Institut's €7 million annual budget.

25 Interview, Freiburg, May 2006.

26 Interview, Darmstadt, May 2006.

27 To protect its hard-earned influence, Öko-Institut researchers now seem largely to refrain from making the kinds of public statements that would have been typical of 1980s counter-science and that some of its membership might still like to hear. In a sense, the institute has opted pragmatically for a gradual effacement of its more radical stance in order to gain influence in state politics. As one of our interviewees explained, if Öko Institut researchers were seen to make comments in public that were too controversial – for example, on sensitive issues such as nuclear energy – this could easily lead to their exclusion from governmental policy advisory committees where such partiality is considered inappropriate. 'Not everything that has publicity value is also politically effective', he concluded.

28 The scepticism can be mutual. Companies are reluctant to cooperate with an institution entangled with environmental NGOs or openly propounding politicised environmental views. Given these pressures to perform its disentanglement from its politicised earlier days, the Öko Institut is keen to demonstrate its respectability, neutrality and credibility in its publicity through long lists of references from commissioning bodies – both public and private. Indeed, the institute can now lend credibility to a company and its

products, although researchers emphasise that they do not allow the institute's name to be used for advertising purposes.

29 The point was taken up in the editorial of *Nature* (2006). For an account of the then Labour government's stress on the value of interdisciplinary research, see House of Commons (2006a).

30 Arguably, the impact of these kinds of funding programmes remains relatively negligible in financial terms, constituting only about four per cent of the institute's overall annual budget in 2005–6 (interview, Freiburg, May 2006).

31 However, the degree to which the institute should be seen to pursue this type of research, and to what extent resources should be set aside to permit the dissemination of research results in peer-reviewed academic journals, remain contested.

32 Interview, Tyndall Centre, 2005.

33 When introducing a series of 'biographies of scientific objects', Daston notes that 'these are not only stories about how interpretations of the world succeed one another, a *vita contemplativa* of scientific objects. They are also stories of the *vita activa*, of practices and products as concrete as the staging of individual atoms and the profits of insurance companies' (Daston 2000: 3, emphasis in original).

34 Whitehead points towards this conclusion in discussing the concept of nature when he notes that 'the red glow of the sunset should be as much part of nature as are the molecules and electric waves by which men of science would explain the phenomena' (Whitehead 1920: 29).

35 Our thanks to Georgina Born, Mike Hulme, Eric Alliez, and Patrice Maniglier for their critical and constructive comments on our work.

References

Acutt, N., Asghar, A., Boyd, E., Hartmann, A., Aeree Kim, J., Lorenzoni, I., Martell, M., Pyhala, A. and Winkels, A. (2000) 'An Interdisciplinary Framework for Research on Global Environmental Issues', *CSERGE Working Paper* GEC 2000–23 www.uea.ac.uk/env/cserge/pub/wp/gec/gec_2000_23.pdf (accessed 9 December 2010).

Adger, W. N., Brown, K. and Hulme, M. (2005) 'Redefining Global Environmental Change', *Global Environmental Change*, 15: 1–4.

Agar, J. (2008) 'What Happened in the Sixties?', *British Journal of the History of Science*, 41, 4: 567–600.

Agrawal, A. (2005) *Environmentality: Technologies of Government and the Making of Subjects*, Durham and London: Duke University Press.

Anderson, K. (2001) 'Reconciling the Electricity Industry with Sustainable Development: Backcasting – a Strategic Alternative', *Futures*, 33: 607–23.

Anderson, K. and Bows, A. (2008) 'Reframing the Climate Change Challenge in Light of Post-2000 Emission Trends', *Philosophical Transactions of the Royal Society – A: Mathematical, Physical and Engineering Sciences*, 366: 3863–82.

Anderson, K., Bows, A., Mander, S., Shackley, S., Agnolucci, P. and Ekins, P. (2006) 'Decarbonising Modern Societies: Integrated Scenarios Process and Workshops', *Tyndall Centre Technical Report*, 48.

Anderson, K. and Braun, B. (eds.) (2008) 'Introduction' to *Environment: Critical Essays in Human Geography*, Aldershot: Ashgate, xi–xx.

Argos, M., Parvez, M. F., Hussain, A. Z. M. I., Momotaj, H., Dhar, R., van Geen, A., Howe, G. R., Graziano, J. G. and Ahsan, H. (2007) 'Influence of Socioeconomic Factors on the Effects of Arsenic on Premalignant Skin Lesions – Results from the Health Effects of Arsenic Longitudinal Study (HEALS)', *American Journal of Public Health*, 97: 825–31.

202 *Gisa Weszkalnys and Andrew Barry*

Arnell, N., Livermore, M., Kovats, S., Levy, P., Nicholls, R., Parry, M. and Gaffin, S. (2004) 'Climate and Socio-Economic Scenarios for Global-scale Climate Change Impacts Assessments: Characterising the SRES Storylines', *Global Environmental Change*, 14: 3–20.

Aspinall, R. (2010) 'Geographical Perspectives on Climate Change', *Annals of the Association of American Geographers*, 100, 4: 715–18.

Barry, A. (2001) *Political Machines: Governing a Technological Society*, London: Athlone.

— (2005) 'Pharmaceutical Matters: The Invention of Informed Materials', *Theory Culture Society*, 22, 1: 51–69.

— (2006) 'Technological Zones', *European Journal of Social Theory*, 9, 2: 239–53.

Barry, A., Born, G. and Weszkalnys, G. (2008) 'Logics of Interdisciplinarity', *Economy and Society*, 37, 1: 20–49.

Barry, J. (1999) *Environment and Social Theory*, London and New York: Routledge.

Beck, U. (1992 [1986]) *Risk Society: Towards a New Modernity*, London: Sage.

Becker, E. (2003) 'Soziale Ökologie: Konturen und Konzepte einer neuen Wissenschaft', in G. Matschonat and A. Gerber (eds.) *Wissenschaftstheoretische Perspektiven für die Umweltwissenschaften*, Wikersheim: Margraf Publishers.

Becker, E. and Jahn, T. (2005) 'Societal Relations to Nature: Outline of a Critical Theory in the Ecological Crisis', published in German in G. Böhme and A. Manzei (eds.) *Kritische Theorie der Technik und der Natur* (2003), München: Wilhelm Fink, 91–112. www.isoe.de/english/person/reload.htm?thj.htm (accessed February 2007).

Benaude-Vincent, B. and Stengers, I. (1996) *The History of Chemistry*, Cambridge, MA: Harvard University Press.

Berglund, E. K. (1998) *Knowing Nature, Knowing Science: An Ethnography of Local Environmental Activism*, Cambridge: The White Horse Press.

Bergmann, M., Brohmann, B., Hoffmann, E., Loibl, M. C., Rehaag, R., Schramm, E. and Voß, J.-P. (2005) *Qualitätskriterien Transdisziplinärer Forschung: Ein Leitfaden für die formative Evaluation von Forschungsprojekten*, Frankfurt am Main: ISOE.

Bergmann, M. and Jahn, T. (2008) 'CITY: mobil: A Model for Integration in Sustainability Research', in Hirsch Hadorn G., Hoffmann-Reim, H., Biber-Klemm S., Grossenbacher-Mansuy, W., Joye, D., Pohl, C., Wiesmann, U., and Zemp, E. (eds.) (2008) Handbook of Transdisciplinary Research (pp. 89–102) Heidelberg: Springer.

Bhaskar, R., Frank, C., Høyer, K. G., Næss, P. and Parker, J. (eds.) (2010) *Interdisciplinarity and Climate Change: Transforming Knowledge and Practice for Our Global Future*, London: Routledge.

Bird Rose, D. and Robin, L. (2004) 'The Ecological Humanities in Action: An Invitation', *Australian Humanities Review*, 31–2, April, www.australianhumanitiesreview.org/archive/Issue-April-2004/rose.html (accessed January 2012).

Bowler, P. (1992) *The Environmental Sciences*, New York and London: W.W. Norton & Company.

Bray, D. and von Storch, H. (1999) 'Climate Science: An Empirical Example of Postnormal Science', *Bulletin of the American Meteorological Society*, 80, 3: 439–55.

Bruce, A., et al. (2004) 'Interdisciplinary Integration in Europe: The Case of the Fifth Framework Programme', *Futures*, 36, 4: 457–70.

Bulkeley, H. and Newell, P. (2010) *Governing Climate Change*, London: Routledge.

Callicott, J. B. (2010) 'The Environment', in R. Frodeman, J. T. Klein and C. Mitcham (eds.) *The Oxford Handbook of Interdisciplinarity*, (pp. 494–507) Oxford: Oxford University Press.

Callon, M., Lascoumes, P. and Barthe, Y. (2001) *Agir dans un Monde Incertain: Essai sur la Démocratie Technique*, Paris: Seuil.

Cane, M. A. (1986) 'El Niño', *Annual Review of Earth and Planetary Sciences*, 14: 43–70.

Carter, N. (2001) *The Politics of the Environment: Ideas, Activism, Policy*, Cambridge: Cambridge University Press.

Castree, N. (2001) 'Socializing Nature: Theory, Practice, and Politics', in N. Castree and B. Braun (eds.) *Social Nature: Theory, Practice, and Politics*, (pp. 1–21). Malden, MA and Oxford: Blackwell.

— (2005) *Nature*, London: Routledge.

Castree, N., Demeritt, D., Liverman, D. and Rhoads, B. (eds.) (2009) *A Companion to Environmental Geography*, Oxford: Basil Blackwell.

Clark, W. C., Crutzen, P. J. and Schellnhuber, H. J. (2004) 'Science for Global Sustainability: Toward a New Paradigm', in H. J. Schellnhuber, P. J. Crutzen, W. C. Clark, M. Clausse, and H. Held (eds.) *Earth System Analysis for Sustainability*, (pp. 1–28) Cambridge, MA: MIT Press.

Crow, M. (2010) 'Organizing Teaching and Research to Address the Grand Challenges of Sustainable Development', *BioScience*, 60, 7: 488–9.

Crow, M. and Bozeman, B. (1998) *Limited by Design: R&D Laboratories in the U.S. National Innovation System*, New York: Columbia University Press.

Daston, L. (2000) 'The Coming into Being of Scientific Objects', in L. Daston (ed.) *Biographies of Scientific Objects*, (pp. 1–14) Chicago: Chicago University Press.

Demeritt, D. (2001) 'The Construction of Global Warming and the Politics of Science', *Annals of the Association of American Geographers*, 91, 2: 307–37.

— (2009) 'Geography and the Promise of Integrative Environmental Research', *Geoforum*, 40, 2: 127–9.

Descola, P. and Pálsson, G. (1996) 'Introduction', in P. Descola and G. Pálsson (eds.) *Nature and Society: Anthropological Perspectives*, (pp.1–22) London and New York: Routledge.

Dessai, S., Adger, W. N., Hulme, M., Turnpenny, J., Köhler, J. and Warren, R. (2004) 'Defining and Experiencing Dangerous Climate Change', *Climatic Change*, 64: 11–25.

Diamond, J. (1997) *Guns, Germs, and Steel: The Fate of Human Societies*, New York: Norton & Co.

Doherty, B. (2002) *Ideas and Action in the Green Movement*, London: Routledge.

Donaldson, A., Ward, N. and Bradley, S. (2010) 'Mess among Disciplines: Interdisciplinarity in Environmental Research', *Environment and Planning A*, 42: 1521–36.

Doubleday, R. (2007) 'Organizing Accountability: Co-Production of Technoscientific and Social Worlds in a Nanoscience Laboratory', *Area*, 39, 2: 166–75.

ECI (2003) *Annual Review 2002–2003*, Oxford: Environmental Change Institute, University of Oxford.

Edwards, P. (2001) 'Representing the Global Atmosphere: Computer Models, Data, and Knowledge about Climate Change', in C. Miller and P. Edwards, *Changing the Atmosphere: Expert Knowledge and Environmental Governance*, (pp. 31–66) Cambridge, MA: MIT Press.

— (2010) *A Vast Machine: Computer Models, Climate Data, and the Politics of Global Warming*, Cambridge, MA: MIT Press.

ESRC (2000) *Annual Report 1999–2000*, Swindon: ESRC.

Ewen, C., Ebinger, F., Gensch, C.-O., Grießhammer, R., Hochfeld, C. and Wollny, V. (1997) *Höchst Nachhaltig: Sustainable Development – Vom Leitbild zum Werkzeug*, Freiburg: Öko-Institut.

Foucault, M. (2000) 'Questions on Method', in *Michel Foucault: Essential Works 1954–1984*, (pp. 223–38) London: Penguin.

Frodeman, R., Klein, J. T. and Mitcham, C. (eds.) (2010) *The Oxford Handbook of Interdisicplinarity*, Oxford: Oxford University Press.

Funtowicz, S. O. and Ravetz, J. R. (1993) 'Science for the Post-Normal Age', *Futures* 25, 739–55.

Gabrys, J. and Yusoff, K. (2012) 'Arts, Sciences and Climate Change: Practices and Politics at the Threshold', *Science as Culture*, 21, 1: 1–24.

Gibbons, M., Limoges, C., Nowotny, H., Schwartzman, S., Scott, P. and Trow, M. (1994) *The New Production of Knowledge: The Dynamics of Science and Research in Contemporary Societies*, London: Sage.

Goodess, C. M., Hanson, C., Hulme, M. and Osborn, T. J. (2003) 'Representing Climate and Extreme Weather Events in Integrated Assessment Models: A Review of Existing Methods and Options for Development', *Integrated Assessment*, 4: 145–71.

Grove, R. (1995) *Green Imperialism: Colonial Expansion, Tropical Island Edens, and the Origins of Environmentalism, 1600–1860*, Cambridge: Cambridge University Press.

Guggenheim, M. (2006) 'Undisciplined Research: Structures of Transdisciplinary Research', *Science and Public Policy*, 33, 6: 394–8.

Hacking, I. (2002) *Historical Ontology*, Cambridge, MA: Harvard University Press.

Halewood, M. (2011) *A. N. Whitehead and Social Theory: Tracing a Culture of Thought*, London: Anthem.

Haraway, D. (1991) *Simians, Cyborgs and Women: The Reinvention of Nature*, New York: Routledge.

Harrison, S., et al. (2004) 'Thinking Across the Divide: Perspectives on the Conversations between Physical and Human Geography', *Area*, 36: 435–42

Harvey, D. (2011) *The Enigma of Capital and the Crisis of Capitalism*, London: Profile.

Haxeltine, A., Turnpenny, J., O'Riordan, T. and Warren, R. (2005) 'The Creation of a Pilot Phase Interactive Integrated Assessment Process for Managing Climate Futures', *Tyndall Technical Report*, 31.

Hinchliffe, S. (2001) 'Indeterminacy In-Decisions – Science, Policy and Politics in the BSE (Bovine Spongiform Encephalopathy) Crisis', *Transactions of the Institute of British Geographers*, 26, 2: 182–204.

— (2007) *Geographies of Nature: Societies, Environments, Ecologies,* London: Sage.

Hirsch Hadorn, G., Hoffmann-Riem, H., Biber-Klemm, S., Grossenbacher-Mansuy, W., Joye, D., Pohl, C., Wiesmann, U. and Zemp, E. (eds.) (2008) *Handbook of Transdisciplinary Research*, Berlin: Springer.

HM Treasury (2006) *Science and Innovation Investment Framework 2004–2014: The Next Steps*, London: HMSO.

Holman, I., Rounsevell, M., Shackley, S., Harrison, H., Nicholls, R., Berry, P. and Audsley, E. (2005) 'A Regional, Multi-Sectoral and Integrated Assessment of the Impacts of Climate and Socio-economic Change in the UK: Part I. Methodology', *Climatic Change*, 71: 9–41.

House of Commons (2006a) 'Select Committee on Science and Technology, Examination of Witnesses', 12 December, www.parliament.the-stationery-office.co.uk/pa/cm200607/cmselect/cmsctech/68/6121203.htm, (accessed February 2012).

— (2006b) 'Select Committee on Science and Technology', *Memorandum from the Tyndall Centre for Climate Change Research*, www.publications.parliament.uk/pa/cm200607/cmselect/cmsctech/68/68we10.htm, (accessed February 2012).

Hulme, M. (2008) 'Geographical Work at the Boundaries of Climate Change', *Transactions of the Institute of British Geographers*, 33: 5–11.
— (2009) *Why We Disagree about Climate Change: Understanding Controversy, Inaction and Opportunity*, Cambridge: Cambridge University Press.
Hulme, M. and Dessai, S. (2008) 'Negotiating Future Climates for Public Policy: A Critical Assessment of the Development of Climate Scenarios for the UK', *Environmental Science and Policy*, 11, 1: 54–70.
Hulme, M. and Minns, A. (2006) 'Truly Useful: Doing Climate Change Research that is Useful for both Theory and Practice', *Tyndall Briefing Note* 14, www.tyndall.ac.uk/sites/default/files/TrulyUsefulTyndall.pdf (accessed December 2010).
Jahn, T. (2003) 'Sozial-ökologische Forschung – Ein neuer Forschungstyp in der Nachhaltigkeitsforschung', in G. Linne and M. Schwarz (eds.) *Handbuch Nachhaltige Entwicklung. Wie ist Nachhaltiges Wirtschaften Machbar?* (pp. 545–55) Opladen: Leske + Budrich.
Jasanoff, S. (1994) 'The Idiom of Co-Production', in S. Jasanoff (ed.) *States of Knowledge: the Co-Production of Science and Social Order*, vol 1 (pp. 1–12) London: Routledge.
Jasanoff, S. and Wynne, B. (1998) 'Science and Decision-making', in Rayner and Malone (eds.), *Human Choice and Climate Change*, pp. 1–88.
Kates, R., Ausubel, J. and Berberian, M. (eds.) (1985) 'Climate Impact Assessment', www.icsu-scope.org/downloadpubs/scope27 (accessed December 2010).
Knorr-Cetina, K. (1999) *Epistemic Cultures: How the Sciences Make Knowledge*, Cambridge, MA: Harvard University Press.
Komiyama, H. and Takeuchi, K. (2006) 'Sustainability Science – Building a New Discipline', *Sustainability Science*, 1, 1: 1–6.
Krohn, P. (1995) 'Solly Zuckerman Baron Zuckerman, of Burnham Thorpe, O.M., K.C.B. 30 May 1904–1 April 1993', *Biographical Memoirs of the Fellows of the Royal Society*, 41: 576–98.
Lamb, H. (1982) *Climate, History and the Modern World*, London: Methuen.
Lamont, M. (2009) *How Professors Think: Inside the Curious World of Academic Judgement*, Cambridge, MA: Harvard University Press.
Latour, B. (1993) *We Have Never Been Modern*, Hemel Hempstead: Harvester Wheatsheaf.
— (1999) *Pandora's Hope: Essays on the Reality of the Sciences*, Cambridge, MA: Harvard University Press.
— (2004) *The Politics of Nature*, Cambridge, MA: Harvard University Press.
Law, J. and Singleton, V. (2005) 'Object Lessons', *Organization*, 12, 3: 331–55.
Liverman, D. (1999) 'Geography and the Global Environment', *Annals of the Association of American Geographers*, 89, 1: 107–20.
Livingstone, D. N. (1992) *The Geographical Tradition: Episodes in the History of a Contested Enterprise*, Oxford and Cambridge, MA: Blackwell.
Lorimer, J. (2007) 'Nonhuman Charisma', *Environment and Planning D: Society and Space*, 25, 5: 911–32.
Lowe, P. and Phillipson, P. (2009) 'Barriers to Research Collaboration across Disciplines: Scientific Paradigms and Institutional Practice', *Environment and Planning A*, 41: 1171–84.
Luke, T. (2006 [1995]) 'On Environmentality: Geo-Power and Eco-Knowledge in the Discourses of Contemporary Environmentalism', in N. Haenn and R. R. Wilk (eds.) *The Environment in Anthropology: A Reader in Ecology, Culture, and Sustainable Living*, New York and London: New York University Press.

Maasen, S., Lengwiler, M. and Guggenheim, M. (2006) 'Practices of Transdisciplinary Research: Close(r) Encounters of Science and Society', *Science and Public Policy*, 33, 6: 394–8.

Mackinder, H. (1962 [1887]) 'The Scope and Methods of Geography', *Proceedings of the Royal Geographical Society*, 9: 141–60, in H. Mackinder *Democratic Ideals and Reality*, Westport: Greenwood Press.

Mansilla, V.B., Feller, I. and Gardner, H. (2006) 'Quality' Assessment in Interdisciplinary Research and Education', *Research Evaluation*, 15, 1: 69–74.

Miller, C. and Edwards, P. (2001) *Changing the Atmosphere: Expert Knowledge and Environmental Governance*, Cambridge, MA: MIT Press.

Mitchell, T. (2011) *Carbon Democracy: Political Power in the Age of Oil*, London: Verso.

Monbiot, G. (2006) 'The Threat is from Those who Accept Climate Change, Not Those Who Deny It', *The Guardian*, 21 September, www.guardian.co.uk/commentisfree/2006/sep/21/comment.georgemonbiot (accessed December 2010).

Nature (2006) 'Special Provision: Some Research Centres are More Equal than Others', *Nature*, 441, 7090: 127–8.

Nowotny, H. (1976) 'Social Aspects of the Nuclear Power Controversy', European Centre for Social Welfare Training and Research and the Joint IAEA/IIASA Research Project, *Research Memorandum*, RM-76–33, 29pp, www.iiasa.ac.at/Admin/PUB/Documents/RM-76–033.pdf (accessed January 2012).

—— (1979) 'Science and its Critics: Reflections on Anti-Science', in H. Nowotny and H. Rose (eds.) *Counter-Movements in the Sciences: The Sociology of Alternatives to Big Science*, Dordrecht: D. Reidel, 1–26.

Nowotny, H., Scott, P. and Gibbons, M. (2001) *Re-Thinking Science: Knowledge and the Public in an Age of Uncertainty*, Cambridge: Polity.

O'Riordan, T. (2004) 'Environmental Science, Sustainability and Politics', *Transactions of the Institute of British Geographers*, 29, 2: 234–47.

Osborne, T. (2004) 'On Mediators: Intellectuals and the Ideas Trade in the Knowledge Society', *Economy and Society*, 33, 4: 430–47.

Owens, S. (2000) '"Engaging the Public": Information and Deliberation in Environmental Policy', Commentary, *Environment and Planning A*, 32: 1141–8.

Petts, J., Owens, S. and Bulkeley, H. (2004) 'Knowledge and Power: Exploring the Science/Society Interface in the Urban Environment Context', *Discussion Paper* for Seminar 6, ESRC Transdisciplinary Seminar Series, University of Birmingham and University of Cambridge, UK.

Power, M. (1997) *The Audit Society: Rituals of Verification*, Oxford: Oxford University Press.

Rayner, S. (1992) 'Global Environmental Change: Understanding the Human Dimensions', in *Environment: Science and Policy for Sustainable Development*, 34, 7: 25–8.

Rayner, S. and Malone, E. L. (eds.) (1998a) *Human Choice and Climate Change,* 4 Volumes, Columbus, Ohio: Battelle Press.

Rayner, S. and Malone, E. L. (1998b) 'Introduction', in S. Rayner and E. L. Malone (eds.) *Human Choice and Climate Change*, volume 1, xiii-xlii.

—— (1998c) 'The Challenge of Climate Change to the Social Sciences', in S. Rayner and E. L. Malone (eds.) *Human Choice and Climate Change*, Volume 4, (33–70).

Rittel, H. and Webber, M. (1973) 'Dilemmas in a General Theory of Planning', *Policy Sciences*, 4: 155–69.

Robinson, J. (1982) 'Energy Backcasting: A Proposed Method of Policy Analysis', *Energy Policy*, 10, 4: 337–344.

Roose, J. (2002) *Made by Öko-Institut: Wissenschaft in Einer bewegten Umwelt*, Freiburg: Öko-Institut.

Rotmans, J. (1998) 'Methods of IA: The Challenges and Opportunities Ahead', *Environmental Modeling and Assessment*, 3: 155–79.

Sachs, J. (2000) 'Tropical Underdevelopment', prepared for Economic History Association Annual Meeting, September 2000 and CID Working Paper No. 57, December 2000, www.cid.harvard.edu/cidwp/057.htm (accessed January 2012).

— (2003) 'Institutions don't Rule: Direct Effects of Geography on Per Capita Income', *Working Paper* 9490, National Bureau of Economic Research, Cambridge, MA, www.nber.org/papers/w9490 (accessed January 2012).

— (2005) *The End of Poverty*, London: Penguin Books.

Sachs, J. and Reid, W. (2006) 'Investments Towards Sustainable Development', *Science*, 312, 1002.

Sachs, J., et al. (2009) 'Biodiversity Conservation and the Millennium Development Goals', *Science*, 325, 5947: 1502–3.

Sachs, W. (1995) 'Zählen oder Erzählen? Natur- und geisteswissenschaftliche Argumente in der Studie "Zukunftsfähiges Deutschland"', *Wechselwirkung*, 76: 20–5.

Saloranta, T. (2001) 'Post-Normal Science and the Global Climate Change Issue', *Climatic Change*, 50: 395–404.

SCA (2010) 'Natureculture: Entangled Relations of Multiplicity', Society for Cultural Anthropology Spring 2010 Meeting, Santa Fe, NM, sca.culanth.org/meetings/sca/2010/intro.html (accessed March 2012).

Schellnhuber, H.-J. (1999) 'Earth Systems Analysis and the Second Copernican Revolution', *Nature* supplement, 402 (2 December): 19–23.

— (2004) *Earth System Analysis for Sustainability*, Cambridge, MA: MIT Press.

Schröder, H. (2010) 'The History of International Climate Change Politics: Three Decades of Progress, Process and Procrastination', in M. Boykoff (ed.) *The Politics of Climate Change: A Survey*, (pp. 26–41), London: Routledge.

Star, S. L. and Griesemer, J. (1989) 'Institutional Ecology, "Translations" and Boundary Objects: Amateurs and Professionals in Berkeley's Museum of Vertebrate Zoology, 1907–39', *Social Studies of Science*, 19, 3: 387–420.

Stengers, I. (2005) 'The Cosmopolitical Proposal', in B. Latour and P. Weibel (eds.) *Making Things Public: Atmospheres of Democracy*, (pp. 94–1003), Cambridge, MA: MIT Press.

Strang, V. (2009) 'Integrating the Social and Natural Sciences in Environmental Research: A Discussion Paper', *Journal of Environment, Development and Sustainability*, 11: 1–18.

Strathern, M. (1991) *Partial Connections*. Savage, MD: Rowman & Littlefield.

— (1992) *After Nature: English Kinship in the Late Twentieth Century*, Cambridge: Cambridge University Press.

— (1999) *Property, Substance, and Effect*, London: Athlone.

— (2000) '"Afterword: Accountabilit and Ethnography', in M. Strathern (ed.) *Audit Cultures: Anthropological Studies in Accountability, Ethics, and the Academy*, (pp. 279–304), London and New York: Routledge.

— (2004) *Commons and Borderlands: Working Papers on Interdisciplinarity, Accountability and the Flow of Knowledge*, Oxon: Sean Kingston.

— (2005) 'Experiments in Interdisciplinarity', *Social Anthropology*, 13, 1: 75–90.

Tansey, J. (2009) 'Integrated Assessment', in N. Castree, D. Demeritt, D. Liverman and B. Rhoads (eds.) *A Companion to Environmental Geography*, (pp. 357–69), Oxford: Wiley-Blackwell.

Thompson, M. and Rayner S. (1998) 'Risk and Governance Part I: The Discourse of Climate Change', *Government and Opposition*, 33, 2:139–66.

Tompkins, E. (2005) 'Review of Interdisciplinary Environmental Centres of Excellence', report to MISTRA, Swedish Foundation for Strategic Environmental Research, www.mistra.org/download/18.61632b5e117dec92f47800097871/Tompkins+report.pdf (accessed January 2012).

Turney, J. (2005) 'Gaia: Nice is Not Enough', *Interdisciplinary Science Reviews*, 30, 1: 1–6.

Turnpenny, J. (2003) 'Post-normal Science and the Tyndall Centre: Some Critical Issues', *Tyndall Briefing Note* 9, www.tyndall.ac.uk/sites/default/files/note09.pdf (accessed December 2010).

Turnpenny, J., Haxeltine, A., Lorenzoni, I., O'Riordan, T. and Jones, M. (2005) 'Mapping Actors Involved in Climate Change Policy Networks in the UK', *Tyndall Working Paper* 66.

Turnpenny, J. and O'Riordan, T. (2007) 'Putting Sustainability Science to Work: Assisting the East of England to Respond to the Challenges of Climate Change', *Transactions of the Institute of British Geographers*, 32: 102–5.

Tyndall Centre (2000) 'The Tyndall Centre for Climate Change Research: Integrated Research for Sustainable Solutions', final proposal, February.

— (2006) 'Memorandam for the Tyndall Centre for Climate Change Research', written evidence, House of Commons Select Committee on Science and Technology.

van der Heijden, K. (2005) *Scenarios: The Art of Strategic Conversation*, Chichester: John Wiley & Sons.

Viveiros de Castro, E. (1998) 'Cosmological Deixis and Amerindian Perspectivism', *Journal of the Royal Anthropological Institute*, 4, 3: 469–88.

Von Weizsäcker, E. U. (1997 [1989]) *Erdpolitik*, 5th edition, Darmstadt: Primus.

Wainwright, J. (2009) 'Earth-System Science', in N. Castree, D. Demeritt, D. Liverman and B. Rhoads (eds.) *A Companion to Environmental Geography*, (pp. 145–67) Oxford: Wiley-Blackwell.

Watts, M. and Peet, R. (2004) 'Liberating Political Ecology', in R. Peet and M. Watts (eds.) *Liberation Ecologies: Environment, Development, Social Movements*, 2nd edition, (pp. 3–47) London: Routledge.

Weszkalnys, G. (2010) *Berlin, Alexanderplatz: Transforming Place in a Unified Germany*, Oxford and New York: Berghahn.

Whatmore, S. (2002) *Hybrid Geographies: Natures, Cultures, Spaces*, London: Sage.

— (2009) 'Mapping Knowledge Controversies: Science, Democracy and the Redistribution of Expertise', *Progress in Human Geography*, 33, 5: 587–98.

Whitehead, A. N. (1920) *The Concept of Nature*, Cambridge: Cambridge University Press.

Whitehead, M., Jones, R. and Jones, M. (2007) *The Nature of the State: Excavating the Political Ecologies of the Modern State*, Oxford: Oxford University Press.

Wissenschaftsrat (2000) 'Thesen zur künftigen Entwicklung des Wissenschaftssystems in Deutschland', www.wissenschaftsrat.de/texte/4594–00.pdf (accessed February 2007).

Zebiak, S. E. and Cane, M. A. (1987) 'A Model El-Niño Southern Oscillation', *Monthly Weather Review*, 115, 10: 2262–78.

9 Ontology and Antidisciplinarity

Andrew Pickering

My aim in this paper is to open up a new front in discussions of interdisciplinarity. The argument hinges on a crude sorting of kinds of science along ontological lines. I distinguish between the 'modern' sciences (more generally: fields of practice and their associated artefacts) and their 'nonmodern' counterparts. Most discussions of interdisciplinarity focus on combinations, juxtapositions and syntheses of modern sciences. But if one focuses instead on the nonmodern sciences a rather different picture comes into view, not so much of the combination of distinct disciplines but of the eruption of a relatively unified approach to the world across the disciplinary map (as marked out by the modern sciences themselves). The nonmodern sciences, one might say, offer us an antidisciplinary rather than an interdisciplinary spectacle, and that is what I want to examine from various angles here.[1]

We can begin with ontology, questions of what the world is like, what its elements are and how they relate to one another. The modern sciences, as defined here, presume a knowable world, of identifiable entities in specifiable interaction with one another, and they take it for granted that their job is to know them. Physics is the obvious example, with its quest to find out about the ultimate constituents of matter: quarks, strings or whatever. But since the scientific revolution many other fields have emulated physics: chemistry with its elements, atoms and molecules; biology and DNA; sociology and its social structures, causes and correlations; economics and markets. The departmental structure of the modern Western university sociologically enshrines these many quests for positive knowledge, and the dominant forms of interdisciplinarity seek to put these various fields together for various purposes. The difficulty, of course, is one of combining positive descriptions of different aspects of the world (physical, biological, economic etc.).

This much is obvious, so we can turn to the other ontology. The nonmodern sciences, as I conceive them, presume a world that is ultimately not fully knowable – a world of endless unpredictable emergence and becoming. These are the sciences of the unknowable. Though it is not obvious what this phrase even means, my feeling is that in the shadows of the modern one can always find traces of the nonmodern and, to bring the argument down to earth, in what follows I will specialise the discussion to the nonmodern science I know best: cybernetics.[2] Cybernetics is often regarded as a paradigmatically interdisciplinary post-war science, but I want to show that interdisciplinarity here entails something different from its manifestation in the modern sciences and is better described as antidisciplinarity.[3]

What was (or is) cybernetics?[4] In 1959, Stafford Beer (1959: 18) defined it as the science of 'exceedingly complex systems' – meaning entities that are either so complicated we can never hope to understand them, or that evolve unpredictably so that our knowledge of them is continually going out of date. The latter, especially, is the nonmodern ontology that I will focus on here. But how can one have a science of entities that are always changing? Clearly one can never get to the bottom of them, which is the aspiration of the modern sciences. Instead, cybernetics is best thought of as focusing on processes of adaptation to the unknown, between elements of the nonhuman world, between humans and the nonhuman, or simply between human entities. Cybernetics, one can say, was a science of adaptation. But still, what might that look like in practice? The trick here is to start with the distinctive machines that were at the heart of early cybernetics, and one example is enough to get the discussion going.

In 1948 Ross Ashby built a machine that echoed through the subsequent history of cybernetics, especially in Britain. The homeostat, as he called it, was an electromechanical device that converted input currents into output ones through some complicated circuitry comprising an electronic valve, a bipolar relay, a stepping switch and some wires, capacitors and resistors. The details are irrelevant here, but the important point is that when two or more homeostats were connected together they would find themselves in one of two conditions. They might be in a stable form of dynamic equilibrium, meaning that the input and output currents of each tended to zero in the face of small disturbances. Or they might be in an unstable condition, meaning that the currents would tend to increase. In that case, once the current within a homeostat exceeded some pre-set limit, the relay would trip, moving the stepping switch to its next position, which in turn changed the resistance or polarity of its circuits at random. The upshot of this might be that the multi-homeostat set-up achieved a state of equilibrium, in which case nothing more would happen. Or it might be that this set-up remained in an unstable state, in which case the relay would trip repeatedly until a state of equilibrium was found. The homeostat was thus an example of an ultrastable machine, as Ashby called it – a machine that could adapt to its environment (other homeostats) by finding its way into stable equilibrium with it.

Norbert Wiener, the man who gave cybernetics its name, called the homeostat 'one of the great philosophical contributions of the present day' (1967: 54) and we should pause to wonder why. Above all, we should think of a multi-homeostat set-up as 'ontological theatre', as staging for us a vision of the nonmodern ontology more generally. None of the homeostats in such a set-up knew anything in a representational sense about the others; each reacted and transformed itself in a performative interaction – a dance of agency, as I call it (Pickering 1995b) – with the unpredictable becomings of the others. This, I take it, is the basic ontology of nonmodern sciences like cybernetics; a multi-homeostat set-up was a simple model of the general picture. Think of the world as built from entities somehow akin to homeostats and you begin to get the hang of the nonmodern ontology.[5]

As ontological theatre, the homeostat can be read as a contribution to philosophy, albeit an odd one – a machine rather than a verbal argument (and we come back to the theme of oddity below). But its significance was by no means solely philosophical. The homeostat figured as the centrepiece of Ashby's 1952 book *Design for a Brain*, and Ashby designed it as a first step towards building a synthetic brain. This is a point that may require some elaboration. If it is not immediately clear how the homeostat might be a model of the brain, that is a reflection of our dominant conception of the brain as a representational organ – an organ that somehow stands apart from the world and contains and manipulates representations thereof. This is the brain as modelled in symbolic AI, where the aim is to reproduce the programmes that the brain runs – a distinctively modern version of brain science. The cybernetic understanding, instead, was of the brain as performative and adaptive – as the organ that helps us get along in situations we have never encountered before, in a world that is ultimately unknowable – and this is the sense in which the homeostat could be seen as a model brain.

Now we can see the homeostat as immediately a contribution to two fields: philosophy (as ontology) and brain science, and we can continue in this direction. Ashby's professional life (until 1960) lay in the psychiatric milieu of the mental hospital, and he typically framed his discussions of the homeostat as contributions to psychiatry. Here he aligned himself with a long-standing tradition that saw mental abnormality as evidence of a lack of adaptability, a feature that he could also model and analyse in terms of his homeostats. So the homeostat was, at once, a contribution to philosophy, brain science and psychiatry.

Going further, cybernetics quickly overflowed the brain – in Ashby's work and more generally. In *Design for a Brain*, for example, Ashby outlined the design of a cybernetic autopilot. If one wires up a conventional autopilot backwards it tends to destabilise flight, the opposite of its intended function. Ashby pointed out that a cybernetic version would not be subject to this pathology: whatever the initial wiring, it would eventually achieve a state of dynamic equilibrium with the aeroplane. Again, in a 1945 note published in *Nature*, he drew on his existing research on stability and instability in multi-element systems to open an argument in economics: that price controls on the British economy might induce economic instabilities, rather than the stability they were intended to encourage. In subsequent work leading up to his second book, *An Introduction to Cybernetics* (1956), he argued that the mathematical analysis in which the homeostat was embedded applied to all 'state-determined systems' – which, in fact, as a class encompassed all physical phenomena. His cybernetics was, then, a theory of everything – or such was the claim.

Philosophy, brain science, psychiatry, engineering, robotics, economics, a theory of everything – the multiplicity of fields crossed by Ashby's cybernetics is one key aspect of what one might be tempted to call the interdisciplinarity of the field. But I can emphasise now how this multiplicity differs from conventional images of interdisciplinary endeavour. Ashby's achievement was not to add up and integrate existing positive knowledge from disciplines such as mathematics, psychiatry and economics. It was rather to show how the model offered by his multi-homeostat set-ups could be further specified and made concrete in those fields and others. This is what I meant earlier by saying that cybernetics erupted across the disciplinary map: at one and the same time, cybernetics could be instantiated, so to speak, in all sorts of fields. And this gets us back to my notion of antidisciplinarity: conventional disciplinary boundaries hardly mattered from a cybernetic perspective; cybernetic approaches crossed them relatively easily – though such crossings always entailed creative work – and tended to efface them.[6]

Perhaps one more observation would be useful before moving on. In getting to grips with the antidisciplinarity of cybernetics it helps to reflect that cybernetic projects differed from conventional ones in a specific way. The modern sciences aim to burrow more and more deeply into specific objects, and they do this by operating specific machineries of instruments, methods and concepts. These machineries, and the objects that they elicit and analyse, are what give the disciplines their distinctive identities and keep them apart, and thus define the boundaries and lacunae that interdisciplinarity struggles with. Cybernetics was not like that. If its defining feature was its nonmodern ontology of exceedingly complex systems engaged in processes of coupled becomings, it did not aim to burrow more deeply into that. There was nowhere to go in that direction. Instead, the research project of cybernetics was precisely to grasp more and more aspects of the world in terms of that ontology, on the model of a multi-homeostat assemblage (or some other cybernetic model). That is why cybernetics was an intrinsically antidisciplinary science.

The theme of antidisciplinary eruption is worth developing further as a way of emphasising its scope, and we can do this by moving beyond Ashby himself and noting some instances in which others developed distinctive approaches growing out of his work. Beyond the phenomenon of adaptation to the unknown, Ashby was interested in the speed of adaptation. The brain would be of no use if it took longer to adapt to its surroundings than, say, the age of the universe, a possibility that readily arose in multi-homeostat set-ups, and Ashby devoted considerable energy to estimating probabilities of stability of differently configured assemblages. This work was taken over directly by Christopher Alexander (1964, 1977) in elaborating his distinctive work in architecture (concerning the fit between elements of buildings and each other and the environment), which fed in turn into his well-known work on 'pattern languages' (of considerable importance in architecture and also computer software design). A stripped down version of the same problematic appears at the origins of Stewart Kauffman's (1969a, 1969b) theoretical biology, where the elements finding equilibrium (or not) are idealised genes. And, though there is no direct historical connection, it appears again in Stephen Wolfram's mathematical work on cellular automata, which fed into the development of what he calls a 'new kind of science' – another theory of everything, a nonmodern one, different in kind from that of the particle physicists (Wolfram 2002).

In the late 1950s a friend of Ashby's, Stafford Beer, founded the field of management cybernetics by considering the relations between elements of organisational structures and between organisations and their environments on the model of multiple homeostats. This led first to some extremely imaginative work in the early 1960s on 'biological computing' (Pickering 2009b). Rather than building adaptive machines like the homeostat, the idea was that nature is already full of adaptive systems which one could seek to entrain in human projects. A pond ecosystem, to give a relevant example, adapts to unpredictable changes in its environment by reconfiguring itself – much like a homeostat, although at a much higher level of complexity. Beer understood the function of management as precisely one of adaptation to an always changing environment, and he therefore explored all sorts of possibilities for substituting naturally occurring adaptive systems for human managers. This project failed, not on any point of principle, but on the practical difficulty of coupling nonhuman systems into the world of human affairs – of getting ponds to care about us. Beer later developed what he called the 'viable system model' (VSM) in which information flows and transformations were designed to turn organisations themselves into performative and adaptive 'brains', again capable of reconfiguring themselves in response to transformations in their business environment. The most spectacular implementation of the VSM was the reorganisation of the entire Chilean economy under the socialist regime of Salvador Allende in the early 1970s, though the approach continues to thrive up to the present – as does an approach to collective decision-making, again modelled on the homeostat, that Beer called 'syntegration' (Beer 1959, 1981, 1994; Pickering 2004).

In the work on biological computing Beer collaborated with Gordon Pask, now remembered principally for his cybernetic approach to the arts. As an undergraduate, Pask built his famous Musicolour machine which turned a musical performance into a light show. Musicolour adapted to the human performer by becoming 'bored' and ceasing to respond to repeated musical tropes, thus obliging the performer to adapt to the machine – again on the lines of a multi-homeostat set-up. A Musicolour performance was thus once more a symmetric dance of agency, now between human and machine, another striking and also literal example of nonmodern ontological theatre (Pask 1971). Pask later pursued this line of development into interactive robotic artworks, interactive theatre and adaptive architecture (Pickering 2007).

This brief run-through of some further cybernetic projects is enough to establish that cybernetic antidisciplinarity was of much wider scope than conventional visions of interdisciplinarity. I began by calling cybernetics a 'science', but this was simply a way of getting the discussion going. Certainly it included threads that one can easily count as 'science' – brain science, theoretical biology, cellular automata – but others not. Along similar lines, we tend to think of interdisciplinarity as a matter of intersections between different university departments, while cybernetics erupted beyond the university into all sorts of institutions and across social life: management, architecture firms, consultancies, the arts wherever they are to be found, and so on. In fact, the centre of gravity of cybernetics was never to be found in the academy, but rather in real-world projects – it was a sort of 'science in the wild'.[7] And, of course, one can see why that might be. The nonmodern ontology is about performance, not representation, while the modern university deals, precisely, in words.[8]

One last remark in this connection. The cybernetic dust cloud extended even further than so far indicated, into realms of the self and spirituality. In fact various forms of mystical and often, although not always, Eastern spirituality continually surface throughout the history of cybernetics. In the late 1920s, Ashby stated that intellectual integrity required him to admit (in the privacy of his notebooks at least) the claims of British spiritualism; in the 1940s, he declared himself a 'time worshipper' (also in his notebooks). Pask wrote a series of unpublished adventure stories about a Victorian psychic detective. Besides his management consultancy, Beer taught tantric yoga and wrote poems expressing, for example, his awe at the computing power of the Irish Sea (see Blohm, Beer and Suzuki 1986).[9]

It would take us too far afield to follow this thread at any length, but I want to note that one can begin to understand what is going on here by returning to the basic nonmodern ontology (Pickering 2008c, 2011). The idea that the world is ultimately unknowable tends directly towards the sort of hylozoist awe at the performativity of matter expressed in Beer's poetry and Ashby's time worship. The idea that we are ourselves exceedingly complex systems points to an endlessly open horizon of possibilities, in which the spirits of the dead (and ESP, nirvana and yogic feats) might find a place. The idea that we are adaptive systems, always mangled in a world of becoming, points to a sort of decentring of the self that resonates strongly with Eastern philosophy and spirituality. Again, the point to grasp here is that cybernetics did not so much combine elements of different fields as cash out the same nonmodern ontology in science, the arts, politics and, now, spirituality. For Beer, the basic diagram of the VSM was at once a map of the adaptive worldly organisation and a great chain of being leading upwards from individual biological cells to the cosmos itself, all elements of which could be grasped in meditative practice. Cybernetics was (or could be) simultaneously a form of science, art and spirit – all of these apparently heterogeneous aspects flowed continuously into one another in an antidisciplinary fashion.[10]

I now want to make explicit another feature of cybernetics that has been close to the surface throughout. Conventional interdisciplinarity is about synthesising objects, concepts and methods from different disciplines, but the eruption of cybernetics across the disciplines did not take that form. As it crossed the terrain of different fields, cybernetics did not typically fit in as an extension of existing projects. It did not solve any already recognised technical or conceptual problems. Against the frame of the conventional disciplines, cybernetics projects and artefacts looked odd. Adaptive machines look odd in comparison with AI computer programmes, and building them was also an odd way of doing psychiatry. Cellular automata are an odd form of mathematics (similarly Benoit Mandelbrot spoke of fractals as 'monsters', Pickering 2005b). Even Gordon Pask had no clear idea of what his Musicolour machine was. He spoke of trying to 'sell it in any possible way: at one extreme as a pure art form, at the other as an attachment for juke-boxes' (Pask 1971: 85). Mainstream architects referred to his style of adaptive architecture as 'anti-architecture' – not really architecture at all (Landau 1968). Hymns of praise to the computing power of water are an unusual form of worship.

The point I want to emphasise, then, is that while it makes some sense to describe cybernetics as interdisciplinary, it is misleading inasmuch as cybernetics almost inevitably implied a transformative displacement of the disciplines as it crossed their paths. Cybernetics unified the disciplines, it is true, but only at the expense of remaking them in its own nonmodern ontological image.

It is perhaps useful to rephrase this point from a more sociological angle. I have been trying to get at the antidisciplinarity of cybernetics by looking at the work of individuals and seeing how it spun off in many directions. The more usual sense of cybernetics as interdisciplinary derives from looking at the variety of fields represented in the field as a whole. The Macy conferences in which cybernetics as a field was born and named are the usual example (Heims 1991). Held in the US between 1946 and 1953, regular attendees came from all sorts of fields: mathematics, physics, engineering, psychology, anthropology, psychiatry. Membership in the formative Ratio Club in Britain and attendances at the European Namur cybernetics conferences were even more diverse, in terms of kinds of institutions as well as fields of study, including hospitals, research institutes and government laboratories besides all sorts of university departments. But we should not think of this heterogeneity as sweeping up disciplines en masse. We should think rather of an accumulation of oddities. Just as cybernetic objects and projects looked odd against the backdrop of the modern disciplines, so the cyberneticians looked odd, too, within their fields and departments. One should probably think in terms of metaphors of attraction and repulsion. The people who came to the Macy and Namur meetings were outsiders in their own fields (if they had one) by virtue of proto-nonmodern interests, and were likewise drawn to one another on a shared ontological basis. Though often coming from fields with familiar names, these cybernetic groupings existed almost orthogonally to their modern counterparts.

This observation might lead us to think further about the social basis of cybernetics. As noted earlier, when we think of interdisciplinarity we usually think of collaborations across departments in the university. But as also noted, the centre of gravity of cybernetics was not in the university at all. Where was it then? The simplest answer is: nowhere. Exaggerating only slightly, one can say that cybernetics has never found a stable home. Ross Ashby was a research psychiatrist by profession, but he referred to his early work on the homeostat as his 'hobby'. The other great first-generation British cybernetician, Grey Walter, built his famous robot tortoises at home using spare parts from clocks and wartime surplus shops. Stafford Beer was the leader of the Operations Research and Cybernetics Department of a major steel company in the early 1960s, but he did his research on biological computing in his spare time, experimenting on his own children and taking them for walks to collect pond water. After a spectacular career in academic physics, Stephen Wolfram founded his own company, Wolfram Research, which is now the institutional foundation of his new kind of science. Collectively, conference series and dining clubs (and now internet chat groups and websites) have provided an always improvised basis for the field to come together.

Two remarks follow. The first returns us to my opening remarks on marginality. Cybernetics flourished in the interstices of a hegemonic modernity, largely lacking access to the means of reproduction: the educational system. If power resides in institutions rather than individuals, the cyberneticians had very little of it. As an antidisciplinary formation, cybernetics grew in the shadows – achieving wider visibility only in the 1960s, no doubt by virtue of ontological intersections with the counterculture, itself quickly forgotten.

Second, at the level of content, the improvised social basis of cybernetics helps to account for another sense in which it has been antidisciplinary – namely, in lacking the disciplinary apparatus that university PhD programmes wield. I talked earlier about 'science in the wild', and cybernetics itself has always been wild and undisciplined in its open-ended capacity for surprising mutation – from brain science to theoretical biology, management, the arts and Eastern spirituality, even finding its way into William Burroughs' *Naked Lunch* (2001 [1959]) and Brian Eno's music (Eno 2003). Lacking an effective police force, individuals have been free to adapt and transplant cybernetic exemplars as they will.[11]

One final distinctive oddity of cybernetics is worth mentioning. As Heidegger (1977) noted, the modern sciences lend themselves readily to projects of domination and the 'enframing' of people and things. The positive knowledge they generate invites a planned reengineering of the world. Cybernetics, in contrast, problematised this stance. In a world built from exceedingly complex systems one should expect such plans to go awry; exceedingly complex systems, by definition, are refractory to 'command and control'. The cybernetic ontology instead invites respect for an uncontrollable other, and translates into a stance not of domination through knowledge, but of open-ended and performative engagement with an ultimately unknowable other – an openness to what the world has to offer us, for better or worse, that we could refer to in Heideggerian terms as a stance of 'revealing' or '*poiesis*' (Pickering 2008a).

This stance of revealing is an enduring thread running through all of the antidisciplinary manifestations of cybernetics, from Ashby's homeostats that explored the behaviour of their environments by reconfiguring themselves, up to Pask's Musicolour machine that searched through coupled spaces of human and nonhuman performativity. What surfaces here, then, is, in a very general but important sense, a political divergence between cybernetics and modern science and engineering, one pointing towards processes of experimental adaptation to the other; the other to asymmetric relations of domination. The latter is, of course, hegemonic today, although the very existence of nonmodern fields such as cybernetics might serve to denaturalise that hegemony. Conversely, one might think that this odd stance of revealing accounts, at least in part, for the marginality of cybernetics – it did not fit in with our usual ways of world-making.

This completes a first pass through cybernetics as an antidisciplinary formation. Despite its reputation as an interdisciplinary science, I have tried to show that cybernetics entailed something other than the combination of existing disciplines. I have argued, instead, that cybernetics amounted to the explosion of a nonmodern ontological stance across, and beyond, the disciplinary map. This is what served to undermine disciplinary boundaries and to bring together practitioners of all sorts of fields and disciplines, but these practitioners and their projects themselves looked odd from the perspective of the modern disciplines, substantively and politically. Alongside this, I have also noted how poorly cybernetics fitted into existing institutional structures, finding its social basis in the cracks and interstices of the modern world.

To conclude, it seems proper to complicate the picture a little. I have so far described cybernetics and the modern sciences as two incommensurable socio-ontological formations, ships that pass in the night. As a first approximation, and as a way of getting the present notion of antidisciplinarity into focus, I think this is right. But, as a matter of fact, the two paradigms could be brought into a variety of relations with one another, and I want to explore some of these intersections briefly at the levels of ontology and politics as an opening into thinking about another form of interdisciplinarity, now of the modern and the nonmodern.[12]

We can start once more with the homeostat. I described a multi-homeostat set-up as ontological theatre inasmuch as it conjures up and instantiates the nonmodern ontology that defines cybernetics. But seen from another angle the homeostat was itself an evidently modern device: its electrical and mechanical components were undoubtedly the products of modern engineering. Somehow, then, the homeostat brought together the modern and the nonmodern, in a way that is worth exploring. My suggestion is that we should see the homeostat as staging a hybrid or mixed ontology in which the two paradigms were fused: an ontological vision of the world as containing both fixed, knowable elements (modelled by the homeostat's valves and capacitors etc.) and exceedingly complex systems (the homeostat's environment) constitutively coupled to one another. We could think of this fusion as entailing, in effect, a pinning down of some but not all of the elements of the basic cybernetic ontology.

The point to note is that under this description the homeostat takes on the character of a bivalued gestalt figure. Grasped one way, the engineering components recede into the background, foregrounding processes of performative adaptation to the unknown. This was the gestalt that characterised the antidisciplinary eruption of cybernetics that I have sketched out thus far. Grasped differently, however, the homeostat's modern elements come into sharp relief, and this was the gestalt in which Ashby could count his cybernetics as a contribution to a modern science of the brain: he was finding out about the sorts of structures an adaptive brain might contain.

This hybrid ontology and the non/modern gestalt switches that go with it deserve more thought than I can give them here, but we can remark that it was the availability of the modern gestalt that put Ashby in a position to align his cybernetics with more conventional approaches to the brain. As just stated, this gestalt allowed Ashby to situate his cybernetics in the same space as neurophysiology, say – both were concerned with understanding the go of the material brain.[13] It also allowed him to offer a cybernetic underpinning for the psychiatric world in which he worked. He used his homeostats, for example, to model the 'great and desperate cures' (Valenstein 1986) – chemical and electrical shock therapy and lobotomy – that dominated psychiatry from the 1930s to the 1960s, and thus offered them an added degree of legitimacy.

Another of Ashby's elaborations of the hybrid ontology is also worth considering in this connection. I described the homeostat as being free to reconfigure itself in response to interactions with its environment. But the machine included a switch which disconnected the relay and stepping switch, so that its circuitry was fixed and non-adaptive. The homeostat itself, as well as its electrical components, could thus be pinned down as a classically modern entity. Ashby also understood psychiatric practice (and warfare) on the asymmetrical model of a homeostat whose parameters were free to vary seeking to come into equilibrium with another whose parameters were fixed. The latter here stood for the psychiatrist, understood as an exemplar of unvarying mental normality, who forces the patient through a series of homeostat-like reconfigurations (via electroshock or whatever) in the hope that one of them will be a return to normality thus defined. This further ontological specification thus located the psychiatrist and the sufferer on opposite sides of the non/modern divide and, in doing so, legitimated the conventional hierarchic power relations of the mental hospital. This ratification of the social status quo is what one can think of as the political aspect of the hybridity of Ashby's ontology.

Far from being ships that pass in the night, then, Ashby found ways to insert his cybernetics into modern brain science and to use it to underpin psychiatric practice. The relay here was the adoption of a modern gestalt for a hybrid ontology. The price of this, of course, was to isolate these aspects of his cybernetics from the overall antidisciplinary explosion that has concerned us here. If the homeostat indeed ran through the wider history of cybernetics, it was not as a scientific model of the efficacy of electroconvulsive therapy; it was as nonmodern ontological theatre.

Having said all that, we can return to the antidisciplinary thrust of cybernetics by noting that in many cybernetic projects the option of adopting the modern gestalt was either not taken or simply unavailable. Pask's Musicolour machine was built from much the same electrical components as the homeostat, but he did not try to read its circuits as contributions to the science of anything: Musicolour was securely within the nonmodern gestalt as a contribution to a strange adaptive art form. Beer and Pask's biological computing project did not pass through modern engineering at all. It staged a purely nonmodern ontology, attempting to insert one exceedingly complex system (a pond ecosystem, say) into others (the firm and its economic environment). In this respect, then, many cybernetic projects indeed sailed straight past their modern cognates. Or, at the other end of the spectrum from Ashby's accommodation to modernity, they collided with their modern counterparts as critique. These collisions were especially acute in contests over common ground, which is where the prefix 'anti-' was often applied to cybernetics, as in the description above of adaptive architecture as 'anti-architecture'. To explore such collisions a little further, we can close with another 'anti': 'anti-psychiatry' as it grew from the work of Gregory Bateson.

Bateson was another of the founders of cybernetics, one of the original participants in the US Macy conferences. He was especially interested in processes of communication, which he understood on the symmetric model of multiple homeostats reciprocally adapting to one another. In 1956 he introduced his famous notion of the 'double-bind' – his name for a situation in which such reciprocal adaptation arrives at an unfortunate form of equilibrium, in which one or more of the partners is left with no good way to go on. Bateson argued that repeated double-binds are what precipitate schizophrenia, and that psychosis is itself a manifestation of some drastic adaptation process which, left to itself, can lead to the undoing of double-binds and spontaneous remission (Bateson et al. 1956).

Various points about Bateson's theory of schizophrenia are worth noting. First, in drawing on the model of the homeostat it remained close to Ashby's cybernetic psychiatry, but with the modern scientific impulse now stripped away. Bateson had no interest in tracing out the electrical (or biochemical) substrates of madness; he was interested in coupled becomings of exceedingly complex systems and their possible pathologies. In this sense, Bateson's approach to psychiatry staged a purely nonmodern ontology from which the hybrid quality of Ashby's, and the possibility of adopting a modern gestalt, was absent. Second, unlike Ashby's, Bateson's symmetric cybernetics functioned as a critique of mainstream psychiatry. On Bateson's account, the great and desperate cures functioned only to stop naturally occurring adaptive processes in their tracks and to leave patients stuck in their double-binds. Bateson's analysis functioned as a critique of the social relations of psychiatry, too. The symmetric model of reciprocal adaptation discouraged the idea of the doctor as a fixed paragon of sanity, and instead pointed to an experimental approach to therapy in which the therapist had to adapt in trying to latch onto the patient and, indeed, to be open to the possibility of learning in the encounter.

Bateson's work was largely theoretical and interpretive, but attempts were made to put these ideas into psychiatric practice within the established mental-health system in Britain in the early 1960s. In the event, however, the mismatch with existing clinical regimes created frictions to the extent that in 1965 R. D. Laing and his colleagues in the Philadelphia Association set up a Batesonian psychiatric community functioning entirely outside the state system, at Kingsley Hall in London. Kingsley Hall was a commune in which doctors and sufferers (and others) lived together in a relatively non-hierarchic relationship. No shock or drug therapy took place; the psychiatrists simply helped the sufferers in their 'inner voyages' in situated ways as best they could, at the same time expecting to be changed themselves. (Laing's argument was that modernity is a form of madness, in its disconnection from the inner self: Laing 1967.)

In this instance, therefore, the socially pressing problem of how to cope with mental illness provided a zone of contestation in which the ships of modernity and nonmodernity collided head on rather than passing in silence. The Bateson–Laing wing of the anti-psychiatry movement, as it became known, constituted both a thoroughgoing and inherently political critique of modern psychiatry and a practical alternative to it.[14]

This is as far as I can go with this discussion of non/modern interdisciplinarity. I have tried to show that the modern and the nonmodern can indeed be brought into relation with one another, and even fused together. In Ashby's work a hybrid ontology supported a modern gestalt in which cybernetics and modern science and engineering could happily coexist. Within this gestalt, cybernetics could take its place as one of the royal sciences, as Deleuze and Guattari (1987) called them, that preserve social order and prop up the state. But when that gestalt was not adopted or simply unavailable, the situation changed. A simple incommensurability of the modern and the nonmodern reigned in practice, which could turn into contestation over shared ground. In this respect, cybernetic anti-psychiatry appears as one of Deleuze and Guattari's nomad sciences that, far from achieving any non/modern interdisciplinary accommodation, sweep in from the steppes to play onto-political havoc with established orders (Pickering 2009c).

Acknowledgements

I am grateful to Andrew Barry, Georgina Born, Antonio Carvalho, Regenia Gagnier and Gisa Weszkalnys for insightful comments on the first draft of this essay, and to Christine Aicardi for access to her unpublished PhD dissertation.

Notes

1 Barry, Born and Weszkalnys (2008) and Born and Barry (2010) identify three underlying 'logics' that variously run through the interdisciplinary projects they examined. The third and most interesting is a 'logic of ontology'. The present essay can be read as an attempt to clarify this ontological thread and explore it further.

2 As defined here and below, a list of contemporary nonmodern sciences would include many of the fields currently grouped under the heading of 'complexity', among them work on cellular automata, dynamical systems theory, self-organising systems, autopoiesis, situated robotics, artificial life, and enactive and embodied strands of cognitive science and philosophy of mind and the emotions. (The fact that these often connect directly to one another and to cybernetics supports my general point about antidisciplinarity.)

Widening the frame, the list extends to include, for example, adaptive architecture and generative music. Some of these fields are discussed briefly below; all of them and more are discussed at length in Pickering (2010). Although my research is not exhaustive, I believe that all of them display the antidisciplinary characteristics discussed below. See, for example, the variety of fields touched upon in Wolfram's *A New Kind of Science* (2002). Aicardi (2010) is an extended account of artificial life research centred on Sussex University and documents in great detail many of the features noted below (and also the fact that the Sussex researchers regard themselves as the current inheritors of the British tradition in cybernetics).

As discussed below, cybernetics began as a science of the brain, and can thus be situated within continuing traditions of research in psychiatry and psychology that focus on processes of adaptation. Alchemy, as I understand it, was both a premodern and nonmodern science (Pickering 2001); Hannaway (1975) draws a beautiful and relevant contrast between a nonmodern Paracelsianism and early modern chemistry, the latter arising in a context of institutionalised disciplinary pedagogy. *Naturphilosophie* in the nineteenth century might also be associated with a nonmodern ontology. Gagnier (2010) discusses Vcitorian 'predisciplinary' and nonmodern forms of knowledge that were eclipsed by the rise of the modern disciplines.

My definition of nonmodernity here emphasises time and emergence, but connects with a simpler notion of ontological nonmodernity as a recognition of non-dualist couplings of the human and the nonhuman (Latour 1993). Contemporary sciences that to some extent undercut Cartesian dualism in this sense, but without foregrounding processes of emergence and becoming, would include ergonomics and operations research (Pickering 1995a; for the contrast between operations research and cybernetics, see Beer 1959). I suspect that the latter sciences tend more towards conventional interdisciplinarity (combining, say, modern mathematics, engineering, social science, psychology and physiology) than the antidisciplinarity at issue here. Studies of the foundations of modern physics are interesting to contemplate in the present context. If one takes seriously the Heisenberg uncertainly principle or the measurement problem in quantum mechanics, the Cartesian distinction between observer and observed becomes problematic, and here one indeed finds antidisciplinary and strikingly nonmodern connections made between physics, consciousness and spirituality (e.g. Capra 1975). See also Fernandez (2010) on connections between David Bohm's quantum mechanics and esoteric thought.

3   For much fuller documentation and analysis of what follows, see Pickering (2010). The novelty of the present essay is the focus on interdisciplinary and antidisciplinary aspects of cybernetics. My interest in cybernetics grew out of my studies of practice in the modern sciences, where I had been led to an antidisciplinary argument from an epistemological angle (Pickering 1993, 1995b). The argument was that mainstream modernist approaches to the history, philosophy and sociology of science systematically obscure the performative and emergent aspects of scientific practice that I refer to as dances of agency, and that what I called 'eclectic interdisciplinarity' can do nothing to remedy this situation. We therefore need what I called an antidisciplinary approach centred on the non-dualist and emergent – nonmodern – phenomena that characterise practice. (For simpler versions of this argument focusing on everyday rather than scientific examples, see Pickering 2005a, 2008a.) The whole 'posthumanist' wing of science and technology studies (Pickering 2008b) can, in this sense, be understood as itself a nonmodern science, and Latour's attempts to forge links between posthumanist STS, politics and the arts dramatise its antidisciplinary aspects: see Latour and Weibel (2002, 2005). For a different political vector of extension of posthumanist theory, see Pickering (2009a). See also Biagioli (2009) on 'postdiscplinary liaisons' between science studies and the humanities.

4   I use the past tense here since the focus is on the history of cybernetics, but the field continues to exist today, less prominently than in the past.

5   The general image should be of indefinite open-ended becomings, and the homeostat only offered a limited model of this. In fact, each homeostat could exist in just 25 different states (corresponding to the 25 settings of its stepping-switch), so that a four-homeostat set-up could take on $25^4 = 390,625$ different states – certainly not infinite, but enough to convey the general idea.

6 To be clear, then: the antidisciplinarity at issue was not necessarily driven by any prior antipathy towards specific disciplines or disciplinarity in general. It was, instead, almost a side-effect of the working out of a nonmodern ontological stance.

7 Discussions of conventional interdisciplinarity often focus on problems of connecting the modern disciplines with 'users' outside the academy. In contrast, cybernetic projects were often real-world enterprises, immediately engaged with their users; no such gap existed to be crossed.

8 For a short but trenchant critique of the representationalist university, see Huxley (1963). For an extended and elaborated version, see Shusterman (2008).

9 One of the best popular introductions to cybernetics, complexity and self-organisation is Capra (1996), which immediately assimilates these worldly sciences to a Buddhist world-view.

10 There remains the question of whether antidisciplinary eruption should be thought of as a *necessary* concomitant of a nonmodern ontology. The answer is probably not. Rodney Brooks' situated robotics, for example, is in a direct line of inheritance from Grey Walter's prototypically cybernetic robot tortoises of the late 1940s, but Brooks (1999) has explicitly declined to explore antidisciplinary readings of his work. More broadly, many contemporary cyberneticians regret the associations of cybernetics with spirituality. What is at issue here, then, is the demonstrable *possibility* of ontologically mediated antidisciplinary extensions, whether taken up in the work of specific individuals or not.

11 Aicardi's (2010) study of artificial life research at Sussex documents in detail many of the above observations, running from a sort of inner antidisciplinarity in the work of specific individuals, to crossovers amongst disparate fields of science, philosophy and art, and the lack of a stable institutional base. A question that arises here is whether institutional instability is inevitably a feature of nonmodern antidisciplinarity. Many of the researchers Aicardi studied were actively opposed to attempts to achieve regular departmental status, precisely on the grounds that it would stifle creativity and openness. On the other hand, there are examples of the achievement of a quasi-stable social basis in the history of cybernetics, most notable Heinz von Foerster's Biological Computing Laboratory at the University of Illinois, where Ashby worked in the 1960s (Müller and Müller, 2007), and the Cybernetics Department at Brunel University, where Gordon Pask held a part-time appointment. Both of these institutions proved ephemeral, pointing not to the impossibility but to the sheer difficulty of maintaining nonmodern antidisciplinarity within the modern disciplinary frame of academia.

Outside the world of the university one thinks of the Santa Fe Institute as a relatively stable institutional base for work on complexity but, significantly, Aicardi notes that artificial life research has been dropped from its agenda as insufficiently scientific and too closely associated with the arts and continental philosophy. Historically, Black Mountain College, North Carolina (1933–1957) appears to have been a fascinating, but in the end also ephemeral, attempt to establish an institutional base for forms of nonmodern antidisciplinarity (www.bmcproject.org). Likewise, the short-lived 'anti-universities' of the countercultural 1960s. (For some information on the Anti-University of London, see Green 1988; for a fictional evocation of the anti-university, see Byatt 2002.) Also in the 1960s, Alexander Trocchi's sigma project imagined the construction of a countercultural institutional base that could grow in parallel with, and eventually displace, the institutions of modernity. A concrete inspiration for Trocchi (1991a [1962], 1991b [1962]) was Kingsley Hall, discussed below.

12 Barry, Born and Weszkalnys' discussions of a 'logic of ontology' (Note 1 above) includes a focus on interdisciplinary projects in 'art-science' where ontological clashes much like those at issue here surface.

13 Despite this accommodation to modernity, Ashby's cybernetics remained a strange science precisely in its hybridity. Since the Scientific Revolution the modern sciences have each presumed its own closed and homogeneous realm of objects. Newtonian

mechanics is a science of point masses and nothing else. Modern interdisciplinarity aims to somehow plug these closed worlds into one another. The nonmodern sciences, in contrast, retain their reference to the constitutive otherness of exceedingly complex systems.

14 Kingsley Hall was also an epicentre for the broader social contestation of the 1960s. It was an institutional base for the British counterculture and a model for other onto-institutional initiatives (Note 11 above).

References

Aicardi, C. (2010) *Harnessing Non-Modernity: A Case Study in Artificial Life*, unpublished PhD thesis, University College London.

Alexander, C. (1964) *Notes on the Synthesis of Form*, Cambridge, MA: Harvard University Press.

Alexander, C., et al. (1977) *A Pattern Language: Towns, Buildings, Construction*, New York: Oxford University Press.

Ashby, W. R. (1945) 'Effect of Controls on Stability', *Nature*, 155: 242–3.

— (1952) *Design for a Brain*, London: Chapman & Hall.

— (1956) *An Introduction to Cybernetics*, New York: Wiley.

Barry, A., Born, G. and Weszkalnys, G. (2008) 'Logics of Interdisciplinarity', *Economy and Society*, 37: 20–49.

Bateson, G., Jackson, D., Haley, J. and Weakland, J. (1956) 'Towards a Theory of Schizophrenia', *Behavioral Science*, 1: 251–64. Reprinted in Bateson (1972) *Steps to an Ecology of Mind*, (pp. 201–27) New York: Ballantine.

Beer, S. (1959) *Cybernetics and Management*, London: English Universities Press.

— (1981) *Brain of the Firm*, 2nd ed., New York: Wiley.

— (1994) *Beyond Dispute: The Invention of Team Syntegrity*, New York: Wiley.

Biagioli, M. (2009) 'Postdisciplinary Liaisons: Science Studies and the Humanities', *Critical Inquiry*, 35: 816–33.

Blohm, H., Beer, S. and Suzuki, D. (1986) *Pebbles to Computers: The Thread*, Toronto: Oxford University Press.

Born, G. and Barry, A. (2010) 'Art-science: From Public Understanding to Public Experiment', *Journal of Cultural Economy*, 3: 103–19.

Brooks, R. (1999 [1995]) 'Intelligence without Representation', *Artificial Intelligence Journal*, 47: 139–60. Reprinted in Brooks (1999) *Cambrian Intelligence: The Early History of the New AI*, (pp. 79–101) Cambridge, MA: MIT Press.

Burroughs, W. S. (2001 [1959]) *Naked Lunch, The Restored Text*, J. Grauerholz and B. Miles (eds.), New York: Grove Press.

Byatt, A. S. (2002) *A Whistling Woman*, London: Chatto & Windus.

Capra, F. (1975) *The Tao of Physics*, London: Wildwood House.

— (1996) *The Web of Life: A New Scientific Understanding of Living Systems*, New York: Anchor Books.

Deleuze, G. and Guattari, F. (1987) *A Thousand Plateaus: Capitalism and Schizophrenia*, Minneapolis: University of Minnesota Press.

Eno, B. (2003) 'An Interview with Brian Eno', in D. Whittaker, *Stafford Beer: A Personal Memoir*, (pp. 53–63) Charlbury: Wavestone Press.

Fernandez, O. (2010) 'Esotericism and the Interpretation of Quantum Mechanics: David Bohm (1917–1992)', paper presented at the 20th IAHR World Congress, Toronto, 15–21 August.

Gagnier, R. (2010) *Individualism, Decadence and Globalization: On the Relationship of Part to Whole,* Basingstoke: Palgrave Macmillan.

Green, J. (1988) *Days in the Life: Voices from the English Underground, 1961–1971,* London: Heinemann.

Hannaway, O. (1975) *The Chemists and the Word: The Didactic Origins of Chemistry,* Baltimore and London: Johns Hopkins University Press.

Heidegger, M. (1977) 'The Question Concerning Technology', in *The Question Concerning Technology and Other Essays,* trans. W. Lovitt, (pp. 3–35) New York: Harper & Row.

Heims, S. J. (1991) *The Cybernetics Group,* Cambridge, MA: MIT Press.

Huxley, A. (1963) *The Doors of Perception, and Heaven and Hell,* New York: Harper & Row.

Kauffman, S. (1969a) 'Homeostasis and Differentiation in Random Genetic Control Networks', *Nature,* 224: 177–8.

— (1969b) 'Metabolic Stability and Epigenesis in Randomly Constructed Genetic Nets', *Journal of Theoretical Biology,* 22: 437–67.

Laing, R. D. (1967) *The Politics of Experience,* New York: Pantheon.

Landau, R. (1968) *New Directions in British Architecture,* London: Studio Vista.

Latour, B. (1993) *We Have Never Been Modern,* Cambridge, MA: Harvard University Press.

Latour, B. and Weibel, P. (eds.) (2002) *Iconoclash: Beyond the Image Wars in Science, Religion, and Art,* Cambridge, MA: MIT Press.

— (2005) *Making Things Public – Atmospheres of Democracy,* Cambridge, MA: MIT Press.

Müller, A. and Müller, K. H. (eds.) (2007) *A Disrupted Revolution? Heinz von Foerster and the Biological Computer Laboratory, 1958–1976,* Vienna: Edition Echoraum.

Pask, G. (1971) 'A Comment, a Case History and a Plan', in J. Reichardt (ed.) *Cybernetics, Art, and Ideas,* (pp. 76–99) Greenwich, CT: New York Graphics Society.

Pickering, A. (1993) 'Anti-discipline or Narratives of Illusion', in E. Messer-Davidow, D. Shumway and D. Sylvan (eds.) *Knowledges: Historical and Critical Studies in Disciplinarity,* (pp.103–22) Charlottesville: University Press of Virginia.

— (1995a) 'Cyborg History and the World War II Regime', *Perspectives on Science,* 3: 1–48.

— (1995b) *The Mangle of Practice: Time, Agency, and Science,* Chicago, IL: University of Chicago Press.

— (2001) 'Science as Alchemy', in J. W. Scott and D. Keates (eds.) *Schools of Thought: Twenty-five Years of Interpretive Social Science,* (pp. 194–206) Princeton, NJ: Princeton University Press.

— (2004) 'The Science of the Unknowable: Stafford Beer's Cybernetic Informatics', *Kybernetes,* 33: 499–521.

— (2005a) 'Asian Eels and Global Warming: A Posthumanist Perspective on Society and the Environment', *Ethics and the Environment,* 10: 29–43.

— (2005b) 'A Gallery of Monsters: Cybernetics and Self-Organisation, 1940–1970', in S. Franchi and G. Güzeldere (eds.) *Mechanical Bodies, Computational Minds: Artificial Intelligence from Automata to Cyborgs,* (pp. 229–45) Cambridge, MA: MIT Press.

— (2007) 'Science as Theatre: Gordon Pask, Cybernetics and the Arts', *Cybernetics & Human Knowing,* 14 (4): 43–57.

— (2008a) 'New Ontologies', in A. Pickering and K. Guzik (eds.) *The Mangle in Practice: Science, Society and Becoming,* (pp. 1–14) Durham, NC: Duke University Press.

— (2008b) 'Culture, Science Studies and Technoscience', in T. Bennett and J. Frow (eds.) *Handbook of Cultural Analysis*, (pp. 291–310) London: Sage.

— (2008c) 'Brains, Selves and the World in the History of Cybernetics', *Global Spiral*, 9(3): www.metanexus.net/essay/h-brains-selves-and-spirituality-history-cybernetics, (accessed November 2012).

— (2009a) 'The Politics of Theory: Producing Another World, with Some Thoughts on Latour', *Journal of Cultural Economy*, 2: 199–214.

— (2009b) 'Beyond Design: Cybernetics, Biological Computers and Hylozoism', *Synthese*, 168: 469–91.

— (2009c) 'Cybernetics as Nomad Science', in C. B. Jensen and K. Rödje (eds.) *Deleuzian Intersections in Science, Technology and Anthropology*, (pp. 155–62) Oxford: Berghahn Books.

— (2010) *The Cybernetic Brain: Sketches of Another Future*, Chicago, IL: University of Chicago Press.

— (2011) 'Cyborg Spirituality', *Medical History*, 55: 349–53.

Shusterman, R. (2008) *Body Consciousness: A Philosophy of Mindfulness and Somaesthetics,* Cambridge: Cambridge University Press.

Trocchi, A. (1991a [1962]) 'The Invisible Insurrection of a Million Minds', in A. Scott (ed.) *Invisible Insurrection of a Million Minds: A Trocchi Reader*, (pp. 177–91) Edinburgh: Polygon. Reprinted from *New Saltire Review* (1962).

— (1991b [1962]) 'Sigma: A Tactical Blueprint', in A. Scott (ed.) *Invisible Insurrection of a Million Minds: A Trocchi Reader*, (pp. 192–203) Edinburgh: Polygon. Reprinted from *New Saltire Review* (1962).

Valenstein, E. S. (1986) *Great and Desperate Cures: The Rise and Decline of Psychosurgery and Other Radical Treatments for Mental Illness*, New York: Basic Books.

Wiener, N. (1967) *The Human Use of Human Beings: Cybernetics and Society*, 2nd ed., New York: Avon Books.

Wolfram, S. (2002) *A New Kind of Science*, Champaign, IL: Wolfram Media Inc.

10 Logics of Interdisciplinarity

The case of medical humanities

Monica Greco

In the winter/spring of 2005, the School of Humanities at King's College London organised a series of public lectures on literature-and-medicine. The series was exceptionally well attended, so much so that a change of venue from the one originally planned was required to accommodate all participants. The opening lecture was offered by the medical and literary historian George Rousseau and was entitled 'The state of the field'. So familiar in its conventionality, this title somewhat belied what Rousseau then went on to do, namely to question whether literature-and-medicine could be said to exist as an academic field at all. Specifically, he asked: is literature-and-medicine a *new* field – born of a transformative encounter across disciplinary divides? Or is it a *false* field – the uneasy sum of two disciplines that remain fundamentally heterogeneous? Or again, is it a *field manqué* – one that permanently fails to fulfil its promise and that exists primarily in the form of wishful thinking and programmatic statements?[1]

The irony is, Rousseau continued, that a preoccupation with these questions of identity is one of the most defining features of literature-and-medicine as a set of practices. Since its early days, one of the main activities taking place under this name has been the compilation of databases – featuring lists of novels on illness or doctors, works of fiction and autobiography written by doctors or patients, and so on – as if to prove and justify the existence of the field as a field. In conclusion, Rousseau proposed to resolve this problem of disciplinary identity by offering another label, a new label that would transcend the old ones: what he hoped to see, he claimed, was the confluence of similarly minded scholars and practitioners from any discipline into a field he would call 'compassion studies'.[2]

Rousseau's intervention was one of many that are currently taking place in the name of interdisciplinarity linking medicine and the humanities, particularly (though not only) in the context of medical education. As an event, it was noteworthy for two reasons: on the one hand, it was a high-profile occasion met with palpable enthusiasm by a very large and very mixed audience, indexing what is clearly no longer a fringe or marginal interest, at least in North America and in the UK.[3] On the other hand, the talk rehearsed a typical form of reflexivity in suggesting that, despite a huge proliferation of activity over more than 30 years, the 'field' remains somewhat embryonic, lacking a clearly defined identity and purpose – although evidently not through a lack of definitional efforts on the part of those who consider themselves part of it. Taken as a whole, such efforts testify rather to an empirical multiplicity of purposes and modes of engagement that is often alluded to, but not explored systematically (see e.g. Shafer 2009; Shapiro et al. 2009; Campo 2005).

It is beyond the scope of this chapter to attempt a systematic mapping of the internal diversity of medical humanities. As Kirklin and Richardson (2001: vx) have put it, medical humanities 'can be held to encompass any interaction between the arts and health', and the breadth of this definition is not merely rhetorical. The field is populated by scholars, researchers and practitioners from disciplines as diverse as theology, philosophy, literature, history, anthropology and sociology, medicine, nursing, social work, visual arts, education, drama and music – many wearing multiple 'hats' at any one time. For some, medical humanities may also include those who use the arts to work directly with patients in a therapeutic capacity (as art or music therapists, for example) or the use of arts within healthcare or community settings (known as arts in health and community arts, respectively). Most commentators, however, will maintain a distinction – either explicitly or implicitly – between hospital-based art therapy and arts-in-health programmes on the one hand, and medical humanities programmes based in universities or medical schools on the other.[4] This distinction reflects a basic heterogeneity of purpose: medical humanities are primarily addressed to the pursuit of educational goals, as distinct from therapeutic goals or the goal of improving healthcare or community environments (Kirklin 2003).

Working with this narrower focus on the academy it is possible to identify a core around which medical humanities may be said to cluster: this is the reflexive meta-discourse heard at conferences, published in the editorials and articles of dedicated journals, and articulated more fully in some key book-length publications.[5] Through this discourse the field gathers around the sense of a 'mission', whose practical expression is primarily pedagogical. This sense of mission binds together educational and research initiatives that otherwise span a very wide range of formats and content.[6]

There is no single model followed in medical humanities programmes and they vary in a number of important ways, including: in terms of whether and how they are integrated within a mainstream medical curriculum and, if so, whether (or what proportion of) courses are compulsory or elective; in terms of whether individual courses are exclusively designed for medical students, or shared with students from humanities faculties; and in terms of the balance between a focus on practical skills and problem-based learning, or theoretical understanding. An entire programme may be methodologically informed by a focus on 'stories', for example, and may draw eclectically on film, literary sources, personal accounts from invited speakers, ethics case reports and drama, to explore a wide range of issues directly pertinent to the practice of medicine (Jones and Verghese 2003). Other programmes, by contrast, may seek to provide a systematic foundation in subjects such as the history and philosophy of medicine, philosophy of science, literature and literary criticism, or law as it pertains to healthcare, drawing on canonical texts in those disciplines.[7] While most programmes offered in medical schools do not follow the blueprint of organ systems-based modules, some are designed to complement organ systems-based instruction closely: a cardiovascular module, for example, might include a medical humanities component where students will engage with artistic and literary representations of the heart; a neuroscience module might include readings from the works of Oliver Sacks.[8] Programmes may also be organised around key topics, offering perspectives informed by a range of humanities disciplines on issues such as death and dying, suffering, the hospital, illness narratives, different aspects of ethics and professionalism, again drawing on an eclectic range of sources. The specific emphases in terms of content and approach will reflect where the programme is based – whether in a medical school or an arts and humanities faculty, for example. Last but not least, in an international context, all these variations are underpinned by cultural and institutional differences informing the structure and content of education more generally, and medical education in particular. A full appreciation of the heterogeneity of medical humanities would thus benefit from a comparative historical analysis of the evolution of concrete initiatives within specific national contexts.

It has been suggested that the absence of anything resembling a 'core' curriculum reflects a persistent ambiguity with regards to whether medical humanities do and should constitute an autonomous academic pursuit – emerging out of developments internal to the humanities themselves – or conversely, whether they are 'parasitic' upon medical education and the requirements of the latter (Evans and Macnaughton 2006). While a normative answer to this question remains the object of theoretical debate, it is worth reflecting on some of the historical ingredients that have contributed to this ambiguous situation.

Medical humanities have emerged, under this name, in close connection with intellectual developments in medical ethics or bioethics – a field defined by a similar ambiguity. In the United States, the genealogical link between medical ethics and medical humanities is easily traceable in the history of several key institutions and journals whose names have changed to reflect an evolution from the former towards the latter. One example is the journal *Bioethics Quarterly*, whose title was changed to *Journal of Medical Humanities and Bioethics* in 1985, and eventually became simply the *Journal of Medical Humanities* in 1989. Another example is that of the *American Society for Bioethics and Humanities*, which was founded in January 1998 as the 'consolidation of three existing associations in the field; the Society for Health and Human Values (SHHV), the Society for Bioethics Consultation (SBC), and the American Association of Bioethics (AAB)'.[9] In this second example, the fact that a reference to the humanities does not figure in any of the former titles is significant. The new umbrella title does not so much reflect the bringing together of previously separate fields of academic interest and research, as a historical development internal to the field of bioethics that opened the field itself to a range of approaches beyond those of traditional moral philosophy. This development was the emergence of narrative ethics, in the wake of postmodern theory and the 'textual turn' (see Lindemann Nelson 1997; Brody 2003). The turn to narrative and to constructionist epistemologies highlighted the relevance of a much wider range of disciplines and perspectives to the 'ethical' practice of medicine, in so far as the latter was understood to require richly textured, situated and reflexive understandings of the lives of patients and communities. Today it is not infrequent for medical education in ethics to be subsumed under a wider medical humanities programme, which will offer a contextualisation of medicine as a social, historical and cultural practice, and a variety of perspectives on the experience of illness, besides addressing more traditional bioethical questions.

In what follows I will examine how different logics of interdisciplinarity (Barry et al. 2008) are at play within medical humanities, including some of the ways in which they blur into each other, and some of their specific inflections in this context. One of Barry et al.'s concerns in proposing the notion of multiple logics of interdisciplinarity is to temper the sense of historical discontinuity that is implied in the narrative of 'Mode-2' knowledge production (cf. Gibbons et al. 1994; Nowotny et al. 2001). Interdisciplinarity, they argue, is neither historically new nor does it necessarily signal a reduction in the autonomy of research. I will argue that this point is particularly salient in relation to medical humanities. In addition to the ways in which medical humanities may be said to exemplify specifically contemporary concerns – particularly around questions of accountability and of public engagement – they can also be regarded as reiterating a set of themes with long genealogies in the history of modern medicine. One of these is the idea that there is an irreducible element of 'art' in the proper practice of medicine, which must be rescued from the increasing dominance of science (or at least scientism). A different but related theme is the idea that medical 'science' is not adequate to the nature of medical subject matter, and thus needs itself to be reformed or transformed – in a variety of possible interpretations of this task. Viewed in this light, the emergence of medical humanities may be set in a line of continuity with other forms of engagement between scientific medicine and its multiple *others* in the course of medicine's recent history. The core intent of this chapter will be to discuss medical humanities in the context of such lines of medium- and long-term continuity, as well as to highlight how the present conjuncture shapes what is original about medical humanities as a field.

From 'Social Medicine' to Disorganised Postmodernism?

A useful starting point from which to develop this core concern is an article by sociologist Bryan Turner that appeared in 1990 with the title: 'The interdisciplinary curriculum: from social medicine to postmodernism'. In this somewhat mournful piece, Turner tells one story of medicine's relationship to the question of interdisciplinarity through the lens of sociology. The narrative begins in the eighteenth century with the advent of social medicine in Germany and France; it continues with the emergence of a critical sociology of health and illness after World War II; and it provisionally ends with what Turner, following Ritzer and Walczak (1988), calls the 'McDonaldisation of medicine' based on a 'research centre model' of interdisciplinarity at the end of the twentieth century.[10]

For Turner this is also the story of a transition from 'positive' forms of interdisciplinarity, defined as such by an underlying rationale that is broadly scientific or philosophical, to a 'negative' form of interdisciplinarity. In this negative connotation, interdisciplinarity occurs as a pragmatic answer to pressures of an economic character, facilitated intellectually by the postmodern demise of meta-narratives. The claim, following Lyotard (1986), is that '[b]ecause the universities are no longer committed to the production of ideals, they become merely instruments for the production of [marketable] skills. . . . the traditional questions about truth are . . . replaced by questions about pragmatics (that is reliability, efficiency and commercial value)' (Turner 1990: 17–18).

An erosion of the traditional autonomy of the medical profession, underpinned by the neoliberalisation of medicine, is part of the general context promoting interdisciplinarity in this new and negative connotation. The irony is, Turner continues, that medical autonomy and dominance had typically been obstacles to the successful integration of other disciplines, such as sociology, within the medical curriculum. While the erosion of medical dominance might have signalled new prospects for interdisciplinary approaches to medical analysis and health-care, 'the challenge of postmodernism would deconstruct the meta-narratives of medicine into fragmented and disorganised claims to power' (ibid: 20).

In the bleak picture Turner presents of recent developments it is possible to recognise, albeit in sketchy and oversimplified form, some of the key features of what Gibbons et al. call Mode-2 knowledge production – namely the growing importance that questions of economic and social accountability play in underpinning interdisciplinary initiatives, in medicine as elsewhere (Gibbons et al. 1994; Nowotny et al. 2001). Conversely, Turner's 'positive' forms of interdisciplinarity – namely social medicine and the sociology of health and illness – point to what Barry et al. call a 'logic of ontology' (2008). Their positive value is given by their particular construction/enactment of the reality of health and illness based on a (supposedly more sophisticated) philosophical and scientific understanding of aetiology, contributing to what Turner calls an 'elegant and coherent map of the sciences' (1990: 16).

It is worth noting that, in Turner's narrative, social medicine and the sociology of health and illness both remain *unrealised* ideals of interdisciplinary collaboration. Social medicine, and the relative importance of socio-economic interventions in tackling health issues, faded into comparative insignificance in the course of the late nineteenth and early twentieth centuries, with the increasing professionalisation of medicine through educational standards based on training in the natural (not social) sciences.[11] The sociology of health and illness, for its part, emerged in a context where the dominance of scientific medicine was already entrenched, such that the reality of interdisciplinary engagement always remained far from the epistemological ideal. The sociological agenda would either be subordinate to the biomedical one, or else inconsequential; alternatively, interdisciplinarity might take the form of critical and sometimes aggressive confrontation, making the prospect of a successful and fruitful mutual engagement between the social and the medical sciences 'remote and untenable' (Turner 1990: 12).

Nevertheless, for Turner social medicine and the sociology of health and illness implied interdisciplinarity as a 'consciously selected epistemological goal', expressing a commitment towards certain ontological assumptions. In his diagnosis, the lack of any such commitment is what the 'Thatcherite' and the 'postmodern' models of science ironically hold in common (ibid: 16).

As a phenomenon emerging most conspicuously in the years following the publication of Turner's article, where do medical humanities stand in this picture? Taken at face value there is much to suggest that medical humanities might exemplify precisely Turner's idea of postmodern, fragmented, disorganised and ultimately toothless interdisciplinarity. His scepticism is mirrored, for example, in some of the more cynical appraisals of the role of the humanities in the medical curriculum, such as the notion that the admission of the humanities into medical training constitutes a purely nominal PR exercise in response to public dissatisfaction with a dehumanising medicine.[12]

Amid an abundance of articles and editorials outlining the potential benefits of humanities teaching for doctors, there are as yet few empirical studies of how such teaching is carried out in practice or received by medical students. But these studies suggest that prevailing responses among students are also broadly sceptical, ranging from the characterisation of humanities courses as 'fun' but ultimately irrelevant, to veritable 'outpourings of anger and contempt' at the prospect of precious curricular time wasted (Wachtler et al. 2006; Shapiro et al. 2009). One study of a MedHum programme at a Danish medical school argues that the 'ideological' rhetoric of interdisciplinarity was especially counterproductive in that it set up an opposition between the humanities and medicine itself, reinforcing the perception that medicine should be identified with natural science. A partial and limited enactment of the humanities, associated with 'soft' and 'vague' qualities of humaneness, was interpellated as medicine's *other* within a medical frame of reference (the MedHum programme under study was administered and financed, as is typical, by the medical faculty). 'In this system', the authors write, 'where the medical perspective was so self-evident, there was no room for the humanities disciplines to define what they wanted from medicine' (Wachtler et al. 2006).[13]

Similar concerns also emerge from reading more enthusiastic appraisals of interdisciplinary engagement. For example, in a paper reflecting on the experience of bringing humanities scholars to a teaching hospital for a month-long institute at Penn State University, Squier and Hawkins (2004) discuss how the enactment of humanities teaching and research differs within academic and clinical settings. Written as a dialogue between the two authors, who are both humanities scholars, but based respectively in an English department and in the University's College of Medicine, the paper highlights how the different settings impact on the types of questions asked and the types of analysis produced, both in the classroom and in publications. Hawkins describes how in the medical context questions and analysis must ultimately pass the 'so what' test – literary works and literary theory must be connected 'to real problems in the real world of doctors and patients' (Squier and Hawkins 2004: 247). While she acknowledges that this puts serious limitations on the pursuit of 'unfiltered critical analysis', she ultimately justifies these limitations on the basis that the academy still exists as a place 'both free and superbly equipped' to engage in analysis of that kind (2004: 248). The continued existence of the academy as such a place is, however, precisely what is in question both according to Turner and to theorists of Mode-2 knowledge production.

To confine attention to the potential for such problematic consequences of interdisciplinarity, however, is to miss both the meaning and the significance of the pedagogical intention that fuels initiatives in medical humanities. More specifically, it overlooks how this pedagogical intention not only does point to an ontological commitment, but also transforms how we might understand and what we might expect as the expression of such a commitment, contributing perhaps to a difficulty in recognising it in those terms. A comparison with how interdisciplinarity has been performed in other social sciences engaging with medicine is again instructive here. The social medicine and medical sociology heralded by Turner as examples of 'good' interdisciplinarity were devoted to the study of social determinants of disease, understood as a specific set of variables within a 'multifactoral' model of disease causation; more recently, collaborations between psychologists, linguists, anthropologists and (psycho)neuroimmuno-logists have explored the role of metaphor in pathogenesis in the attempt to define aspects of what has been termed 'cultural biology' (see Wilce 2003). In other words, the ontological commitment of these interdisciplinary efforts focuses on a redefinition of the medical object as a cultural and a social object, with a view to producing supplementary or alternative models of aetiology and pathogenesis – that is, alternative models of disease explanation. To the extent that medical humanities do not engage with questions of aetiology, and to the extent that they do not seek to supplant orthodox biomedical explanations *qua* explanations, their ontological commitment defies expectations based on the precedents set by social science.

Key to grasping the character of the ontological commitment that is specific to medical humanities, I propose, is a serious appreciation of the *pedagogical* as a value in its own right – that is, as something not merely instrumental to the transmission of otherwise established knowledge and/or skills, but something transformative of both the subjects and the objects of knowledge. In what follows I propose to explore this point along two closely related dimensions that I distinguish here mainly for heuristic purposes. In broad outline: the first dimension speaks to the theme of medicine comprising an irreducible element of 'art', whose increasing marginalisation is detrimental both to the practice of medicine itself and to the relations between medicine and the public. In the context of this theme or narrative, the adequacy of the science underpinning current medical practice is not in question, but the reductive understanding of medicine as science is. The second dimension speaks to the question of a paradigm shift in medicine, and thus involves a problematisation not only of the assumption that medicine is or can be scientific, but also the assumption that the (mechanistic, reductive) scientific approach currently employed in the context of medicine is adequate to its purpose. While the first dimension is explicitly addressed in the discourse of medical humanities, the second remains mostly implicit but, I propose, is compatible with it in significant and consequential ways. Let us then examine them in turn.

A Restraint Upon Specialists, an Enlargement of their Imagination

Alfred North Whitehead famously described philosophy as 'the welding of imagination and common sense into a restraint upon specialists, and also into an enlargement of their imaginations' (1978: 17). This description may be taken to synthesise what key practitioners see as the function of the humanities for medicine. As a good synthesis would, it embraces the contrast often drawn between the 'instrumental' and 'non-instrumental' value of humanities teaching for doctors (e.g. Macnaughton 2000). The instrumental value refers to interpretive and communicative skills considered to be of practical benefit to doctors within clinical and non-clinical situations. An eloquent and often cited account of these benefits is the one given by Rita Charon in what has become something like a manifesto for what she calls 'narrative medicine', and for medical humanities more generally. Charon, a general internist with a PhD in literature and founder of the *Narrative Medicine Program* at Columbia, defines narrative medicine as medicine marked by a capacity to understand 'complex narrative situations, including the situations between the physician and the patient, the physician and himself or herself, the physician and colleagues, and physicians and society' (Charon 2001: 1897). The *Narrative Medicine Program* is designed to teach 'narrative competence' as the precondition for the successful practice of narrative medicine.[14]

Charon explicitly presents the programme as the development and formalisation of the idea that there is an art to medicine. The designation of the interpretive nature of clinical reasoning as 'art' is misleading, she claims, because 'art' bears similar connotations to the term 'genius': both are generally assumed to be matters of natural talent rather than something that can be taught. The idea of narrative competence stems from the opposite assumption, namely that skills of interpretation and communication *can* be taught, by turning to those disciplines that have developed methods specifically for this purpose – that is, the humanities in general, literary studies and narratology in particular.

The *Narrative Medicine Program* involves medical students in the reading of literary theory and literary texts, and in exercises of active and reflective writing. Students and residents are also asked to keep what is called a *parallel chart*. As the name implies, this is a chart that is written up alongside the traditional hospital chart for each patient. Students are invited to become introspective and to record their feelings and thoughts – be these feelings of impotence or victory or uncertainty, their fear of mistakes or their sadness at the worsening of a patient's condition. The exercise is designed to promote awareness of their implicit assumptions, prejudices and expectations, and of how their own narrative intersects with that of the patient.

Although the frequent reference to narratology in Charon's work carries suggestions of technical specialism, what is at stake in humanities teaching for doctors is a partial undoing of their specialist training *as doctors*, specifically with regard to the process of 'distancing' that is such a key feature of the hidden medical curriculum.[15] As Deborah Kirklin has put it, the aim of teaching humanities for medical students is to restore to them many 'common sense' qualities of empathic understanding that they come to lose in the course of medical training and that they would normally possess, as part of their experience of life, before they enter medical school.[16]

It is worth stressing that, even in its instrumental connotations, the relevance of humanities teaching is not seen as confined to the clinic, or to relations between doctors and patients. Charon offers four keywords through which her approach can be summarised – empathy, reflection, profession and trust – each of them indexed to a relational dimension of the doctor's work that narrative competence is designed to improve. While *empathy* refers to the doctor/patient relationship and *reflection* refers to a doctor's relation to herself, *professionalism* refers to the relationship between medical colleagues as a community, and *trustworthiness* to the relationship between the medical profession and society more widely. 'Only sophisticated narrative powers', she writes, 'will lead to the conversations that society needs to have about its medical system': not only because physicians need to learn to talk 'simply, honestly and deeply' to other stakeholders, but ultimately because they are conversations about questions of 'meaning and value' that cannot be settled by 'scientific or rational debates' (2001: 1900; see also Engel et al. 2008).

The last point illustrates how medical humanities may be said to enact a logic of accountability, mediating the relationship between medicine and the public (Nowotny et al. 2001; Barry et al. 2008). Crucially however, and in contrast to a 'public understanding of science' paradigm, the pedagogical effort here is not directed at the public – if the public is understood as *other* with respect to the expert or the professional. On the one hand, this effort is directed at educating *doctors* about the experiential and narrative dimensions of illness, and to recognise these as a source of knowledge and authority in their own right. On the other hand, it is directed at correcting a profound misunderstanding of the character of medical knowledge and practice in which both the lay public *and* the medical profession are seen to partake.

A book by sociologist Arthur Frank which, like the article by Charon, has become a standard reference in the field, might serve to illustrate the first aspect in more detail. *The Wounded Storyteller* (1995) stems from Frank's close association with patients' grassroots movements, motivated also by his own experience as a cancer patient, and reflects a broader agenda of political activism on the author's part in the form of mediating dialogue between illness sufferers and the medical profession.

Frank's concern is that in relatively recent times people have learned to tell their own stories of illness in medical terms, and this is not necessarily to their own benefit. What he calls the 'narrative surrender' to medicine, or also 'narrative colonisation' of the experience of the ill person, is presented as a byproduct of the modern professionalisation of doctors and of the corresponding features of the 'sick role' – features that Talcott Parsons (1951) famously described as a structure of specific rights and duties incumbent on anyone who falls ill.

Like other sociologists before him, Frank argues that in the postmodern context – a context characterised by the prevalence of chronic rather than acute illness – both the rights and the duties implicit in the 'sick role', as Parsons described it, no longer hold. Chronically ill people are not excused from their responsibilities, and their compliance with medical authority is not matched by an expectation that they will be able to relinquish the sick role itself. On this basis, Frank draws an analogy between the situation of ill people in postmodernity and the situation of post-colonialism. In terms of a question of *representation*, post-colonialism constitutes the demand to speak rather than being spoken for. In the context of health and illness, the same demand is expressed in refusing 'narrative surrender' to medicine. In terms of a question of *reciprocity*, just as colonised peoples claim recognition of what their labour has contributed to the prosperity and civilisation of colonising powers, the ill 'are demanding, in various and often frustrated ways, that medicine recognize its need for them' (Frank 1995: 12). The pedagogical importance of case history in clinical texts and the participation of volunteers in randomised control trials are only two among many examples of the way in which the development and dissemination of medical knowledge relies on the contribution of patients.

In Frank's work we see the rationale for medical humanities articulated from the perspective of the patient activist, for whom the problem is not how to acquire skills of empathy or communication but rather one of how to resist misplaced authority – claiming recognition of experiential narratives as both valid and useful for the purpose of living with chronic illness and disability. A logic of accountability is evident in medical humanities as the professional response to this type of demand. What is involved in this response, however, is more than a political concession towards non-professional stakeholders, and it is more than the admission of different 'perspectives' on the medical reality of disease to produce, as Turner would have it, a set of 'fragmented and disorganized claims to power' (1990: 20). What is also involved is an endeavour to enlarge the medical imagination, an endeavour that pertains to an ontological logic in that it simultaneously concerns the construction of the subjects of medical knowledge and the character of the reality they profess to address.

What is meant here by an 'enlargement of the medical imagination'? If the development of skills of empathy and communication might rely quite literally on an instrumental exercise of the imagination through engagement with literary and other texts, the 'non-instrumental' value of the humanities for medicine may be said to address the collective imagination as to what medicine is and what it can or should be. This collective imagination transcends the lay–expert divide, particularly in light of the proto-professionalisation of the lay public (De Swaan 1988). And, in its current mainstream expression, it involves the perception of medicine as a science – or 'the mistaken idea of medicine as a body of objective, scientific knowledge that has only to be mastered to bring reliable results' (Montgomery Hunter 1991: xix). In this broader sense, then, the pedagogical intention of medical humanities is addressed to correcting a culture of scientism that is shared by the profession and by patients alike, and that shapes their (often frustrated) mutual expectations, as well as research and policy agendas based on these.

This broader pedagogical intention is articulated through two related but different types of argument. The first type of argument is perhaps most explicitly presented in the work of Kathryn Montgomery (Montgomery Hunter 1991; Montgomery 2006), and proceeds by highlighting isomorphisms between medical and hermeneutic ways of knowing.[17] Based on her ethnography of medical education at the University of Rochester School of Medicine and Dentistry, Montgomery's work foregrounds the inescapability of uncertainty and indeterminacy in the practice of medicine, and the range of (hermeneutical) skills that are routinely deployed to manage them in the clinical context. Montgomery's description testifies to the specificity of medicine as a practice distinct from science, and indeed a practice that is often at its most rational when it does not exclude subjectivity. In this sense, an explicit recognition of medicine's kinship with interpretive approaches typical of the humanities serves to reinforce medical autonomy in the name of a distinctive professional ethos, against exogenous pressures in the name of other rationalities of accountability or success (e.g. financial or scientific).[18] These pressures are frequently alluded to in the medical humanities literature, both through general remarks to the effect that 'the humane is being supplanted by unfeeling science and uncaring economics' (Campo 2005: 1009), and through more detailed accounts of how marketplace-driven healthcare and the competitive drive towards individual distinction or reward have led to an erosion of professionalism and public trust (Charon 2001).[19]

The second type of argument, more eclectic in terms of the range of theoretical and empirical sources it mobilises, is similarly concerned with exposing the inapplicability of determinist assumptions in medicine. But the argument goes further, in this case, to illustrate how assumptions of this kind are explicitly or implicitly embedded in the framing of health policy, and particularly of questions around resource allocation (Greaves 1996). Again, the invitation here is to reimagine not only the practice of medicine as something different from an applied science, but also the theoretical conception of 'health care needs' as something amenable to objective description rather than matters of moral debate (1996: 133). This conclusion is not particularly original in itself, and the argument as a whole may be regarded as a recent addition to a long line of critiques of Western medicine.[20] What makes it noteworthy, however, is its location within a different circuit of reception and dissemination, one associated with a pedagogical agenda that aims to be effective at a capillary level.

In sum, I have argued here that an ontological logic is apparent in the pedagogical intention that lies at the core of medical humanities. Contrary to the expectation that an ontological commitment should refer to the nature of the medical *object* – leaving the subject of knowledge unproblematised – this logic is addressed in the first instance to fostering processes of 'aesthetic and ethical self-forming' (Bleakley et al. 2006) with the aim of producing (and legitimating) doctors as different kinds of *subjects*.[21] These are reflexive practitioners educated in the dangers of 'misplaced concreteness' (Whitehead 1925, quoted in Greenhalgh 1998: 251), and in the creative use of their imagination; subjects more explicitly committed to acknowledging the multiple dimensions of subjectivity in medicine, which range from the uncertainty and indeterminacy of clinical situations to the emotionally textured stories that underlie them. At the same time, this pedagogical intention addresses itself to 'culture' as something like a collective subject, with the hope of effecting an equivalent transformation at that level.

'Better Doctors' – Better Medical Scientists?

If the pedagogical intention of medical humanities is focused, at least as its point of departure, on the subjectivity of the medical practitioner, an ontological commitment towards a different conception of the medical *object*, or a different model of medical science, is also apparent. At the same time, such a model remains highly unspecified, through a deferral of its enactment to future generations. The ambition, in other words, is not simply to produce better doctors in the sense of doctors who are more 'humane', but also to produce better medical scientists in the sense of scientists interested in questions more directly relevant to human beings.[22] The medical humanities movement can thus be regarded, as historian Charles Rosenberg has put it, as one among many 'reformist strategies' addressed at questioning 'the power and efficacy of a fragmented, reductionist, procedure-oriented medicine' (1998: 344).

The essays collected by Lawrence and Weisz (1998) under the rubric of 'holism' in biomedicine illustrate that forms of mainstream resistance to reductionist models have existed as an ongoing counterpoint to scientific medicine throughout the course of the twentieth century, spanning a wide variety of approaches and propositions.[23] This historical work is useful for the purpose of highlighting both historical and thematic continuity between medical humanities and various earlier movements and programmes of reform. At the same time, in presenting current developments through a unifying lens focused on the past, historical comparative analysis can foreclose attention to potentialities, and to the underdetermined character of the present.

Theodore Brown, for example, draws an explicit line of continuity between medical humanities and the influential project of educational reform carried out at Johns Hopkins by Dr George Canby Robinson in the 1930s with a view to restoring relevance to the 'patient as a whole' within the medical curriculum (Brown 1998). In Brown's reading, current efforts in medical humanities share some of the problematic features of Robinson's approach – most notably, perhaps, the translation of the 'social' dimensions of pathology into 'personal' ones. More fundamentally, however, Brown is critical of what he sees as the simultaneously naïve and ideological character of both movements. They are naïve, he claims, in their belief that a 'quick injection' of alternative teaching in the fourth year of medical school can counteract the harm done in the remainder of medical training. And they are ideological in their reliance on 'the crucial but superficially examined assumption that educational change will reform a faulty present by transforming future generations' (ibid: 154). The historian's verdict is thus in line with some of the more cynical or pessimistic appraisals of the significance of medical humanities: at best, the naïvety of their ambition would make them ineffective; at worst, their ideological character would mask their subservience to agendas reinforcing the status quo. From Brown's perspective, not only is the phenomenon nothing new, but it might be described as 'anti-inventive' (Barry 2001: 212).

What is indeed striking about the discourse of medical humanities is the consistently conciliatory and non-confrontational tone in which the transformative ambitions of the movement are articulated. Charon's foreword to what may be described as the first textbook of narrative medicine is indicative in this regard: 'The design of the book is coy', she writes, 'its early sedate presentation of self as a scholarly account of work from many intellectual disciplines acting as a cover for a subversive invitation to radical change' (Charon in Engel et al. 2008: ix).

The project of medical humanities is not promoted in the name of a medical 'revolution' (cf. Foss and Rothenberg 1987). Indeed, narrative medicine is some-times referred to also as 'narrative-based' medicine – a label deliberately selected to convey the suggestion of a profound compatibility between narrative medicine and 'evidence-based' medicine as the current gold standard of medical practice (see e.g. Greenhalgh 1998). At least *prima facie*, advocates and practitioners in the field seem happy if not eager to slot into a division of labour that excludes medical humanities from the task of contributing to research on questions of aetiology, ensuring that 'meaning' and 'causation' remain distinct provinces assigned to the 'art' and the 'science' of medicine respectively. One might go as far as to say that references to bodies of work that might pose a direct challenge to biomedical models in terms of aetiological reasoning seem to be actively avoided – references to psychoanalysis, for example, are mostly conspicuous for their absence.[24] Indeed, this absence of overt commitment to alternative conceptions of aetiology does distinguish the field from its historical predecessors, as well as from other examples of interdisciplinarity in medicine.[25]

On this basis it might be tempting to infer that, as a self-consciously pragmatic form of 'holism', medical humanities implicitly subscribe to the idea that ultimately their fate is to coexist with reductionist science as their constitutive *other* (Rosenberg 1998: 349). Yet the field is rife with claims that the purpose and function of the humanities should not be understood as providing a mere counterweight to biomedical science, 'in such a way as to humanize the medical enterprise but without producing any fundamental challenge to it' (Greaves 2001: 15). Rather than dismiss such claims as empty or ideological, it may be useful to read them, in conjunction with claims as to the cultural misapprehension of medicine as a positivist science, as pointing to the relevance of 'second order' questions of medical ontology (Foss 2002). With this expression, Foss refers to questions addressed to the adequacy not of specific aetiological hypotheses, but of more fundamental constitutive assumptions of explanatory strategies currently operant in medical science. The agnosticism implicitly professed within medical humanities on the question of aetiology, in other words, should be regarded as just that – and not as an endorsement of reductionist models of disease causation, as some commentators suggest. Indeed, in some instances, explicit reference is made to the need to recognise the inadequacy of the scientific model that remains operant in medical practice, despite having long been discredited among natural scientists themselves. Only then, it is claimed, will the full medical potential of an engagement with the humanities really come into its own (Engel et al. 2008).

It has been argued that this type of reference to the possibility of a different science underpinning medical practice – a science capable of admitting 'downward causation' and of addressing living beings as subjects – should be distinguished from the claim that medicine is not, and cannot ever be, scientific (Foss 2002: 285; cf. Montgomery Hunter 1991). The latter claim would serve to perpetuate a dualistic settlement whereby, as suggested above, biomedical explanations based on an obsolete scientific model are deemed still necessary but insufficient to the medical task, and should be 'compensated' accordingly by a parallel focus on the subjective dimensions of illness, care and person.

Critics such as Foss insist that the way out of the dualist deadlock is to lobby not against the cultural association of medicine with science (as Montgomery would argue), but against the identification of scientific explanation with its seventeenth-century ideal. There is no reason, however, to suppose that these positions are mutually exclusive, particularly if we consider that a new medical model informed by the sciences of complexity is not likely to narrow the gap between scientific (medical) theory and medical practice in terms of reducing uncertainty and indeterminacy. Lobbying for a new scientific medical model has its rhetorical justification in the notion that it would legitimate a drastic reorientation of both policy and research priorities, in the quest to tap 'the therapeutic potential of the patient's subjective state' (Foss 2002: 91). But there is a paradox in suggesting that this legitimation should occur in the name of 'science', since the force of the claim relies on a culture of scientism which is itself informed and theoretically supported by reductionist principles.[26] Similarly, a form of scientism underlies the assumption that the benefits of a new medical model – in this case, the benefits of tapping the therapeutic potential of subjectivity – are self-evidently desirable, in so far as the model itself is deemed to be scientifically more adequate. In fact, the desirability of a medicine intervening on subjectivity is far from self-evident, and is certainly not a question that can be settled in scientific terms.[27]

In sum, the reference to a new medical model informed by the sciences of complexity, and the relative absence of such a reference within the discourse of medical humanities, does not authorise a judgment whereby the latter should be identified with forms of conservatism or resistance to change, or indeed a judgment that their relevance to the possibility of change is overstated. On the contrary, the understated way in which the question of a successor model is alluded to, but not regarded in itself as the answer to the limitations posed by objectivist science, may reflect an awareness and respect for the truly complex nature of the relationship between medicine and society.

Conclusions

I have argued that the key to understanding the specificity of medical humanities as a form of interdisciplinarity is a focus on its pedagogical intention, and that an ontological commitment is apparent in the latter. In a pragmatic sense, this ontological commitment is primarily addressed not at the object of medical knowledge and intervention but at the subjectivity of the medical practitioner, which it seeks to transform. A different subject of medical knowledge also implies, by extension, the apprehension of the object of medical knowledge as a different kind of object – in fact, one that can no longer be characterised as an object at all. If we might describe this pedagogical intention by reference to a single requirement, a single exhortation, it would be the one voiced by a maverick free spirit of the medical profession, Georg Groddeck: 'Remember', he wrote, 'that the human being in front of you is but a figment of your lack of imagination' (1977 [1927]: 243).

In underlining this dimension of ontology, I have deliberately constructed my argument in contrast to readings of medical humanities that would reduce them to a logic of accountability or, in the parlance of detractors from the movement, to a PR exercise designed to pacify public opinion and pander to political agendas. If I have framed my description in these terms it is not because such readings do not have a certain plausibility, but because they are too easy and, arguably, themselves anti-political (Barry 2001) in their effects.

Notes

1 I am grateful to Paul Stenner for extensive discussion of the ideas presented in this chapter.
2 Author's notes on G. S. Rousseau 'Literature and Medicine: The State of the Field', lecture held on 27 January 2005 at King's College London.
3 In the US, a trend towards including the humanities as a component of medical education dates back to the mid-1960s, when Penn State University College of Medicine was founded, under the deanship of George T. Harrell, to include a Humanities Department – the first academic department of humanities to be established within a medical school (Hunsaker Hawkins, Ballard and Hufford 2003). The Institute of Medical Humanities at University of Texas (Galveston) soon followed, in 1973; a number of dedicated journals began to emerge from the mid-1970s, including the *Journal of Medicine and Philosophy* (from 1976), *Literature and Medicine* (1981) and the *Journal of Medical Humanities* (previously the *Bioethics Quarterly*, renamed *Journal of Bioethics and Humanities* in 1985 and again renamed in 1989, in conjunction with an announcement of the journal's expansion both in size and frequency); this trend has intensified considerably in the last 20 years or so, with a proliferation of medical humanities centres and programmes across the US (see Dittrich 2003).
  In the UK, the presence of humanities within medical schools has a much shorter history, dating back to the mid 1990s, particularly following the publication in 1993 of *Tomorrow's Doctors: Recommendations on Undergraduate Medical Education* by the education committee of the General Medical Council, which allowed for the opening of up to 30 per cent of the medical curriculum to elective 'special study modules'. After a slower start, the field is expanding in the UK with a similarly quickening pace (see Hurwitz and Dakin 2009). The Wellcome Trust has recently regrouped its funding initiatives in biomedical ethics and history of medicine under a single department of

Medical Humanities. In 2008, the Trust announced a major funding investment through the Centre for Arts and Humanities in Health and Medicine at Durham University, and in support of the foundation of a new Centre for the Humanities and Health at King's College in 2009 (see www.wellcome.ac.uk/News/Media-office/Press-releases/2008/WTX049941.htm, accessed November 2012). The medical humanities movement is not limited to the US and the UK, with examples of academic programmes in Latin America, Australia, New Zealand, Hong Kong and Scandinavian countries among others – an overview is provided in a special issue of the journal *Academic Medicine* (2003, vol 78, no. 10).

4 Shafer (2009), writing from a US perspective, claims that the extent of the interaction between hospital-based art-therapy programmes and medical-school-based medical humanities programmes is variable, and tends to be greater in the UK – where supposedly the boundaries between them are more blurred – than in the US.

5 Contributions are too numerous to cite individually here, but among the most notable examples see: Charon 2001 and 2006, Evans and Finlay 2001, Kirklin and Richardson 2001, Greenhalgh and Hurwitz 1998, Engel et al. 2008.

6 See the special theme issue of the journal *Academic Medicine* (2003), as mentioned in Note 2 above. The selection made by the editors focuses on curricula that are 'substantive and/or comprehensive (as opposed to single courses) and/or . . . innovative', but is otherwise designed to represent a diversity of programmes, geographic locales, and private and public institutions (Dittrich 2003).

7 For two examples, see the intercalated BA in Medical Humanities offered by the University of Bristol: www.bris.ac.uk/philosophy/prospective/undergrad/ibamh_details.html (accessed August 2010), and the MA in Medical Humanities offered by the School of Human and Health Sciences at Swansea University.

8 The examples are drawn from the programme offered by the Center for Medical Humanities and Ethics at the University of Texas Health Science Center at San Antonio, see Jones and Verghese (2003).

9 www.asbh.org/about/history/index.html (accessed August 2010).

10 On social medicine and medical police see Ackerknecht (1953), Rosen (1979), Foucault (1980).

11 The years between 1890 and 1920 saw the emergence of a university standard of medical education across France, Germany, Britain and the United States. Spurred by the revolution in bacteriology, this standard was centred on laboratory science as the 'foundation stone of all medical teaching' (Bonner 1995: 289). While tensions and disagreements persisted as to the relative importance of scientific versus clinical training and as to the ultimate usefulness of the former in the context of practical medicine, the efforts of reformers focused on how the two might be more closely aligned through, for example, the building of laboratories within teaching hospitals.

12 Author's conversation with Deborah Kirklin, then (2002) Director of the Centre for Medical Humanities at UCL, currently chief editor of the BMJ journal *Medical Humanities*. These sceptical views were reported by Dr Kirklin as common among the medical profession at large, but obviously did not reflect her own.

13 This point about the partial enactment of the humanities in the context of medical training echoes the more general point on some problematic consequences of interdisciplinarity made by Marilyn Strathern (2004) through the example of social anthropology.

14 Dissemination and research are also part of the programme's mission statement and form an important part of the activities carried out within it. Details of this range of activities can be found at www.narrativemedicine.org/ (accessed November 2012).

15 The concept of a hidden medical curriculum has a long genealogy in the sociology of medical education. For a review of the concept written in the wake of the

recommendations of the General Medical Council (1993) on *Tomorrow's Doctors* (often cited as a landmark development in terms of enabling humanities teaching within the medical curriculum in the UK) see Cribb and Bignold (1999); specifically relevant to the emotional socialisation of doctors is the piece by Smith and Kleinman (1989); on 'distancing' and communication see Mintz (1992).

16 Personal communication, 2002.

17 Kathryn Montgomery has contributed to shaping the field of medical humanities since its earliest days, having chaired the committee that studied the inclusion of the humanities and social sciences in the medical curriculum at Morehouse Medical School already in the late 1970s (see Montgomery Hunter and Axelsen 1982 for an account of that process).

18 Montgomery's intervention is similar, in this respect, to Annemarie Mol's in *The Logic of Care* (2008). Mol too seeks to make explicit a specifically clinical 'logic' that 'is silently incorporated in practices and does not speak for itself. . . . The aim is to articulate the specificities of good care so that we may talk about it' (2008: 2). Mol's intervention is constructed against a 'logic of choice' that, pertinent as it may be in the fields of state politics and of the market, is largely misplaced in the clinic.

19 For a more detailed discussion of the medical profession as an 'unhealthy community' see Engel et al. (2008).

20 Greaves (1996) discusses the critiques of Dubos (1960), Cochrane (1972), Illich (1976), McKeown (1979), Fulford (1989) and Cassell (1991) among others.

21 In this sense, the aim of medical humanities bears significant resemblances to Michael Balint's work with general medical practitioners in post-war Britain. Balint mobilised psychoanalysis to act upon the personality of the doctor as a therapeutic instrument addressed to the patient as a 'whole person' (see Osborne 1993). An exploration of some important differences between the problematisation of the subjectivity of doctors in Balint's case and in that of medical humanities – differences that pivot on the conspicuous absence of psychoanalysis from the discourse of medical humanities – I defer to another occasion.

22 Kirklin, personal communication.

23 In their introduction to the volume, Lawrence and Weisz distinguish for example between varieties of medical holism addressed to the individual, to the environment or to populations; between those that focus on the *human body* in systemic fashion, either in terms of biological or psycho-biological processes; on relations between the (physical or socio-cultural) *environment and the organism*; on the *nature of medical knowledge*, and particularly on the respective roles of synthesis and analysis, including across scientific and humanistic disciplines; and on the *quality of human relations* within medicine (1998: 3–4).

24 There are exceptions, of course, both in connection with the problem of aetiology and in connection with the reference to psychoanalysis. As to the former, see for example the discussion of the therapeutic uses of placebos (implying mental causality) in Spiro (1998), selected here as an example for being published under the auspices of the Program for Humanities in Medicine at Yale University School of Medicine; see also work by psychologist and linguist James W. Pennebaker on the therapeutic power of narrative self-expression (Pennebaker 1990, 1995). Because of its focus on linguistic and artistic expression, Pennebaker's work is cited in the medical humanities literature, but I am not aware of any authors in the field engaging systematically with this work at a theoretical or methodological level. This type of engagement, on the other hand, is evident among medical anthropologists collaborating with psychoneuroimmunologists and with Pennebaker himself (see Wilce 2003). With regard to engaging with psychoanalysis, a recently published collection edited by Rudnytsky and Charon (2008) addresses the relationship between psychoanalysis and narrative medicine. The editors present it as an invitation for narrative medicine 'to claim an insufficiently acknowledged portion of its history' (p. 2).

25 Robinson's approach, for example, actively incorporated 'psychogenic assumptions' about the patient's condition (Brown 1998). The aetiological focus of medical sociology and of interdisciplinary research involving other social sciences was mentioned above.
26 See Isabelle Stengers on the conceptual significance of the notion of complexity (1997). It is within the framework of reductionism that the general relevance of scientific models is affirmed. As Stengers puts it: 'if, a priori, the discourse of complexity has meaning, that meaning cannot be homogenous to the science it critiques. The vision of a complex world per se cannot be substituted for another scientific vision of the world; it is the notion of a vision of the world, from the point of view of which a general and unifying discourse can be held, that in one way or another must be called into question' (1997: 4–5).
27 The proposition that medicine should be radically transformed by way of acknowledging the relevance of subjectivity is historically not new, and the socio-political implications of it have been debated in more explicit terms than Foss does. Elsewhere I have explored this issue through an analysis of the contrasting positions of Viktor Von Weizsäcker and Karl Jaspers on the question of whether an institute for psychotherapy should be established within the medical faculty of the University of Heidelberg (Greco 2008).

References

Ackerknecht, E. H. (1953) *Rudolf Virchow: Doctor, Statesman, Anthropologist*, Wisconsin: University of Wisconsin Press.
Barry, A. (2001) *Political Machines: Governing a Technological Society*, London: Athlone.
Barry, A., Born, G. and Wezskalnys, G. (2008) 'Logics of Interdisciplinarity', *Economy & Society*, 37: 20–49.
Bleakley, A., Marshall, R. and Brömer, R. (2006) 'Toward an Aesthetic Medicine: Developing a Core Medical Humanities Undergraduate Curriculum', *Journal of Medical Humanities*, 27: 197–213.
Bonner, T. N. (1995) *Becoming a Physician: Medical Education in Britain, France, Germany, and the United States, 1750–1945*, Baltimore, MD and London: Johns Hopkins University Press.
Brody, H. (2003) *Stories of Sickness*, New York and Oxford: Oxford University Press.
Brown, T. M. (1998) 'George Canby Robinson and "the Patient as a Person"', in C. Lawrence and G. Weisz (eds.) *Greater Than the Parts. Holism in Biomedicine 1920–1950*, (pp. 135–160) New York and Oxford: Oxford University Press.
Campo, R. (2005) '"The Medical Humanities", For Lack of a Better Term', *JAMA*, 294: 1009–11.
Cassell, E. J. (1991) *The Nature of Suffering and the Goals of Medicine*, Oxford: Oxford University Press.
Charon, R. (2001) 'Narrative Medicine: A Model for Empathy, Reflection, Profession, and Trust', *JAMA*, 286: 1897–902.
— (2006) *Narrative Medicine: Honoring the Stories of Illness*, New York and Oxford: Oxford University Press.
— (2008) 'Foreword', in J. D. Engel, J. Zarconi, L. L. Pethtel, S. A. Missimi *Narrative in Health Care: Healing Patients, Practitioners, Profession, and Community*, (pp. ix–xii) New York and Oxford: Radcliffe Publishing.
Cochrane, A. L. (1972) *Effectiveness and Efficiency*, London: The Nuffield Provincial Hospitals Trust.
Cribb, A. and Bignold, S. (1999) 'Towards the Reflexive Medical School: The Hidden Curriculum and Medical Education Research', *Studies in Higher Education*, 24: 195–209.

De Swaan, A. (1988) *In the Care of the State: Health Care, Education and Welfare in Europe and America*, Cambridge: Polity.

Dittrich, L. R. (2003) '"Preface" to a Special Theme Issue on Medical Humanities', *Academic Medicine*, 78: 951–2.

Dubos, R. (1960) *Mirage of Health*, London: George Allen and Unwin Ltd.

Engel, J. D., Zarconi, J., Pethtel, L. L. and Missimi, S. A. (2008) *Narrative in Health Care: Healing Patients, Practitioners, Profession, and Community*, New York and Oxford: Radcliffe Publishing.

Evans, M. and Finlay, I. G. (eds.) (2001) *Medical Humanities*, London: BMJ Books.

Evans, M. and Macnaughton, R. (2006) 'A "Core Curriculum" for the Medical Humanities?', *Medical Humanities*, 32: 65–6.

Foss, L. (2002) *The End of Modern Medicine: Biomedical Science Under a Microscope*, Albany: State University of New York Press.

Foss, L. and Rothenberg, K. (1987) *The Second Medical Revolution: From Biomedicine to Infomedicine*, Boston: New Science Library, Shambhala.

Foucault, M. (1980) 'The Politics of Health in The Eighteenth Century', in C. Gordon (ed.) *Power/Knowledge*, (pp. 166–182) Brighton: Harvester Press.

Frank, A. (1995) *The Wounded Storyteller*, Chicago, IL: University of Chicago Press.

Fulford, K. W. M. (1989) *Moral Theory and Medical Practice*, Cambridge: Cambridge University Press.

Gibbons, M., Limoges, C., Nowotny, H., Schwartzmann, S., Scott, P. and Trow, M. (1994) *the New Production of Knowledge*, London: Sage.

Greaves, D. (1996) *Mystery in Medicine*, Aldershot: Avebury.

— (2001) 'The Nature and Role of Medical Humanities', in M. Evans and I. G. Finlay (eds.) *Medical Humanities*, (pp. 13–22) London: BMJ Books.

Greco, M. (2008) 'On the Art of Life: a Vitalist Reading of Medical Humanities', *Sociological Review*, 56: 23–45.

Greenhalgh, T. (1998) 'Narrative Based Medicine in an Evidence Based World', in T. Greenhalgh and B. Hurwitz (eds.) *Narrative Based Medicine: Dialogue and Discourse in Medical Practice*, (pp. 247–265) London: BMJ Books.

Greenhalgh, T. and Hurwitz, B. (eds.) (1998) *Narrative Based Medicine: Dialogue and Discourse in Medical Practice*, London: BMJ Books.

Groddeck, G. (1977 [1927]) 'The Human Being, Not the Patient, Requires Help', in G. Groddeck (ed.) *The Meaning of Illness: Selected Psychoanalytic Writings*, (pp. 241–247) New York: International Universities Press, Inc.

Hunsaker Hawkins, A., Ballard, J. and Hufford, D. (2003) 'Humanities Education at Pennsylvania State University College of Medicine, Hershey, Pennsylvania', *Academic Medicine*, 78: 1001–5.

Hurwitz, B. and Dakin, P. (2009) 'Welcome Developments in UK Medical Humanities', *Journal of the Royal Society of Medicine*, 102: 84–5.

Illich, I. (1976) *Limits to Medicine*, London: Marion Boyars.

Jones, T. and Verghese, A. (2003) 'On Becoming a Humanities Curriculum: the Center for Medical Humanities and Ethics at the University of Texas Health Center at San Antonio', *Academic Medicine*, 78: 1010–14.

Kirklin, D. (2003) 'The Centre for Medical Humanities, Royal Free and University College medical school, London, England', *Academic Medicine*, 78(10): 1048–53.

Kirklin, D. and Richardson, R. (eds.) (2001) *Medical Humanities: A Practical Introduction*, London: Royal College of Physicians of London.

Lawrence, C. and Weisz, G. (eds.) (1998) *Greater Than the Parts: Holism in Biomedicine 1920–1950*, New York and Oxford: Oxford University Press.

Lindemann Nelson, H. (ed.) (1997) *Stories and Their Limits: Narrative Approaches to Bioethics*, London: Routledge.

Lyotard, J. (1986) *The Postmodern Condition: a Report on Knowledge*, Manchester: University of Manchester Press.

Macnaughton, J. (2000) 'The Humanities in Medical Education: Context, Outcomes and Structure', *Medical Humanities*, 26: 23–30.

McKeown, T. (1979) *The Role of Medicine*, Oxford: Blackwell.

Mintz, D. (1992) 'What's in a Word: the Distancing Function of Language in Medicine', *Journal of Medical Humanities*, 13: 223–33.

Mol, A. (2008) *The Logic of Care: Health and the Problem of Patient Choice*, New York and London: Routledge.

Montgomery, K. (2006) *How Doctors Think: Clinical Judgment and the Practice of Medicine*, New York and Oxford: Oxford University Press.

Montgomery Hunter, K. (1991) *Doctors' Stories: the Narrative Structure of Medical Knowledge*, Princeton, NJ: Princeton University Press.

Montgomery Hunter, K. and Axelsen, D. (1982) 'The Morehouse Human Values in Medicine Program, 1978–1980: Reinforcing a Commitment to Primary Care', *Journal of Medical Education*, 57: 121–3.

Nowotny, H., Scott, P. and Gibbons, M. (2001) *Re-Thinking Science: Knowledge and the Public in an Age of Uncertainty*, Cambridge: Polity.

Osborne, T. (1993) 'Mobilizing Psychoanalysis: Michael Balint and the General Practitioners', *Social Studies of Science*, 23: 175–200.

Parsons, T. (1951) *The Social System*, London: Routledge & Kegan Paul.

Pennebaker, J. W. (1990) *Opening Up: the Healing Power of Confiding in Others*, New York: William Morrow.

Pennebaker, J. W. (ed.) (1995) *Emotion, Disclosure, and Health*, Washington, DC: American Psychological Association.

Ritzer, G. and Walczak, D. (1988) 'Rationalization and the Deprofessionalization of Physicians', *Social Forces*, 67: 1–22.

Rosen (1979) 'The Evolution of Scientific Medicine', in H. E. Freeman, S. Levine and L. G. Reeder (eds.) *Handbook of Medical Sociology*, Englewood Cliffs, NJ: Prentice-Hall.

Rosenberg, C. E. (1998) 'Holism in Twentieth-Century Medicine', in C. Lawrence and G. Weisz (eds.) *Greater Than the Parts. Holism in Biomedicine 1920–1950*, (pp. 335–355) New York and Oxford: Oxford University Press.

Rudnytsky, P. L. and Charon, R. (eds.) (2008) *Psychoanalysis and Narrative Medicine*, Albany: State University of New York Press.

Shafer, A. (2009) 'Medical Humanities: Demarcations, Dilemmas and Delights', *Medical Humanities*, 35: 3–4.

Shapiro, J., Coulehan, J., Wear, D. and Montello, M. (2009) 'Medical Humanities and their Discontents: Definitions, Critiques, and Implications', *Academic Medicine*, 84: 192–8.

Smith, A. and Kleinman, S. (1989) 'Managing Emotions in Medical Schools: Students' Contact with the Living and the Dead', *Social Psychology Quarterly*, 52: 56–69.

Spiro, H. (1998) *The Power of Hope: A Doctor's Perspective*, New Haven, CT and London: Yale University Press.

Squier, S. M. and Hawkins, A. H. (2004) 'Medical Humanities and Cultural Studies: Lessons Learned from an NEH Institute', *Journal of Medical Humanities*, 25: 243–53.

Stengers, I. (1997) 'Complexity: A Fad?' in *Power and Invention*, (pp. 3–20) Minneapolis and London: University of Minnesota Press.

Strathern, M. (2004) 'Laudable Aims and Problematic Consequences, Or: The "Flow" Of Knowledge is Not Neutral', *Economy & Society*, 33: 550–61.

Turner, B. (1990) 'The Interdisciplinary Curriculum: From Social Medicine to Postmodernism', *Sociology of Health and Illness*, 12: 1–23.

Wachtler, C., Lundin, S. and Troein, M. (2006) 'Humanities for Medical Students? A Qualitative Study of a Medical Humanities Curriculum in a Medical School Program', *BMC Medical Education*, 6. Available from www.biomedcentral.com/1472–6920/6/16, (accessed November 2012).

Whitehead, A. N. (1978) *Process and Reality*, New York: The Free Press.

Wilce, J. M. (ed.) (2003) *Social and Cultural Lives of Immune Systems*, New York and London: Routledge.

11 Art-Science

From public understanding to public experiment

Georgina Born and Andrew Barry

One of the most significant arguments in Nowotny et al.'s *Re-Thinking Science* (2001), as has become clear in previous chapters, is the commitment to a model in which scientific knowledge in the present is purported to be 'more responsive to public expectations' (ibid: 227). One manifestation, in this account, is the way that numerous publics, NGOs and social movements – including feminism, environmental and patients' movements – engage in critique and contestation of scientific research, so that science and society 'co-mingle' and play out their confrontation in a 'special kind of public space': what Nowotny et al. term the agora (ibid: 211, Chapter 13).

The idea of 'contextualization' sums up these claims. It depicts a greater level of interaction than before between the production of knowledge, the context of its application and relations with citizens or publics: 'Giving a place to people in our knowledge refers to the ways that they are being conceptualised, which may – or may not – be supported by various forms of interaction, communication and participatory engagement with "real people"' (ibid: 256–7). At stake is a process in which the context of knowledge production is something that has to be made, not just through the work of scientists but through interdisciplinary practices involving a series of other institutions and professions as well as publics. Crucially, for Nowotny et al., contextualisation multiplies the connectedness of the institutions of scientific knowledge production to other institutions and publics and to forms of activity that are not considered scientific and technical, including those that 'take subjective experience seriously' (ibid: 257).

More questionable, perhaps, is the underlying claim in *Re-Thinking Science* that this situation results from a 'co-evolution' of science and society in recent decades along a number of axes, notably from certainty to uncertainty, and from linearity to complexity (ibid: 47). For, by presuming certain macro-social trends in advance, this kind of claim sits uncomfortably with any imperative to interrogate more closely just how the 'co-mingling' of scientific practices and their various publics takes place, as well as the need to assess the fruits of these processes. The suggestion that we live in a world in which science and society are increasingly 'mutually invasive' (ibid: 54), where the environment in which knowledge is generated has become more plural and democratic, and in which expertise is distributed across new groups, sites and institutional settings, raises the challenge of identifying and analysing – rather than assuming – these new forms and sites.

In this chapter we open up these questions of the existence and the production of new publics for science, as well as the contributions made by interdisciplinary practices to the generation of novel and even inventive forms of 'publicness' (cf. Latour and Weibel 2005). We do so by giving a particular perspective on these issues through the burgeoning in recent decades of a spate of initiatives around the interdisciplinary field of 'art-science'. It is tempting to view art-science as a good example of the kinds of practices associated with Nowotny et al.'s Mode-2 knowledge production. Institutional support for art-science is associated, in part, with a broad array of activities intended to foster growing interaction between the production of scientific knowledge and non-expert citizens, while establishing connections between scientific knowledge and those forms of human and 'subjective experience' that lie outside the domain of scientific investigation. As we will show, many of the institutions involved in supporting art-science claim – apparently in the terms of Nowotny et al.'s analysis – that art-science renders scientific and technical knowledge more accessible and comprehensible as well as more accountable to its publics. They contend, then, that it contributes to the contextualisation of science in the sense outlined above.

But another emphatic aim of our chapter is to allow art-science its singularity, rather than reducing it to an exemplification of contextualisation. Thus, while there are resonances between aspects of the history of art-science and Nowotny et al.'s analysis, we suggest that the further development of these arguments requires greater attention to the diversity of forms of interdisciplinarity associated specifically with art-science. We propose that art-science should be understood as a multiplicity, and that part of its interest lies in not being reducible to the imperative to render scientific knowledge more accessible or accountable. Indeed art-science poses definitional and conceptual challenges since, while it exists as a practical, intentional category for artists and scientists, cultural institutions and funding bodies, it forms part of a larger heterogeneous space of overlapping interdisciplinary practices at the intersection of the arts, sciences and technologies. This includes new media art and digital art, interactive art and immersive art, bio art and wet art (Wilson 2002; Da Costa and Philip 2008; Leonardo 2012), while these domains abut adjacent interdisciplinary scientific and technological fields from robotics, informatics, and artificial and embodied intelligence to tissue engineering and systems biology. There is thus a ferment of activity but little codification: 'art-science' amounts to a pool of shifting practices and categories that are themselves relational and in formation.

The notion of contextualisation, then, fails to capture the ways in which the emergent field of art-science exhibits its own complex trajectories, which cannot be grasped primarily as a consequence or corollary of a unitary, epochal transition in the co-evolution of science and society. Drawing on ethnographic research on art-science institutions, practitioners and administrators in the UK, US and Australia,[1] in what follows we develop this argument in two ways. First, we indicate the heterogeneity of art-science and of the experiments carried out under its name by contrasting distinctive forms and genealogies of art-science. We suggest that art-science can be understood as evidencing what we have identified as three logics of interdisciplinarity (Barry, Born and Weszkalnys 2008; Barry and Born, this volume). As described in the introduction to this volume, in our comparative study of interdisciplinary fields we found three logics – of accountability, innovation and ontology – pervasive across these fields, and probed their provenance in each. By the logic of accountability we refer to a series of ways in which scientific research is increasingly required to make itself accountable to society. By the logic of innovation we draw attention to a range of arguments about the need for scientific research to fuel industrial or technological innovation and economic growth – a discourse that, while it has a long history, has exhibited a particular intensity in recent decades (Barry 2001: Chapter 1).

However, interdisciplinarity can also be informed by a logic of ontology: an orientation in interdisciplinary practices towards effecting ontological transformation in both the object(s) of research and relations between the subjects and objects of research. As we will show, certain art-science initiatives are concerned less with making art or science accountable or innovative than with altering existing ways of thinking about the nature of art and science, as well as transforming the relations between artists and scientists and their objects and publics. The three logics of interdisciplinarity, then, have a different prominence and distribution, and are differently entangled, in the sites of art-science that we researched. Our second aim, in indicating the ways in which art-science manifests the three logics, is to suggest that it evidences diverse modes of publicness or of making connections with 'society'. Rather than simply multiplying the connections between science and its publics, art-science is instructive in highlighting alternative conceptions and practices of publicness.

The chapter is in two parts, contrasting two radically different forms of art-science and their construal of publicness. In the first part we examine the logics of accountability and innovation in the guise of their association with the development of art-science in the UK, addressing interventions in the relations between science and culture from C. P. Snow's essay on the 'two cultures' to the recent activities of the Wellcome Trust and Arts Council England. In these developments, art that is in dialogue with science is understood as a means by which the (absent) public for science can be assembled or interpellated. Science is conceived as finished or complete, and as needing only to be communicated, understood or applied, while art provides the means through which the public is mobilised and stimulated in the quest for greater understanding of science.

In the second part we develop an analysis of the logic of ontology in art-science. We do this by focusing ethnographically on a striking institutional experiment in art-science based at the University of California at Irvine (UCI): the Masters program in Arts, Computation and Engineering (ACE).[2] As we will show, ACE became a crucible for experimentation in interdisciplinary pedagogies and practices, as well as for confronting the institutional shape and challenges of a strong interdisciplinarity. The case of art-science at UCI is instructive, then, not because it is either unique or typical of art-science in general, but because it indicates the possibility of a type of art-science that articulates the logic of ontology. At the same time ACE evidences a distinctive form of publicness in relation to art-science, one in which science is understood not as self-sufficient or complete but as transformed and enhanced through its engagement with art, just as art is transformed and enhanced through engagement with science. Here the public conceived by art-science is not assembled or interpellated. Rather art-science performs the mutual transformation of both the objects and practices of, and the relations between, science and art. In this way art-science becomes not so much a way of producing a public for science, but what we term a public experiment. At the same time, the comparison between the practice of ACE and prevalent approaches to art-science in the UK highlights the difference between those modes of contextualisation that politicise the relations between science and its publics and those that effectively depoliticise those relations.

The Two Cultures: Art-Science in the UK

In Britain, more than 50 years after its delivery, C. P. Snow's lecture on *The Two Cultures* (1959) still powerfully informs contemporary accounts of the relations between the arts and sciences, and the economic importance of these relations. In the lecture Snow reflected on the potential that might be released if only there were greater interaction between the arts and sciences:

> The clashing point of two subjects, two disciplines, two cultures – of two galaxies, so far as that goes – ought to produce creative chances. In the history of mental activity that has been where some of the breakthroughs came.

But in practice, Snow continued, 'the two cultures can't talk to each other. It is bizarre how very little of twentieth-century science has been assimilated into twentieth-century art' (Snow 1959: 16). According to Snow, Western society was being split into 'two polar groups': on the one hand, the literary intellectuals; on the other, 'and as the most representative, the physical scientists' (ibid: 4). In his view, if Britain was to remain a successful industrial economy, this split needed to be overcome and the value of the sciences to cultural and economic life needed to be fully recognised. The cultural divide was not just an 'English phenomenon', but it seemed 'at its sharpest in England' (ibid: 17). One of its consequences, Snow argued, was that arts graduates had little knowledge or understanding of science and technology, while being disproportionately represented in the executive class in government and industry: not 'one in ten [of men getting firsts in arts subjects at Cambridge] could give the loosest analysis of human organization which [technology] needs' (ibid: 30). Snow himself was subsequently to become a minister in the Wilson government's new Ministry of Technology (Gummett 1980: 45).

David Edgerton, in a recent book (2006), has argued that Snow should be understood as an influential exponent of British 'declinism', a term that Edgerton takes from Martin Wiener's text *English Culture and the Decline of the Industrial Spirit* (1981). For declinists, according to Edgerton, Britain has always underinvested in science and engineering – whether in comparison with Germany

(1880–1890s), the US (1950–1960s and 1990s), Japan (1970s–1980s), or China and India today. Snow's lecture, as is well known, elicited a stinging response from the literary critic F. R. Leavis, criticisms that Edgerton broadly endorses. Anticipating more recent academic critics of the New Labour government of Tony Blair, Leavis viewed Snow as a technocrat who, in his lack of understanding of culture and value, was a 'spokesman for the "technologico-Benthamite" reduction of human experience to the quantifiable' (Collini 1993: xxxiii).

But despite Edgerton's interest in the afterlife of Snow's 'two cultures' lecture, he has little to say about its central thesis, namely the lack of communication between the arts and sciences, nor about its continuing importance in the political imaginary of British science. In this political imaginary, as Snow's essay indicates, the question of the relation between the sciences and arts is not just considered an intellectual issue, but one that has critical significance for economic life. In this context one figure is notably absent from Edgerton's discussion: Raymond Williams, who came to Cambridge shortly after the Snow–Leavis exchange. Williams, in his 1958 *Culture and Society*, had chided Leavis for reducing the study of culture to literature and for failing in this way to acknowledge the importance of 'history, building, painting, music, philosophy, theology, political and social theory, *the physical and natural sciences,* anthropology and the whole body of learning' (Williams 1963 [1958]: 248, our emphasis). Where Edgerton lends support to Leavis's criticisms of Snow, Williams argued that Leavis's educational project was marked by profound ignorance and hostility towards science, technology and industry.

The significance of Williams for our analysis, and of noting his absence from Edgerton's history of this era, is not that he provides a diagnosis of British culture that we wish to endorse. Rather, it is that Williams is suggestive of the need for a more complex conception of the multidimensional relations between the arts, humanities and sciences, and between research and cultural and economic life, than is given in the polarised debate between Leavis and Snow.[3] For Williams, the problem was not so much the relations between the arts and sciences in general, but the disdain of both literary and scientific intellectuals for popular and vernacular forms of knowledge and cultural practice. In this way Williams's analysis prefigures the ways in which interdisciplinarity between the arts and sciences became associated in the 1990s and 2000s not only with the view that the political elite should be scientifically literate, as Snow argued, but with a growing concern to rethink the relations between scientific experts and the public. Moreover, Williams's attention to the history of cultural forms points to the importance of framing any analysis of art-science in terms of the history not only of relations between science and the public, as Nowotny et al. suggest, but of art's relations with the public.

Public Understanding, Public Engagement and Innovation

As we have seen, in his account of the problem of the relations between the disciplines, Snow showed little interest in the public. He was preoccupied by what he perceived to be ignorance about science among the academic and political establishments. Yet in the 1980s and 1990s, when British scientists again pointed to the existence of a cultural division between the arts and sciences, as well as to the putative deleterious economic consequences of this division, they placed great emphasis on the public as a key element in responding to these challenges.

Critical to the revival of interest in the relations between the arts and sciences in Britain in the 1980s was the preparation of a report on the public understanding of science by an ad hoc group of the Royal Society under the Chairmanship of the statistician and geneticist Walter Bodmer (Royal Society 1985; Bodmer 1986). The report came at a time when scientists saw themselves as under attack from two directions. On the one hand, it drew attention to what was perceived to be 'anti-scientific feeling' associated with a revival of romanticism (Wolpert and Richards 1988: 1; cf. Barry 2001: Chapter 6) as well as a broad 'erosion' of public support for science (Royal Society 1985: 14). On the other hand, the neoliberal economic policies of the Conservative government had resulted in substantial cuts to basic scientific research (Edgerton and Hughes 1989).

Indeed, while the circumstances of its publication were entirely different, the Bodmer report replicated closely some of Snow's arguments. It proposed that 'no pupil should study only arts, or only science, even after the age of 16' (Royal Society 1985: 6), and called for greater efforts on the part of scientists to 'communicate with the public'. This 'public' included not only the political and academic elites, but a series of other categories including 'private individuals', 'people employed in skilled or semi-skilled occupations' and the 'middle ranks of management' (ibid: 7). Like Snow, the Royal Society argued that it was particularly important that the higher echelons of the civil service should understand science. In effect, for the Royal Society, the public was conceived as a broad aggregate, one that was differentiated by occupation and class; and as the public understanding of science paradigm 'became something of an international movement during the 1990s', it saw as its purpose engaging 'in a kind of missionary work' that emphasised the educational and civilising role of science (Elam and Bertilsson 2003: 12–13).[4] But the Bodmer report had a second influential theme. Again echoing Snow, it argued that public education was essential in enhancing science's contribution to economic progress, indeed that economic growth depended on all factions of the public having some understanding of science:

[T]here is a strong prima facie case for the existence of a link between public understanding of science and national prosperity, though the link may be as difficult to quantify as that between a company's research and development effort and its overall profitability.

(Royal Society 1985: 9)

By the mid-1990s, in the wake of the Bodmer report, it appeared that the wisdom of Snow's thesis was finally being recognised in the UK and was leading to practical proposals as a spate of initiatives arose that aimed to support and promote the rapidly emerging interdisciplinary field of 'science-art'.[5] Most of the funding initiatives, each offering about £0.5 million per annum, gave relatively small grants for collaborative projects. In 1996 the Wellcome Trust, one of the foremost funders of British medical research, launched the first in a series of funding programmes for art-science projects. The Trust's 'sciart' programme was explicitly intended to bridge the two cultures by enlisting artists to foster the public's relationship with science; over ten years, from 1996 to 2006, it supported 124 projects with £3 million of funding. An art-science administrator explained that although some of the public are completely uninterested in or even suspicious of science, contemporary art exhibits that happen to be about science can sometimes reach them, getting people who would not ordinarily be interested to think about and connect with science.[6] The Wellcome Trust's programme was followed in 1998 by the Invention and Innovation scheme funded by the National Endowment for Science, Technology and the Arts (NESTA), and from 1999 to 2002 by the formation of the Sciart Consortium, in which the Trust was joined by Arts Council England, NESTA, the Calouste Gulbenkian Foundation, the Scottish Arts Council and the British Council (Webster 2006: 76). From 2003–2006 the Wellcome Trust reinstated its sciart awards, while in 2003 Arts Council England established an interdisciplinary arts department which, together with the Arts and Humanities Research Board, initiated the Art and Science Research Fellowship programme, funding additional collaborative projects between artists and scientists. Versions of these initiatives continue to the present day.[7]

Despite differences between these initiatives, they broadly followed Snow and the Royal Society in drawing connections between the lack of communication between the arts and sciences and the challenge of responding to the economic demands of a technological society. They articulate, that is to say, the logic of innovation. In the words of an Arts Council England executive, the ACE/ AHRB Fellowship scheme 'would be an ideal ground for . . . connecting art and science and [privileging] openness and knowledge sharing across disciplines'. At the same time it met the wider public interest 'in using public funding to support research and development in the interests of "new knowledge" and innovation' (Ferran 2006: 443). Formative in the design of the ACE/AHRB scheme were both the EU Lisbon Agenda of 2000, with its knowledge economy focus, and a 2001 report by the UK Council on Science and Technology which 'declared that the divisions in education and research between the arts, humanities and science were anachronistic and detrimental to the future of Britain's economy' (ibid).

But in addition to the rationale of fostering innovation, a number of art-science funding initiatives from the mid-1990s articulated the logic of accountability, evident in their increasing orientation towards the discourse that succeeded the public understanding of science: what was called 'public engagement' (Elam and Bertilsson 2003; Irwin and Michael 2003; Turney 2006; cf. Callon and Rabeharisoa 2004). In the words of the Wellcome Trust:

> We believe the arts are an effective way of stimulating debate and engaging people with biomedical science. Visual art, music, moving image, creative

writing and performance can reach new audiences which may not traditionally be interested in science. Collaborative and interdisciplinary practice across the arts and sciences can help to provide new perspectives on both fields. The arts can also provide imaginative ways of engaging and educating young people in the field of science.

(Wellcome Trust 2009)

In part, the shift to public engagement represented a response by the funding agencies to a critique by social scientists – one that echoes Williams's earlier critique of Leavis's culturalism – of the assumption implicit in the idea of public understanding of science that the public was conceived in terms of a lack, a conception that failed to recognise the existence of 'alternative, more culturally rooted and legitimate forms of collective public knowledge' (Wynne 1996: 46). But the concept of public engagement responded also to a sense of declining trust in scientific institutions associated with growing public anxiety over environmental and health risks (Poortinga and Pidgeon 2005). Thus in 2000, in the aftermath of the BSE debacle, the House of Lords Select Committee on Science and Technology declared that there was a 'crisis' in the relations between science and society: 'Public unease, mistrust and occasional outright hostility are breeding a climate of deep anxiety among scientists themselves' (House of Lords 2000: 1.1).[8]

In this situation the conviction took hold among the funding bodies that art-science, along with other practices of public engagement, would make it possible to manage and improve the ways in which the public can develop not only cognitive but interactive and affective involvements with science. In this view, in place of a mistrustful, disengaged and anxious population, art-science could assist by assembling a public that was not only ready to participate in debate about the risks raised by scientific research, but excited and entranced by science. At best, art-science might align the public's hopes and passions more precisely with the hopes and passions of research institutions: art-science could become a device for the governance of affect (cf. Anderson 2007).

In the history outlined, then, art-science is conceived as rendering science more accountable and communicable to the public, whether through its capacity to attract the public to science through its aestheticisation, or by bringing affective and expressive experience into the domain of science. Art-science promises to assemble a public for science in a form to which science can then consider itself accountable; science is rendered accountable to a public that is, in turn, properly disposed towards it.

There are three points to note. First, the type of public envisaged here is one that, in Michael Warner's Althusserian formulation, 'exists by virtue of being addressed' (Warner 2005: 67). Scientific research is taken as a given, and art provides a means through which the public can be assembled and then engaged in relation to it. Second, the role of art-science in assembling this public is explicitly an instrumental one. Such a conception was acknowledged by administrators, some of whom spoke of the appeal of art-science to the funding bodies as being essentially a pragmatic and instrumental one based on what it could accomplish for science. Indeed, it was a critique of instrumental notions of art-science that generated some of the funding schemes from the later 1990s in which, as an alternative justification, innovation came to the fore. But – and a final point – whether motivated by accountability or innovation, in the trajectories of UK art-science that we have sketched, interdisciplinarity is uniformly conceived in the terms of what we have called the service-subordination mode, auguring hierarchical relations in which art is enrolled in the service of science (Barry, Born and Weszkalnys 2008; Barry and Born, this volume).

Art-Science and Conceptual Art: Genealogies and Emergence

It is striking that in accounts given by the British funding bodies, art-science is not portrayed as a field that has any substantial existence in itself – unlike, say, biochemistry or nanotechnology. In effect, the rationale for supporting art-science is given not by its relation to art but to science, extending the capacities of research institutions to assemble a public that will be engaged or to contribute to the promotion of a knowledge economy.

In contrast, an influential Rockefeller-funded research report on art-science in 1999 sought to give an alternative account of art-science (Century 1999). This was achieved by construing the prehistory of art-science in terms of the evolution of a particular social form, the 'studio lab', seen as a privileged site of hybrid, innovative practices 'where new media technologies are . . . developed in co-evolution with their creative application' (ibid: 2). The Rockefeller report therefore aimed to legitimise the field, and specifically the 'studio lab' (examples mentioned include Bell Labs, the MIT Media Laboratory, Xerox PARC, IRCAM and ZKM), as a valuable incubus for innovation in the knowledge economy: as an institutional form worth investing in. However, like the British funding agencies, the Rockefeller report again presents a restricted account of the field: one that domesticates the ramifying and sometimes controversial links between art, science and technology across the twentieth century. Thus, in the funding institutions' concern with the service that art can perform for innovation or scientific accountability, the conception that practitioners and art theorists themselves have of art-science, the assessments they make of its potential and value, and the genealogies of art-science as a category of specifically art-historical practice, all tend to be backgrounded or obscured (cf. Boltanski and Thévenot 2006).

A clear difficulty facing any analysis of art-science, then, stems from the difference between the way that the category has been deployed by the funding institutions and its existence as a category for artists. Indeed, among the practitioners that we interviewed, art-science and its cognates are portrayed as stemming from a much larger, heterogeneous – if contested – space of historical coordinates. They are experienced as having their genesis in the mutual disturbances or interferences thrown up at the intersection of three distinct but related genealogies. The first is conceptual and post-conceptual art, including performance, installation, public and activist art; the second encompasses historical art and technology movements, as they issue in the multi-, inter- and trans-media arts of the present; and the third comprises, broadly, developments and debates around the computational and bio sciences and technologies. In relation to art these coordinates are traced, depending on the individual artist, through origins in the work of Muybridge and Duchamp (often taken to be the founding father of conceptual art); via such mid-twentieth-century figures and groups as John Cage, Jean Tinguely, Billy Kluver and Experiments in Art and Technology, Nam June Paik, Jack Burnham, Jim Pomeroy, Hans Haacke, Fluxus, Art and Language, and the Artist Placement Group; to contemporary artists including Laurie Anderson, Perry Hoberman, Natalie Jeremijenko, Geert Lovink, Stelarc, Eduardo Kac, Oron Catts and groups such as Adbusters, RTMark, Critical Art Ensemble, Survival Research Labs, the Red Group at Xerox PARC, and SymbioticA (Osborne 2002; Wilson 2002; Corris 2004; Weszkalnys 2005; Buchmann 2006).

Clearly these coordinates portray a series of decidedly artistic trajectories – trajectories, however, that intersect with technological and scientific experimentation and controversy. The various genealogies given by practitioners of art-science, then, are not definitive. Rather, they generate together a type of perspectivism (Viveiros de Castro 2012), one that etches out a diachronic map of practices and potentials. At stake are artists' varying constructions of the lineages and networks of retentions and protentions – that is, of practices and events that matter and that are considered generative – within which they situate their current practices (Gell 1998; Born 2005, 2010).

Despite the attempts to construe historical foundations, practitioners working in an emergent interdisciplinary field like art-science nonetheless inhabit a state of radical uncertainty stemming from the underdetermined and ongoing formation of the field, in which their own practices may play a role, along with the inevitably contested and suspended nature of its identity. While practitioners acknowledge both the significance of genre and the genealogical orientation of their work, these uncertainties take several forms. They concern the definition and very conception of the historical lineages that their work and that of other art-scientists aspires to prolong or protend into the future; they concern the adequacy of their own work with respect to this aspiration and their placement within these unfurling lineages, sometimes expressed in terms of an existential dilemma or hiatus; and they concern the expectation of and the drive to achieve originality or novelty in conditions of considerable flux. These sentiments were articulated by individual art-scientists based at UCI when reflecting critically on their own and others' practices:

> I never claim that everything I do is brand new; I'm much more interested in the idea that art is clear about its claims to historical linkage. . . . [But] I can get very early on in a project to a point where I say, 'This has been done already, it's a total waste of time. I'm re-inventing the wheel'. So some of the kind of external referentiality that I know is there, I have to push aside and not deal with for some phases of the project or actually I can't make any progress at all. It's a kind of 'as-if' period – a suspension of belief, and it can last quite a long time.[9]

In these interdisciplinary fields you have artists that are *genre-hunting*, looking for the next big thing – like Eduardo Kac: if you look at his history, it's *firstism*, going through genres and finding new niches to be the first. I think that's an important role that art can play, but when there's no content there, it can be a little tiresome.[10]

These uncertainties, thrown up for art-scientists by inhabiting the condition of emergence, are multiplied by the way that practice inevitably runs ahead of art theory and art criticism:

For me, installation and machine work challenge the passive connoisseurship model [of art]; ... they need a completely new realm of aesthetics to be developed – the aesthetics of behaviour. Speaking as someone who has been practicing in this field for twenty years, it's astonishing that even now the art historical and critical establishments are in the majority completely ignorant of the aesthetic resources that could be brought to bear in assessing these kinds of work. There is no theoretical basis for discussing the entire experience of the work! [Even] in the Studio Art department here at UCI, ... with a strong representation of feminist and interventionist approaches and performance, there is still a fixation with the image as opposed to process: there is a real resistance to machine-mediated practices.[11]

What is at stake, then, is the struggle engaged in by both practitioners and their works to protend the emergent genealogy that they are attempting to co-produce, as well as the imperative to effect both a sense of the genre's coalescence or consolidation and of its forward movement in time. This co-production of genealogy, genre and temporality by practitioners and their objects or works is one that will later, of course, be either endorsed or overwritten by the art historians and theorists.

ACE is the Space:[12] Pedagogy and the Formation of Interdisciplinary Subjectivities

Having indicated the plural genealogies of art-science and the condition of emergence that practitioners inhabit, in what follows we do not attempt definitively to map the multiplicity of the field. Instead we zoom in ethnographically on a particular example: an institutional experiment in art-science pedagogy based at UCI, in the guise of the Masters program in Arts, Computation and Engineering (ACE). While, as we have explained, this example cannot be taken as typical of art-science in general, it nonetheless makes clear what we argue are critical features of the work of some practitioners: an orientation towards what we have termed the logic of ontology, and in some instances a concern with the production of what we will call public experiments.[13] The particular significance of ACE for this chapter and this volume is therefore twofold. First, ACE exemplifies the critical importance of inventive pedagogies in catalysing interdisciplinary subjectivities and thus in the formation of interdisciplines. Second, as we will show, ACE and its practitioners indicate how interdisciplinary subjects can become skilled in and sensitised to the complex imbrication of component disciplines such that they are endowed with a reflexive sense of the capacity of experimental practices to enrol publics in novel ways.

If we attend to the intellectual and practical contents of the ACE teaching program at the time of fieldwork (2006), an elaborate space of contemporary genealogies of art-science comes into view. In outlining these genealogies we draw on the substance of and the teaching materials provided for a core seminar of the ACE program taught by artist-engineer Simon Penny, founding Director of ACE.[14]

One trajectory begins with the critique of artificial intelligence (AI) via phenomenological notions of embodiment and situatedness (Dreyfus, Agre); through the 'bottom-up', biologically-based simulation of embodiment and situatedness in intelligent robotics (Brooks); through automatic design and evolvable robotic lifeforms (Lipson and Pollack); through artificial life (ALife), using biological concepts as a basis for computation via 'self-reproducing cellular automata' (Langton); through the problem of emergence – that is, designing 'open-state' artificial organisms capable of creative and learning behaviour (Cariani); through artificial cultures – the design of 'dynamically-evolving mobile autonomous agents that serve to embody hypotheses for understanding cultural behaviour' (Gessler); through computational modelling of a grammar to describe the morphology and nervous systems of virtual creatures, so as to achieve 'dynamic systems with emergent complexity' in the guise of autonomous behaviour, as well as their evolution via 'mating' and 'competition' (Sims); through the design of interactive systems with rudimentary agency as artworks, generating an 'aesthetics of behaviour' (Penny);[15] through computer-based generative art, with reference to cybernetics and ALife, which envisages creative behaviour in artificial systems and gestures to the 'computational sublime' (McCormack and Dorin); to interactive artworks that use 'expressive AI' to generate avatars with emotion (Mateas). Meanwhile the phenomenological critique of AI (which draws on Husserl, Heidegger and Schutz) takes another route through the field of 'human computer interaction' and its 'embodied interaction' paradigm, manifest in the tangible, ubiquitous and social computing advocated by Paul Dourish (Dourish 2001; Dourish and Bell 2011), an ACE faculty member and iconic UCI interdisciplinary figure who was based in 2006 in Informatics with affiliations not only to ACE but to a host of other UCI interdisciplinary initiatives, including CalIT[2] and the Center for Ethnography.[16]

In the ACE curriculum this trajectory runs in parallel with another, starting from the 'non-modern' epistemology and ontology of the early British cyberneticists Beer and Pask and their work on biological computing, self-organisation and dynamic equilibrium (Pickering 2002, 2005, this volume). Beer and Pask offer a vision of symmetrical, non-hierarchical relations (or assemblages) between entities – nature and culture, human and non-human, ponds and electrolytic cells – as they are mobilised by their performative qualities into adaptive systems, which are themselves liable to open-ended transformation in dialogue with environmental conditions. The trope of self-organisation migrates from cybernetics into the biology of cognition and the idea of autopoiesis (Maturana and Varela), from where it folds back to meet the challenge for robotics of simulating autonomy, sentience and environmental responsiveness in artificial organisms.

A third trajectory in ACE pedagogy, finally, cuts through and destabilises these universes via feminist and critical cultural studies of science and technology (Fox Keller, Haraway, Martin, Kember), throwing into relief the ideological underpinnings of, for instance, the alliance between the new biology and artificial life, as well as charting the collusive materialisation and reengineering of these new sciences in the guise of 'posthuman', ALife technological systems.[17]

What does this space of overlapping genealogies portend? First, it is essential to note the importance of these multiple genealogies of art-science to practitioners, which are strikingly different from the kinds of rationales that – as we have seen – animate the actions of the funding bodies.[18] Second, we want to draw out the variance between these ACE genealogies and the rationales of the funding bodies along two axes: on the one hand, the presence or absence in them of an engagement with the politicised elements of conceptual art, as well as of critical and feminist science and technology studies; on the other hand, and following on, the degree to which they entertain or not the basic premise of conceptual art: its commitment to an entirely distinctive ontology of art. Originating in responses in the 1960s to the impasses of formalist modernisms, conceptual art has itself been a heterogeneous movement entailing a questioning of art as object, as site and as social relations, each of which has been targeted for transformation by particular conceptual lineages. Conceptual art can be sketched, then, through a series of negations: negation of the primacy of visual and material objects and forms – in favour of the temporality of intermedia and multimedia performances and events; negation of art's commodity form – in favour of installations, site-specific and performance works that insist on the value of presence, embodied experience and place; and negation of the philosophy of art's autonomy, and this in several ways – in favour of works that address the politics of everyday life through interventions in existing media and publicity; works allied to wider political movements and ideological conflicts; works that probe the politics of art as an institution; and works that foreground art's social mediation, reconceiving art as various kinds of social practice and research (Bourriaud 2002; Newman 2002; Osborne 2002: 18–19; Bishop 2004, 2006; Corris 2004, 2006; Doherty 2004; Fraser 2005; Buchmann 2006).

Running through the rock of conceptual art, then, is a constitutive tension between orientations that are primarily formal and to do with medium and materials, and those that are primarily concerned with the production of political, social and cultural experimentation (Newman 2002): a tension recapitulated in art-science and, in microcosm, in fissures palpable within the ACE program. To return, then, to the variance: while the ACE genealogies encompass both critical science studies and conceptual art's reworking of art's ontology, the funding institutions' cleaving to accountability and innovation tends to obscure if not occlude these potentials. ACE pedagogy places the radical ontological shift proffered by conceptual art smack in the middle of its interrogation of the categories not only of art, but science, technology, agency, life and the human. In light of ACE's ambitions it is possible to argue that art-science can be allied to an ontological politics which, proffered by conceptual art, predates it; that art-science affords, although it does not guarantee, its expression in contemporary art practice.

How were the ACE program's interdisciplinary ambitions in evidence in its teaching sessions? In what follows we want to indicate ethnographically how these sessions illustrate the shifting between epistemic and ontological registers that might be expected when training students to become adept in the various component disciplines identified earlier, with their entirely different styles. This can be equated with the 'trading-zone' behaviour identified by Galison (1996) in his account of the development of the interlanguages that enable dialogues between the several subcultures of physics.

ACE teaching sessions wove between discussion of intellectual history, current topics, technics and mechanics across the range of disciplines described earlier – computer science, human–computer interaction (HCI) and robotics, biotechnology, philosophy, science and technology studies (STS), media and critical theory – and various arts practices. One of the core ACE seminars, led by Simon Penny, took a route through the critique of AI, a consequent reactive shift to biological computation influenced by cybernetics, to robotic architectures based on recent models of embodied intelligence. Here discussion might switch instantaneously from theoretical to very concrete questions to do with robot design, as when the question arose as to what happens to the 'search' function when it moves from an AI paradigm to an embodied-situated robotics context: how can you establish the 'search space' as discrete and limited when a mobile robotic 'agent' is operating in unlimited physical space? How can you model an encounter with, or recognition of, a human hand? How can the continuous, complex variables of the analogue world be translated into discrete digital values? Can it be done with sensors? Simon teases: 'In the digital domain everything is inherently knowable – why? Because it's been set up that way!', and reminds the students that all technologies encode particular theories of perception and of the world, explaining that one response to these problems was the rise of work on situated cognition. A student offers as an alternative the 'brute force' Cartesian solution: 'What if we had infinite computing power and all the possible representations of a hand?'; which leads to a discussion of the limits to sheer computational power and the potential discrepancies between even massively powered digital representations and the subtleties of the analogue world, which can escape and exceed such representations – at which point the ethnographer (Born) was able to join in and illustrate the same issue from computer music[19] – and thence to feminist commentaries on the gendering of 'infinite power' argumentation. Such linguistic- and register-shifting was a remarkable feature of this attempt at forming interdisciplinary subjects; it seemed both intellectually effective and, to the ethnographer, quite moving.

A Public Experiment: PigeonBlog

How does such a pedagogy inform the art-science practices associated with ACE and its faculty? At this point we move outside the seminar room and consider these practices through the work of ACE faculty member Beatriz da Costa. At the same time we consider the question: what do we mean by a public experiment? And what is the relation between a public experiment and the types of experimentation found in scientific research?

Da Costa's work can exemplify an orientation towards the production of public experiments in a way that cuts across distinctions between scientific and artistic experimentation, and that manifests a particular conception of publicness. At ACE, da Costa has engaged in close collaboration with scientists; two of her UCI collaborators, from systems biology and environmental health science, had previously experienced successful multi-disciplinary scientific projects and were predisposed to think positively about interdisciplinary work. Da Costa described herself as omnivorous: her technique was to get extremely close to current scientific problematics through several years of immersion in the work of scientific colleagues – a process appreciated by her collaborators. Far from providing a 'service' to science, da Costa attempted to reach the state of inhabiting and, on that basis, reinflecting or re-empractising current scientific problematics. The resulting projects promised to generate not only artistic interest but scientific gains. Indeed, they were intended to be trebly inventive: to generate at once scientific, artistic and political value. Her project PigeonBlog (2006) was a public art event, a 'social experiment between human and non-human animals', which centred on the provision for ordinary people living in southern California of low-tech means of collecting data on air pollution in their locality.

In PigeonBlog homing pigeons were released equipped with GPS-enabled electronic sensors which, as they flew over urban areas, sent back real-time location-based pollution data and imaging to an online mapping and blogging site. The information was analysed and modelled on the website, where it sat next to educational material. The aim was to increase both awareness of pollution exposure and participation in its monitoring. In da Costa's words:

> By using homing pigeons as the reporters of current air pollution levels we are hoping to achieve two main goals: 1) to re-invoke urgency around a topic that has serious health consequences, but lacks public action and commitment to change; and 2) to broaden the notion of grassroots scientific data gathering while building bridges between scientific research agendas and activist-oriented citizen concerns.[20]

But the project also answered a gap in the science and technology of air pollution monitoring. Typically, air pollution monitoring in major cities depends on an array of fixed monitoring stations. In Los Angeles in 2006, for example, 37 monitoring stations served 17 million people. However, readings from these stations, since they are derived only from specific points, provide a very limited basis for estimating the state of the air mass over extremely large areas. In PigeonBlog the limitations of this approach to the construction of a metrological regime (Barry 2002) are considered to be, in part, political. As da Costa's scientist collaborator, Rufus Edwards, explained:

> People living in poor neighbourhoods where more pollution sources are located will individually have greater exposure than the air monitoring station would have you believe; so they are less protected by our regulations. Whereas, the affluent people who live here [in Orange County] on hillsides have cleaner air than the monitoring site suggests. When you have these systematic differences in exposure, you have the potential for environmental injustice, with certain segments of the population receiving a greater pollution burden. If you look at this worldwide, the populations that receive more of the air pollution are the poor.[21]

He continued that for PigeonBlog, da Costa had herself researched and developed a cheap, portable monitor, and he had also developed one:

> It became clear that we could combine our monitors and make what would be a new and interesting monitor that measures multiple pollutants together. So in addition to her art demonstration, there are other applications for such a monitor in improving the way we do health research. Releasing the pigeons, depending on their flight paths, tells us a lot about how pollution is dispersing spatially over the city, which we had no way of calibrating before. . . . [Moreover] what a pigeon can carry is ideally suited in size and weight for one person to carry, so we can start to get individual information that will allow us to look at our epidemiology and health research in a new way; in fact I'd like to do a full-scale epidemiological study using these sensors. Where it's also very powerful is that it can measure continuously for an extended period of time, so on an individual level you start to get longitudinal measurements.[22]

Three observations follow from da Costa and Edwards's project. The first is how PigeonBlog intervenes in scientific practice by pointing towards a reconceptualisation of air quality as an object of measurement. As we have noted, air quality is measured at a number of fixed points in most major cities, as is the case in Los Angeles. However, such an approach is problematic on two grounds, as the project makes apparent. On the one hand, it fails to describe the ways in which air pollution moves and disperses in time and space. Through the use of pigeons and potentially humans as carriers of monitoring devices, da Costa and Edwards's project makes it possible to map the dynamic geography of air quality. On the other hand, existing air quality monitoring regimes fail to address the question of how individuals interact with air, by breathing particular mixtures and quantities of pollutants during the course of their everyday activity in the city (Barry 2001: 170). In making measurement mobile, da Costa and Edwards's approach points to a recognition that air quality should not be considered a property of air, but understood as a relation between air and those who breathe and are affected by it, who are in turn differentiated by class, location and other variables. In this way, da Costa and Edwards's work does not simply offer a service to science as it exists: it makes a significant scientific contribution by pointing out the need to reconceptualise the object of air quality research. It enacts a logic of ontology: reconfiguring air quality not as a property of air, but as a relation between pollution and those who are affected by it. In this way art-science projects such as PigeonBlog do something more than present ready-made science to the public. Rather, they contribute inventively to the generation of something new within scientific practice itself, challenging the boundaries of disciplinary authority (cf. Stengers 1997: 18).

A second observation turns on distinctive practices of public-making: it is that da Costa and Edwards's project points to the difference between the provision of public information and the practice of a public experiment. Air quality monitoring data are typically presented in public as finished or inert information. Such information reports the results of a standardised type of metrological practice, governed by national or international standards and based on a science of air pollution that is well-established. The data are presented as public information in order that the abstract public interpellated by the data can become informed (Barry 2001: 153).

In contrast, the informational outputs of PigeonBlog are less substantial and systematic, and the practice of measurement takes an experimental and local form. The aim of the project is not to provide public information while hailing the formation of an abstract public. Instead it is to develop a different kind of public knowledge of air quality: one that highlights the critical significance of its social-geographical variation, and that invites those most affected by this variation to participate in the practices of knowledge production. This is a type of public knowledge, then, that is in principle unfinished, in process and dialogical, developing through the reflexive relations between participants *who are both the subjects and objects of knowledge*, a public knowledge that enfolds both themselves and their relations with their immediate environment.

A third observation concerns PigeonBlog's implications for artistic practice; for its effect is to transform and multiply art such that it encompasses enduring processes of scientific and social research, public performance event, website, scientific papers, and social relations between art-scientists and affected local populations, who become co-producers of the work. Dadaesque and deadly serious, PigeonBlog traverses the boundaries that would contain it. In an original design for PigeonBlog it was intended that the pigeons conducting air quality monitoring would be accompanied by 'embedded reporter' pigeons carrying cameras, thereby providing a visual record of the localities. The idea for PigeonBlog derived in part from the work of Julius Neubronner, a German engineer who in 1903 patented the idea of a pigeon-born camera as a reconnaissance device. Likewise, PigeonBlog was intended visually to record the devastated and polluted terrain of Los Angeles county, one of 'the most polluted areas' of the

US, and one in which the 'economic concerns of the automotive industry tend to motivate policy decisions far more than human health'.[23] A war zone of a kind, which only pigeons would be able to map.

Thus, as we have stressed, while PigeonBlog was an interdisciplinary experiment in art-science, it should be understood in relation to the broader history of the multiple lineages of conceptual and post-conceptual art. This is because it gathers within itself and unleashes the cumulative, protentive power and imagination of over 40 years of conceptual art, as relayed through a decade of contemporary art-science. It augurs art as a new kind of experience by reference to and retention of this rich prehistory (Gell 1998; Born 2010), both concretising and extending conceptual art's protean ontological ambitions. At the same time, rather than adopt the service-subordination mode of interdisciplinarity in the communication of a finished science, here art-science draws upon but augments the resources of science. PigeonBlog makes a scientific contribution, while reconfiguring the objects both of art and of scientific research.

Art-Science, the Public, and their Relation

For some commentators on art-science, projects like da Costa's risk an excessive moralism (Zylinska 2009: 208);[24] they might be accused of taking on a political education function that is not so distant from the educational mission envisaged by the proponents of public understanding of science. But we want finally to draw out a critical distinction that disturbs that equation. Our case is that PigeonBlog was not addressed to a pre-formed public (Bell 2007), one that would come into existence through its interpellation by a pre-formed scientific knowledge. Rather, PigeonBlog amounted to an experiment through which the public, knowledge, and their relation were expected to emerge in a different form.

One way to grasp this difference would be to hold Warner's Althusserian formulation of the public interpellated through practices of cultural production, which privileges a textual model, up against an Arendtian, anti-teleological conception of the public, which takes as its model the public performance event (Barry and Kimbell 2005; Born 2008, 2013). If Arendt's concern was with the systematic renewal of political praxis and the public realm, her preferred idiom for political action was the performing arts. For Arendt, plurality was the fundamental condition for such action, the essence of which was continuous, direct civic participation. As Dana Villa suggests, Arendt's performance model 'emphasises the embeddedness of action in the "already existing web of human relationships" while stressing its phenomenality, its need for an audience. . . . [She] directly links the meaning-creative capacity of initiatory action to its "futility, boundlessness, and uncertainty of outcome"', where 'boundless' implies the creation of 'myriad new relationships [and] unforeseen constellations'. Moreover, Arendt insists that the public realm constituted through political action or performance has a 'unique *revelatory* capacity' by virtue of being both artificial and autonomous (Villa 1996: 84–5, citing Arendt 1989 [1958]: 190–2 and 184). The public experiment that is PigeonBlog recalls such a conception of an agonistic, participatory, performance-engendered public – a performance that is artificial, oriented to political action, and the outcome of which is uncertain.

We can pursue this difference through Barbara Cassin's productive discussion, drawing in part on Arendt, of the contrasting Greek rhetorical forms apodeixis and epideixis. Cassin begins with a paradox: 'Truth is sometimes defeated. When it happens, it's man's fault, a human wrong against nature. . . . This is precisely why men [sic] need rhetoric: we need rhetoric to help truth . . . against rhetoric' (Cassin 2005: 858–60). Apodeixis refers to a kind of 'proof-demonstration', 'the art of showing "from" (*apo*) that which is shown', a faithful showing from the (finished) knowledge or truth. Cassin continues that epideixis, in contrast, 'is the art of "showing" (*deiknumi*) "in front" (*epi*), in the presence of a public, to make a show. . . . *Epideixis*: you speak *to*, audience-oriented; *apodeixis*: you speak *of*, object-oriented' (ibid: 862, emphases in the original). But the difference extends also to the performative qualities of the two rhetorical modes. Where apodeixis follows the object by confirming 'what is or seems to be, epideixis *makes it be*' (ibid, our emphasis). Epideixis is therefore the most rhetorical or artful of rhetorical genres. Crucially, for Cassin, epideixis is 'an active maker' of the world: a rhetorical demonstration that is intended to move (in both senses) its interlocutors towards both new objects and new common values (*koina*), new matters of concern (Latour and Weibel 2005; Fraser 2006) – a shift from 'consensus . . . to invention, from liturgy to *happening*' (Cassin 2005: 863, emphasis in the original). Epideixis, that is to say, encapsulates the transformative power of speech and art, a power to move that can reconfigure not only the substance of the knowledge that is held in common but, simultaneously, the publics that coalesce around and the social relations that are referenced by that knowledge.

By now, in outlining Cassin's argument, our rhetorical intention should be plain. It is to create a kind of proof-effect or equation in which [apodeixis : epideixis] stands for [public understanding : public experiment]. As a form of epideixis, public experiments do not so much present existing scientific knowledge to the public, as forge relations between new knowledge, things, locations and persons that did not exist before – in this way producing truth, public, and their relation at the same time. Cassin herself draws a distinction between the presentation of 'pre-existing proofs' and managing evidence: '"managing evidence" does not mean . . . dealing with pre-existent proofs but contriving new types of obviousness' (Cassin 2005: 864).

It should be obvious, after PigeonBlog, that air quality is not just a property of urban air, but a matter of social knowledge and social justice. While PigeonBlog cannot be seen as typical of art-science, it demonstrates the difference between a project of public understanding and a project of public experiment – and between the logics of accountability and innovation, and the logic of ontology. In doing so, rather than conceive of art-science as a manifestation of a broader transformation in the mode of production of knowledge, PigeonBlog insists on the need to attend to the specificity, heterogeneity and complexity of the genealogies of art-science, and in this light it makes obvious the fertility and inventiveness of this public experiment.

Epilogue: Anatomy of a Crisis of Interdisciplinary Evaluation

We end this chapter, and this book, with brief reflections on changes that have occurred since we published an earlier version of our research on art-science (Born and Barry 2010). In particular, we want to relate and draw out the implications of the closure of the ACE Masters program, which took in its last students in 2009 and wound up in 2011.

ACE had been set up in an innovative structural arrangement in which it was suspended independently between, and received funds from, three UCI Schools: the Claire Trevor School of the Arts, the Donald Bren School of Information and Computer Sciences, and the Henry Samueli School of Engineering. Students were admitted into a 'home School' based on their undergraduate academic achievements, but had in addition to demonstrate through a portfolio or position statement their commitment to art-science interdisciplinary practice. While this arrangement provided ACE with deep contacts in each disciplinary area, as well as a certain mobility and a diverse inflow of students into the program, it also meant that no one School had responsibility to administer or support it, to champion ACE within the political culture of the university, nor to plan for its future – for example by expanding its staffing or by the creation of an ACE PhD program. Apart from its small group of core staff, ACE drew on a large pool of affiliate 'program faculty' who contributed teaching and supervision largely on the basis of good will, with no credit or remission of duties in their home departments.

In all, throughout its short life (2003 to 2011), ACE inhabited a contradiction. It is hard to convey the extent to which, in 2006, ACE seemed to be the sunny locus at UCI of campus-wide hopes that it might fulfil the long-standing, collective aspirations for a transcendent interdisciplinarity. Everyone to whom the ethnographer (Born) spoke at UCI – from very senior figures across the entire range of the arts, humanities, social and natural sciences to students from other programs – knew something about and voiced benign and excited expectations of ACE. Much was also known about the works and projects of some ACE faculty, who attracted admiration, not least because they sometimes attracted positive attention from the mainstream media. Yet for all its ambition, and despite the approbation, the ACE program was far from stable and unified; indeed it was permanently embattled. In being the servant of three masters, set up in the interstices of three Schools, it was also answerable to all three and vulnerable to political changes. The modest funding for ACE was subject to periodic review, and – signifying its uncertain and impoverished status – ACE was located physically in portacabins on the grassy lots behind the monumental UCI Science Library. The extraordinary teaching session described earlier took place in a ramshackle shed resembling nothing so much as a domestic garage.

In 2006, at the time of fieldwork, this ambivalent situation had reached a turning point as ACE was subjected to an external review chaired by a senior academic from elsewhere in the University of California system. The remit was to assess 'whither ACE'. In a core meeting held as part of the review, one aspiration of ACE faculty was for the program to expand its interconnections with other parts of UCI; by this time, significant links had been made and sympathetic faculty had become involved in ACE both from the School of Social Sciences and from the School of Biological Sciences. The talk was, in part, of a 'five School' ACE, and plans were also being discussed for an undergraduate 'major concentration' and a PhD program.

On the other hand, the cracks in ACE's foundations were also becoming apparent. Recruitment, beyond arts students, was proving difficult. Engineering students admitted to ACE, someone noted, were seriously disincentivised because they were unable to count their ACE courses towards their final degree. Critical comments were made about the shoestring budget on which ACE operated; one manifestation was that the comprehensive financial support available routinely to students entering other UCI graduate programs was simply missing for those admitted to ACE. Another was that the technical infrastructure at ACE was woefully inadequate; as the review Chair quipped, 'Kids in the program have more technology in their bedrooms than ACE has!'. Three affiliate faculty from different parts of UCI spoke of their problems of overwork given that no resources or credit followed their teaching for ACE; nor did their involvement contribute in any way towards their tenure or promotion profile. One of the scientists present commented, 'There's a lip service paid to interdisciplinarity here [at UCI], but in reality there's a very confined, precise list of the journals that count for promotion: it's incredibly narrow'. Someone else spoke of the Chair of one of the art departments seeing ACE as a rival for students and resources.

Overall, it seemed quite unclear in this review meeting, and in 2006, whether or when more resources would be forthcoming from any one of the Schools, as well as whether a PhD program would eventuate. The discussion of how an involvement in ACE affected and indeed might blight tenure prospects was concretised in highly concerned discussions among sympathetic colleagues of a core ACE faculty member whose interdisciplinary work, occupying a terrain between the School of Arts and one of the two science Schools, they felt could not be adequately assessed or evaluated in the 'additive' terms institutionalised at UCI: a committee made up simply of members of those two schools, with all the unbreachable 'two cultures' realities enshrined in such an arrangement.

The immediate cause of ACE's closure was a withdrawal of funding and administrative support from the School of Information and Computer Sciences, which resulted in technical and administrative staff being fired. The long-anticipated ACE PhD program, which had been drawn up and was waiting to be signed off, was shelved. An obvious higher cause was the ramifying effect of the severe financial crisis affecting the University of California as a whole, in which $50 million of cuts had been handed down to be implemented in six months and radiated throughout the system. According to an informant, ACE was just 'low-hanging fruit', easy to pick off and not the core of anyone's business. More locally, following the 2006 review, ACE's structural problems appeared to have been solved when it was given administrative shelter by the School of Information and

Computer Sciences. Just a couple of years later, however, it was this school that determined that ACE should be closed.

But there is no doubt that the chronic problems encountered by ACE were deeper, and come to the core of this book. They stemmed from the difficulty of evaluating and legitimising as interdisciplinary an entity as ACE, signalled by its split reception at UCI: apparently highly valued, recognised as a site of invention and a source of fascination, and yet starved of security and adequate funding. The problems of evaluation and legitimation, then, ricocheted across scales (Strathern and Khlinovskaya Rockhill, this volume): they affected ACE as a program within the university, and they affected its individual faculty in their quest for promotion and tenure. The fate of ACE, the program and its people, therefore highlights in turn the larger challenges both of recognising and metabolising the value of particular forms of interdisciplinarity, in all their ineluctable singularity, and of institutionalising the means of identifying and acting on that value (Barry and Born 2007). We hope in this volume to have pointed to some of the irreductionist methodologies and mechanisms that are necessary in order to meet just these challenges.

Notes

1 The study formed part of the ESRC project, A. Barry, G. Born and M. Strathern, 'Interdisciplinarity and Society: A Critical Comparative Study' (2003-6, RES-151-25-0042-A). We thank warmly all those who allowed us to observe and interview them, in particular those involved in the British and Australian art-science scenes, and a number of faculty and students based at the University of California, Irvine, including Tom Boellstorff, Beatriz da Costa, Paul Dourish, Rufus Edwards, David Theo Goldberg, Garnet Hertz, Antoinette Lafarge, Robert Nideffer, Simon Penny, Kavita Philip and others. We are also grateful to Gisa Weszkalnys for valuable fieldwork, and to Lucy Kimbell, Bill Maurer and others for comments on the paper. None of them are responsible for the analysis given here.
2 See ace.uci.edu/ and simonpenny.net/ace_archive/index.php (accessed September 2012).
3 As others have argued, Snow also failed to address the ways in which the sciences were themselves divided between sub-specialisms, rendering scientists outsiders to the culture of other specialisms (e.g. Knight 2006: 108).
4 Central to the educational mission of the evolving paradigm of the public understanding of science was its influence on science museums: see, in particular, Macdonald (1998, 2002) and Barry (1998).
5 The terms 'science-art' or 'sciart' are often preferred in the UK, and these terms and 'art-science' should be considered interchangeable. The funding initiatives grew around foundations created by the Arts Catalyst, a small independent organisation which from the early 1990s pioneered art-science in the UK, which it envisaged in terms of encouraging 'artists' engagement with science, and [with] critical discourse around this field'; see www.artscatalyst.org/about (accessed May 2012), and, on a recent Arts Catalyst project, Triscott and La Frenais (2005). The version of 'science-art' cultivated by the funding bodies, however, is widely thought to have relatively neglected 'critical discourse' on science.
6 Interview, 2005.
7 In the UK, funding for art-science continues to be supported by the Wellcome Trust ('Art awards'), the Arts Council of England, which supports the Arts Catalyst organisation, and

the AHRC 'Science in Culture' programme, which funds a broad range of projects that 'develop the reciprocal relationship between the sciences, on the one hand, and arts and humanities, on the other': see AHRC (2012) 'Science in Culture' research theme, www.ahrc.ac.uk/FundingOpportunities/Pages/scienceinculture.aspx (accessed May 2012).

8 The idea that there is a 'crisis' in the relations between science and society is not, of course, a new one (Agar 2008: 571).

9 Interview, 2006.

10 Interview, 2006 (our emphasis).

11 Interview, 2006.

12 With knowing allusion to Sun Ra's 'Space is the Place' (1974).

13 In the UK, a similar orientation is evident in the work of the Arts Catalyst (note 5) and some individual artists and curators. The activities of the Arts Catalyst during the 1990s came to be driven in part, like the later ACE/AHRB Fellowship programme, by dissatisfaction with the perceived instrumentalism of 'public understanding of science' funding for art-science. At the same time, centres and pedagogies similar to those embodied in ACE developed in the 1990s in several British universities, such as the Centre for Electronic Arts and the MA Computing in Art and Design at Middlesex University, the Royal College of Art's department and MA in Computer Related Design, now called MA in Design Interactions, and Westminster University's Hypermedia Research Centre. However, they tended not to be set up across departmental or School boundaries, as ACE was, and paid less attention than ACE to critical feminist and science studies. We are grateful to Lucy Kimbell for these insights and comparisons.

14 We are grateful to Simon Penny for allowing us to use this material.

15 This concept underlies Simon Penny's interaction design work, Fugitive: see www.ace. uci.edu/penny/works/fugitive2.html and www.simonpenny.net (accessed September 2012).

16 CalIT² and the Center for Ethnography are two of numerous interdisciplinary institutes and research centres based at the University of California, Irvine, itself founded in the 1960s as a model of the interdisciplinary university: see www.calit2.net/index.php, www.ethnography.uci.edu/, and www.lib.uci.edu/ucihistory/index.php?page=academic (accessed September 2012).

17 It is significant that, according to key UCI interlocutors from the social sciences and humanities, while critical science and technology studies were represented in the ACE curriculum, in general they were marginal to the intellectual culture of UCI, which is predominantly a large science and engineering university. For these interlocutors, some of them very senior figures in the University, that ACE was a locus for STS at Irvine, and for its translation into practical art-science work, was a key indicator of its value to the University.

18 It is worth noting that the genealogies related here concern the theoretical agenda of ACE pedagogy; the practical dimensions of ACE pedagogy, which turned centrally on how to negotiate the often contradictory criteria and methodologies of science research and art research, has not been addressed.

19 For a precisely analogous discussion of the way that the subtleties of the behaviour of analogue musical sounds can exceed their digital representation, see Born (1995), pp. 247–250.

20 See www.beatrizdacosta.net/pigeonblog/statement.php (accessed September 2012).

21 Interview, 2006.

22 Interview, 2006.

23 See www.beatrizdacosta.net/pigeonblog/statement.php (accessed September 2012).

24 This issue is itself a point of contention among some art-science practitioners.

References

Agar, J. (2008) 'What Happened in the Sixties', *British Journal for the History of Science*, 41 (4): 567–600.

Anderson, B. (2007) 'Hope for Nanotechnology: Anticipatory Knowledge and the Governance of Affect', *Area*, 19: 156–65.

Arendt, H. (1989 [1958]) *The Human Condition*, Chicago, IL: University of Chicago Press.

Barry, A. (1998) 'On Interactivity: Consumers, Citizens, and Culture', in Macdonald S. (ed.) *The Politics of Display: Museums, Science, Culture*, (pp. 98–117) London: Routledge.

— (2001) *Political Machines: Governing a Technological Society*, London: Athlone.

— (2002) 'The Anti-Political Economy', *Economy and Society*, 31 (2): 268–84.

Barry, A. and Born, G. (2007) 'Interdisciplinary Research and Evaluation', Unpublished Manuscript, Prepared for the Economic and Social Research Council, 5pp.

Barry, A., Born, G. and Weszkalnys, G. (2008) 'Logics of Interdisciplinarity', *Economy and Society*, 37 (1): 20–49.

Barry, A. and Kimbell, L. (2005) 'Pindices', in Latour, B. and Weibel, P. (eds.) *Making Things Public: Atmospheres of Democracy* (pp. 872–3), Cambridge, MA: MIT Press.

Bell, V. (2007) *Culture and Performance: The Challenge of Ethics, Politics and Feminist Theory*, Oxford: Berg.

Bishop, C. (2004) 'Antagonism and Relational Aesthetics', *October*, 110: 51–79.

— (ed.) (2006) *Participation*, London: Whitechapel Gallery and MIT Press.

Bodmer, W. (1986) 'The Public Understanding of Science', *Bernal Lecture*, Birkbeck College, London, 30 April.

Boltanski, L. and Thévenot, L. (2006) *On Justification: Economies of Worth*, Princeton, NJ: Princeton University Press.

Born, G. (1995) *Rationalizing Culture: IRCAM, Boulez, and the Institutionalization of the Musical Avant-garde*, Berkeley, CA and London: University of California Press.

— (2005) 'On Musical Mediation: Ontology, Technology and Creativity', *Twentieth Century Music*, 2 (1): 7–36.

— (2008) 'On the Public-Isation and Privatisation of Music', paper presented to the conference Music, Sound and the Reconfiguration of Public and Private Space, Centre for Research in the Arts, Social Sciences and Humanities, Cambridge University, 18–19 April.

— (2010) 'The Social and the Aesthetic: For a Post-Bourdieuian Theory of Cultural Production', *Cultural Sociology*, 4 (2): 171–208.

— (2013) 'Introduction – on Musical and Sonic Publics', in Born, G. (ed.) *Music, Sound and Space: Transformations of Public and Private Experience* (pp. 35–40), Cambridge: Cambridge University Press.

Born, G. and Barry, A. (2010) 'Art-Science: From Public Understanding to Public Experiment', *Journal of Cultural Economy*, 3 (1): 107–23.

Bourriaud, N. (2002) *Relational Aesthetics*, trans. S. Pleasance and F. Woods. Dijon: Les Presses du Reel.

Buchmann, S. (2006) 'From Systems-Oriented Art to Biopolitical Art Practice', in Francis, M.-A., Walsh, J., Sykes, L. and Vishmidt, M. (eds.) (2006) *Media Mutandis: Surveying Art, Technologies and Politics*, London: NODE.

Callon, M. and Rabeharisoa, V. (2004) 'Gino's Lesson on Humanity: Genetics, Mutual Entanglements and the Sociologist's Role', *Economy and Society*, 33: 1–27.

Cassin, B. (2005) 'Managing Evidence', in Latour, B. and Weibel, P. (eds.) *Making Things Public: Atmospheres of Democracy* (pp. 858–65), Cambridge, MA: MIT Press.

Century, M. (1999) 'Pathways to Innovation in Digital Culture', report Published by the Centre for Research on Canadian Cultural Industries and Institutions, McGill University, Montreal.

Collini, S. (1993) 'Introduction', in Snow, C. P. (ed.) *The Two Cultures* (pp. vii–lxxi), Cambridge: Cambridge University Press.

Corris, M. (ed.) (2004) *Conceptual Art: Theory, Myth and Practice*, Cambridge: Cambridge University Press.

Corris, M. (2006) 'The Dialogical Imagination: The Conversational Aesthetic of Conceptual Art', in D. Hopkins (ed.) *Neo-Avant-Garde* (pp. 301–10), Amsterdam: Rodopi.

Da Costa, B. and Philip, K. (eds.) (2008) *Tactical Biopolitics: Art, Activism, and Technoscience*, Cambridge, MA and London: MIT Press.

Doherty, C. (ed.) (2004) *Contemporary Art: From Studio to Situation*, London: Black Dog Publishing.

Dourish, P. (2001) *Where the Action Is: The Foundations of Embodied Interaction*, Cambridge, MA: MIT Press.

Dourish, P. and Bell, D. (2011) *Digital Future: Mass and Mythology in Ubiquitous Computing*. Cambridge, MA: MIT Press.

Edgerton, D. (2006) *Warfare State: Britain 1920–1970*, Cambridge: Cambridge University Press.

Edgerton, D. and Hughes, K. (1989) 'The Poverty of Science: A Critical Analysis of Scientific and Industrial Policy under Mrs Thatcher', *Public Administration*, 67, 4: 419–33.

Elam, M. and Bertilsson, M. (2003) 'Consuming, Engaging and Confronting Science: The Emerging Dimensions of Scientific Citizenship', *European Journal of Social Theory*, 6: 233–51.

Ferran, B. (2006) 'Creating a Program of Support for Art and Science Collaborations', *Leonardo*, 39 (5): 442–6.

Fraser, A. (2005) 'From the Critique of Institutions to an Institution of Critique', *Artforum*, September: 100–106.

Fraser, M. (2006) 'The Ethics of Reality and Virtual Reality: Latour, Facts and Values', *History of the Human Sciences*, 5(19): 45–72.

Galison, P. (1996) 'The Context of Disunity', in Galison, P. and Stump, D. (eds.) *The Disunity of Science: Boundaries, Contexts, and Power* (pp. 1–36), Stanford, CA: Stanford University Press.

Gell, A. (1998) *Art and Agency*, Oxford: Oxford University Press.

Gummett, P. (1980) *Scientists in Whitehall*, Manchester: Manchester University Press.

House of Lords (2000) *Science and Society*, Third Report of the House of Lords Select Committee on Science and Technology Session 1999–2000, HL38.

Irwin, A. and Michael, M. (2003) *Science, Social Theory and Public Knowledge*, Maidenhead: Open University Press.

Jennings, P. (2000) *New Media Arts/New Funding Models*, prepared for Creativity and Culture, The Rockefeller Foundation.

Knight, D. (2006) *Public Understanding of Science: A History of Communicating Scientific Ideas*, London: Routledge.

Latour, B. and Weibel, P. (eds.) (2005) *Making Things Public: Atmospheres of Democracy*, Cambridge, MA: MIT Press.

Leonardo (2012) 'The Leonardo Story', www.leonardo.info/isast/leostory.html (accessed September 2012).

Macdonald, S. (ed.) (1998) *The Politics of Display: Museums, Science, Culture*, London: Routledge.

— (2002) *Behind the Scenes at the Science Museum*, Oxford: Berg.

Naimark, M. (2003) *Truth, Beauty, Freedom, and Money: Technology-Based Art and the Dynamics of Sustainability*, www.artslab.net: Leonardo Journal, supported by the Rockefeller Foundation.

Newman, M. (2002) 'Conceptual Art from the 1960s to the 1990s: An Unfinished Project?', in Osborne, P. (ed.) *Conceptual Art* (pp. 288–9), London: Phaidon.

Nowotny, H., Scott, P. and Gibbons, M. (2001) *Re-Thinking Science: Knowledge and the Public in the Age of Uncertainty*, Cambridge: Polity.

Osborne, P. (ed.) (2002) *Conceptual Art*, London: Phaidon.

Pickering, A. (2002) 'Cybernetics and the Mangle: Ashby, Beer and Pask', *Social Studies of Science*, 32: 413–37.

— (2005) 'Beyond Design: Cybernetics, Biological Computers and Hylozoism', International Conference on the Philosophy of Technology, Copenhagen, 13–15 October. Reprinted in ACE teaching materials.

Poortinga, W. and Pidgeon, N. F. (2005) 'Trust in Risk Regulation: Cause or Consequence of the Acceptability of GM Food?', *Risk Analysis*, 25: 199–209.

Royal Society (1985) 'Report of the Ad Hoc Committee on the Public Understanding of Science', London (online), available at: www.royalsociety.org/displaypagedoc.asp?id_26406 (accessed September 2012).

Snow, C. P. (1959) *The Two Cultures*, Cambridge: Cambridge University Press.

Stengers, I. (1997) *Power and Invention*, Minneapolis: Minnesota University Press.

Triscott, N. and La Frenais, R. (eds.) (2005) *Zero Gravity*, London: The Arts Catalyst.

Turney, J. (ed.) (2006) *Engaging Science: Thoughts, Deeds, Analysis, and Action*, London: Wellcome Trust.

Villa, D. (1996) *Arendt and Heidegger: The Fate of the Political*, Princeton, NJ: Princeton University Press.

Viveiros de Castro, E. (2012) *Cosmological Perspectivism in Amazonia and Elsewhere*, Manchester: HAU Network of Ethnographic Theory.

Warner, M. (2005) *Publics and Counterpublics*, New York: Zone.

Webster, S. (2006) 'Art, Science and the Public', in Turney, J. (ed.) *Science: Thoughts, Deeds, Analysis, and Action* (pp. 74–9), London: Wellcome Trust.

Wellcome Trust (2009) 'Arts Awards', available at: www.wellcome.ac.uk/Funding/Public-engagement/Grants/Arts-Awards/index.htm (accessed September 2012).

Weszkalnys, G. (2005) 'Science/Art: A Preliminary Report', Goldsmiths College, Centre for the Study of Invention and Social Process, unpublished research report.

Wiener, M. (1981) *English Culture and the Decline of the Industrial Spirit, 1850–1980*, Cambridge: Cambridge University Press.

Williams, R. (1963 [1958]) *Culture and Society 1780–1950*, London: Chatto and Windus.

Wilson, S. (2002) *Information Arts: Intersections of Art, Science and Technology*, Cambridge, MA: MIT Press.

Wolpert, L. and Richards, A. (eds.) (1988) *A Passion for Science*, Oxford: Oxford University Press.

Wynne, B. (1996) 'May the Sheep Safely Graze? A Reflexive View of the Expert–Lay Knowledge Divide', in Lash, S. and Szersynski, B. (eds.) *Risk, Environment and Modernity: Towards a New Ecology* (pp. 44–83), London: Sage.

Zylinska, J. (2009) *Bioethics in the Age of New Media*, Cambridge, MA: MIT Press.

Index

Abbott, Andrew 40–1
'academic left' 104
accountability, logic of 14–17, 24–5, 32, 35–8, 43, 164, 178–9, 185, 235, 240, 249, 253, 266
actor-network theory (ANT) 103, 112
agonistic-antagonistic mode of interdisciplin-arity 12–13, 21, 33, 37, 41, 58, 74, 156
air quality, reconceptualisation of 262–6
Akerloff, George 89
Alexander, Christopher 212
Allende, Salvador 36, 213
Althusser, Louis 61
American Union of Concerned Scientists 181
'antecedent disciplines' 10, 12
anthropology 30, 33, 42, 86–9, 96; in business settings 141–57; of exotic *other* 151–2
anti-psychiatry movement 36, 220
antidisciplines and antidisciplinarity 36, 209–18
apodeixis 265
Apostel, Leo 8–9
'applied metaphysics' (Daston) 18, 196
Arendt, Hannah 264–5
Arizona State University (ASU) 99
Art and Science Research Fellowship programme 28
art-science 11–12, 15–16, 27–9, 32, 38–9, 91–5, 248–66; in the United Kingdom 250–1
artificial intelligence (AI) 211, 258, 260
Arts, Computation and Engineering (ACE) Masters programme at UCI 13, 29, 38–41, 249–50, 257–61, 266–8
Arts Council England 249, 253
Ashby, Ross 36, 210–20
autonomy, academic 4, 43

Babu, Senthil 71
Bachelard, Gaston 83
Bateson, Gregory 36, 219–20
Beck, Ulrich 35, 102, 181
Becker, Gary 89
Beckett, Samuel 82
Beer, Stafford 210, 213–15, 218, 259
Bell, Andrew 29, 57, 67–73
benefit sharing in research 134
Bennett, Jane 163
Bentham, Jeremy 29–30, 64–8, 73
Bentham, Samuel 65
Bernard, Thomas 68, 72
Biagioli, Mario 106–11
'bifurcation of nature' 20
bioethics 228–9
'biological computing' 213, 218, 259–60
Bloor, David 102–5
Bodmer, Walter (and Bodmer Report) 252–3
Boguski, Mark 154–5
Boyle, Robert 60
brain science 36, 211, 217–18
brand-building 152–3
Briggs, Asa 9, 60–1
Brown, Theodore 237–8
Browner, C. 144
Burroughs, William 216
Bush, George W. 112–13

California Department of Transportation (Caltrans) 148–50
Callon, Michel 33, 112, 141, 147, 169
Cambridge Genetics Knowledge Park (CGKP) 3, 32–3, 39, 41, 119–35
Campo, R. 236
Canguilhem, Georges 87
Carlile, Richard 64–5
Cassin, Barbara 24, 38, 265
cellular automata 212, 214, 258

Center for International Earth Science Information Network (CIESIN) 183–4, 193
Charon, Rita 233–4, 238
Chernobyl crisis (1986) 182
Chibnik, M. 144
Chile 213
Chrestomathia project 65–7, 73
Clark, Nigel 173
Clark, William 60
climate change research 11, 24–5, 35, 89–90, 110–13, 162, 182–3, 186, 193–6
Cohen, Bernard 60
Coleridge, Samuel Taylor 64, 68
collaboration in ethnography 24
Collini, Stefan 8
communities of practice 16, 155
competency groups (CGs) 34, 39, 164, 167, 170–3
computer-supported cooperative work (CSCW) 21–2
conceptual art 27, 38, 93, 256, 259–60, 264
contagion in ethnography 23
contextualisation of research 247; *strong* and *weak* 178, 197
Coombe, Rosemary 150
Council on Science and Technology (2001 report) 28, 253
social movements 15
Crow, Michael 99–100, 114, 181, 184
'culturisation' of economics and organisations 143–4
cybernetics 36, 39, 41, 61, 209–20, 259–60; definition of 210; social basis of 215–16

da Costa, Beatriz 38, 261–4
Daston, Lorraine 18, 108–11, 196
Deleuze, G. 34, 163, 169, 220
deliberative mapping 15
de Solla Price, Derek 106–7
Dessai, S. 195
Deutsch, Claudia 150–1
D'Hooge, H. 17
Dickens, Charles 62, 64
disciplinarity 3–8, 30, 57–61, 64, 68, 74, 85, 88, 91–6, 100, 105, 114, 217; in the social sciences and humanities 82; value of 7
disciplines, heterogeneity of 8
document-handling systems 148–50
'double-bind' situation (Bateson) 219
Doubleday, Robert 11, 112

Dourish, Paul 258
Drayton, Richard 69
Duchamp, Marcel 93
du Gay, P. 143–4

Earth Institute, Columbia University 35, 178, 181, 184–93
earth systems analysis 25
East India Company 72–3
Economic and Social Research Council (ESRC) 83, 126
economics 89–90; *see also* utilitarian economics
Edgerton, David 250–1
Edwards, Paul 24
Edwards, Rufus 262–3
Ellery, George 58
Elster, Jon 89, 94
Engineering and Physical Sciences Research Council 83
Eno, Brian 216
Environment Agency 170
environmental crises 180, 182
environmental debates 25–6
environmental research 17, 24–6, 32, 35, 39, 41, 162–3, 169, 173–4, 178–80, 184–7, 195–8
epideixis 265
epistemic cultures 193
epistemology 18–19, 82–3; neo-Kantian 18
ethical, legal and social implications (ELSI) of new genetic knowledge 32, 41, 120–6, 129–35
ethnography 12, 16–17, 33–4, 38–9, 86, 96, 102, 142–3, 260; of the IT industry 20–4, 26, 39; rationale for use of 23
ethnomethodology 21–2
Ezrahi, Yaron 110–11

Ferran, B. 253
Feynman, Richard 84
flood risk management 34, 164, 167–72
Foss, L. 239
Foucault, Michel 5, 30, 59, 62–3, 84, 90, 105
Frank, Arthur 234–5
Fuller, S. 7

Galison, Peter 7, 260
Gardner, H. 2, 10–11
genetically-modified (GM) crops 112
genetics knowledge parks (GKPs) 119–22, 126, 131, 134; *see also* Cambridge Genetics Knowledge Park

Geographical Association 162
geography, discipline of 34–5, 42, 161–9,
    172–4, 179
Gibbons, Michael 1, 230
Gibson-Graham, J.K. 157
glaciology 85–6
global financial crisis (2008) 110
globalisation 74, 151
Goffman, Erving 84
'going native' 87
Golinksi, Jan 59
Goodman, Nelson 94
Greaves, D. 238
Groddeck, Georg 240
Gross, Paul 102, 104
Guattari, F. 34, 163, 169, 220
Guillemin, Roger 103

Hacking, Ian 8, 88–91, 95
Hadley Centre 183
Halewood, Michael 20
Halle programme 69
Hammerstein, Notker 59
*Handbook of Science and Technology
    Studies* 31, 106–11
Hawkins, A.H. 231–2
Haxeltine, A. 194
Hayden, C. 133–4
Heidegger, Martin 216
Herschel, William 58
Hirsch, E. 121–2
Hirschman, Albert 88–9
historicity of scientific objects 18
history of science 18, 60
Holman, I. 196
homeostat devices and assemblages 36,
    210–19
Hoskin, Keith 63
Huggan, Graham 74
Hulme, Mike 190, 195–7
human–computer interaction (HCI) 21,
    258
hybrid disciplines 92–3

'idiot sciences' 96
imperialism, disciplinary 30, 89–90
information technology (IT) industry,
    ethnography of 20–4, 26, 39
innovation: 'defensive' 6; logic of
    16–17, 21, 23, 28–9, 38, 43, 164,
    249, 266
Institute for Social Ecological Research
    (ISOE) 180, 190
integrated assessment 93

integration in environmental research
    191–5
integrative-synthesis mode of
    interdisciplin-arity 10–13, 35
Interactive Integrated Assessment Process
    (IIAP) 195–6
'interdisciplinarism' (Abbott) 40
interdisciplinarity 1–17, 29–32, 36, 40–2,
    57–64, 73–4, 82, 86–96, 99–101,
    105–10, 114, 124–9, 147, 154–5,
    161–9, 180–93, 198, 209–13; of ACE
    programme 268; of art-science 249, 256,
    258; between arts and sciences 251;
    bottom-up and *top-down* 99–100;
    contemporary concept of 1–4; of
    cybernetics 210; definition of 9–10; as
    distinct from multidisciplinarity and
    transdisciplinarity 8; in environmental
    research 191–2; of geography 168–9,
    172–4; ideology of 4; institutional form
    of 119; instrumental value of 5;
    literature on 6; logics of 14–17, 229,
    249; of medical humanities 231, 240;
    modes of 10–14, 101; and novelty 6;
    politics of 61, 105–9; *positive* and
    negative forms of 230; *superficial*,
    functional and *radical* forms of 166–7;
    temporalities of 41; typology of 42;
    unity and heterogeneity of 5; within one
    discipline 86; within one person 29
'Interdisciplinarity and Society' research
    project 2
interdisciplinary knowledge, status of 7
Interdisciplinary Studies Project,
    Harvard 2
interdisciplines 40–3
Intergovernmental Panel on Climate
    Change (IPCC) 183
interlanguages 38, 260
International Research Institute for
    Climate and Society (IRI) 184, 186, 192
invention and inventiveness 5–6, 43

Jantsch, Erich 9, 61
Jean-Klein, Iris 134
Jones, Sir William 69
Julius, Nikolaus Heinrich 62–5

Kac, Eduardo 257
Kaiser, David 59
Kaplan, Martha 73
Kauffman, Stewart 212
Kelley, Donald 60
Kepler, Johannes 58

Kings College, London 226
Kingsley Hall 219
Kirklin, Deborah 227, 234
Klein, Naomi 152–3
knowledge, types of 94
Kohler, Robert 59–62
Kuhn, T. 100
Kundera, Milan 94

Laing, R.D. 36, 219–20
Lamb, Hubert 184
Lane, Stuart 165
Langley, Samuel 58
Lash, S. 143
Latour, Bruno 18–19, 59, 88, 102–5,
    111–13, 169
Law, J. 157
Lawrence, C. 237
Leavis, F.R. 251, 254
Leibniz, Gottfried 88
Lenoir, T. 61
Leroy, P. 11
Lévi-Strauss, Claude 144
Levitt, Norman 31, 102, 104
Lichnerowizc, André 9
Lingua Franca (journal) 104
literature-and-medicine 226
Liu, Alan 58
Lloyd, Geoffrey 60
Los Angeles 262–4
Lury, Celia 153
Lyotard, J. 230

'McDonaldisation' of medicine 229–30
Mackenzie, John 74
Mackinder, Halford 179
MacLeod, Roy 106
Macy conferences (1946 to 1953) 215, 219
mad cow disease 112
Maddox, John 106
'Madras system' 29, 69–73
Malone, E.L. 192
management cybernetics 213
Mandelbrot, Benoit 214
Mansilla, V.B. 2, 10–11
Marcus, George 156
Markle, Gerald 106
mathematical modelling 193–4
medical humanities 37–41, 227–9, 232–9
mental illness 219–20
Merton, Robert K. 108
Messer-Davidow, E. 59
metaphor, use of 90–1
methodological symmetry 104–5

metonymy 23
Mill, James 66, 73
Mode-1 and *Mode-2* knowledge production
    1–4, 9, 13, 40–1, 91, 100, 164, 173, 185,
    188, 190, 229–32, 248
Mol, Annemarie 18, 173
Montgomery Hunter, Kathryn 236
Mulkay, Michael 106
multidisciplinarity 8, 61, 123, 127–30,
    186
Musicolour machine 213–18

Nair, Savithri Preetha 70
Namur cybernetics conferences 215
'narrative medicine' (Charon) 233, 238
National Endowment for Science,
    Technology and the Arts (NESTA) 253
network formation 129
Neubronner, Julius 264
Nietzsche, Friedrich 96
Nissani, Moti 82
'nomad sciences' 220
non-governmental organisations (NGOs)
    187
Nowotny, Helga 1–2, 9, 15, 26, 35, 40–1,
    164, 178, 181, 185–90, 197, 247–8,
    251

Öko Institut 15, 35, 178–91, 197
'ontological politics' (Mol) 18, 173
ontology 19, 209–20, 232, 240; cybernetic
    216–17; logic of 13–14, 18–21, 24, 27,
    29, 32, 37–9, 42, 169, 179, 191, 196,
    230, 237, 249–50, 258, 263, 266;
    nonmodern 213–19
open model of research 23
'outformations' (Ezrahi) 110–11
Oxford Handbook of Interdisciplinarity 58

Palo Alto Research Center (PARC) 33–4,
    41, 142–6, 149–51, 155
panopticon principle 62–6
'parallel charts' 233–4
parasitism 30–1, 86–8
Parsons, Talcott 235
participatory practices 15, 33–4
Pask, Gordon 213–18, 259
Pasteur, Louis 19
Pauling, Linus 84
pedagogy and pedagogical initiatives 31–2,
    37–9
peer review 35, 167–8
Penny, Simon 12–13, 258, 260
performance indicators 127, 189–90

Pestre, Dominique 61
Petersen, James 106
philosophy 96, 233; of science 31, 87
Piaget, Jean 9
PigeonBlog project 38, 261–6
Pinch, Trevor 106
Platonic research 92–3
'poaching' 90
postmodernism 30, 230–1, 235
problem-focused orientation 17
problem-solving linked to interdisciplinarity 8
Pryke, M. 143–4
public engagement in research 124, 127–31, 167, 172, 253–5
public experiments 261–6
Public Health Genetics Unit (PHGU) 122–3, 126–7
public understanding of science 15–16, 28, 38, 164, 234, 252, 254, 264, 266

quantitative and qualitative social science 192

Rabinow, Paul 154
Randall, D. 22
Ratio Club 215
rational choice theory 31, 89
Rayner, S. 192
Rees, Martin 85
research councils 83, 126, 189–90
rhetoric 265
Richardson, R. 227
'ricochet effect' 32–3, 38, 121
Rip, A. 122
Ritzer, G. 229–30
Robinson, George Canby 237–8
Rosenberg, Charles 237
Ross, Andrew 104
Rousseau, George 226
Royal Geographical Society 162
Royal Society 252–3
'rules of method' 103
Rulifson, Jeff 144–5
Rumsfeld, Donald 83
Rural Economy and Land Use (RELU) programme 34, 164–72

Sachs, Jeffrey 181, 184
Sachs, Wolfgang 192
Sacks, Oliver 228
Sacy, Antoine Silvestre de 66
Said, Edward 58, 66, 74
scenario work 194–6

Schelling, Thomas 89
Schellnhuber, John 25, 193–4
schizophrenia 219
Schlecker, M. 121–2
school systems 63–4, 68, 71–3
Sciart Consortium 253
science: boundaries of 109; *modern* and *nonmodern* 209–12, 216–17, 220
Science Studies Reader (1999) 31, 106–11
science and technology studies (STS) 31–2, 36, 41, 100–14, 167, 169; interdisciplinarity of 101; normativity of 101–2; quarrels with science and with technology 102
'science wars' 31, 101–5, 110, 113
Sciences Po 111–12
scientific disciplines 59–62, 65
scientific research 18, 20, 24; *see also* environmental research
scientism 239
Scott, Peter 1
Sebald, W.G. 94
security studies 90
September 11th 2001 attacks 110
Serfoji II, Raja of Tanjore 70
Severn Tidal Power Feasibility Study 92
Shapin, Steven 106
Shove, E. 122
'sick role' 235
Skole, D. 162
Slater, D. 142–3, 150
Smith, Adam 68
Snow, C.P. 30, 84, 249–53
social anthropology 145–6
social medicine 229–32
social sciences 11, 15–17, 25, 30, 32, 40, 42, 82–90, 101, 113, 119, 121, 125, 134, 147, 151–3, 156–7, 186, 192–3
Social Text (journal) 104
Society for Social Studies of Science (4S) 106–8
sociology 31, 42, 95–6; of health and illness 230–1; of science and scientific knowledge 18, 96, 102–3, 108, 114
Sokal, Alan 31, 102
Sokal's hoax 104–5
Southey, Robert 68
Spiegel-Rösing, Ina 106–7
spirituality 214
Squier, S.M. 231
stakeholders in the research process 35, 172, 185–6, 192
statistics as a discipline 86

Stehr, N. 59
Stengers, Isabelle 169–70, 197
Stern Report (2006) 89–90
Stichweh, Rudolf 59
subordination-service mode of
    interdisciplin-arity 11–13, 255, 264
Sunder Rajan, Kaushik 154–5
sustainable technology 17
symmetry principle of scientific knowledge
    31, 103

technoscience 108, 110
tenure track system 189
Thatcher, Margaret 183
Thrift, Nigel 155–6
Tipu Sahib 72
Toulmin, Stephen 106, 110
transdisciplinarity 8–10, 35, 40–2, 60–1,
    74, 181, 184–5, 188, 190, 198
transportation in ethnography 24
Treasury, British 3
'trespassing' 30, 88–9
Trigg, Randall 149–50
Tsing, A. 154
turf wars in STS 110
Turner, Bryan 229–32, 235
Turnpenny, J. 195
Tyndall Centre for Climate Change
    Research 35, 178, 181–96

University of California at Irvine (UCI)
    249, 266–8
university-linked research 22–3, 29
Ure, Andrew 67–8
Urry, J. 143
utilitarian economics 31, 89

Verran, H. 154
viable system model (VSM) (Beer) 213–14
Villa, Dana 264–5
'virtual' corporations 152
von Weizsäcker, Ernst Ulrich 182

Wachtler, C. 231
Wajcman, J. 147
Walczak, D. 229–30
Walter, Grey 215
Ward, Neil 165
Warner, Michael 254, 264
Warwick, Andrew 59
Weibel, Peter 112
Weingart, P. 59
Weizs, G. 237
Wellcome Trust 27, 249, 253–4
Werrett, Simon 65
Westman, Robert 60
whistle-blowing 113
Whitehead, Alfred North 20–1, 233
Wiener, Martin 250–1
Wiener, Norbert 210
Williams, Raymond 251, 254
Wolfram, Stephen 212–16
Woolgar, Steve 103
Wuppertal Institute for Environment,
    Climate and Energy Research 182
Wynn, Eleanor 144
Wynne, Brian 25, 112, 254

Xerox Corporation *see* Palo Alto Research
    Center

Ziegenbalg, B. 71
Zuckerman, Solly 183–4

14500014R00168

Printed in Poland
by Amazon Fulfillment
Poland Sp. z o.o., Wrocław